They Saw Beyond Death

They Saw Beyond Death

NEW INSIGHTS ON NEAR-DEATH EXPERIENCES

Arvin S. Gibson

Other Contributing Authors:
B. Grant Bishop
Sandra L. Cherry
Duane S. Crowther
Lynn D. Johnson
David R. Larson
Harold A. Widdison

Horizon Publishers
Springville, UT

ISBN 13: 978-0-88290-788-3
ISBN 10: 0-88290-788-3
Order Number: C2998

Published by Horizon Publishers, an imprint of Cedar Fort, Inc.
925 N. Main, Springville, UT, 84663
Distributed by Cedar Fort, Inc. www.cedarfort.com

Cover design by Nicole Williams
Cover design © 2006 by Lyle Mortimer
Printed in the United States of America

10   9   8   7   6   5   4   3   2   1

Printed on acid-free paper

Dedication

This book is dedicated to Bill English. Bill's near-death experience changed his life and made him the person most of us know and love today. He has been an inspiration for countless people who have witnessed the courage and good humor of this indomitable man. Without Bill, it is doubtful that IANDS of Utah would have continued to exist as the vital organization it is today.

Table of Contents

Memorial

Arvin S. Gibson was born in Salt Lake City but was raised and graduated from high school in rural northern California. He served in the U.S. Army during World War II, participating in one of the most crucial battles on the Pacific front: the struggle for the island of Iwo Jima.

After completing his military service, he attended the University of California, where he graduated with a bachelor of science degree in mechanical engineering. He took post-graduate courses from the International School of Nuclear Science and Engineering, UCLA, General Electric, and the Edison Electric Institute. For many years he worked and performed research in the field of nuclear engineering, and much of his working career was devoted to research and development of nuclear energy.

Arvin met his wife, Carol, at the University of California at Berkley, and they were married in 1950. They raised their four children in California. They moved their family to Utah in 1977 for Arvin to accept employment as a manager in the Utah Power and Light Company. He rose through the ranks and became the firm's executive vice president. In that capacity he was responsible for engineering power plant and major transmission systems, construction, operations, planning and budgeting, and supervising 1,600 employees until he retired in 1987.

Following his retirement, Arvin and Carol became interested in near-death accounts due to an earlier experience of his father. They began active research in the field in 1990 and began recording the results of their research. Arvin wrote a series of books that have enjoyed wide-spread distribution. Three of his books, *Glimpses of Eternity, Echoes from Eternity,* and *Journeys Beyond Life,* contain numerous interviews with people who have had NDE experiences. These added numerous insights to the general body of knowledge in the field; they also earned him the respect of many who are engaged in ongoing research in the fields of near-death and life-after-death research.

He also took time to write an autobiographical work, *In Search of Angels,* and a unique piece of romantic fiction based on insights drawn from various near-death experiences he had recorded and analyzed: *Love's Eternal Legacy.*

During this period, also, he was a driving force in the founding and stabilizing of the Utah chapter of the *International Association for Near-Death Studies.* The chapter, which has become one of the most active in the organization, hosted the association's international convention in Salt Lake City in 1995.

Though he thought it was time to retire, he returned to writing by crafting *Fingerprints of God: Evidences from Near-Death Studies, Scientific Research on Creation, and Mormon Theology,* harmonizing his extensive insights in all three fields of research into a meaningful and comprehensive whole. In 2003, he undertook this work, *They Saw Beyond Death,* as a summary of Latter-day Saint writings and research in the field and as a tool for providing ongoing direction for future studies among LDS scholars.

Beginning with his adult years in California, Arvin has held numerous teaching and service positions in The Church of Jesus Christ of Latter-day Saints, including counselor in a stake presidency, bishop, high councilor, elders quorum president, Sunday School teacher, and many other ward callings.

Health problems became serious for Arvin as he worked on this book, and they interrupted his efforts and progress. In October 2004 he underwent open-heart surgery, but he continued his writing and book-orchestration efforts even as he was recovering from that ordeal. He had to return to the hospital several times during the next two months.

In November 2004, he was stricken with pneumonia, which caused him to return to the hospital on November 19. During the next several days he enjoyed loving and memorable visits from his close family members, but he passed away peacefully in his sleep on November 24. As Carol, his wife of fifty-four years, observed at the time, no man has ever been more informed and aware of what lay ahead for him as he left the darkness of this earth and ventured onward toward the light, the joyful reunions, and future service in the realm where spirit beings are receiving further education and training and awaiting their resurrection and eternal assignments.

Many tributes have come concerning Arvin's numerous contributions, from both within and outside of the Latter-day Saint faith. Perhaps one that summarizes them all is the communication from Reverend Howard Storm, who had a significant near-death experience and developed an ongoing friendship and working relationship with the Gibsons. He wrote:

> Arvin Gibson radiated God's love to those who knew him. I had the good fortune to know him and work with him. Arvin has a brilliant mind, a wonderful wit, and an inclusive love. He was and is a Godly man. This book is his last testament to his desire to build faith in God and propagate the love of God to the world. My hopes and interests in Arvin Gibson's research and book are learning from my friend and supporting the direction he is pursuing—of oneness with God. Through his examination of NDEs and Mormon doctrine, both areas of inquiry have been enhanced.

Preface

A Terrible Accident and the NDE that Followed

In May 1990 **Eloise Weaver,** her husband, Dave, and their seventeen-year-old daughter made a trip to Montana to go biking. While they were a few miles outside of Dillon, Montana, another car drifted into their lane and hit them on the driver's side. An older couple were in the colliding car, and the man driving apparently dozed off. They both survived the crash. My interview of Eloise occurred in July 1992 (Gibson, pp. 23–29). A portion of that interview follows:

"The paramedics got my daughter out first. Then they began to pry on the door where my husband was. Dave kept saying how badly he hurt, and they were afraid he was dying. He turned toward me, and that's when everything in the car got really bright, very warm, and very quiet. I didn't hear my daughter screaming anymore, and I didn't hear any voices coming from outside the car.

"I felt Dave's presence very close to me, and suddenly we were above our bodies. He held me really tight, and he said: 'Hang in there babe; I love you.' That's what he always called me. Then he said, 'I'm being called home, and you need to go back and raise our girls.'

"I remember telling Dave that I really didn't want to go back without him, but he told me I had to return. Then the warm feeling left, and I was hit with pain—immense pain. The pain was more horrible than when the car hit us.

"I could hear the people again, and I saw Dave as they were pulling him out of the car. He winked at me. Then they began doing CPR on him; I knew he was gone. . . ."

"Eloise, can you describe the light you saw?" I asked.

"It was just radiant and brilliant; it was soft and warm. The experience was almost as if I were sitting by a mountain stream and hearing the creek babbling, and the little birds. It was the most peaceful feeling I have ever felt, probably more peaceful than sitting in the temple—just absolutely wonderful."

"Why did you use the word peaceful?"

"I felt so great. I didn't feel any pain."

"When you went out of your body could you see your physical body in the car?"

"Yes. I could see myself with my knees pulled up, and I could see Dave slumped over."

"As you were embraced by Dave, how did your spirit body feel?"

"It felt just like me. I was exhilarated from the embrace."

"When you were out of your body, did you see anything or anyone else?"

"No, I've read about other experiences, but I didn't see a tunnel or flowers or trees. . . . There were just Dave and I and the soft, beautiful brightness. It was soft, just so soft."

"Why did you use the word *soft?*"

"It was kind of a pastel color—just soft. When I saw the two personages, they were radiant and breathtaking. But with Dave in the light, it was just a soft . . . it reminded me of a cloud that puffed around us in a soft, cuddly, warm way."

"Earlier in your story you mentioned that two personages appeared to you. Could you tell us a little more about the two personages? What did they look like?"

"I could see them from the waist up. When I first saw them I couldn't tell whether they were men or women, but after I heard the tone of voice of the one I assumed they were men. They were dressed in white—very, very white. Everything was white."

"After seeing Dave, when you were out of your body, do you remember going back into your body?"

"I just remember him kissing me and hugging me, and then the noise came back. The pain—it was so terrible."

"You said that you looked at Dave as they were removing him from the car, and he winked at you. He must have been back in his body?"

"Yes, he must have been back too. They were just starting

to take him out when he gave me that little wink that he always gave me. They pronounced him dead at the hospital, but I think he was dead right after they took him out. I felt him brushing my hair with his hand shortly after they got him out."

Eloise had a long and difficult recuperation from a broken neck and from multiple internal injuries. The trauma of Dave's death was ameliorated by Eloise's near-death experience (NDE). She was overwhelmed by the light and the glory of the two beings she had witnessed.

What was equally amazing about the accident was the aftermath. In March 2004, I contacted Eloise to get an update of her situation. Her children had grown up and she was living a happy life surrounded by her children, grandchildren, and one great-grandchild. She excitedly explained that she had recently accepted a temple service mission for the LDS Church to London, England. She felt that such a call could help repay Heavenly Father for the many blessings she had received.

As she described her life since the accident, she told me how she felt about the two people who had crashed into the car Dave was driving. She knew that they must have felt terrible about the damage they had caused, and she wanted to reassure them that she bore them no ill will. She knew their names, Jim and Jane Smith (not their real names), and that they lived in Cardston, Canada, but little else about them. She prayed for them to feel of her forgiveness.

Some years later, Eloise attended a conference at Brigham Young University. During a meal break, she began a conversation with a young man sitting across from her. He mentioned his name and said he was from Cardston. Without expecting an answer, she asked him if he happened to know Jim and Jane Smith. He replied, "Yes, they are my neighbors."

After Eloise recovered from the surprise, she explained why she wanted to get in touch with them. He observed that they had suffered considerable physical and emotional distress over the accident, and it would be helpful for her to contact them. This she did, first by letter and then in person. It turned out that the Smiths were also members of the LDS Church.

These circumstances, like many analogous coincidences of those having NDEs, seem more than just serendipity. Eloise was, indeed, blessed to see the glory of God and to feel of his guiding hand in her life.

A Similar Near-Death Experience

In the process of reviewing material for this book, I happened to reread portions of Dr. Cherie Sutherland's book *Within the Light.* Sutherland is a sociologist who lives in Australia. She had an NDE that launched her into the research of such experiences.

Imagine my surprise when I read an almost duplicate NDE to that of Eloise. Portions of that experience are repeated below. The lady who had the experience, **Joy,** was a friend of Cherrie's, and she, like Eloise, did not want to leave her husband and return to earth.

> We died together, he and I, and as entities of energy, we moved together to a place outside of time and space. . . .
>
> I moved to another plane where my Being expanded until I was One-With-All. It is the ultimate coming home. There is only Oneness, total belonging. And there is only ecstasy. I knew I wanted to be here where I belonged, forever One with the Light. I was told I must return to earth because I had not completed my work there. I did not want to go, yet I understood many things. My husband would stay, and I would go, and that was just the way it was. (Sutherland, pp. 171–72)

The Purposes of this Book

This book is about NDEs and how they relate to the doctrine and teachings of The Church of Jesus Christ of Latter-day Saints (the Mormons). Those doctrines, for example, speak of the glory of God as it is reflected in the all-embracing light and love, witnessed by those who were engulfed in its magnificence, although but for a moment. Modern LDS scriptures reinforce the Bible concerning the glory of God. Indeed, one chapter of this book is devoted to accounts of Joseph Smith's visions and the fallout from them. Many scriptural examples could be given, but the writings of Luke give us one biblical example of the glory of God:

> And it came to pass about eight days after these sayings, he took Peter and John and James, and went up into a mountain to pray. And as he prayed, the fashion of his countenance was altered, and his raiment was white and glistening. And, behold, there talked with him two men, which were Moses and Elias: Who appeared in glory, and spake of his decease which he should accomplish at Jerusalem. But Peter and they that were with him were heavy with sleep: and when they were awake,

they saw his glory, and the two men that stood with him. (Luke 9:28–32)

This book, then, concerns the many-faceted aspects of NDEs and how they do or do not correlate with LDS teachings. The book considers research findings that have accumulated from various scientific disciplines over the past thirty years or so. Thus, it not only gives a Mormon perspective of NDEs but also an updated view of NDE findings.

The book illustrates primary findings—including some of the controversies and uncertainties still remaining, and it speculates on the future course of research in the NDE realm. Most important, it compares NDE-related events with LDS teachings and scriptures, and it draws some conclusions.

The Process and the Goal: Heading Toward Omega

The last chapter of the book derives some conclusions from the work presented. In that chapter, as well as in other portions of the book, Kenneth Ring's concept of "Omega" is discussed. As Ring conceived the term, he wrote of the "ascent toward Omega" in which a higher human evolutionary state would be reached, at least in part, due to NDEs. That concept is considered in the final chapter. A subjective evaluation is made of how successful our march to Omega has been and what role, if any, NDEs and Mormon philosophy have played.

Also in the concluding chapter, the question, "Why the inordinate interest in NDEs by the LDS community?" is addressed. Evidence for this strong interest is demonstrated by the large number of LDS authors who write on the subject.

As with most research work, any conclusions presented in this book are limited and tentative. As Kenneth Ring wrote when he completed the book *Heading Toward Omega:*

> To prevent any misunderstanding of this point, I must not only repeat but also emphasize that nothing in this book *proves* any of these propositions or, of course, the overall thesis that they represent. It is just a framework supported by some of my data and suggested by others. Only further research and the passage of time can demonstrate its validity. I offer it here as the outcome of my personal search for understanding of these extraordinary experiences. (Ring, 1984, p. 259)

Although twenty years have elapsed since Dr. Ring wrote that paragraph, the basic statement is still true. Readers can draw their own conclusions relative to the data shown, bearing in mind that NDE information is, by its very nature, uncertain.

In the process of spending approximately fifteen years of my life actively involved in near-death research and studies, I have become acquainted with—and in many cases, made close friends with—other professional researchers, teachers, and those who have had NDEs. I confess to taking advantage of my relationships with these people. You will find contributions by some of them in this book, for which I am supremely grateful.

My purpose in getting others in the near-death field to add their contribution to this volume was to add some balance to the overall theme. The book cannot hope to present all of the varying claims and counterclaims related to NDE research, but it can offer a glimpse from other LDS professionals actively working in the field.

Who This Book Is For

This book is directed in part to LDS readers but with a broad outreach to others involved in near-death studies, or just to interested folks. As a book written for both an LDS audience and for others with particular NDE interests, the materials selected for this book are deliberately chosen with those interests in mind.

Books and articles about NDEs have been written by LDS authors (amply illustrated in later portions of the book), but none to my knowledge has comprehensively reviewed past and recent research findings in which both agreement and possible disagreement between NDE's and LDS theology have been examined.

This book is not an unbiased exposition on all of the possibilities that other religions may have for claims on NDE research findings. That is better left to the believers of those religions. Neither is this book an invitation to debate the merit of one philosophic or religious point of view versus that of other religions or of The Church of Jesus Christ of Latter-day Saints. The material is presented as selected and diagnosed by the authors, and readers are invited to draw their own conclusions.

Inevitably there may be some, both LDS and non-LDS, who may seek to challenge some of the representations of the LDS position or to compare and even refute them with claims of their own. That is their privilege in a free society. I hope, however, that in the spirit of LDS teachings and overwhelming pleas by those who have glimpsed another world during an NDE, the work will be accepted as an offering of love.

Use of "Mormon" Terms

Throughout this book we will frequently refer to members of The Church of Jesus Christ of Latter-day Saints as "LDS" members, or "Mormons," and their corollary, "Mormon doctrine," or "LDS teachings" will be used to describe Church teachings. In a technical sense, there is no such thing as "Mormon doctrine," or a "Mormon Church." The nickname "Mormon" was given to early members of the church by nonmembers, primarily because of their use of the Book of Mormon.

Mormon was an ancient American prophet, descended from Israel, who compiled the history and religious teachings of his ancestors from the time they left Jerusalem in 600 B.C. until his death in the Americas in about A.D. 435. These writings, on golden plates, were translated by Joseph Smith and published as *The Book of Mormon—Another Testament of Jesus Christ.*

The use of Mormon's name—and the acronym LDS—has remained as a convenient shortcut for describing the Church and its members. Church members, who accept and use these shortcuts themselves, believe that the Church is, indeed, the church of Jesus Christ. To distinguish it from the ancient church during Christ's ministry, the designation of "Latter-day Saints" is part of its official title. Thus, the doctrines and teachings are, in reality, not Mormon teachings or LDS teachings but are, rather, the doctrines and teachings of Jesus Christ.

Responsibility and Authorship

This book seeks to address some of the questions implied by the foregoing material. Many of them are tackled by me, and the presentations and conclusions are my own. I make no claim to authoritative representation of The Church of Jesus Christ of Latter-day Saints. That privilege is reserved to the Church president, revered by Latter-day Saints as a prophet, and other General Authorities of the Church. Neither do I claim any significant academic credentials in the fields of medicine, psychology, social studies, or other such disciplines. Any errors of the data or conclusions presented in my name are my responsibility.

Others who contribute to the work are in an analogous position, except that many have substantial academic credentials directly related to the study and research of NDEs. They have final approval of their material included in the book.

Finally, lest there be any question about my particular beliefs, the research I have carried out in the near-death field convinces me that there is overwhelming evidence—suitable for any number of scientific tests—that human consciousness survives death. Moreover, I believe that NDE research and studies, together with an aggressive promotion of Mormon philosophy, have carried us closer to Omega in a dramatic way. While it is true that in some ways these are the worst of times, these are also the best of times. There are millions of people trying to do their best and to help their fellow beings. And though rare, there are still Mother Teresas in the world. All of us are, in the end, sons and daughters of the Creator, and we carry the embryonic light from that Creator within us. It is the light that speaks of an ethereal love, a love beyond earthly comprehension or description.

Most important, I am a dedicated and believing member of The Church of Jesus Christ of Latter-day Saints. I believe that Joseph Smith was the first prophet of the Church, which is a restoration of the primitive church established by Jesus Christ, and I believe that the Church is today directed by a modern-day prophet.

So, to all of the readers of this book, I wish a pleasant reading journey. May you feel of the spirit of Love described so emotionally and so forcefully by those who have taken a timeless journey to a place of peace, a peace spoken of in Phillipians 4:7: "The peace of God, which passeth all understanding."

That death does, indeed, open a door to the peace of God was brought home forcefully recently when a marvelous friend of mine died. He succumbed to Lou Gehrig's disease after several months of debilitating suffering. In commenting on his passing, Kenneth Ring wrote an e-mail to me in which he said, "Death is certainly the great antidote to dying, and it's the dying we witnesses see, which causes us, and not just the person dying, such distress."

Think about that for a moment. If its true impact does not immediately seize you, read on. The many experiences documented in this book will add their testimony to Ken's truism.

Acknowledgments

This book is the result of the effort of many people. First among those is Duane Crowther, president and senior editor of Horizon Publishers and Distributors, Inc., my publisher. In 2003 Duane asked me if I wanted to write another book on near-death experiences that drew upon the expertise of other experts in the field. At the time I was involved in a major family history project for my grandchildren, and I declined. By the time 2004 arrived, I had completed my grandchildren project—with much appreciation from them—so I called Duane and told him I had some time. He suggested that I put together an outline and proposed premise for the book. As I viewed the proposed book at the time, it would draw upon the experience of numerous individuals involved in near-death research. It would examine NDE studies on a broad front.

With the major parameters of the book set and agreed upon, I was faced with the problem of selecting a group of participating LDS authors who were both knowledgeable in Mormon theology and thoroughly competent in the field of NDE research. With much care I selected B. Grant Bishop, Sandra Cherry, Duane Crowther, Lynn Johnson, David Larsen, and Harold Widdison. To my surprise, they all agreed upon my initial request. Their biographies, included in the book, as well as their finished chapters, both testify to their competence. I owe them my gratitude.

For reasons explained in the book, I decided to reinterview several of those I had interviewed thirteen years ago. In addition, I intended to add some NDEs that had not been published previously. In particular, I am indebted to the following individuals for their involvement in this project (in the order they appear in the book): Eloise Weaver; Don and Wanda Wood and their boys; Ella Jensen; Lucinda Hecker; Ruby and Bill Essex; David Herard; John Hernandez and his son Sebastian; John Stirling; Derald Evans; Bill English and his daughter Cam; Elizabeth, Crystal and John Clark; Vern Swanson; Ann; Sylvia; Gary Gillum; Joe Swick; Jack Wait; Maxine Zawodniak; DeAnne Anderson Shelley and Melvin Shelley; Renee Zamora; and Beverly Brodsky.

Beverly Brodsky was particularly helpful in providing information about her proposed new book and in granting an interview that is included in chapter 17 of this book. Her perspective of the climb to Omega—the concept advanced by Ken Ring in 1984—and how successful that climb has been, materially strengthened that chapter.

Another of the pioneers who cheerfully provided important information regarding prospective NDE research being carried out at the University of Virginia is Bruce Greyson. The nature of the proposed work lends itself to a unique corroborative type of research.

A number of readers reviewed the book and provided an assessment of their feelings about the work. Included in this group are Jan Holden, Nan Hunter, Ralph Maybe, David Conklin, Phil Pluta, and Melvin Morse. My fellow authors and I owe them a debt of gratitude.

This book would not exist except for the many researchers, Mormon and non-Mormon, who provided the informational foundation that the book draws upon. There are too many to list here, but their contributions are discussed in chapters 2, 3, 9, and 10.

Finally, and most important, I must acknowledge the Word produced under revelation from God by prophets through the centuries. That Word has come down to us as scriptures and other prophetic utterances that represent pure light and truth.

Although the data included in this book comes from many sources—as witnessed by the References Section—the thoughts that tie them together are my own and those of my fellow authors. If there are overstatements based on the facts presented, please, dear reader, accept our apology. It is my hope and prayer, however, that you will sense, as I did in gathering the information, the awesome import of the evolving story derived from the different sources.

Part 1:

Latter-day Saint Perspectives on Near-Death Experiences

O my Father, thou that dwellest
In the high and glorious place,
When shall I regain thy presence,
And again behold thy face?

In thy holy habitation,
Did my spirit once reside?
In my first primeval childhood,
Was I nurtured near thy side?

For a wise and glorious purpose
Thou hast placed me here on earth,
And withheld the recollection
Of my former friends and birth.

Yet oft-times a secret something
Whispered, "You're a stranger here,"
And I felt that I had wandered
From a more exalted sphere.

I had learned to call thee Father,
Through thy Spirit from on high;
But until the key of knowledge
Was restored, I knew not why.

In the heavens are parents single?
No, the thought makes reason stare!
Truth is reason, truth eternal
Tells me I've a mother there.

When I leave this frail existence,
When I lay this mortal by,
Father, Mother, may I meet you
In your royal courts on high?

Then, at length, when I've completed
All you sent me forth to do,
With your mutual approbation
Let me come and dwell with you.

("O My Father," *Hymns*, no. 292)

1: Joseph Smith's Experiences and Their Aftermath

Joseph Smith

Their Pertinence to NDEs

As will be evident upon reading this chapter, the visions that Joseph Smith and his colleagues had contain some remarkable parallels to what those who have had near-death experiences or analogous epiphanies claim to have happened to them. Indeed, it is impossible to speak of The Church of Jesus Christ of Latter-day Saints without recognizing Joseph Smith's claims to have seen and spoken with God, his son, Jesus Christ, and with many of the early prophets of the Bible.

Also, inextricably connected to Joseph Smith and his claims are the Book of Mormon, the Pearl of Great Price, and the Doctrine and Covenants—modern-day scriptures—which were given by revelation to the prophet Joseph. In particular, the Book of Mormon purports to be an ancient history of three groups of people who migrated from ancient Israel to America under the direction of God. Joseph translated the book from ancient writings that were engraved on gold plates.

These astonishing claims are unique in religious history in that the details of their foundation are backed by volumes of relatively current—beginning in the early 1800s—available documentation. Thus, checks and counter-checks have been made on their authenticity. It is beyond the scope of this book to detail all the material, pro and con, regarding Joseph Smith, the Book of Mormon and other latter-day scriptures. One excellent recent work which summarizes many of the diverse arguments about Joseph Smith and the Book of Mormon is by Professor Terry L. Givens of the University of Virginia. His book *By the Hand of Mormon,* attempts to present a balanced view of the LDS experience, with particular attention to the claims and counter-claims of the Book of Mormon (Givens, 2002).

So, what is the pertinence of these materials to the NDE phenomenon? It is that they are readily available for scholarly study; and other works, such as NDE documentaries, can easily be checked against them. And, just as any active and believing Latter-day Saint must perforce accept Joseph Smith's historical account, so also must that same Latter-day Saint accept many of the claims associated with the near-death experience. To do otherwise would be to deny the origins of his/her own religion—including ancestral spiritual documentaries which form a sacred part of many Mormon libraries. It should be noted that there are, of course, Latter-day Saints who do not accept the claims of those who have had NDEs.

The history which follows is not a comprehensive history of Joseph Smith and the Mormon Church. There are ample books written on that subject to which the reader can refer. Instead, it is a selected history which documents visions and other epiphanies associated with the foundation of the religion. That most of the materials were written—or translated—by a relatively illiterate farm boy in the 1820–1840 time period makes them even more interesting.

The First Vision of Joseph Smith

Joseph Smith Jr., the Mormon Prophet, was born on December 23, 1805 in Sharon Vermont. The family moved to New York in 1815 where they farmed a one-hundred-acre unimproved plot of land two miles south of Palmyra. Young Joseph's education was limited; school was held in his home, except for periods in Vermont where he attended "common schools," and where he learned to read, write and cipher. In his home schooling, Joseph was largely taught from the Bible by his mother. From his early youth Joseph and his older brother, Alvin, labored diligently to help the family and to obtain money by hiring themselves out.

Bible reading and family prayers were a daily practice in the Smith home, and Joseph was aware of basic Christian beliefs. He was confused, however by the various religious sects which contended for members in the area. He had his initial vision when he was fourteen years of age. His account of what happened follows (Joseph Smith–History 1:12–20):

> While I was laboring under the extreme difficulties caused by the contests of these parties of religionists, I was one day reading the Epistle of James, first chapter and fifth verse, which reads: If any of you lack wisdom, let him ask of God, that giveth to all men liberally, and upbraideth not; and it shall be given him. Never did any passage of scripture come with more power to the heart of man than this did at this time to mine. It seemed to enter with great force into every feeling of my heart. I reflected on it again and again, knowing that if any person needed wisdom from God, I did; for how to act I did not know, and unless I could get more wisdom than I then had, I would never know; for the teachers of religion of the different sects understood the same passages of scripture so differently as to destroy all confidence in settling the question by an appeal to the Bible.
>
> At length I came to the conclusion that I must either remain in darkness and confusion, or else I must do as James directs, that is, ask of God. I at length came to the determination to "ask of God," concluding that if he gave wisdom to them that lacked wisdom, and would give liberally, and not upbraid, I might venture. So, in accordance with this, my determination to ask of God, I retired to the woods to make the attempt. It was on the morning of a beautiful, clear day, early in the spring of eighteen hundred and twenty. It was the first time in my life that I had made such an attempt, for amidst all my anxieties I had never as yet made the attempt to pray vocally.
>
> After I had retired to the place where I had previously designed to go, having looked around me, and finding myself alone, I kneeled down and began to offer up the desires of my

heart to God. I had scarcely done so, when immediately I was seized upon by some power which entirely overcame me, and had such an astonishing influence over me as to bind my tongue so that I could not speak. Thick darkness gathered around me, and it seemed to me for a time as if I were doomed to sudden destruction. But, exerting all my powers to call upon God to deliver me out of the power of this enemy which had seized upon me, and at the very moment when I was ready to sink into despair and abandon myself to destruction—not to an imaginary ruin, but to the power of some actual being from the unseen world, who had such marvelous power as I had never before felt in any being—just at this moment of great alarm, I saw a pillar of light exactly over my head, above the brightness of the sun, which descended gradually until it fell upon me.

It no sooner appeared than I found myself delivered from the enemy which held me bound. When the light rested upon me I saw two Personages, whose brightness and glory defy all description, standing above me in the air. One of them spake unto me, calling me by name and said, pointing to the other— This is My Beloved Son. Hear Him!

My object in going to inquire of the Lord was to know which of all the sects was right, that I might know which to join. No sooner, therefore, did I get possession of myself, so as to be able to speak, than I asked the Personages who stood above me in the light, which of all the sects was right (for at this time it had never entered into my heart that all were wrong)—and which I should join. I was answered that I must join none of them, for they were all wrong; and the Personage who addressed me said that all their creeds were an abomination in his sight; that those professors were all corrupt; that: "they draw near to me with their lips, but their hearts are far from me, they teach for doctrines the commandments of men, having a form of godliness, but they deny the power thereof." He again forbade me to join with any of them; and many other things did he say unto me, which I cannot write at this time. When I came to myself again, I found myself lying on my back, looking up into heaven. When the light had departed, I had no strength; but soon recovering in some degree, I went home.

Visits of the Angel Moroni

Joseph told his parents and his siblings of his vision and they believed him. He also told others, including Christian Ministers, for which he was soundly derided. However, on the evening of September

21, 1823, Joseph retired to his bed "in quite a serious and contemplative state of mind" (Barrett, 1973, p. 61). His account of what happened next follows (Joseph Smtih–History 1:29–34):

> After I had retired to my bed for the night, I betook myself to prayer and supplication to Almighty God for forgiveness of all my sins and follies, and also for a manifestation to me, that I might know of my state and standing before him; for I had full confidence in obtaining a divine manifestation, as I previously had one.
>
> While I was thus in the act of calling upon God, I discovered a light appearing in my room, which continued to increase until the room was lighter than at noonday, when immediately a personage appeared at my bedside, standing in the air, for his feet did not touch the floor. He had on a loose robe of most exquisite whiteness. It was a whiteness beyond anything earthly I had ever seen; nor do I believe that any earthly thing could be made to appear so exceedingly white and brilliant. His hands were naked, and his arms also, a little above the wrist; so, also, were his feet naked, as were his legs, a little above the ankles. His head and neck were also bare. I could discover that he had no other clothing on but this robe, as it was open, so that I could see into his bosom.
>
> Not only was his robe exceedingly white, but his whole person was glorious beyond description, and his countenance truly like lightning. The room was exceedingly light, but not so very bright as immediately around his person. When I first looked upon him, I was afraid; but the fear soon left me.
>
> He called me by name, and said unto me that he was a messenger sent from the presence of God to me, and that his name was Moroni; that God had a work for me to do; and that my name should be had for good and evil among all nations, kindreds, and tongues, or that it should be both good and evil spoken of among all people. He said there was a book deposited, written upon gold plates, giving an account of the former inhabitants of this continent, and the source from whence they sprang. He also said that the fulness of the everlasting Gospel was contained in it, as delivered by the Savior to the ancient inhabitants.

The angel gave further instructions to Joseph Smith, and he quoted extensively from Malachi, Isaiah, Acts, Joel and other scriptures from the Bible. Then as the instructions from Moroni seemed about to cease, Joseph Smith recorded this (Joseph Smith–History 1:43–45):

> After this communication, I saw the light in the room begin

to gather immediately around the person of him who had been speaking to me, and it continued to do so until the room was again left dark, except just around him; when, instantly I saw, as it were, a conduit open right up into heaven, and he ascended till he entirely disappeared, and the room was left as it had been before this heavenly light had made its appearance.

I lay musing on the singularity of the scene, and marveling greatly at what had been told to me by this extraordinary messenger; when, in the midst of my meditation, I suddenly discovered that my room was again beginning to get lighted, and in an instant, as it were, the same heavenly messenger was again by my bedside. He commenced, and again related the very same things which he had done at his first visit, without the least variation. . . .

Moroni repeated this same message a total of three times. As part of these messages, Joseph was told that at the proper time he would be given the golden plates and, through the power of the Lord, would be able to translate the ancient writings contained on them. After these visits to Joseph by Moroni, which took most of the night, daylight broke and Joseph went to the field to harvest the grain as usual. His father observed that Joseph was not able to vigorously work as he normally did, and thinking him ill, told him to go home. Joseph left and in attempting to climb a fence collapsed. Immediately he heard a voice speaking his name. Looking up, he again saw Moroni, who repeated the same message from the previous evening, and he told Joseph to tell his father what had transpired. (Barrett, 1973, pp. 64–65)

The Translating of the Book of Mormon

In his vision Joseph had seen where the golden plates were buried in a hill four miles south of Palmyra. Joseph went to the spot of the vision and was able to find the plates and other materials. He attempted to remove them but was unable to do so as he was commanded by Moroni, who again appeared, to leave them until he was given permission to remove them. He was told to visit the hill each year, on September 22, to be instructed further (Barrett, 1973, pp. 66–67).

Joseph did as he was instructed for four years, and on September 22, 1827, Joseph was given the plates by the Angel Moroni. He was cautioned that he would be responsible for the record, and should the record be lost through his neglect God would cut him off. In addition to the plates, Joseph was given a Urim and Thummim, which was an ancient translating device, and which would later aid him in the translation. He took the plates home and hid them (Barrett, 1973, p. 75).

Joseph wrote this description of the plates:

> These records were engraven on plates which had the appearance of gold, each plate was six inches wide and eight inches long, and not quite so thick as common tin. They were . . . bound together in a volume as the leaves of a book, with three rings running through the whole. The volume was something near six inches in thickness, a part of which was sealed. The characters of the unsealed part were small, and beautifully engraved. The whole book exhibited many marks of antiquity in its construction, and much skill in the art of engraving. (Barrett, 1973, p. 78)

As to the method of translation, Joseph said that he translated the plates "by the Gift and Power of God." A number of witnesses have described how the process worked. A summary of the process is as follows:

> Joseph Smith viewed the interpreters (either the Urim and Thummim or a seer stone) and dictated for long periods of time without reference to any books, papers, manuscripts, or even the plates themselves. Joseph also spelled out unfamiliar Book of Mormon names. After each dictated sequence, the scribe read back to Joseph what was written so that Joseph could check the correctness of the manuscript. Joseph started each dictation session without prompting from the scribe about where the previous session had ended, and without notes. (Reynolds, 1997, Chap. 4)

Throughout the translation of the Book of Mormon the plates stayed with Joseph Smith except for a brief period when Moroni retrieved them, then later returned them to Joseph. Upon completion of the translation, Moroni reclaimed the plates from Joseph.

The Witnesses of the Book of Mormon

During the translation of the Book of Mormon, Joseph and Oliver Cowdery discovered that some of the text spoke of witnesses who would "bear record of same." Ultimately, eleven witnesses would be chosen, eight who would view and handle the plates, and three who would have the greater privilege of an angelic visitation. The three chosen witnesses were Martin Harris, Oliver Cowdery and David Whitmer. The eight witnesses were Christian, Jacob, Peter, and John Whitmer, Hiram Page, Joseph Smith, Sr., and Joseph's brothers, Hyrum and Samuel Smith.

In June of 1829, as the translation was almost complete, Joseph took Martin, Oliver and David into the woods where they prayed to have a vision. Notwithstanding their prayer, nothing happened, and Martin asked to be excused so that he could pray separately. He was excused and Oliver, David and Joseph resumed praying. Joseph described what happened next in this manner:

> When presently we beheld a light above us in the air, of exceeding brightness; and behold, an angel stood before us. In his hands he held the plates which we had been praying for these to have a view of. He turned over the leaves one by one, so that we could see them, and discern the engravings thereon distinctly. He then addressed himself to David Whitmer, and said, "David, blessed is the Lord, and he that keeps His commandments;" when immediately afterwards, we heard a voice from out of the bright light above us, saying, "These plates have been revealed by the power of God, and they have been translated by the power of God. The translation of them which you have seen is correct, and I command you to bear record of what you now see and hear."
>
> After this experience, David and Oliver left, and Joseph went in search of Martin. He found him praying a short distance away. They joined in prayer, and Martin and Joseph then had a similar experience. (Barrett, 1973, pp. 101–2)

A few days after these experiences, the Whitmers and Hiram Page visited the Smiths in Manchester. The Prophet invited them, his father and brothers into the woods. There he took the plates from a cloth container and laid them before the eight men. They saw and handled the plates. There was no vision or voice that spoke to them—just the plates (Barrett, 1973, p. 103).

All of the eleven witnesses signed a statement bearing witness to what they had seen and heard. The statements appear at the beginning of each Book of Mormon. Later in their lives, some of the witnesses left the Church for various reasons, but they never denied their testimonies (Barrett, 1973, pp. 100–116).

Baptism under the Direction of an Angelic Messenger

While translating the Book of Mormon, Joseph and Oliver discovered that baptism for the remission of sins was mentioned several times by prophets described in the text. The mode of baptism prescribed was baptism by immersion. They also determined that baptism was for those eight years of age and older—for those capable of sinning.

Little children and those not capable of sinning were saved through the atonement of Jesus Christ without baptism.

As a result of these passages of scripture, on May 15, 1829 they retired to a riverbank on the edge of the Susquehanna River where they commenced to pray for enlightenment. They had scarcely commenced their prayer when a heavenly messenger descended in a cloud of glory, surrounded by light which surpassed the glitter of the May sunbeams and shed its brilliancy over the face of nature (Barrett, 1973, p. 121).

The messenger introduced himself as John the Baptist, and said that he was acting under the direction of Peter, James and John—Christ's Apostles from the Old World—and that he was to bestow upon them the Aaronic Priesthood, which held the keys of the ministering of angels and of the gospel of repentance, and of baptism by immersion for the remission of sins.

Oliver Cowdery, the school teacher and scribe of the Book of Mormon, was one of the more eloquent speakers and writers in the early Church. He later wrote an account of what he felt and saw during this experience. His description follows (Joseph Smith–History, note at end):

> I shall not attempt to paint to you the feelings of this heart, or the majestic beauty and glory which surrounded us on this occasion; but you will believe me when I say, that earth, nor men, with the eloquence of time, cannot begin to clothe language in as interesting and sublime a manner as this holy personage. No; nor has this earth power to give the joy, to bestow the peace, or comprehend the wisdom which was contained in each sentence as they were delivered by the power of the Holy Spirit! Man may deceive his fellow-men, deception may follow deception, and the children of the wicked one may have power to seduce the foolish and untaught, till naught but fiction feeds the many, and the fruit of falsehood carries in its current the giddy to the grave; but one touch with the finger of his love, yes, one ray of glory from the upper world, or one word from the mouth of the Savior, from the bosom of eternity, strikes it all into insignificance, and blots it forever from the mind. The assurance that we were in the presence of an angel, the certainty that we heard the voice of Jesus, and the truth unsullied as it flowed from a pure personage, dictated by the will of God, is to me past description, and I shall ever look upon this expression of the Savior's goodness with wonder and thanksgiving while I am permitted to tarry; and in those mansions where

perfection dwells and sin never comes, I hope to adore in that day which shall never cease.

A View of Jesus Christ in the Kirtland, Ohio, Temple

On Sunday, April 3, 1836, while in the temple, a marvelous vision was revealed to Joseph Smith and Oliver Cowdery. Joseph described what happened in these terms:

> In the afternoon, I assisted the other Presidents in distributing the Lord's Supper to the Church, receiving it from the Twelve, whose privilege it was to officiate at the sacred desk this day. After having performed this service to my brethren, I retired to the pulpit, the veils being dropped, and bowed myself, with Oliver Cowdery, in solemn and silent prayer. After rising from the prayer, the following vision was opened to both of us.
>
> The veil was taken from our minds, and the eyes of our understanding were opened. We saw the Lord standing upon the breastwork of the pulpit, before us; and under his feet was a paved work of pure gold, in color like amber. His eyes were as a flame of fire; the hair of his head was white like the pure snow; his countenance shone above the brightness of the sun; and his voice was as the sound of the rushing of great waters, even the voice of Jehovah, saying: I am the first and the last; I am he who liveth, I am he who was slain; I am your advocate with the Father.
>
> Behold, your sins are forgiven you; you are clean before me; therefore, lift up your heads and rejoice. Let the hearts of your brethren rejoice, and let the hearts of all my people rejoice, who have, with their might, built this house to my name. For behold, I have accepted this house, and my name shall be here; and I will manifest myself to my people in mercy in this house. (D&C 110:1–7)

After the vision of the Savior, Moses appeared and committed to Joseph and Oliver the keys of the gathering of Israel from the four parts of the earth; Elias appeared and committed the dispensation of the gospel of Abraham, and Elijah appeared saying: "Behold, the time has fully come which was spoken of by the mouth of Malachi—testifying that he [Elijah] should be sent, before the great and dreadful day of the Lord to come—to turn the hearts of the fathers to the children, and the children to the fathers, lest the whole earth be smitten with a curse" (D&C 110:11–15).

The Reaction of Professional Religionists
to Joseph Smith's Testimony

Just as with those who first timidly told their NDE stories—prior to Moody, Ritchie and Ring—and found a disbelieving audience, so too did Joseph Smith collide with entrenched belief systems which denied that an unschooled fourteen-year-old could have spoken with God. Joseph wrote this about these reactions (Joseph Smith–History 1:22–25):

I soon found, however, that my telling the story had excited a great deal of prejudice against me among professors of religion, and was the cause of great persecution, which continued to increase; and though I was an obscure boy, only between fourteen and fifteen years of age, and my circumstances in life such as to make a boy of no consequence in the world, yet men of high standing would take notice sufficient to excite the public mind against me, and create a bitter persecution; and this was common among all the sects—all united to persecute me.

It caused me serious reflection then, and often has since, how very strange it was that an obscure boy, of a little over fourteen years of age, and one, too, who was doomed to the necessity of obtaining a scanty maintenance by his daily labor, should be thought a character of sufficient importance to attract the attention of the great ones of the most popular sects of the day, and in a manner to create in them a spirit of the most bitter persecution and reviling. But strange or not, so it was, and it was often the cause of great sorrow to myself.

However, it was nevertheless a fact that I had beheld a vision. I have thought since, that I felt much like Paul, when he made his defense before King Agrippa, and related the account of the vision he had when he saw a light, and heard a voice; but still there were but few who believed him; some said he was dishonest, others said he was mad; and he was ridiculed and reviled. But all this did not destroy the reality of his vision. He had seen a vision, he knew he had, and all the persecution under heaven could not make it otherwise; and though they should persecute him unto death, yet he knew, and would know to his latest breath, that he had both seen a light and heard a voice speaking unto him, and all the world could not make him think or believe otherwise.

So it was with me. I had actually seen a light, and in the midst of that light I saw two Personages, and they did in reality speak to me; and though I was hated and persecuted for saying that I had seen a vision, yet it was true; and while they were persecuting me, reviling me, and speaking all manner of evil against me falsely for so saying, I was led to say in my heart: Why persecute me for telling the truth? I have actually seen a vision; and who am I that I can withstand God, or why does the world think to make me deny what I have actually seen? For I had seen a vision; I knew it, and I knew that God knew it, and I could not deny it, neither dared I do it; at least I knew that by so doing I would offend God, and come under condemnation.

The Ubiquitous Nature of Spiritual Experiences

Joseph was not unique in having visions such as those described above. Spiritual stories among the early saints were ubiquitous. They became part of the documented histories of many pioneer families. And as such, just as in the primitive Church during Christ's and Paul's time, these stories became a prime impetus in attracting members into the Church. Going back even further in time, it was the prophets of the Old Testament, and the miracles which they performed, which kept ancient Israel close to God. One might legitimately ask, if there were prophets during the Old and New Testament times, why not now? Or has God ceased to be interested in his children? That God still speaks to his children would receive a strong Amen from the members of The Church of Jesus Christ of Latter-day Saints, and, if NDE accounts are to be believed, that Amen would be echoed by those having had such NDEs.

Joseph Smith's Impact and Accomplishments

Joseph Smith, in his 38 ½ years accomplished more than most men accomplish in twice that time. He founded a new religion—or rather he helped God reestablish Christ's original religion. In that religion Joseph established, by authority of the Lord, the Priesthood offices and authority that existed in Christ's pristine Church. He set into place the means to continue with that organization after his departure with follow-on "prophets, seers and revelators."

He translated an ancient record, The Book of Mormon, within a ninety-day elapsed period, with no reference to other materials or sources other than those provided by the Angel Moroni. He did that with less than a fourth-grade education, and he included complex materials about a complete civilization on this continent which developed from the descendants of some ancient prophets and their families who were led by the Lord from ancient Israel. The book describes Christ's visit to those ancient peoples, and it details many other instances of the Lord's dealings with them during their periods of peace and war. It includes new information on doctrinal matters which are incomplete in the Bible. It displays evidence of being an ancient work, the technical nature of which could not have been understood by Joseph Smith when the book was written. Despite challenges by numerous scholars attempting to disprove the book or its origin, it has stood the test of time. Millions of copies have been printed in many languages and distributed throughout the world.

Joseph attracted thousands of dedicated followers, and he initiated an aggressive missionary program which survives to this day. Temples were reestablished by him as a central part of the religion—with ordinances and covenants binding man to God and God to man.

Several other documents of scripture were added to the standard works of the Church by revelation to Joseph. These included the Doctrine and Covenants and the Pearl of Great Price. The Pearl of Great Price contained additional writings of Moses and Abraham. All of these writings were to act as complements to the Bible and were additional witnesses that Jesus is the Christ.

In the area of civil and national government, Joseph planned cities, established a welfare system for the care of the needy, became mayor of the largest city in Illinois, directed the Nauvoo Legion as its commanding general, and ran for the Presidency of the United States.

During all of this time, Joseph met his accusers with civility and in accordance with established laws. He defended the Constitution of the United States as an inspired document, and he met with President Van Buren and members of the U.S. Congress in an attempt to get redress for the Saints. Van Buren's response was, "Gentlemen, your cause is just, but I can do nothing for you. . . . If I take up for you I shall lose the vote of Missouri" (Barrett, 1973, p. 449).

The LDS Church Today

The Church, today, is dynamic and growing. Joseph Smith understood that he was the instrument in the Lord's hand which had launched a world-wide religion, but even he might be amazed at what started as a congregation of about 50 members on April 6, 1830. There are obviously a number of factors which affect growth. These include such ingredients as the number and effectiveness of the missionaries; the birth rate of Church members; geopolitical issues; availability of Church leadership in the area being proselyted; the strength of the message being delivered; and most importantly, the individual revelatory testimony of the members. Without an analysis of all of these factors, precise causative effects are impossible. A rough feeling, however, for the dynamics of Church growth can be obtained from a total membership chart. Such a chart is given here (Data from Church statistical records). As can be seen, from a period beginning about 1960, the Church showed an accelerating growth trend. This was also the time when the Church missionary activity was increased significantly.

The official data as of October 31, 2005 showed the Church at 12.49 million members. Unofficial estimates as this book goes to press in early 2006 show the Church approaching 13 million members.

A Catholic organization, "The Glenmary Research Center" in Nashville, Tennessee recently (September 17, 2002) published "The 2000 Religious Congregations Membership Study." They studied data from 149 participating faiths and adjusted the information to make it comparable. Their findings showed that The Church of Jesus Christ of Latter-day Saints was the fastest-growing faith in the nation during the 1990s.

2: Mormons and Near-Death Experiences—Preparing the Way

By Duane Crowther, MA, MBA

About the Author

Duane S. Crowther graduated from Brigham Young University with a Bachelor of Arts degree in music education in 1959, and stayed on to earn a Master of Arts degree in Old and New Testament in 1960. He also earned an MBA from the University of Phoenix in 1987 and completed all the course work for a Ph.D. in music education from the University of Utah, writing a dissertation which became a choir-instruction curriculum used in numerous high schools across the nation.

Since the publication of his first book in 1962, he has played a significant role in the Latter-day Saint marketplace, not only as a widely-read author, but also by preparing and supervising the publication of numerous works that have added important insights on a wide variety of doctrinal and educational themes. He has guided and helped more than 300 other authors get into print. He is the President and Senior Editor for Horizon Publishers & Distributors, Inc., a publishing company formed in 1971. In that capacity he has personally edited and produced more than eight hundred books. He is the author of more than fifty of those books himself.

With his training and background in teaching, he has taught in various church and secular capacities over the years.

He is a former LDS Seminary teacher and principal, as well as a former public school band and orchestra conductor. For years he taught thesis-writing and business courses for the University of Phoenix. He has been a speaker on numerous religious subjects as well as a seminar instructor on various writing and business topics. His LDS Church service is extensive, both as a teacher and in various leadership positions.

How *Life Everlasting* Was Researched and Written

As my good friend Arvin Gibson asked each of the authors in this book to write a chapter, he presented us with a detailed outline of points he suggested that we cover. The first task he assigned me was to relate how my book *Life Everlasting* came into being.

The period: 1965–1966. The place: our home in Smithfield, Utah. My full-time occupation: proprietor of two music and book stores—one in downtown Logan, the other in the rear of our home in Smithfield, seven miles north of Logan. My time availability: limited—I was then the father of four sweet but very young children, working full-time-plus in the Logan store, serving as the Elders Quorum President for the Smithfield First Ward and the nearby Amalga Ward, and learning that the best time to write was from 4:30 to 6:30 each morning. This put my workload up to between seventy to eighty hours a week. The four books I had previously written were still being well received and I was filling more than 150 requests per year to speak at firesides, youth conferences, youth camps, and other Church meetings.

As I pondered what my fifth book should be, I felt that a valuable contribution would be to compile what the scriptures and the brethren had said on the nature of death, the spirit world, and the kingdoms of glory and exaltation, including all the related topics such as the resurrection, the judgment, hell, the sons of perdition, etc.

By this time I had developed a research routine that had proved very helpful. Each time I would embark on a new gospel topic, I would devote about six weeks to rapid but very intense scanning of the major sources. During that time I would typically scan all four of the Standard Works, the seven-volume *History of the Church,* the six-volume *Comprehensive History of the Church,* and two or three other books related to the subject I was pursuing. I would force myself to ignore all the other intriguing but unrelated new concepts that would jump out of the books at me, but would carefully note every reference pertaining to the subject of the book in process with a source and a brief one-line summary statement. The only exception would be that I compiled an extensive list of titles and publication sources of articles and books that I felt would be helpful in researching and writing on other topics.

Key ideas would receive an asterisk beside the reference. I would organize as I went along, establishing a new, lined notebook sheet for each sub-topic.

At this point I had begun to find my writing niches. My role as an author, in great measure, has been to identify newly perceived patterns of understanding on many aspects of gospel subjects—not by interjecting remarkable new sources, but by linking passages and ideas that had been there for many years but never associated with the patterns I was laying out for the readers' consumption. The scriptures are so full of conceptual pearls that there's always something new to be gleaned from them, though their texts have been there for hundreds or thousands of years. That's what I sought to do in this fifth book. Another of my niche roles has been to document thoroughly and fully, so that the sources are available to readers everywhere. Other authors have the skill to do this, but many are unwilling to put in the extra effort to document fully and well.

During the months while I was compiling all these doctrinal insights, I had not yet told the editors at Bookcraft that the manuscript was in process. (Since becoming a publisher I have quickly learned the folly of such a course of action—the publisher should be involved from very early after a book's inception.) I had the manuscript finished and almost completely polished. I was only a day or two away from taking it down to Bookcraft when I opened my *Deseret News* and saw a Bookcraft advertisement for a brand new book: *If a Man Die.* It only took the moment to read the description of the book in that newspaper ad and to realize that my timing was off. I took my manuscript and put it up on the bookshelf to wait till they would be ready for another book on life after death.

An Agonizing Loss—The Death of Laura Jean Crowther

It was several months later, in July 1966, while enjoying a family gathering at the Grand Canyon, that our daughter, **Laura Jean Crowther,** hemorrhaged a bit onto her pillow as she slept. My mother-in-law, Helen Decker, looked at her the next day, commented that she didn't look well, and suggested that we should take Laura to the doctor when we returned home. It was a week later when I received Jean's tearful phone call saying, "Honey—the doctor says it's leukemia!"

Stricken with two virulent adult forms of the disease at once, Laura passed away on September 5, less than two months after her illness was diagnosed. She left us as the family was driving home from a speaking engagement Jean and I had both participated in at a young-adult encampment in Richland, Washington. She died just as we reached Cascade, Idaho, in our southward journey back to Utah. After pronouncing her dead in the small hospital at Cascade, the doctor advised us that we would need to take her body back north to McCall, where there was a mortician who could care for her. It was as we backtracked on that hour-long journey that Laura appeared to Jean. Jeanie described to me what she had seen as we drove northward (Crowther, 1997, pp. 255–56). Needless to say, Laura's death and appearance to Jean created an emotional turmoil in us and raised as many questions as it answered. It certainly affected the direction I was taking on the book.

A Changed Direction—Adding Near-Death Experiences

In my manuscript which was then collecting dust on my shelf, waiting for the "appropriate time" to be submitted, I hadn't incorporated any of those many life-after-death and near-death experiences I had noted in my past researching. I'd fallen into the "it's got to be a statement by a General Authority to be accepted as authoritative" school of thought. Yet limiting my research to the scriptures and to their discourses left numerous questions unanswered—for me and for all those who would eventually read the book.

I resolved that I would go back to those first-person experiences and look for further insights. Having their sources previously noted and listed, I quickly found them, photo-copied them, and sat down to read them, one after another. It wasn't long before numerous patterns began to emerge. Sometimes a single account would comment on dozens of different topics. I decided that my approach would be to chop all the accounts into useable pieces that would address only a single subject at one time. Again, my goal was to build patterns of evidence, where numerous people were reporting the same situation or activity, giving the weight of numbers in establishing the veracity of the event, location, environment or activity.

As I added these pages to the manuscript, I saw my book move from being a stodgy, scholarly doctrinal study to being a life-filled book with new concepts and perceptions for the reader to discover on almost every page. My experience as an author told me that it would be a widely read book that would touch many lives, and that perception most certainly has proven to be true.

I have often wondered if the passing of my sweet daughter, Laura, was not timed by the powers on high so her death would be a catalyst for me to add these many experiences to the book. I presume that she died when she was supposed to pass through the veil, yet her death and subsequent appearances lit in me the fires of curiosity that motivated me to action. The changes I made to the manuscript, by including many patterns of evidence drawn from beyond-the-veil personal experiences, have had a profound effect on hundreds of thousands of people. I feel blessed that I became a tool in the Lord's hands to bring that work to pass.

Bookcraft gladly accepted the manuscript and agreed to publish it. As publishers often do, they changed the name I'd proposed to _Life Everlasting_ (Crowther, 1967). (At the time, I liked my selected title better, but time has proven their choice to be the correct one, and now I can't even recall what title I had suggested.) The book came into print in 1967, gained rapid acceptance, and went through numerous printings, selling several hundred thousand copies while Bookcraft was the publisher.

As publishers reach retirement age and want to make sure their rocking chairs are functioning correctly, publishing houses tend to change hands. That happened when Bookcraft was sold to Deseret Book Company in 1996. As the change was in progress, Bookcraft was willing to release the copyrights on several of their old-time favorites, and I was very pleased that _Life Everlasting_ was one of them. As both the author of the book and the owner of Horizon Publishers, I was quick to acquire the copyright and to keep the book in print.

New Versions and Translations

But I wanted to do more than just reprint the book. During the almost 30 years of the book's existence, I had learned a great deal more about the nature of life after death, and I wanted to add many of those later-acquired insights to the book. So, in 1997, Horizon Publishers produced a new revised edition of *Life Everlasting,* with about 175 pages of intriguing new details and patterns added to the book.

During 2000–2001, when Jean and I were on a couples mission serving in the Mexico City East Mission, many of the saints there knew of the book. A good number of bi-lingual members had acquired it in English. Many others knew of the book's existence and were hungry to gain the insights it contained. Since Horizon Publishers had published the book in Spanish several years before and made it available in the United States, I procured some copies and brought them down to Mexico to be distributed there. The available supply was purchased so rapidly by the Mexican members there that I arranged to have an edition printed in Mexico City. That edition, *La Vida Sempiterna,* was a translation of only the original Bookcraft version, so I arranged for the pages added in English in 1997 to be translated into Spanish also, and published there and also back in the States as *La Vida Sempiterna, volumen 2.* Since returning from our mission in 2001, I've worked hard to have several other of my books translated into Spanish.

In December 2005, a second revised edition was published and the book was reprinted in paperback with a durable, "plasticized" cover.

How Was *Life Everlasting* Received by the Latter-day Saints?

As mentioned earlier, *Life Everlasting* has sold over half a million copies, and continues to sell well each month and year. Why has it gone so well? Let me suggest several reasons.

First, the book has supplied a wealth of knowledge which was previously unknown to the majority of LDS readers. It has lots of answers! It provides knowledge and security to those who are worried about going beyond the veil and experiencing the next phase of their eternal journey.

Second, it has added acceptance and respectability to those who have experienced communications from beyond the veil. Before, some who shared such experiences were regarded as odd, strange, or peculiar, and sometimes were told by family members not to discuss such things.

Some "do not share" advocates tried to class all the next-life things being divulged by those who came back from the spirit world as "religious doctrines" and inappropriately tried to apply "doctrinal" tests concerning who should or should not be the recipient of a "revelation from God." This book caused a lot of that unfortunate "labeling" to be removed, and people began to recognize what that labeling really was: prejudice, and fear of the unknown.

Third, the book is unique in that, by the very nature of the sources which I had explored, the book is a recounting of experiences in the lives of Mormon pioneers and other early Utah inhabitants. These experiences had resided for decades in personal journals written by individuals who had actually experienced communications beyond the veil, or in biographies written by descendants of those faithful pioneers who tapped their forefathers' records, both written and oral. Many of those whose experiences are recorded were highly respected in their day and locale, and that lingering respect has added to the acceptance of the experiences they recorded. Yet the many insights reported in experiences were not common knowledge while those people were alive—their accounts remained separate and "uncontaminated" by other accounts, which adds to the power of their combined messages.

Fourth, the book provides tremendous comfort to those who are approaching death, as well as to those who have just lost a loved one. One of the sweetest aspects of my adult life has been to repeatedly hear, week after week and month after month, expressions of gratitude for the comfort the book has supplied for many families (in combined form, many thousands).

Fifth, it became apparent to me, as time went by, that the book was known by those who now reside beyond the veil. In several instances (about a dozen, over the years), I have been told by individual recipients (or close family members of those recipients), of communications they had received from beyond the veil, counseling them to obtain and read the book. On several particular occasions, they were even instructed to read a specific account, on a particular page, because it held an answer for a question or need the person was trying to resolve.

Sixth, in retrospect, it now clearly appears, in the eternal scheme of things, that the time came when the Lord chose to open up the windows of heaven and pour out more knowledge about the life to come—not only to Latter-day Saints, but to people throughout the world. Uniquely, *Life Everlasting* was a significant part of that pouring out of increased knowledge concerning what lies beyond the veil.

The Beginning of a World-wide Expansion of Knowledge

Viewed from the perspective of thirty-some years later, it is obvious that *Life Everlasting* was an early pioneer venture in the field of life-after-death studies, and it was a pivotal one. It is equally apparent to me that the same Spirit which moved and inspired me to write on the subject moved numerous others to write also. Our mission was to make the nature of life after death a very important area of knowledge and understanding, and to make it available to the world. I count it a privilege to be a part of such an important endeavor, and to realize that *Life Everlasting* was a forerunner of other significant and important works.

As noted in chapters 9 and 10, a new type of scholarly inquiry began during the past four decades of the twentieth century. Millions of people discovered that innumerable individuals have experienced temporary separation of their consciousness from their bodies. Indeed, this research strongly implied that human consciousness survives death. During those experiences, we Latter-day Saints believe that their spirits went into the spirit world, and those individuals observed a great many aspects of life there before being sent back into their physical bodies to resume mortal life. Scholars and scientists began collecting the accounts of those spirit-world excursions and studying them. Terms such as "out-of-body experiences (OBEs)," "near-death experiences (NDEs)," "verge-of-death experiences," "spontaneous contacts with the dead," "life panoramas," and "life reviews" were coined to refer to various aspects of such experiences. Numerous repeated evidences of the same types of experiences were gathered, and it became increasingly evident that broad patterns of similar experiences existed.

Books on Near-Death Experiences

After *Life Everlasting* was published in 1967, it was soon followed by other important books on the subject. In 1969, Dr. Elizabeth Kübler-Ross published *On Death and Dying,* the first of several volumes she wrote relating to the death experience (Kübler-Ross, 1969). In 1975, Dr. Raymond A. Moody, Jr. released *Life After Life,* which caught the attention of the nation, became a national best-seller, made the subject popular, and opened the way for numerous other studies (Moody, 1975). George W. Ritchie published an account of his near-death experience, *Return From Tomorrow,* which was widely read in this era (Ritchie, 1978). Many dozens of other books on the subject, usually based on the collecting of true accounts of near-death and after-life experiences, soon followed. A significant number of them are found in the references list of this volume.

The following is a list of some (but certainly not all) of the most-influential books in the flood of works that followed the publication of *Life Everlasting.* The list was prepared with the help of Arvin Gibson. The publication dates it shows provide a "highlights time line" for this worldwide out-pouring of knowledge concerning death and the spirit world which occurred during the past forty years. Excluded are a host of foreign publications and hundreds of scholarly journal, magazine, and newspaper articles:

1967	*Life Everlasting*	Duane S. Crowther
1969	*On Death and Dying*	Elizabeth Kubler-Ross
1975	*Life After Life*	Raymond Moody Jr.
1978	*Return from Tomorrow*	George G. Ritchie and Elizabeth Sherrill
1979	*Beyond Death's Door*	Maurice Rawlings
1980	*Life at Death*	Kenneth Ring
1982	*Adventures in Immortality*	George Gallup, Jr.
1982	*A Collection of Near-death Research Readings*	Craig R. Lundahl
1982	*Recollections of Death*	Michael B. Sabom
1984	*Heading Toward Omega*	Kenneth Ring
1984	*On the Other Side of Life*	Evelyn Elsaesser Valarino
1987	*The After Death Experience*	Ian Wilson
1987	*Otherworld Journeys*	Carol Zaleski
1988	*Coming Back to Life*	Atwater, p.m.H.
1988	*Beyond the Veil, Vol. 1*	Lee Nelson
1989	*Beyond the Veil, Vol. 2*	Lee Nelson
1990	*Closer to the Light*	Melvin Morse
1990	*Heaven and Hell*	Emanuel Swedenborg
1991	*My Life After Dying*	George G. Ritchie
1992	*Glimpses of Eternity*	Arvin S. Gibson

1992	*Transformed by the Light*	Melvin Morse with Paul Perry
1992	*Transformed by the Light*	Cherie Sutherland
1993	*Echoes from Eternity*	Arvin S. Gibson
1993	*Beyond Death's Door*	Brent L. Top and Wendy C. Top
1994	*Coming from the Light*	Sarah Hinze
1994	*The Burning Within*	Ranelle Wallace with Curtis Taylor
1995	*After the Light*	Kimberly Clark Sharp
1995	*Reborn in the Light*	Cherie Sutherland
1995	*Children of the Light*	Cherie Sutherland
1995	*Beyond the Darkness*	Angie Fenimore
1996	*Experiences Near Death*	Allan Kellehear
1996	*Absent From the Body*	Don Brubaker
1997	*I Saw Heaven!*	Lawrence E. Tooley
1997	*The Eternal Journey*	Craig R. Lundahl and Harold A. Widdison
1997	*Heavenly Answers for Earthly Challenges*	Joyce H. Brown
1998	*Lessons from the Light*	Kenneth Ring and Evelyn Elsaesser Valarino
1998	*The LDS Gospel of Light*	B. Grant Bishop
1998	*I Stand All Amazed*	Elane Durham
1999	*Fingerprints of God*	Arvin S. Gibson
1999	*Mindsight*	Kenneth Ring and Sharon Cooper
1999	*The Soul's Remembrance*	Roy Mills
2000	*Blessing in Disguise*	Barbara R. Romer
2000	*My Descent into Death*	Howard Storm
2001	*The Truth the Whole Truth and Anything But the Truth*	Bill Essex
2002	*Nothing Better than Death*	Kevin R. Williams
2003	*Religion, Spirituality and the Near-death Experience*	Mark Fox
2003	*Fast Lane to Heaven*	Ned Dougherty
2003	*If Morning Never Comes*	Bill VandenBush
2004	*Trailing Clouds of Glory*	Harold A. Widdison

Some Evidences of the March to Omega

It is interesting to note that this world-wide surge of increased knowledge concerning life after death was officially commemorated within the LDS Church. Two often-quoted but as yet uncanonized visions of after-death conditions received by Latter-day Saint Prophets more than a century earlier were canonized and accepted as scripture. The *2003 Church Almanac* records that on April 3, 1976 "Members attending general conference accepted Joseph Smith's Vision of the Celestial Kingdom and Joseph F. Smith's Vision of the Redemption of the Dead for addition to the *Pearl of Great Price.* These scriptures became part of the *Doctrine and Covenants* on June 6, 1979" (*Deseret News 2003 Church Almanac,* 564).

A national poll taken in 1981 by George Gallup, Jr., and published in 1982 under the title *Adventures in Immortality,* showed that an amazing fifteen percent of Americans have been involved in "verge-of-death experiences." His survey did much to move public perception of near-death experiences toward acceptance and toward their being an area for legitimate inquiry and study. Another important pioneer in the field was Dr. Kenneth Ring, with his books *Life at Death* and *Heading Toward Omega.* He founded and was the first president of the International Association for Near-Death Studies (IANDS). Publication began, under his direction, for the *Journal of Near-Death Studies.* Hundreds of other books and numerous scientific studies on death and life after death followed and are continuing.

A significant result of these widely disseminated works is that people, worldwide, became aware that millions have had life-after-death and spirit-world experiences. No longer is it "strange" to have a near-death experience, and no longer is it felt necessary to keep such experiences secret for fear of being branded odd, or a sensationalist, or a liar, or a dreamer who couldn't distinguish fantasy from reality. Fewer near-death accounts are circulated anonymously. Evidence is easier to gather. More patterns are evident. Among those who believed that all life ended at death (the "eat, drink, and be merry" crowd), a great many came to believe that life truly does continue, and that they will someday face some type of judgment and encounter with Deity for their mortal actions. For many others, previously held faith in the afterlife has blossomed into knowledge. The commonality of near-death experiences between people of all nations, races and religions removed their experiences from the realms of "secret" to the realm of knowledge which is available to all and which is a legitimate field for personal, clinical, and scholarly study and research.

Insights on the Lord's Concept of Timing of "Revealed" Information

Since part of this chapter is devoted to the chronicling of various aspects of the opening up of knowledge concerning the spirit world to people world-wide—the Omega effect—I feel it appropriate to comment on the timing of this remarkable event. The "Preacher," who wrote the book of Ecclesiastes, observed that "To every thing there is a season, and a time to every purpose under the heaven" (Eccles. 3:1). It appears that in the past, there may have been some restriction on (1) who, from beyond the veil, could communicate some of the details concerning life in the spirit world, and (2) what information it was appropriate to communicate.

An example is found in the life sketch of my great-grandfather, **Thomas Crowther.** He and his wife, Sarah Thomason, were baptized into the church on October 13, 1850, in the Tipton Branch of the Birmingham Conference in England. Four years later, they and their 3-year-old daughter emigrated with other English saints to the United States, coming through New Orleans and up the Mississippi River to St. Louis, arriving on January 10, 1855. Two months later, Sarah gave birth to a stillborn son, and death claimed her two days later. Thomas and his young daughter made their way across the plains, with him driving a team of oxen and Mary Ann perched in the back of the wagon in front of him. Along the route, he had this experience:

> At Sweet Water a false alarm of an Indian raid gave us quite a scare. But in all our journey we were wonderfully blessed. At this place my wife that is dead visited me, put her arms around my neck, *told me of many things I have seen come to pass since that time.* She looked so beautiful. *When I asked her how it was in the sphere where she moved she signified that she was not at liberty to tell.* I knew that she was dead and where she was buried. At this point I was aroused by the false alarm. (Keller, 1998, p. 39)

As I researched numerous pioneer records while writing *Life Everlasting,* I occasionally but rarely found other situations where the visitor from beyond the veil was not at liberty to fully communicate details concerning his or her situation there.

Perhaps the conveying of the requested information was a matter which required the needed confidentiality because of the labor the individual was performing (such as would be expected of a temple worker today). Perhaps, too, it was a matter of limiting what the particular individual was to confide because of that person's lack of experience (just as in the mission field, the senior companion typically will speak up if he perceives that his young new junior companion is getting in "over his head"). Perhaps it was a matter of the individual not being at liberty to announce a pending change of organization, leadership or program (just as it is today when certain people "in the know" are not at liberty to divulge who the new bishop of the ward will be); those changes are reserved for the person designated as the spokesman by the presiding authority to make the announcement.

LDS Scriptural References
to the Timing of Information

A perusal of the scriptures shows that the Lord, in his wisdom, has chosen to direct both the writing-down and also the timing of dissemination of information on many significant events. A few brief examples should clarify this matter.

One of the most important and significant revelations of all time is the appearance of the Lord to the Brother of Jared, recorded in the book of Ether in the Book of Mormon. Concerning the details of the manifestation, the Brother of Jared was instructed by the Lord that he was to "write them," but he also was told, "thou shalt not suffer these things which ye have seen and heard to go forth unto the world, until the time cometh that I shall glorify my name in the flesh" (Ether 3:21–22). Moroni, when he translated the book of Ether, noted that when plates of the book of Ether came into the possession of King Mosiah, the king discovered that the Lord had commanded the Brother of Jared that "they were forbidden to come unto the children of men *until after that he should be lifted up upon the cross,*" and Moroni wrote that "for this cause did king Mosiah keep them, that they should not come unto the world until after Christ should show himself unto his people." But then Moroni added: "After Christ truly had showed himself unto his people he [King Mosiah] commanded that *they should be made manifest.*" (Ether 4:1–2).

A similar instruction was given by the Lord to Peter, James and John concerning their bearing witness to the reality of Christ's transfiguration. He told them to "Tell the vision to no man, *until the Son of man be risen again from the dead*" (Matthew 17:9). Obviously, for reasons he has not revealed to us, our Savior wanted these highly sacred events to be quietly preserved until after the completion of his atoning sacrifice was consummated.

Nephi was shown many end-time events as he received his revealed explanation of Lehi's vision of the Tree of Life. But when he reached a certain point in his revelation, he was told that he was not to write about any of the events beyond that point because a later prophet, "one of the twelve apostles of the Lamb," would "see and write the remainder of these things" (1 Nephi 14:18–25). Almost a millennium later, Moroni was told by the Lord that in the last days, after some of the Gentiles and the house of Israel had heard the gospel, that *"then shall my revelations which I have caused to be written by my servant John be unfolded in the eyes of all the people"* (Ether 4:13–16).

The Doctrine and Covenants also gives interesting insights on the Lord's desire to time the release of specific information. In September 1830 he began alluding to the building of a great city of Zion, saying that "It is not revealed, and no man knoweth where the city Zion shall be built, but it shall be given hereafter" (D&C 28:9). During the eleven months that followed, numerous revelations were given concerning events related to the future city of Zion, but it wasn't until July 20, 1831, that the Lord finally revealed that "the place which is now called Independence is the center place; and a spot for the temple is lying westward, upon a lot which is not far from the courthouse" (D&C 57:3). After that revelation, of course, the location of the future city of Zion immediately passed into the realm of general knowledge among the Saints.

When the earliest revelations of the Doctrine and Covenants were given, the counsel was to "show not these things unto the world *until it is wisdom in me*" (D&C 19:21; March, 1830). Yet by July 20, 1833, the church was publishing them in Independence, Missouri as portions of the *Book of Commandments*.

As part of the "times of restitution of all things" (Acts 3:21), the Lord has repeatedly promised the pouring out of great fountains of information—not only to his saints, but to all the inhabitants of the earth. *"He will give unto the faithful line upon line, precept upon precept"* (D&C 98:12); *"here a little, and there a little: giving us consolation by holding forth that which is to come, confirming our hope!"* (D&C 128:21).

Even back in Nephi's day, the Lord's promise was that "I will give unto the children of men line upon line, precept upon precept, here a little and there a little; and blessed are those who hearken unto my precepts, and lend an ear unto my counsel, for they shall learn wisdom; *for unto him that receiveth I will give more*" (2 Nephi 28:30).

There are promises of *"knowledge . . . to be revealed in the last times, . . . a time to come in the which nothing shall be withheld,"* a time to come when nothing shall "hinder the Almighty from *pouring down knowledge from heaven*" (D&C 121:26–33). But especially, there are rich promises of forthcoming knowledge linked to the eternal plan of salvation and the saving and perfecting of the dead: a "welding link of some kind or other between the fathers and the children" upon the subject of "baptism for the dead. . . . for it is necessary in the ushering in of the dispensation of the fulness of times, which dispensation is now beginning to usher in, that a whole and complete and perfect union, and welding together of dispensations, and keys, and powers, and glories should take place, and be revealed from the days of Adam even to the present time. And not only this, but *those things which never have been revealed from the foundation of the world, but have been kept hid from the wise and prudent, shall be revealed unto babes and sucklings* in this, the dispensation of the fulness of times" (D&C 128:18).

My mortal mind can't comprehend all the realms of knowledge that will be poured out, but I have observed one aspect of it very clearly. I have observed, first hand, that during the past half-century, the powers from on high have made knowledge of many aspects of life after death, in the glorious world of spirits, much more available—not only to the Latter-day Saints but to millions of others throughout the world. And to Mormons, especially, the flood of increased knowledge is merely another indication of God's communication—on his time scale—of momentous events long predicted by prophets. After all, only one-third of the plates from which the Book of Mormon was translated by Joseph Smith were available to him. Two-thirds were sealed, to come forth at some undisclosed future date.

Do Mormons Experience More NDEs Than Others?

While the writing of this chapter was in process, I shared a pleasant mid-day meal with several other Latter-day Saints as we conversed with a Jewish woman—Beverly Brodsky (see chapter 17)—who had related her very interesting NDE to the local IANDS chapter the previous evening. During the conversation, she expressed the opinion that LDS members apparently experience far more NDEs than comparable non-LDS populations do. Was she right? No one knows for sure, but I was asked to express my opinion and reasoning on the subject in this chapter because of that conversation.

So, do Mormons have more NDEs and life-after-death experiences and communications? What's my opinion? Yes, we do. Here are my reasons:

1. Among the first events in the restoration process were the appearances of the angel Moroni to Joseph Smith, during which he thrice-repeated the prophet Malachi's prophecy found in Malachi 4:5–6. The way it was repeated to Joseph is found in Joseph Smith–History 1:38–39 and D&C 2:1–3. It was the prophecy of the future return of the prophet Elijah:

> Behold, I will reveal unto you the Priesthood, by the hand of Elijah the prophet, before the coming of the great and dreadful day of the Lord. . . . *And he shall plant in the hearts of the children the promises made to the fathers, and the hearts of the children shall turn to their fathers.* If it were not so, the whole earth would be utterly wasted at his coming.

We learn in D&C 110:13–16 that this prophesied appearance took place on April 3, 1836, in the new Kirtland Temple. D&C 128:17–18 tells us that

> It is sufficient to know, in this case, that the earth will be smitten with a curse unless there is a welding link of some kind or other between the fathers and the children, upon some subject or other—and behold what is that subject? It is the baptism for the dead . . . it is necessary in the ushering in of the dispensation of the fulness of times, which dispensation is now beginning to usher in, that a whole and complete and perfect union, and *welding together of dispensations, and keys, and powers, and glories should take place, and be revealed.*

I believe that a significant part of this welding together of dispensations through genealogical research and work for the dead has been a major increase in communications to living Latter-day Saints from the world of spirits. Thousands of LDS members are actively engaged in genealogical research and in performing temple work in behalf of many of their progenitors. This work, by its very nature, involves extensive record keeping and the preserving of significant dates and events from the lives of their forefathers. According to an instructional epistle written to the Saints by Joseph Smith (which now is recorded as Doctrine and Covenants Section 128), records kept on earth are designed to correspond to records kept beyond the veil (D&C 128: 6–9). Thousands of communications to mortals from beyond the veil show that many individuals in the spirit world are extremely anxious and desirous that temple ordinances be performed on their behalf here on earth. This is so they can accept them there and be enabled to move forward in their eternal progression (for examples, see Crowther, 1997, pp. 299–326).

This intense beyond-the-veil interest in vicarious work for the dead being performed here on earth is significant. It is the source of numerous communications which come only to Latter-day Saints, because only they are in a position to accomplish the temple work the potential recipients desire.

2. D&C Section 13 tells of another of the significant events in the restoration: the coming on May 15, 1829 of John the Baptist to convey the Priesthood of Aaron to Joseph Smith and Oliver Cowdery. As John enumerated to them the major keys of this priesthood authority, he announced that *"I confer the Priesthood of Aaron, which holds the keys of the ministering of angels, . . ."* (D&C 13:1). The history of the Church is replete with accounts of the appearance of angelic beings bringing both specific directives from God on high and conveying personal messages of comfort, counsel, warning, admonition, and information. When millions of Latter-day Saint priesthood holders possess the keys to the ministering of angels for themselves and their families, while others outside the Church do not possess such keys, it seems logical that more angelic communications concerning the afterlife would flow through LDS channels than would be found among non-Mormons.

3. Latter-day Saints have been admonished since the earliest days of the restoration to keep personal, family and other historical records. Record keeping is a significant theme in the Book of Mormon (see 1 Ne. 1:1, 17; 3:3, 19; 5:12, 16; 6:1; 13:23; 19:1; 2 Ne. 5:29; Enos 1:13–15; Omni 1:9, 17; W. of M. 1:1; etc.). The Doctrine and Covenants records that from the very day in which the restored Church was organized, the church was instructed to keep records of membership transactions and procedures (D&C 20:63–64, 81–84; 21:1), and Church record-keepers

and historians were appointed (D&C 47:1–4). But by commandment, records were to extend beyond basic Church history: they were to cover *"all things that transpire in Zion,"* and were to extend to *"their manner of life, their faith, and works"* (D&C 85:1–2).

For many years, Church leaders have admonished the Saints to keep personal journals and records, and to include therein the experiences which they hold dear and which have shaped their lives. Thus, Latter-day Saints are accustomed to recording significant life events, and those records often will include details of near-death and life-after-death experiences. It can easily be hypothesized that accounts of near-death experiences are more available among LDS members because they keep better personal records than other population groups. This doesn't address the issue of whether they actually receive more of these experiences, but it does explain why their accounts are more readily available.

4. The Latter-day Saints are, by and large, a "believing people," and a people to whom gifts of discernment have been promised and bestowed. The Lord has promised that "I will show miracles, signs, and wonders, unto all those who believe on my name" (D&C 35:8). Communications from beyond the veil easily qualify as part of this glorious promise. Again, those who have not yet accepted Christ and his gospel are presumed to have fewer opportunities to receive some of the communications discussed in this chapter, perhaps because of lower levels of expectations and spiritual receptivity, and inability to discern incoming communications from the spirit world.

For these four reasons, then, I believe that more near-death and life-after-death experiences and communications occur within Mormondom than within any other population across the earth. But, after expressing this opinion, I acknowledge the obvious occurrence of many thousands of near-death and life-after-death experiences to non-Mormons throughout the world. In the matter of who may receive such experiences, it is clear that "God is no respecter of persons" (Acts 10:34; D&C 1:35), and that their reception does not depend on nationality, race, gender, or religious faith. Rather, it is a matter of specific need and desire (whether on the mortal or spirit-world side of the veil), and also of the degree of personal receptivity of the recipient. It also appears to be clearly linked to the closeness of family ties as they bridge the veil of death.

And how prevalent are these experiences among Latter-day Saints? I still remember quite vividly, back in 1967, gaining a first perspective on this question. I was asked to speak in a meeting of the Bountiful First Ward, of the Bountiful Utah Stake. (Since we now reside in that stake, I'm aware that this is the "grey-haired area" of the stake where many elderly Saints reside.) When I asked the audience, for the first time, the question: "How many of you either have had some kind of personal life-beyond-the-veil experience or communication, or are intimately acquainted with the details of such an experience received by one of your close family members?" I was amazed when almost three-fourths of the congregation raised their hands! Later, having asked the same question on numerous other occasions in LDS gatherings, I've found that a more typical result is that slightly over fifty percent respond affirmatively. Obviously, the younger the congregation, the fewer there are who are intimately connected with one or more life-beyond-the-veil experiences; but fifty percent seems a very reasonable figure for estimating purposes.

Are All These Communications from the Spirit World "Doctrine"?

The answer to this question is obvious: No, they are not the doctrine of The Church of Jesus Christ of Latter-day Saints. The doctrines which we Latter-day Saints have concerning death, the spirit world, paradise, hell, the spirit prison, the resurrections, the time of judgment, the degrees of glory and who attains them, and the nature of exaltation, are all based on passages in the four standard works of the church. What made them doctrine? They were "canonized," or made the doctrines of the Church, by their being accepted as doctrine by the affirmative votes of our representatives who were in attendance at the general conferences in which they were canonized.

There have been, and still are, many often-quoted near-death and life-after-death experiences within the annals of Mormondom which are not canonized as doctrine by the Church. The "Vision of the Redemption of the Dead" was one such item for more than a half-century. It was received on October 3, 1918 by Church President Joseph F. Smith. On October 31, 1918, "it was submitted to the counselors in the First Presidency, the Council of the Twelve, and the Patriarch, and it was unanimously accepted by them" (heading to D&C 138). Did that make the many insights recorded in his vision the doctrine of the Church at that time? No, because the vision had not yet been canonized by the common consent of the Church. Though often quoted during that interim period, the "Vision of the Redemption of the Dead" did not become "doctrine" and part of the scripture of the Church until it was canonized during General Conference on April 3, 1976.

The same is true of Joseph Smith's vision of the celestial kingdom. He received it on January 21, 1836, but it didn't become "doctrine" and part of the scripture of the Church until it was canonized during the same General Conference on April 3, 1976.

But while the numerous scriptural statements concerning the spirit world and all the other topics listed above provide a sound footing and doctrinal framework for understanding these events, they leave a myriad questions unanswered. They are like the foundation and studs of a house under construction—there still is much to be added. Numerous descriptive patterns of places, populations, work and social conditions, qualities and capabilities of spirit beings, missionary labors beyond the veil, and dozens of other topics are found in the thousands of life-beyond-the-veil experiences which now have been collected and analyzed, and which continue to join the historical base from which such patterns and explanations are drawn. A multitude of questions have been answered and a host of valuable insights have been gleaned.

But are these additional insights and answers to significant questions the doctrine of the Church? Obviously, they are not, and no one is claiming that they are, nor asserting that they will or should be.

The Church of Jesus Christ of Latter-day Saints has been restrictive in adding new items to its canon of scripture. Perhaps the observation that "the Church membership needs to better understand and utilize the revealed doctrines which have been canonized before other, new doctrines are canonized" is pertinent in this context. (I don't know if this persistent comment is true, but it is a frequently mentioned observation or opinion voiced by Church members.) I'm not an authorized spokesman for The Church of Jesus Christ of Latter-day Saints, so my personal views should be regarded as just that: personal opinions of a loyal and somewhat informed lay member who is not, and does not represent himself as being, an authorized Church spokesman.

While it is proper, appropriate, beneficial, and often Spirit-led for researchers and scholars to gather and analyze these insights, it must be clearly recognized that these gleaned items are only peripheral insights which have not, and probably never will be, canonized doctrine.

Regarding the source of canonized doctrine, we believe that these doctrines did not originate with Joseph Smith or Brigham Young or Mormon, or any of their contemporary associates (although each of them will be quoted as authoritative purveyors of LDS doctrine) but the true source, we believe, is Jesus Christ and his Father, our Father in Heaven. We believe these doctrines, for the most part, originated or were well known before this world was created. They were revealed to prophets by God down through the ages, and reiterated again by Jesus during his time here in mortality. They were taught in large measure to the early saints—his disciples and later members of his church—first by himself and later by his apostles. However, not all of these teachings made it into the Bible. It is important to understand that while the Bible contains the "milk" of the gospel, it does not necessarily contain all of the "meat," or more-spiritual doctrines of Christ (1 Cor 3:2; Heb 5:12), although many of them are alluded to in that great book.

After the apostles died off, much of this knowledge was lost or distorted, but we believe it was restored once again in large measure, "line upon line, precept upon precept" through a series of revelations over time, to Joseph Smith and succeeding prophets in the Church since him.

Different Criteria and Definitions
for "Truth" and "Doctrine"

The question may be asked, "Is it appropriate to study and discuss personal revelatory experiences, both privately and in gatherings of the Saints?" Let me point out that the answer to the question "What is doctrine?" is clearly different than the answer to the query, "Oh say, what is truth?" Doctrine requires canonization; truth requires only veracity. In effect, canonization enjoys a more stringent sieve than does truth. There are many truths, in and out of the LDS Church, which have not been canonized. That does not make those truths less meaningful in a spiritual or any other sense. It merely means that they do not have the authoritative consequence that canonized doctrinal statements can have.

In chapters 4 and 5 of this book, for example, when NDEs are compared with LDS teachings, the references used may either be canonized doctrine or other teachings originating with church leaders, including the current LDS Church Prophet. Such quotations are just as informative as canonized doctrine; they just will not have the same authoritative basis as the official church doctrine. Again, the question, "Is it the official canonized doctrine of the church?" is far more stringent than the question, "Is it true, or of good report, or praiseworthy?"

The Lord has revealed that *"truth is knowledge of things as they are, and as they were, and as they are to come"* (D&C 93:24). Certainly many past and present life-after-death experiences fall under this mantel, and with the greatly increased outpouring of such experiences in recent decades, there is no reason to doubt there will be many more such experiences received and recorded in the future. The Lord also has instructed his Church to teach one another not only the "doctrine of the kingdom" but also to diligently teach *all things that pertain unto the kingdom of God, that are expedient for you to understand,* of things both in heaven and in the earth, and under the earth; *things which have been, things which are, things which must shortly come to pass;* things which are abroad; . . . Of countries and kingdoms" (D&C 88:77–79). And he also instructed the saints that they should hasten *"to obtain a knowledge of history, and of countries, and of kingdoms, of laws of God and man,* and all this for the salvation of Zion" (D&C 93:53).

From the preceding discussion, it is clear that a strong case can be made for the appropriateness of studying and discussing life-after-death experiences in LDS gatherings. This is true from any number of different approaches. And, as a matter of interest, all of the above-referenced quotations are from canonized doctrine. One more passage is pertinent in this context: *"if there is anything virtuous, lovely, or of good report or praiseworthy, we seek after these things"* (Article of Faith 13).

For general information, as I wrote this chapter I contacted the Public Affairs Office of the LDS Church at Church headquarters in Salt Lake City and asked the question: "Does the Church have any official policy or statement concerning near-death experiences?" The answer was: "No, there is no official policy or statement concerning near-death experiences."

"Shared," or "Secret"?

One other item I was asked to comment on in this chapter was my personal opinion concerning whether communications received from the spirit world should be shared with others or kept confidential. This "informal debate" sometimes arises in Sunday School classes and other

Church gatherings, and it is quite clear that two schools of thought on this question exist within Mormondom. Both viewpoints have some sound scriptural basis, and various statements by living and past General Authorities can be cited to support the defense of either of the two philosophical positions.

It should be noted in this regard that when it comes to the "first principles of the gospel," the Latter-day Saints are essentially of one mind.

"We believe that the first principles and ordinances of the Gospel are: first, Faith in the Lord Jesus Christ; second, Repentance; third, Baptism by immersion for the remission of sins; fourth, Laying on of hands for the gift of the Holy Ghost" (Article of Faith 4).

On other less portentous issues there is sometimes a spectrum of opinions. Adherents to one or another position can sometimes vigorously defend their beliefs, and the Church can and does accept those adherents who espouse different points of view as good and faithful Latter-day Saints. One such issue has to do with the sharing of "sacred" personal experiences.

Some of the Saints are in the "Let your light so shine before men, that they may see your good works, and glorify your Father which is in heaven" camp (Matt. 5:16). Their effort is to gain more knowledge and then to inform and enlighten others. They firmly believe that the sharing of accounts of near-death and life-after-death experiences and communications is informative, faith-promoting, and of general benefit to almost everyone who hears and reads them. They know that key writings on these subjects have been instrumental in leading many to accept the gospel and the great plan of salvation. They are seeking to expand the body of knowledge on numerous after-mortality subjects, and they feel that their efforts, most definitely, are inspired by the Holy Ghost (when the individual has properly prepared and placed himself "in tune"), and that they are furthering the Lord's work in these last days through their efforts.

In the other camp are those who base their position in another of the Master's injunctions in his great Sermon on the Mount: "Give not that which is holy unto the dogs, neither cast your pearls before swine, lest they trample them under their feet, and turn again and rend you" (Matt. 7:6). These individuals seem to be deeply concerned with "who" can receive "what" revelations. In the extreme, they tend to regard themselves as "protectors of the faith."

These two philosophies sometimes reside side-by-side in our Church organizations. When an issue is raised which relates to these philosophic differences we sometimes hear comments from both proponents and opponents in both camps. Typically, the scenario arises when someone from the "light shine before men" philosophy makes a statement or cites a quotation which is beyond the other camp's accepted definition of doctrine, so a spokesman for the "cast not your pearls" philosophy speaks up and attempts to protect the listeners from something he feels may be "not accepted as doctrine" because it doesn't meet his stringent "straining" criteria.

I remember, quite vividly, a Spirit-filled meeting I attended several years ago in the Woods Cross Regional Center which many of the stakes in south Davis County, Utah utilize for stake conferences and other large gatherings. The occasion was a gathering of temple workers who were serving in the Bountiful Temple, and their spouses. The main speakers were a General Authority (a member of the First Quorum of the Seventy), who was to be followed by the temple president. During his discourse, which lasted the better part of an hour, the General Authority recounted numerous "beyond the veil" faith-promoting experiences related to genealogical and temple work. Indeed, those experiences constituted his entire discourse. The temple president, obviously, hadn't expected the numerous experiences to be the subject of the visiting authority's talk, and had prepared a talk in a different vein. Rather than changing his talk to correspond more closely with the previous speaker's comments, he opted to proceed with his prepared remarks. Those remarks included a lengthy exhortation based on his opinion that such personal experiences were "private" and should *not* be shared with others. The interesting thing about the meeting was that we felt the Spirit as each of the two brethren was speaking, but I had never heard the two philosophies set forth so vigorously and in such direct contrast to each other in the same meeting by two acknowledged Church leaders.

So, I expect the two points of view are able to coexist, side by side. But there is danger if we ever come to a point where a person in a position of authority exerts his personal viewpoint from one camp or the other to the point that it is presented to those in his sphere of influence as "the doctrine" or "the official Church policy" on the subject, and attempts to exert restrictive, punitive or disciplinary action against individuals with the opposing point of view simply because that is their viewpoint.

When either camp is setting forth its viewpoints in a Church meeting, I find it beneficial to evaluate (1) whether I and others are feeling the Spirit as we listen to them speak, and (2) whether I perceive them to be speaking under the influence of that Holy Spirit. In other words, I believe that LDS members have the right—and the obligation—to determine the ethereal legitimacy of various teachings through personal revelation.

I have observed that there is one line of assertion, by the "cast not your pearls" believers, that repeatedly turns off the Spirit of the discussion. That occurs when they vigorously assert, or even subtly imply, that *any* communication from beyond the veil that is received is (1) either from God or the devil, with no other source allowed, (2) is subject to the tests of "authority" typically applied to theological revelations directing Church actions, (3) is "sacred" simply because it is dealing with some aspect of the spirit world, (4) can be judged as true or false based on the supposed character of the recipient or the church membership or leadership status of the recipient. Their approach invariably brings an element of contention into the meeting, and they forget the Lord's command "that they should not contend one with another" (2 Ne. 26:32; see also Mosiah 2:32 and 3 Ne. 11:29).

The Logic of Information Divulgence

Since I obviously am firmly entrenched in the "let your light shine" camp, and have been invited to comment in this chapter on "tactics" of the opposite viewpoint, let me pose a few examples to point out situations when these "either-or" positions of the "cast not your pearls" camp are inappropriate. They tend to exclude such obvious realities as the following, which I'll number to correspond to the points listed above:

1. *The majority of communications from beyond the veil come from individuals to their family members who are still in mortality, and typically do not include any instructions or messages from Deity.* If a mother, or father, or grandparent gives counsel to a child here on earth, it is readily accepted. Is it different if the individual has passed beyond the veil, but returns to instruct the child? Does his/her coming from a different locale somehow make the communication a "revelation from God" in the theological sense of the word, rather than merely parental counsel? (Crowther, 1997, pp. 189–90, 43, 150–51, 121, 188, 197, 233, 250). I doubt it. Another situation: When Elder Parley P. Pratt was

41

unjustly imprisoned in a Missouri dungeon in 1839, and was visited and comforted by his deceased wife in a "vision," was that a "revelation from God"? (Crowther, 1997, p. 252, 261–62). I think not—I believe that was only a love-filled communication from his former wife who was there in the spirit-world Paradise of the righteous.

2. *Personal communications from beyond the veil typically do not conform with "line of authority" logic which holds that one is entitled only to inspiration or revelation for his own ecclesiastical station, and that any "inspiration" regarding someone else's position or sphere of responsibility should be considered as "false."* For instance, when Keith Burt (who drowned when the ship sank which was taking him to serve as a missionary in South Africa) appeared in the Celestial Room of the Cardston Temple to console his grieving father and tell him he had been called, instead, to do missionary work in the Spirit World, was that a communication on a family matter, or was it a "revelation from God" which should have come through Church channels? I believe it was a communication only from a son to his father. And when the departed missionary provided his father a sign so he could know of a surety that his son truly had communicated with him, the sign was that the father's priesthood leader, temple president Edward J. Wood, would call him into the nearby sealing room to bear his testimony (which President Wood had never done before, but did in this instance). Obviously, President Wood was prompted to ask the brother to bear his testimony, but the entire situation was not revealed to him, even though he was the presiding ecclesiastical authority (Crowther, 1997, p. 254). Should we follow the "cast not your pearls" camp's logic that the son's communication was a false revelation because it didn't flow through the correct line of authority? I think not; the problem lies with the line of logic rather than with the line of communication from beyond the veil.

3. *The term "sacred" has very precise, tightly limited definitions, but its broad definition does not fit nor apply to most spirit-world communication situations.* In the typical dictionary, the term "sacred" is defined as "a place or object that is entitled to reverence or veneration because of its direct relationship to God," or "something that is set apart for the service or worship of deity." We learn more of the term when we consider its antonym, or "word of opposite meaning." The antonym for "sacred" is "sacrilegious," which means "theft or violation of something consecrated to God" or "gross irreverence toward a hallowed person, place or thing."

Unfortunately, the dictionary also lists a too-broad, general definition for "sacred": merely "of or related to religion." Those in the "cast not your pearls" camp apparently think it appropriate to use this too-broad definition. They apparently consider anything and everything to do with life after death or the spirit world as being "of or related to religion," and they therefore regard it as something "sacred"—something which they believe should be kept "secret."

Let me draw a parallel that perhaps will demonstrate the ineptness of this line of reasoning. Salt Lake City, Utah, is the headquarters city for The Church of Jesus Christ of Latter-day Saints, and the home and repository for its records, leadership, organizational staffs, and many Church-related functions. But does that make the city itself, and all its inhabitants, "sacred"? Should we believe that any communication we receive from anyone in Salt Lake City should be regarded as a message from God? If a relative from Salt Lake City contacts me to commiserate with me because I have the flu, or to ask me to buy him tickets for the next Jazz game, should I consider that to be a message from deity—a communication which I should regard as "sacred"? What's the difference between labeling the entire Salt Lake City sacred and labeling the entire spirit world "sacred"? Both have religious inhabitants and activities. But, quite obviously, it is far beyond the mark to assert that any and every communication from either locale is directly sent by God. True, He ultimately rules in both places, but He allows inhabitants in both areas their free will and a wide latitude in whom they contact and what they say. His direct intervention in daily affairs and communications is the "rare" exception, not the common everyday mode of operation.

4. *Across the earth, people of all character traits and levels of personal character communicate with one another, and that is typical of many or most communications from the spirit world also. The majority of the communications from the spirit world received by mortals do not have theological origins and implications.* In the spirit world, the vast majority of inhabitants are neither in the paradise of the righteous, nor the hell of the wicked who have already been damned. Instead, they are in a third area, by far the largest of the three areas, which is peopled by those who have yet to hear and/or accept the gospel of Jesus Christ. Though individuals from paradise do not enter into hell, and vice versa (see Crowther, 1997, pp. 328–31), representatives from both areas constantly conduct their missionary efforts in this third area, which many refer to as the "spirit

prison" (see Crowther, 1997, pp. 275–98).

Mormon research (including my research for *Life Everlasting)* concerning who comes from the spirit world to communicate with individuals on earth has, admittedly, been filtered through an LDS perspective, listing various purposes for their communications which tend to have religious meanings (see Crowther, 1997, pp. 229–74). But it must be acknowledged that many spirit-world to earth experiences recorded in both Latter-day Saint and non-Mormon sources do not all fit into that convenient theological mold. It should be recognized that personal needs and desires (from either side of the veil), and the personal receptivity of the individual receiving the communication seem to govern who receives these communications and when they receive them. It is presumptuous and erroneous to assume that every, or even the majority of communications to mortals from those residing beyond death have theological origins and implications.

5. *It must be recognized that many who receive near-death or life-after-death experiences undergo major life changes. Many of them discover they have specific tasks to perform during their mortal existence on earth, and many learn that they are not prepared to "pass" the expectations they will encounter at their day of judgment. These "life conversions" have a very similar effect to the "conversions" of those who hear and learn the gospel of Jesus Christ and his grand plan of salvation for all mankind. In both instances, they receive a type of "spiritual rebirth" and a type of "testimony."* In many instances, they acquire a strong desire to share their experience and life-changing lessons with others. They very willingly speak and tell of their experiences. They are willing to write magazine articles and books to share their joyful news. They feel the "good news" they have received is too important to keep to themselves.

I firmly believe it is just as appropriate for them to share their "testimony" of the near-death and life-beyond-the veil experiences they have undergone as it is for new converts to the Church and gospel to bear their testimonies of the truthfulness of the gospel and how they came to hear the good news of Christ to others. And I just as firmly feel it is inappropriate for "cast not your pearls"-type individuals to criticize them for doing so.

These "cast not your pearls"-type individuals have an unbecoming bias that prevents them from utilizing the true spirit of discernment. I suspect that some of them may find themselves in the same situation as those who will say concerning the gospel in the last days: "We have received, and we need no more!" Of that group, the Book of Mormon prophecy says that "from them that say, We have enough, from them shall be taken away even that which they have" (2 Nephi 28:27, 30). Those of this persuasion, whom I and others have occasionally encountered as authors and publishers of books concerning the spirit world and after-life events, certainly seem to be devoid of understanding of the field of study to which this book is devoted.

My hope and desire is that advocates of both philosophical viewpoints concerning "sacred" or "secret" issues be charitable, kind, and thoroughly informed and documented when expressing their views on the subject. They should be sure that they are being guided by the Spirit in their thoughts and manner of expression if such issues arise, that they are not being motivated by personal or group prejudices or biases, and that they are heeding the injunction to "do no harm" and to avoid contention as they speak or write.

Summary

In this chapter I have attempted to fulfill the assignments made to me by the author and organizer of this book: Arvin Gibson. I'm well aware of the many hours of effort he has put into the project and the vision he has for the good it can accomplish, both among Latter-day Saints in general and those who have devoted their efforts to understanding the next phases of our path to eternal life. I can see that it will have real value, also, to non-Latter-day Saints who are pursuing various avenues of research pertaining to near-death and life-after-death experiences.

I have summarized my personal background, told how the book *Life Everlasting* was written and came into print, and commented on its broad and continuing acceptance among Latter-day Saints.

The role of *Life Everlasting* as a pioneering effort in the new but quickly evolving field of near-death studies which spread world-wide in less than four decades has been described, portraying that rapid spread of knowledge concerning the inhabitants of the spirit world as part of the fulfillment for God's promise that great truths would be poured out in the last days.

As requested, I listed the various books pertaining to this field of study, which, in the aggregate, served to "popularize" the study of near-death and life-after-death experiences and lift the "social taboos" on sharing personal experiences of this nature. *Life Everlasting* was one of the very first of such books to be published as this cultural and religious change took place.

Comment has been made concerning how God has intentionally

managed the timing of various revelations, events, and the introduction of various inventions which have coincided with his purposes and great plan for the betterment of all mankind. The assertion has been made that the great outpouring of increased knowledge on the spirit world is a significant and noteworthy part of this orchestrated timing of last-days events.

The opinion that Mormons, as a unique population, experience significantly more near-death and life-after-death experiences than other populations has been set forth, with reasons cited for that hypothesis and perspective.

Observations on the limited and protected nature of official Church doctrine in The Church of Jesus Christ of Latter-day Saints have been made, with the forthright acknowledgment that most NDEs and similar experiences, though they may be both true and highly informative, are not Church doctrine and probably never will nor should be.

A contrast has been made between two different attitudinal philosophies within Mormondom, the "Let your light shine before men" philosophy and the "Cast not your pearls before swine" philosophy, with an appeal for moderation from adherents of both viewpoints.

I sincerely hope that these observations will help advance the cause of gleaning further light and understanding in the broad field of near-death studies, and I express my hope that trained and qualified researchers and analysts will step forward to increase knowledge and understanding which will be of value to people of all belief systems and personal religious perspectives. Indeed, this book is devoted to that goal. Hopefully all who read it will find increased devotion to the message of love which threads through the experiences of those who have, if briefly, glimpsed a holier realm.

I close with the very significant statement made by the first Latter-day Saint prophet, Joseph Smith Jr., concerning this subject, when he said:

> All men know that they must die. And it is important that we should understand . . . our departure hence. . . . It is but reasonable to suppose that God would reveal something in reference to the matter, and it is a subject we ought to study more than any other. We ought to study it day and night, for the world is ignorant in reference to their true condition and relation. If we have any claim on our Heavenly Father for anything, it is for knowledge on this important subject. (*History of the Church*, 6:50)

3: Mormon Contributions
to NDE Research

Prior to the publication of *Life Everlasting* in 1967, Mormon interest in near-death experiences (before the term NDE was coined by Raymond Moody) was on an ad hoc basis by the members. As observed in chapter 2, it was common—since the days of Joseph Smith—for LDS members to keep detailed records of family members who had undergone special spiritual events in their lives. The keeping of such family records was encouraged by the General Authorities. Often, those stories were copied and sent to other members of the family. Inevitably, they were also forwarded to friends and acquaintances, sometimes anonymously, and thereby circulated as a sort of underground network of spiritually uplifting stories.

Duane Crowther

Undoubtedly the most important formal LDS research on NDEs was that done by Duane Crowther. Duane did more than formalize the NDE research process for LDS investigators. He awakened, amongst Mormons, an understanding of the great depth of such accounts. When his book *Life Everlasting* was published in 1967, it became clear that there was a rich history of NDEs that were, literally, a part of LDS culture. Why this was so is explained in chapter 2.

Duane's work preceded the general public's awareness of the NDE phenomenon by eight years—until Raymond Moody's book *Life after Life* was published in 1975. Although *Life Everlasting* was not well known with the general public, it was enormously popular with LDS members. Moreover, it helped spawn interest in NDE research among a significant group of academic and other professionals who were adherents of the LDS faith.

In his book, Duane drew attention to the remarkable parallels of some of the historically recorded events with major aspects of Mormon doctrine. In so doing, he established a pattern of study and explanation that was often mimicked by LDS researchers who followed him. In the process of making these comparisons, Duane became the first to divulge some parallels which uniquely support certain aspects of LDS theology. In *Life Everlasting,* for instance, Crowther documented a story of Niels P. L. Eskildz, a Danish convert to the LDS Church. He was seriously crippled and deformed when ten years of age, and suffered terribly for many years. In 1862 he had a spiritual experience in which he saw himself in a premortal environment. A portion of his account follows (Crowther, 1967, pp. 39–40; 1997, p. 103):

> He beheld as with his natural sight, but he realized afterwards that it was with the eye of the spirit that he saw what he did. His understanding was appealed to as well as his sight. What was shown him related to his existence in the spirit world, mortal experience and future rewards. He comprehended, as if by intuition, that he had witnessed a somewhat similar scene in his premortal state, and been given the opportunity of choosing the class of reward he would like to attain to. He knew that he had deliberately made his choice. He realized which of the rewards he had selected, and understood that such a reward was only to be gained by mortal suffering—that, in fact, he must be a cripple and endure severe physical pain, privation and ignominy. He was conscious too that he still insisted upon having that reward, and accepted and agreed to the conditions.

Craig Lundahl and Harold Widdison

Beginning in 1983, articles authored by Lundahl and Widdison began to appear in *Anabiosis* (later to be renamed *The Journal of Near-Death Studies*). At the time, Lundahl and Widdison were Professors of Sociology at, respectively, Western New Mexico University and Northern Arizona University. Their first article in this journal was *The Mormon Explanation of Near-Death Experiences* (Lundahl and Widdison, 1983), and it pointed out some of the similarities of Mormon doctrine with particular NDE events.

Craig began his research on the near-death phenomenon in 1977. He taught the first course offered exclusively on the near-death experience at a university in the United States. His first book on the subject was *A Collection of Near-Death Research Readings* (Lundahl, 1982).

Hal is a pioneer in the field of death education. He taught a college-level course on death, grief, and bereavement in 1972. He lectured extensively on the subject of death and near-death experiences, frequently at professional conferences devoted to those subjects.

Breadth of their work does not allow a full exposition of the many contributions to the near-death literature by Lundahl and Widdison. A feeling for the scope of their work, though, may be illustrated by listing some of the titles of Journal articles they authored:

- Angels in Near-Death Experiences (Lundahl, Fall 1992).
- Near-Death Visions of Unborn Children: Indications of a Pre-Earth Life (Lundahl, Winter 1992).
- Social Positions in the City of Light (Lundahl and Widdison, Summer 1993).
- The Physical Environment in the City of Light (Lundahl and Widdison, Summer 1993).
- The Near-Death Experience: A Theoretical Summarization (Lundahl, Winter 1993).
- Near-Death Studies and Modern Physics (Lundahl and Gibson, Spring 2000).
- A Comparison of Other World Perceptions, by Near-Death Experiencers and by the Marian Visionaries of Medjugorje (Lundahl, Fall 2000).
- Prophetic Revelations in Near-Death Experiences (Lundahl, Summer 2001).

Craig and Hal also co-authored the book *The Eternal Journey: How Near-Death Experiences Illuminate our Earthly Lives* (Lundahl and Widdison, 1997). As observed in chapter 9, their book did an extensive categorization of events into various subjects known to be a part of many NDEs. Indeed, Lundahl's and Widdison's particular choices for categorization became a source of controversy and criticism of the book. To quote from the reviewer, Jenny Wade: "'The book seeks to enlighten us about the reality, purposes, and meaning of life and death' (p. 11). However, the authors never state that their version of enlightenment, purpose, and meaning comes largely from a single source: The Church of Jesus Christ of Latter-day Saints. . . . Mormon ideology permeates the entire book, but identification with this organization is not apparent to the average reader who is the audience for this mass-market book" (Wade, Fall 1999, p. 51).

Hal responded to the critique of Jenny in a later edition of the Journal (Widdison, Fall 2000). His rebuttal amply defended the book, and it is beyond the scope of this book to re-argue the various points raised by Wade and Widdison. Interested readers may go to the original sources for detailed information. There is one point, however, which deserves further elaboration; namely, why it is that even less-than-friendly reviewers can see strong Mormon ideology in the writings of so many NDE researchers who happen to be of that faith. Is it truly a matter of bias, as Jenny implies, or is something else in play? This question will be further explored later in this chapter.

Most recently, Harold wrote the book *Trailing Clouds of Glory* (Widdison, 2004). In this work he examined the evidence for a multi-faceted life before mortality. His work in this area was the first which investigated this aspect of NDEs. Also, as is evident from reading chapter 13, Harold has taken a lead among investigators in demonstrating the proper use of statistics in performing NDE research.

Brent and Wendy Top

Brent Top is an associate professor of Church History and Doctrine at Brigham Young University. He has lectured extensively and is an especially popular speaker for the "Know Your Religion" and "Education Week" series which the LDS Church sponsors. As well as being an expert in LDS Church theology, he has studied near-death phenomena for many years. His wife, Wendy, attended BYU and has also studied NDEs for some years. Together, they wrote the book *Beyond Death's Door: Understanding Near-Death Experiences in Light of the Restored Gospel* (Top, 1993).

In their book, the Tops set out to deliberately compare LDS scriptural references and other teachings with particular events commonly associated with NDEs. They wrote of this effort: "We were amazed at the similarities and consistencies between near-death accounts and the doctrines of the restored Gospel." In particular, they discussed the "being of light"; the sense of many who had an NDE of being in a perfect, vitalized spirit body; the rapid, graphic review of one's mortal life; populated cities of dazzling brilliance; meeting with loved ones; communication by thought transference; spirits in radiant white robes;

an intense, dynamic light that does not hurt the spirit eyes; travel at phenomenal speeds; all levels of beauty and brilliance in the different realms and conditions; expanded comprehension and memory powers; gorgeously beautiful scenery and vegetation; an out-of-this-world reality which cannot readily be described with earthly words; and a sense of ineffable light and love.

In each of these areas, the Tops took care to make comparisons that could be documented with authentic LDS references. As only one example, they wrote the following concerning our difficulty in describing a world for which we have very inadequate vocabulary and only limited comprehension. The reference they used was from a talk by Elder Parley P. Pratt (one of the early church leaders from the Quorum of Twelve Apostles). Elder Pratt delivered his talk—which was quite long—in Salt Lake City on April 7, 1853. The text is given in its entirety in the *Journal of Discourses*, Volume 1. The pertinent section is from page 12 (Top, 1993, 21–22). Elder Pratt was discussing what kind of information one could expect from some believing Christian who had died and returned to life:

> They expected to go to that place called heaven, as soon as they were dead, and that their doom would then and there be fixed, without any further alteration or preparation. Suppose they should come back, with liberty to tell all they know? How much light could we get from them? They could only tell you about the nature of things in the world in which they live. And even that world you could not comprehend, by their description thereof, any more than you can describe colours to a man born blind, or sounds to those who have never heard.

The Tops were the first investigators to give a detailed description of the writings of Emanuel Swedenborg and to compare those writings with both LDS teachings and NDEs. Swedenborg was an immensely influential eighteenth-century Swedish scientist, engineer, and religious philosopher who claimed to have traveled to heaven and hell. He documented much of what he experienced in the book *Heaven and Hell* (Swedenborg, 1990). In introducing the subject of Swedenborg's works, the Tops wrote this:

> Swedenborg insisted that "he was not exaggerating or telling lies, or speaking in parables." Those who met him "agreed that he was a polite, logical man with a kindly manner and a sense of humor." For our—the authors'—part, in studying

his book *Heaven and Hell* we too have found the preponderance of his work to be consistent, rational, genuine, and filled with true principles and doctrines, many of which are consistent with doctrines unique to Mormonism and which must have seemed heretical in his day. We believe that he actually did experience the things he attempts to describe. However, while he may have been blessed to receive more enlightenment than most who lack the restored gospel, he was still limited in what he was allowed to see or comprehend. . . . Another point to remember as we read Swedenborg is that he was trying to describe a world for which we have very inadequate vocabulary and only limited comprehension, even within the gospel framework. (Top, 1993, p. 21)

Arvin Gibson

This particular section, dealing with the author's achievements, was difficult to write. Since it was about me and my NDE research, I had to wrestle with *humility* and its antonym, *pride*. I'm afraid, dear reader, that humility succumbed to pride. Please forgive me.

Gibson was the first Mormon researcher to do extensive interviewing of those who claimed to have had NDEs. In consultation with his wife, Carol, the Gibsons developed a pattern for the work which was similar, in some respects, to what Kenneth Ring had done at the University of Connecticut. To find suitable candidates they used two methods: referrals from friends, relatives, and associates; and advertisements in local papers and publications. Both methods were fruitful.

During the period from December 1990 through June 1991 they interviewed 45 respondents, of whom 38 first-hand experiences were included in the book *Glimpses of Eternity* (Gibson, 1992). There were also four second-party experiences which were incorporated. Two first-hand experiences from other sources were included, bringing the total of first-hand accounts to 40. Numerous others were rejected because they didn't meet certain criteria having to do with the types of experiences.

In soliciting candidates to interview, no attempt was made to screen for religious or non-religious beliefs. The only criterion that had to be met was that the candidate had undergone some type of NDE, or other incident, which led to an out-of-body or related spiritual event. By reason of the location of the interviews, in the greater Salt Lake City region, most of those interviewed (71 percent) professed membership in The Church of Jesus Christ of Latter-day Saints.

The interviews were conducted in the Gibson's home or in the home of the respondent, except for one which was conducted by telephone. Where women were involved, Carol, was usually present and she assisted in the interviews.

The results of this effort were so productive that it was difficult to stop interviewing people. So, encouraged by the publisher, beginning in the summer of 1992 and extending through the spring of 1993 they interviewed twenty-nine candidates whose firsthand stories were detailed in the book *Echoes From Eternity* (Gibson, 1993).

During this period of intense study concerning NDEs, the Gibsons, together with Dr. Lynn Johnson, Martin Tanner, and Fred Beckett, founded a local chapter of the International Association for Near-Death Studies (IANDS of Utah). The founders established monthly meetings in which various individuals who had experienced an NDE or who were involved in research—or who needed support—could meet and trade information. Gradually that effort expanded until today (2004), from 90 to 120 individuals meet monthly in formal meetings. The chapter has also developed their own web site on the Internet.

Gibson contributed to the near-death literature with many professional articles in the *Journal of Near-Death Studies*. Perhaps the most important of these was the cowritten study with Craig Lundahl titled *Near-Death Studies and Modern Physics* (Lundahl and Gibson, "Near-death Studies and Modern Physics"). In this study Lundahl examined the many alternative explanations for NDEs, and Gibson related the possible role of modern physics to various aspects of the NDE.

Partially as a result of his work on the modern physics article, Gibson did the research for and wrote the book *Fingerprints of God: Evidences from Near-Death Studies, Scientific Research on Creation, and Mormon Theology*. This was the first (and to this date, only) book which attempted to reconcile modern science's view of creation with Mormon theology and with evidence from NDEs.

Fingerprints of God was not without controversy. Although most of those who reviewed the book wrote favorably of it, some saw it in a contrary light. Two of those who provided favorable reviews were Dr. Kenneth Ring (Gibson, 1999, p. 20) and Dr. B. Grant Bishop (Bishop, Fall 2002, pp. 35–41). Ring wrote this in his Foreword to Gibson's book:

And indeed in this domain, Arvin and I do share a lot of common ground, particularly in regard to our skepticism that anyone will be able to frame a convincing reductive, purely physical or biological explanation of the NDE and in our viewpoint that God's fingerprints are all over this phenomenon. In any event, both the research that Arvin cites in this connection and the many case histories from his own investigations he offers in this book certainly make a powerful and, to me, compelling brief for his thesis.

Unfavorable reviews were provided in the 2001 edition of *FARMS Review of Books* by three professors from Brigham Young University. The reviewers were Philip D. LaFleur, Kevin Livingstone and Bruce Schaalje (LeFleur, Livingstone and Schaalje, 2001). There were a number of points that they took issue with, including the statistical data provided by Gibson, but perhaps most offensive to them was the frequent references to individuals who had undergone NDEs, and use of this information as "evidence" of the "fingerprints" of God.

LaFleur put it this way:

> "My biggest concern with this book is its over-reliance on near-death experiences (NDEs). That NDEs happen seems certain. Why and how they happen and what, if anything, they really mean are other issues that have yet to be resolved. The NDE Literature varies from purely neurological approach to the metaphysical." All three of them also confessed that they were not well versed in the subject. LaFleur wrote: "While I do not have a great deal of experience in studying NDEs, some things seem unanswered: for example, why are NDE experiences so varied?"

Gibson wrote a rebuttal to the points raised by the three professors and sent it to FARMS (as well as to the professors). It was never published. It is beyond the scope of this book to repeat the arguments and rebuttals made by the professors and Gibson. For those interested, they are encouraged to seek the original sources and decide for themselves wherein lies the truth.

Gibson was the first researcher to interview and write the published story of an individual who had a group NDE with many other individuals. This was the story of Jake (a pseudonym, the real name is **John Hernandez**), whose experience is described in *Fingerprints* (Gibson, 1999, pp. 128–31). An update concerning John and his experience is given in chapter 7.

Gibson was one of several Mormon researchers to record the experience of individuals who found themselves in a premortal condition, making decisions about their future life on earth. One such experience documented by Gibson was the story of DeLyn (a pseudonym), who was afflicted with cystic fibrosis. After a heroic battle with the disease, **Don Wood** (his real name) passed away. He accomplished, in his relatively short life, all that he set out to do. Portions of his experience follows (Gibson, 1993, pp. 117–31):

> At this point in my experience I became aware of a voice talking to me. My surroundings, and my analysis of them, had so interested me that I had not paid attention to the voice at first. It was a soft, fatherly voice that kept repeating my name. Facing the light, and then turning 90 degrees to my left and looking up at a slight angle, I looked to see where the voice was coming from. There was no one that I could see—but the voice persisted, not in my ears, but in my mind. I finally responded by asking the voice: *What?*
>
> The voice didn't immediately respond. I wondered how I could hear with my mind and not my ears, and I learned that it wasn't necessary for me to understand the process just then. My mind next thought the questions: *Why am I here? Why me? I'm a good guy—why did I die?*
>
> The voice answered: *You are here because you have earned the right to be here based on what you did on earth. The pain you have suffered qualifies you to be here. You have suffered as much pain in 37 years as a normal person might have suffered in 87 years.*
>
> I asked: *It's pain that gets me here?* and the answer was yes.
>
> This still puzzled me, so I asked: *But why was it necessary for me to suffer so? I was a worthy member of the Church; I kept all the commandments. Why me?*
>
> Then I received a most startling answer. He said to me: *You chose your disease and the amount of pain you would be willing to suffer before this life—when you were in a premortal state. It was your choice.*
>
> While I was hearing this voice, I became aware that it was a familiar voice—it was one that I knew. It was a voice that I had not heard during my mortal lifetime. When it was speaking to me, though, there was no question but that I knew who it was. There was enormous love for me in the voice.
>
> **You said, Don, that you knew who the voice was. Who was it?**
>
> It was my Father in Heaven.
>
> **It was not Jesus Christ?**
>
> No.

And you felt love in the voice?

We don't have a word that would describe what I felt from Him toward me. The closest word we have is *love,* but it doesn't begin to describe the feeling. There is no appropriate description in mortal tongue that can explain the feeling—you have to feel it.

When He told me that it was my choice, in a premortal environment, to suffer when I came to earth, I was both astonished and incredulous. He must have understood my incredulity, because I was immediately transported to my premortal existence. There was a room that I was viewing from above and to the side, but at the same time I was sitting in it. In a sense I was both an observer and a participant. About thirty people were in the room, both men and women, and we were all dressed in the white jumpsuit type of garment.

An instructor was in the front of the room, and he was teaching about accountability and responsibility—and about pain. He was instructing us about things we had to know in order to come to earth and get our bodies. Then he said, and I'll never forget this: *You can learn lessons one of two ways. You can move through life slowly, and have certain experiences, or there are ways that you can learn the lessons very quickly through pain and disease.* He wrote on the board the words: *Cystic Fibrosis,* and he turned and asked for volunteers. I was a volunteer; I saw me raise my hand and offer to take the challenge.

The instructor looked at me and agreed to accept me. That was the end of the scene, and it changed forever my perspective of the disease that I previously felt was a plague on my life. No longer did I consider myself a victim. Rather, I was a privileged participant, by choice, in an eternal plan. That plan, if I measured up to the potential of my choice, would allow me to advance in mortal life in the fastest way possible. True, I would not be able to control the inevitable slow deterioration of my mortal body, but I could control how I chose to handle my illness emotionally and psychologically. The specific choice of cystic fibrosis was to help me learn dignity in suffering. My understanding in the eternal sense was complete—I knew that I was a powerful, spiritual being that chose to have a short, but marvelous, mortal existence.

Gibson also found and documented other interesting effects and patterns, some of which were related to LDS doctrine and some were not. He was the first, for example, to write of particular words which those who have had NDEs repeatedly use, almost as if they were programmed. This was documented in this manner (Gibson, 1993, p. 267):

Several words were repeated often enough in the interviews that they attracted my attention. These were words that the candidates used in their attempts to describe what they felt. The words were: *Energy* (7.2%), *Peace* (45.7%), *Love* (47.0%), *Warmth* (20.5%), and *Pure* (4.8%). In many instances, as with the word *love*, the individuals said that this was an improper word to describe what they felt. Don Wood put it this way: "We don't have a word that would describe what I felt from Him toward me. The closest word we have is *love*, but it doesn't begin to describe the feeling. There is not an appropriate description in mortal tongue that can explain the feeling—you have to feel it."

Gibson coined the term "corroborative NDEs" to identify those types of experiences that could be verified by medical and other objective observers of the events said to have occurred by the individuals undergoing the experiences. Corroborative NDEs are especially useful in demonstrating the reality of NDEs because there seems to be no other way to explain them except as an out-of-body occurrence in some other dimension or spiritual reality. Gibson gave examples of such NDEs, both from cases he was personally familiar with, and from documented other cases. More is written about this type of NDE in chapter 9 of this book.

Sarah Hinze

Several researchers have documented NDEs in which individuals claim to have lived in a celestial type of premortal existence. The cases given above by Crowther and Gibson—and Maxine's story detailed in chapter 16 by Gibson—are but three examples among many. Sarah Heinze was the first researcher to do a major study devoted solely to the subject of researching individuals who claimed to have had prebirth memories of a previous life. In particular, she reviewed thirty cases in which fifty-seven prebirth experiences (PBEs) are documented for her book *Coming From the Light: Spiritual Accounts of Life Before Life* (Hinze, 1994, 1997, p. 173).

Sarah and her husband, Brent, developed—in much the same way that Moody, Ring and others did for NDEs—a set of characteristics or events that often is a part of PBEs (Hinze, 1994, 1997, pp. 177–78). These include: (1) Radiation of love from a preborn entity to the person with the prebirth experience, (2) a celestial light in the preearth environment, (3) a thankful feeling about the forthcoming experience on earth,

(4) a sense of leaving a loving heavenly home, (5) a time to come to earth, (6) a unique earthly mission for the preborn, (7) messages brought from the preborn to parents and others on earth, and (8) the light. As with NDEs, all events are rarely present in a single experience.

Lee Nelson

Lee Nelson is a full-time writer who lives on a small farm in cental Utah. He has written and had published in excess of fifteen books, including the popular *Storm Testament* series of historical novels. He is well versed in Mormon theology, having served a mission for the Church in Southern Germany. He has held numerous teaching and administrative positions in the Church. Lee became interested in NDEs several years ago. Three of his popular non-fiction books which deal with the NDE are *Beyond the Veil—Volume One*, *Beyond the Veil—Volume Two*, and *Beyond the Veil—Volume Three*. These books include compilations of personal accounts of people who have briefly stepped through the veil, and returned (Nelson, 1988, 1989 Vol. Two and Vol. Three). A large fraction of the accounts are by those of the LDS faith. Nelson also wrote the book *NDE: Near Death Experiences*, which gave examples of NDEs from different individuals who were interviewed.

Richard Eyre

Richard Eyre is a Harvard-educated management consultant and has authored twenty-six books, at least one of which reached the *New York Times* number one bestseller list. His book *Life Before Life*, although not about NDEs as they are usually considered, does examine the question, "If we are spiritual beings, where did our spirits originate?" The author draws on numerous sources for the development of his premise, including C.S. Lewis, T. S. Eliot, the Old and New Testaments, and different apocryphal writings. His thesis coincides with his LDS religious background, but perhaps the most persuasive argument is a personal epiphany experienced during his climb of the highest mountain in Africa, 19,400-feet-high Kilimanjaro (Eyre, 2000, pp. 69–91).

Kevin Christensen

Kevin Christensen, with a B.A. from San Jose State University, is a freelance technical writer with special interest in Mormon theology. His article, *"Nigh unto Death": NDE Research and the Book of Mormon,* is perhaps the most comprehensive review of NDE parallels which can be found in the Book of Mormon (Christensen, Spring 1993). In particular, it examines the life and teachings of Alma, a prophet leader in the Book of Mormon, and compares many of the events in Alma's life—including a life review—with NDEs. He also studies Lehi's dream sequence in the Book of Mormon and evaluates it in the context of other NDE writings such as that of Zaleski and her *Otherworld Journeys.*

Other LDS Professionals Involved in Near-Death Research

A number of LDS professionals have been involved in various aspects of NDE research. Several of them are contributors to this book. Their biographies and their particular chapter contributions speak for themselves. A summary of some of the unique contributions by these professionals is given below.

Sandra Cherry has been involved in NDE research and in a college teaching environment for about ten years. For several months she helped Kenneth Ring in his research at the University of Connecticut. She has been a member of the Board of Directors for the Utah chapter of IANDS. As such she helped arrange scheduled speakers for the monthly meetings. Her enthusiasm is infectious and helps keep the organization functioning smoothly. She takes special interest in working with those involved in NDE research. Her own understanding of the NDE phenomenon is comprehensive.

As a result of being an LDS Chaplain in the military, and of being the Director of the Organizational Health Center at Hill Air Force Base, **David Larsen** is well versed in LDS theology. He is also on the Board of Directors for Utah IANDS. He wrote two of the key chapters for this book—chapters 4 and 5.

Lynn Johnson was also one of the founders of the Utah chapter of IANDS, and one of its first Presidents. In his practice as a psychologist, he has worked with and treated many who have had NDEs. His most recent contribution is included in chapter 12 of this book.

Martin Tanner also was one of the founders of the Utah chapter of IANDS. He is currently the Chairman of the Board of Directors.

Martin's interest in near-death experiences reverts back to 1982. Since that time he has been an active participant in the work of the Utah chapter, including spearheading the 1999 Annual IANDS Conference held in Salt Lake City. Commencing in 1989 and continuing through to the present, Martin has been the host of a weekly radio talk show, *Religion Today,* on KSL Radio. The show deals with various religious and spiritual subjects, including near-death experiences.

B. Grant Bishop is a clinical professor of dermatology at the University of Utah School of Medicine. He has expertise in LDS philosophy and in NDE research. His contribution in chapter 11 of this book speaks partially to his interest in the Light as expressed in LDS doctrine and as described by those having NDEs. He wrote the book *The LDS Gospel of Light* as a consequence of these interests.

Robert Fillerup presented a paper titled "Early Mormon Visions & Near-Death Experiences." The paper was delivered at a Sunstone Symposium in Salt Lake City in 1990. This was an attempt to show, in a relatively abbreviated form, many of the LDS-NDE correlations that Crowther, Widdison, and Lundahl presented in a more complete form in their books.

Personal-NDE Researchers

A number of LDS members had deep NDEs that prompted them to write books and contribute in other ways to the growing database of knowledge. These include Ranelle Wallace, whose NDE happened as the result of a light-plane crash. The ensuing fire burned Ranelle horribly, yet she and her husband escaped from the crash and staggered from a snow-bound mountain to reach help. Their miraculous escape from death is told in the book *The Burning Within.* Ranelle has lectured to many groups about the lessons she learned from the experience.

Joyce H. Brown literally willed herself to die, and then had an NDE which taught her the value of life. Her story is told in the book *Heavenly Answers for Earthly Challenges: How to be Certain you Enjoy the Other Side When you Get There* (Brown, 1997). Joyce has lectured extensively to medical groups, and to others susceptible to suicide, about how her NDE taught her to avoid that action at all costs.

Elane Durham, in her book *I Stand All Amazed: Love and Healing from Higher Realms,* describes her sweeping NDE in detail. Elane has been sharing her experience with numerous groups since 1976. She was on the Board of IANDS of Utah, and she has worked with several other IANDS groups. Unique in Elane's book is the testimony of the Catholic Deacon, Stanley Cebrzynski, who administered to Elane at the Mercy Hospital in Chicago. He saw that Elane had been dead for fifteen or twenty minutes before he arrived, and they were preparing her body for the morgue. A week or two later, he returned, and this was his reaction (Durham, 1998, p. 97):

> Then when I got back, I think maybe a week or two later, I looked in one of the beds and I thought, "Oh, my God!" So I said to this woman . . . Elane Durham, "What happened to you? You were dead!" She looked at me funny and said, "No, I'm not dead."
>
> "Yes," I said, "yes, you were!" I was shocked, and I'll be honest about it. I knew it was the same person I had said "Last Rites" for, and that she had been dead. . . . But I was absolutely amazed, for I knew that she had been dead, and here she was, alive as could be. . . . I've been in on many, many deaths, and that is the only time I ever ran across something like that.

Angie Fenimore, in her book *Beyond the Darkness*, described how, in the depth of depression, she emptied a pill bottle in an attempt to commit suicide (Fenimore, 1995). She was seeking relief from the agony and pain of her depression. Instead, she was transported to a realm of hopelessly forlorn spirits who could not or would not get relief. A voice spoke to her and asked: "Is this what you want?" She subsequently had a painful "life's review" in which she felt again the emotions of those she had hurt during the twenty-seven years of her lifetime. Ultimately, she was brought to an enormous light and basked in its radiance in the presence of the Father and the Son. She learned, through her extensive NDE, that suicide was the worst of all the choices she could have made.

Bias among Mormon Researchers?

Earlier in this chapter it was noted that some critics claim that Mormon authors show a bias in their NDE research that reflects their LDS background. Among academics, one of the most damaging accusations is to affirm that someone's work reflects a bias. In the scientific community, "proof" of bias is to guarantee that the work deserves only scorn from those "objective" observers asserting bias. This aversion to bias occurs despite the obvious influence that social, psychological, physiological, religious, and educational effects have on the behavior and psyche of every living person.

Thus, to accuse someone of bias is to state the obvious. Anyone who has lived on this planet cannot escape the prejudices and biases resulting from having lived on earth. Indeed, one of the claims against the reality of the various events which occur in an NDE is that each NDE seems tailored, at least to a certain extent, by the philosophical, cultural and religious background of the individual undergoing the epiphany—hence it merely reflects the biases of the one having the NDE.

The key question, then, is not whether some work is biased or not, but rather whether that bias interferes with the premises and conclusions of the investigator. To insist that a single attribute, such as the religion of the author or researcher, be disclosed prior to exhibiting the work is to ignore all of the other factors which might override this particular parameter. Worse yet, such insistence by a critic or other reviewer reflects more on the reviewer than on the researcher. It tends to suggest that the reviewer's primary objection is that the author of the work has different biases than those of the reviewer, and the reviewer's biases are somehow superior to those of the researcher. It also implies that the reviewer does not have the capability for properly judging the validity of the data used by the investigator to develop his or her premises and conclusions.

In addition to these problems, with accusations of bias, is a more fundamental weakness. What the reviewer sees as bias may, in fact, be just the opposite. If one grants the possibility that the NDE data gathered by the researcher may be supportive of LDS theological positions because they are reflective of the truth given by God, then the answer is simple. The data correlates with LDS doctrine because both the data and LDS doctrine correspond to ultimate truth. Such truth becomes almost binding if the data from other, non-LDS investigators, also correlates well with that of the LDS investigators.

One may correctly argue that where the basic premise of a book—or research paper—is to test a hypothesis about the supernal truth of a set of data, then the religious background of the investigators becomes a primary issue and should be disclosed. In the case of the book *Eternal Journey*, by Lundahl and Widdison, and the book *Coming From the Light*, by Sarah Hinze, this was not the case. They presented the data, and the particular patterns they saw from the data, and allowed the readers to draw their own conclusions about the cogency of the patterns. On the other hand, Duane Crowther, in the book *Life Everlasting,* Brent and Wendy Top, in their book *Beyond Death's Door;* and Arvin Gibson, in the book *Fingerprints of God,* either stated or implied a premise involving the supernal truth of LDS doctrine. In these latter cases, the authors all identified themselves as believing Mormons.

As stated in the Preface, this book concerns the many-faceted aspects of the NDE, and how they do or do not correlate with LDS teachings. As such, it falls in the latter category given in the preceding paragraph. The religious affiliations and backgrounds of each contributing author is clearly identified.

Summary of Mormon Contributions to NDE Research

Latter-day Saint contribution to the evolution and depth of NDE research has been substantial. With Duane Crowther's work, the Mormons were probably the first group to recognize the vast body of recorded spiritual and personal revelatory experiences available within the group. These stories resided in thousands of treasured family history journals, and they were largely untapped by researchers and authors until Duane decided to write a book about them.

As Ring, Moody, Ritchie, Morse, Greyson and others spawned a world-wide effort on NDE research, LDS researchers and authors joined in the burgeoning search for data and patterns in the epiphanies. From the beginning, the LDS investigators frequently made comparisons of the data with Mormon theology. Often, word pictures from LDS doctrine were matched with analogous word pictures from these ephemeral experiences. While such comparisons might, at first, seem a natural outgrowth of overeager LDS apologists, there was a more essential and subtle reason having to do with the concept of Omega. This action by LDS investigators is explored in some detail in chapter 17.

In his book *The Light Beyond,* Raymond Moody comments on his view of Mormon interest in the NDE. A portion of his comments follow:

> There are many religions around the world that readily accept NDEs as the doorway to the spiritual world. The most prominent of the Western religions to do this is the Church

of the Latter Day Saints [sic], more commonly known as the Mormon Church. The Mormon Doctrine supports the NDE as a peek into the spirit world. . . .

The Mormon *Journal of Discourses*, a commentary on Mormon beliefs written by church elders, says that the spirit body retains the five senses of the physical body (sight, hearing, feeling, taste, and smell) while having "enhanced capacities" and the ability to consider many different ideas at the same time. It can also move with lightning speed, see in many different directions at the same time, and communicate in many ways other than speech. And it is free of disability and illness.

Mormon doctrine says that the spirit enters the body at birth and leaves upon death. It defines death as "merely a change from one status or sphere of existence to another."

Many of the traits of the NDE are described by Mormon leaders. One says, "The brightness and glory of the next apartment is inexpressible," which is basically the same as being engulfed by the soothing light. (*The Light Beyond*, 68–71)

Raymond Moody continues with his discussion of LDS beliefs by quoting from several areas of the *Journal of Discourses*. It is rare for a non-Mormon researcher or author to quote from the twenty-six-volume *Journal of Discourses*. It is no simple matter to search through the books and computerized libraries to find what a particular leader said. It is believed, for example, that the quotation above of traveling at great speed was made by Brigham Young. Brigham was speaking at the funeral of a friend, and among other things he said:

As quickly as the spirit is unlocked from this house of clay, it is free to travel with lightning speed to any planet, or fixed star, or to the uttermost part of the earth, or to the depths of the sea, according to the will of Him who dictates. Every faithful man's labor will continue as long as the labor of Jesus, until all things are redeemed that can be redeemed, and presented to the Father. (*Journal of Discourses*, 13:77)

The *Journal* includes dozens of authors of various speeches and articles. At the very least, therefore, Raymond Moody should receive credit for doing his homework.

In addition to contributing substantially to the general NDE database which was evolving from the effort of numerous researchers, the LDS were unique in a number of areas. These included the concept—backed by supporting data—of a premortal existence (see chapters 4 and 15). Also unique was the recognition that the premortal place of our origin was our real "home," and when we left this mortal existence, we—and *everyone* who has ever lived—would simply be returning home. In concert with these concepts was the idea that life was eternal—but without any recognition of reincarnation as a valid explanation for eternal life.

A key correlation with LDS doctrine was the repeated assertion by those having NDEs that their spirit, soul, essence, or energy field separated from their physical body upon death. Human consciousness continued to reside in this separated entity—in point of fact, upon separation it was enhanced in its ability to absorb and communicate knowledge. Moreover, this spirit form, energy field, or whatever, was able to pass through solid objects and travel immense distances at speeds which implicitly exceeded the speed of light. The arithmetic of the universe was immediately accessible and understood by the separated spiritual consciousness.

Another discovery unique to LDS research stemmed from the firsthand interview of John Hernandez, who, with his workmates, underwent multiple NDEs (see chapter 7). Similarly, the firsthand interview of Eloise Weaver revealed another case in which more than one person shared the NDE (see Preface).

Since many of those interviewed and/or documented by Mormon researchers were LDS, it was possible to search for differences between their experiences and those who were non-LDS. A relatively complete comparison of LDS teachings and scriptures with NDEs is given in chapters 4, 5, and 15. Readers can draw their conclusions relative to the validity of the comparisons.

One interesting observation is that the LDS membership is approximately 2 percent of the overall population of the United States. Although the number of LDS professionals and others involved in NDE research compared with those not of the Church is unknown, from the data included in this book, it appears that the contribution of Latter-day Saints is larger than the proportion of general population density.

4: Near-Death Experience Correlations with LDS Teachings on Death and God

By David R. Larsen, MS

About the Author

David R. Larsen was born and raised on a farm in Logan, Utah. He served a mission in Argentina from 1969–1972. Following his mission he enlisted in the Army as a Chaplain's assistant, serving primarily Protestant and Catholic Chaplains in the 101st Airborne and 1st Infantry Division in Germany.

In 1975, David was married in the Bern Switzerland Temple to Maureen Kulinicz of Coventry England. A Catholic priest was his best man in a prior civil ceremony. Later that year, he returned to Utah to resume his schooling. He obtained a bachelor's degree in psychology in 1978 and master's degree in family and human development in 1982, at which time he received a commission in the Navy as a chaplain.

He served two years with the Marine Corps and two years with the Navy before moving over to the Air Force in 1986. He then served in Mountain Home, Idaho; Hill Air Force Base, Utah; and Mildenhall, England, as a civilian in their family-support program. He continued to serve as a Chaplain with the Navy and Marine Corps Reserves until 1997.

In 2001 David was selected as the Organizational Health Center director at Hill Air Force Base, where he is currently employed. In the Church he has served as elders quorum president, high priests group leader, stake mission president, and a member of three high councils and two bishoprics, where he now serves as first counselor.

Context of Chapters 4 and 5

This chapter and the one that follows describe in some detail the teachings, and to a certain extent, the origin and history, of The Church of Jesus Christ of Latter-day Saints. They draw from other chapters in the book, as well as other sources, to show areas of correlation—or non-correlation—of the teachings with NDE accounts. The emphasis here (in Part I of the book) is on the doctrinal data rather than the NDEs. As such, the NDE examples are sparse and given solely as reinforcement of the main theological message being discussed.

On the other hand, in Part IV of the book, the chapter titled *A Comparison* provides a more complete NDE exhibit of particular LDS teachings. And in this latter portion, the NDE is emphasized rather than the particular LDS teaching and its scriptural origins. This technique was adopted so that each area could get relatively complete exposure within a limited space. It has the advantage of full coverage of the subject, but the disadvantage of some duplication.

Death—An Important Subject for Latter-day Saints

Death and dying were frequent topics for discussion among the early members of The Church of Jesus Christ of Latter-day Saints. This wasn't due so much to their fascination with the topic as to their frequent participation in the process. As a result of the early persecution of church members, the "extermination order," and resulting mobbings in Missouri, the infested swamp lands of Nauvoo, Illinois, and the arduous trek to Utah, hundreds of these early saints died. Many had given up their homes, their native lands, and livelihoods to heed the call of their prophet to "gather to Zion" to build the kingdom of God.

How trying this must have been to make such sacrifices, only to have to watch as family and friends died from accidents, were murdered, or became sick and died.

Fortunately, due to the love and foresight of their benevolent God, their new faith, scriptures, and prophet provided a variety of reassuring doctrines and promises. These teachings not only helped them endure these trials, but enabled them to persevere optimistically in the hope of a better life after death.

Their new scripture, the Book of Mormon, provided a second witness that Jesus Christ had indeed overcome death, as in the following statement from the book's compiler, the ancient American prophet Mormon. In talking about a group of his ancestors converted to Christ, Mormon wrote, "And they never did look upon death with any degree of terror, for their hope and views of Christ and the resurrection; therefore, death was swallowed up to them by the victory of Christ over it" (Alma 27:28).

Later in a revelation received by Joseph Smith on February 9, 1831, he was told, "Thou shalt live together in love, insomuch that thou shalt weep for the loss of them that die, and more especially for those that have not hope of a glorious resurrection. And it shall come to pass that those that die in me shall not taste of death, for it shall be sweet unto them (D&C 42:45–46).

According to LDS historian M. Guy Bishop:

> In its early stages, the philosophy of Mormonism in regard to dying and the hereafter could not be easily distinguished from the contemporary beliefs. It focused primarily on the promise of a resurrection and individual post-mortal rewards for the righteous . . . by the mid-nineteenth century many Americans regarded dying as a transition to a state of blessedness for the faithful. [But as time went on], though many conventional sentiments continued to characterize Mormon thinking about death, a more distinctive note gradually came in. ("To Overcome the 'Last Enemy,'" pp. 64–65)

The Father, Son, and Holy Spirit

While most Christian creeds referred to a triune, "three-in-one" God in transcendent ethereal terms, without body parts or mortal passions, as noted in chapter 1, Joseph Smith declared the Father and Son to be two separate glorified persons "whose brightness and glory defy all description," but in form like men (see chapter 15 for more details).

Joseph later wrote: "The Father has a body of flesh and bones as tangible as man's; the Son also; but the Holy Ghost has not a body of flesh and bones, but is a personage of Spirit" (D&C 130:22).

Joseph Smith did not describe God as being in the image of mortal man; rather, his emphasis was as Moses in Genesis—that man was created in the image of the gods (Genesis 1:26). Moreover, he declared God the Father to be the literal premortal father of the spirits of all flesh (Hebrews 12:9; see below, and chapter 11 by Grant Bishop). He declared Jesus Christ to be the literal Son of God, a perfect representative or agent of his Father, our mediator between God and man.

Latter-day Saints see Jesus as the "executor" or administrator of the Father's will regarding the children of men on earth. As the perfect representative of God, his Father, Jesus was the great Jehovah of the Old Testament. The Book of Mormon refers to him as "the God of heaven, . . . and of earth." (Alma 11:3).

President Brigham Young taught that in the spirit realm the faithful would have the privilege of communing with both the Father and the Son—an idea which was incompatible with most Christian theologies:

> Here, we are continually troubled with ills and ailments of various kinds, and our ears are saluted with the expressions. "My head aches," "My shoulders ache." "My back aches," "I am hungry, or tired;" but in the spirit world we are free from all this and enjoy life, glory, and intelligence, and we have the Father to speak to us. Jesus to speak to us, and angels to speak to us, and we shall enjoy, the society of the just and the pure who are in the spirit world until the resurrection." (*Journal of Discourses,* 14:231–32).

The Holy Ghost and Spirit Matter

From the D&C reference to The Holy Ghost in section 130, as well as Luke 24:39, we learn that a spirit does not have a body of flesh and bones. LDS doctrine teaches, however, that spirits do have unique identities, i.e. bodies, but of a more refined nature. In Section 131 Joseph Smith declared, "All spirit is matter, but it is more fine or pure, and can only be discerned by purer eyes" (D&C 131:7).

Latter-day Saints believe each of us has a spirit within, the true seat of our intelligence. We believe this spirit existed for some time before we were born (see *premortal life,* below). The body is merely the tabernacle or temple of our spirit. It is this spirit that leaves the body at death, and as a result of the atonement of Jesus Christ, we believe this spirit will be reunited with its glorified body in the resurrection.

An example of an NDE in which the spirit was clearly separate from the body, and was able to pass through the dense matter of a separate physical body, is that of **Margaret Amodt.** Margaret's NDE was as a result of an ectopic pregnancy in which the fetus exploded in the tube and Margaret bled profusely. Her experience was in 1983. She had been rushed to Holy Cross Hospital for treatment when the medical crisis developed.

Carol and Arvin Gibson interviewed Margaret and her husband Bob in 1991 (Gibson, 1992, pp. 82–83). A portion of their interview follows. It begins after she found herself out of her body.

> **"What do you remember next, Margaret?"**
> "I knew I was . . . I felt so good. And I thought: Wow, this is beautiful. I really liked it, the feeling I had."
> **"The pain was gone?"**
> "Yes, the pain was gone."
> **"Did you see yourself—your body?"**
> "No, the first thing I saw was my kids. They had been taken to my parents' house. They were running around, laughing."
> **"How many children did you have?"**
> "Two little girls. They were playing and I was in my parents' house. I remember, I wasn't standing, I was, like, floating. And then my oldest daughter ran right through me."
> **"Did that surprise you?"**
> "Yes. I tried to hold her and I couldn't. And she started screaming . . . I could hear her scream, 'Mamma.' Shortly after that I was back in the hospital and I felt pain. It was awful . . ."
> **"When you were in your parents' home, did your body feel like a body?"**
> "No."
> **"What did it feel like?"**
> Margaret thought for a moment. "It didn't feel like air either . . . energy!"
> **"Did this energy have arms and legs?"**
> "Just like me . . ."

"**And you actually tried to embrace your child?**"

"Yes, my daughter. She was running and I reached out to hold her, and she ran through me. I saw her just run through me."

We Lived Before We Were Born: The Offspring of God

In 1830, although most Christian ministers repeated the words of Jesus, referring to God as "our Father which art in heaven," few if any believed men and women to be the literal offspring of God, born in His image (Acts 17:28). Nor was it common to believe our spirits dwelt with God before coming to earth. This belief is alluded to in the Bible (Genesis 2:1,5; Jeremiah 1:5; John 9:2), and there is evidence that early Christians held such beliefs. But once the church embraced the doctrine of creation *ex nihilo* (from nothing), this ancient teaching vanished from Christian thought. That does not mean, however, that Christians abandoned the idea of a premortal or pre-earth existence of beings altogether. It was widely accepted that Jesus was the premortal logos, or word of God, who existed with God prior to his coming to earth (although the nature of that relationship was and still is, hotly debated). Also, it was quite widely accepted that angels, and demons, existed with God prior to the formation of the earth, this having been plainly revealed in several passages of both the Old and the New Testaments (Gen 1:26; Job 38:4–7; Jude 1:6; Rev 12:4).

In his book *The Life Before,* Brent Top chronicles the shift in Christianity from a belief in a premortal existence to disbelief. He notes that Origen of Alexandria, *perhaps the greatest theologian of the third century,* wrote of a judgment in a premortal state that, to a certain extent, affected our position in our earthly existence. These writings caused such a furor in the hierarchy of the church that in A.D. 543 a council was called to consider Origen's writings. The council viewed Origen's writings as heretical and rejected the concept of premortal life of man. Brent Top summarized today's Christian thought on premortality in this manner:

> Today conventional Christianity vehemently rejects the notion of a premortal existence but fails to remember that the doctrine was widely taught and accepted prior to the Council of A.D. 543. Even today, some modern Christian scholars view this council and its repudiation of Origen's teachings with a degree of regret and skepticism. (Top, 1988, pp. 18–19)

LDS Belief Regarding a Premortal Existence

In 1835 Joseph Smith purchased a bundle of ancient scrolls believed to contain a record of the teachings of Abraham. As he reviewed this ancient parchment, it was revealed to him that God had informed Abraham of a premortal existence for all of mankind, where prophets and others leaders were chosen by the Lord for unique earthly missions.

> Now the Lord had shown unto me, Abraham, the intelligences that were organized before the world was; and among all these there were many of the noble and great ones; And God saw these souls that they were good, and he stood in the midst of them, and he said:
>
> These I will make my rulers; for he stood among those that were spirits, and he saw that they were good; and he said unto me: Abraham, thou art one of them; thou wast chosen before thou wast born. (Abraham 3:22–23)

From this and ensuing revelations, Joseph Smith learned that indeed mankind had lived in a premortal existence with God, as intelligent spirits. And not only was God our creator, but He is literally the Father of our spirits, as Jesus and Paul had declared (Matthew 6:9; John 20:17; Acts 17:28–29; Hebrews 12:9).

Do NDEs Verify LDS Beliefs Regarding God, Heaven, and a Premortal Home?

Latter-day Saints who study NDEs are curious to hear how people who have had NDEs, including an encounter with a divine being, describe Him. Do they describe Him in ethereal terms, as just energy or light, or in form like a glorified man? Are there ever two? And if so, do they ever refer to one of them as their Father? And do they ever feel as though death is a homecoming, a return to prior knowledge and a previous state?

In chapter 15 and other chapters of the book, examples are given of NDE accounts of encounters with Christ and his Father. For example, **Angie Fenimore** states:

> From the light I felt love directed toward me as an individual, and I was baffled by it. I had never felt deserving of God's love. . . . I had grossly underestimated my importance and the nature of my origin—I am literally the spirit offspring of God.
>
> I even looked like Him. I was surprised that He really had a body with arms and legs and features like mine. . . . As I

studied the features of God, I marveled to see that what I had learned in church and from the scriptures, which I had assumed was figurative or symbolic, was apparently literally true. We are actually, physically created in His image. This realization was staggering.

While NDE descriptions of a divine encounter vary, almost everyone describes the being that greets them as Joseph Smith did (see chapter 1), as a personage of indescribable brilliance, or light. Some who have had more in-depth experiences affirm this person to be their Savior or creator. Moreover, most of these (though not all) affirm that this was indeed a man—usually described as having blue eyes. Also, many have noted that he embraced them, that they felt his arms and the warmth of his body (see Liz Clark—chapter 8). They all describe Him as a very personal God indeed, who always knows their name.

Seeing, Hearing, and Touching Jesus

The description of George Ritchie's encounter with Christ is especially interesting since it encompasses two aspects of Mormon theology. First, that man can see God and Christ and still live, and second, that this is possible only if the individual is changed—either in spirit form or "quickened" in the flesh.

One of the early arguments against Joseph Smith was that he could not have seen God because the Bible said, "No man hath seen God at any time" (1 John 4:12). Joseph Smith later clarified that by noting: "For no man has seen God at any time in the flesh, except quickened by the Spirit of God" (D&C 67:11).

George Ritchie was given that privilege and recorded:

> I stared in astonishment as the brightness increased, coming from nowhere, seeming to shine everywhere at once. . . . It was impossibly bright: it was like a million welders' lamps all blazing at once. And right in the middle of my amazement came a prosaic thought probably born of some biology lecture back at the university: "I'm glad I don't have physical eyes at this moment," I thought. "This light would destroy the retina in a tenth of a second."
>
> No, I corrected myself, not the light.
>
> He.
>
> . . . He would be too bright to look at. For now I saw that it was not light but a Man who had entered the room, or rather, a Man made out of light, though this seemed no more possible

to my mind than the incredible intensity of the brightness that made up His form.

The instant I perceived Him, a command formed itself in my mind. "Stand up!" the words came from inside me, yet that had an authority my mere thoughts had never had. I got to my feet, and as I did came the stupendous certainty: "You are in the presence of *the* Son of God."

. . . This Person was power itself, older than time and yet more modern than anyone I had ever met.

One of the more dramatic descriptions of an individual being touched by Christ is that of **David Chevalier** (Gibson, 1993, pp. 197–206). David's multiple NDEs occurred in 1981 and were the result of a drunken uncle shooting him in the abdomen with a shotgun. The medical trauma was enormous—essentially the doctors has to remove his bowels by placing them on a gurney while they were still attached to Dave, and then repair or cut lengths away. A brief portion of his interview, as it was recorded by Gibson, follows:

"One night, about a week after entering the hospital, while in Intensive Care, I slipped away and they again had to resuscitate me with the paddles. During that night, with my room darkened, I became fully aware of what was going on in my room. Looking around the room I could see everything—and standing by one side of my bed was my Savior. He was as plain to me then as you are now.

"Reaching over to me, He ran His hands up and down my body, and all the tubes, all the staples and other attachments to my body were gone. His right hand reached out, as if to beckon me; I reached back to touch His hand. . . .

"In [that] event, Dave, you said that your Savior was standing near the bed?"

"Yes, He was on my left as I was lying in bed."

"What was He wearing?"

"Exactly as I imagined my Savior would look, with a white robe, and a sash tied in the center of the robe. He had a beard and long hair."

"Was He, or was the room, bathed in light?"

"Not that I noticed—except when He put his hands on me. The sheets seemed to get brighter during that instant."

"What were your feelings when He put his hands on you?"

"It was comforting. There were no feelings of fear or pain."

"How did you know it was your Savior?"

"I know Jesus Christ when I see Him."

"**How did you know?**"

David chuckled as he thought. Then he said:

"Probably it was the sense of goodwill and the sense of comfort that I felt—together with the other events that I witnessed. The fact is, I just knew. I knew!"

A particularly interesting feature of David's experience was how closely it paralleled what happened to Howard Storm when Christ healed his spiritual wounds (Storm, 2000, p. 30). Another aspect of David Chevalier's experience will be explored in the next chapter.

Both **Don Wood** (Gibson, 1993, pp. 117–31) and Elder David B. Haight (chapter 10) were also shown portions of Jesus' earthly ministry, including his suffering in Gethsemane. Don declared:

"While I was marveling at this new-found knowledge, or rather, from the reawakened knowledge that I previously had, I was again transported to another era. This time I found myself looking on a different scene—the scene was the Garden of Gethsemane. Looking down from above, I saw Christ undergoing his ordeal of pain with dignified endurance."

"**When you were transported to these different scenes in time, [Don], did you ask to see them?**"

"No, they were completely automatic. The first one seemed to be in response to my astonishment when the voice told me that I chose the disease, cystic fibrosis, in a premortal life. I suspect that the second scene, in Gethsemane, was to teach me more about the value of a dignified endurance of pain."

Encounters with Our Father in Heaven

A far fewer, yet significant number, have also mentioned an encounter with their "Father in Heaven." And some have seen both together. **Rocky** was a thirteen-year-old boy when the Gibsons interviewed him and his mother Berta. Berta and her husband were nominal Protestants, but not active in their faith. Rocky was four years old when he fell from an upstairs window to the concrete below. Among other things young Rocky reported seeing both Jesus and his Father (Gibson, 1993, pp. 100–106).

Through the following months, Rocky told me [Berta] that Jesus had taken him by the hand and taken him to heaven. When I asked him what it was like there, he said that there were homes there, too, only they were kind of cloud-like. People had families, he said, and they live in homes like here.

Jesus visited Rocky and gave him an apple. Heavenly Father also visited him. Rocky's frequent reference to Heavenly Father and Jesus caused me to ask: "How do you know the difference between Heavenly Father and Jesus?" He responded: "Heavenly Father has light hair and Jesus has dark hair." Explaining how they communicated he said: "They talk to you but they don't move their mouths."

These vignettes continued to come from my son for some months. It was as if he had an inner knowledge of some distant place—a place that I had not taught him about. Once, for example, he told me that Jesus and Heavenly Father had power. I looked up passages in the Bible, such as Mark 12:24, where it referred to God's power, and I wondered how a five-year-old could know that. I certainly didn't teach it to him.

With time, a rather complete picture emerged of Rocky's visit to another world where Jesus and Heavenly Father dwelled. So, I asked him why he came back. He cried and said: "I'm sorry, Mom, I liked heaven. It was wonderful there and I didn't want to come home. But Jesus said I had to come back. He told me that my mother needed me."

Wondering about this further I asked Rocky: "How did you get back?" "Jesus has powers," he said, and then he put his hand to his lips and motioned outward. When Rocky did that the thought came to me: *It's no more said than it is done. . . .*

Once I asked him: "You saw God?"and he said: "He prefers that we call him *Heavenly Father.*"

One other example not mentioned in later chapters is the experience of **Gayleen Williams,** a victim of years of spouse abuse. In sharing her experience with the Salt Lake chapter of IANDS, in May 2004, she noted that she was visited by both Jesus and her Father in Heaven, who asked:

> "Daughter, why weepest thou?" Although He already knew.
>
> My response was—as I again hung my head in shame, "Because I am not worthy, Father, to be with you and my Lord and Savior."
>
> As he spoke—his tenderness filled my soul—his voice was so soothing that I felt completely serene, and I no longer felt ashamed. Then he said to me, "Oh my daughter, how I love thee. You are worthy, my child, or you would not be here. The one

who has led you to believe [this] and has caused thee to mourn is not filled with truth, but he is a mockery to heaven and has become a servant of the dark son. You are not what you have been convinced you are.

"You are my daughter—now I take you in my arms." At this point He gently held out his hand towards me and the son also held out a hand towards me. As I set one of my hands in each of theirs, they helped raise me to my feet and they wrapped themselves around me. Their loving arms of love. As they did this, my body was completely filled. Every fiber of my being was filled with love. All fear, all doubt, all anguish, self-disgust, self-doubt and self-disdain were removed from deep within me. Instantly I was healed to the very depth of my being. I now felt such wonder, such awe; complete tranquility and bliss. My entire self was so complete, so whole, and so pure. The light so often referred to in the presence of glory and eternity is not only brightness and glory, but freedom. . . . It truly has shown me a new meaning to the light and knowledge that Adam and Eve sought to get from Father.

NDE Evidence for Premortal Existence

There are ample examples in the literature of individuals who had NDEs and believed they were returning "home" to a place they had lived before, and to their Heavenly Father, as Rocky noted above. Three dramatic cases are included in this book.

Chapter 15 includes Julie's experience of seeing herself in a premortal environment. Chapter 16 details Maxine Zawodniak's recollections. Chapter 3 reviewed Don Wood's experience where he was taken back in time to a premortal existence where he actually saw himself making choices that would affect his mortal life. To recap **Don Wood's** experience:

> When He told me that it was my choice, in a premortal environment, to suffer when I came to earth, I was both astonished and incredulous. He must have understood my incredulity, because I was immediately transported to my premortal existence. There was a room that I was viewing from above and to the side, but at the same time I was sitting in it. In a sense I was both an observer and a participant.

In the next chapter I will comment further on the continuation of the family after death. It is worth noting here, however, that LDS teachings acknowledge that we lived in a premortal environment with the Lord Jesus Christ and his Father (as noted above). Mortal death, therefore, is a return to that home and glory which we once knew.

And a Little Child Shall Teach Them

The expression of death as being a return to our premortal home is not unique to NDEs of Latter-day Saints. This is perhaps best illustrated by a moving experience described by Ken Ring (*Lessons from the Light*, pp. 118–21). He was attending a conference in which notable scholars were present and presented material in their areas of specialty. The conference was for the purpose of establishing a dialogue between Western scholars and Tibetan Buddhism on the subject of death and dying. The conference was headed by the Dalai Lama. Attending the conference, and a last-minute replacement on the panel of speakers, was a nine-year-old boy by the name of **Marc Beaulieu**. He was dying of leukemia.

According to Dr. Ring, Marc was frail in appearance, almost as if he were one of the Holocaust survivors. Marc gave a very brief address to the assembled scholars, and then retired into himself with his translating head-phones for making the mostly English speakers understandable in his native French. After a rather boring group of speakers finished, and during the questioning period, Marc was asked what he thought of all the erudite speeches he had heard, and especially to give his own views about death. As Ken Ring sat transfixed with the rest of the audience, he heard the translation of Marc's response:

> I think that when you die, it's not over. It *can't be over*, because in my mind, it's just impossible. It continues—we just go back home. We go back home where we were before we were in this life. And that [this] life is only something that we have to learn something. And when we learn that thing, then we go back home. We go back where we were before. And that life, of course, is limited to a certain time period. That is, exterior life. But the life that's inside is infinite, it never ends.

Ken's statement as to the reaction of the audience to Marc's remarks was, "With that comment, the panelists seemed to be at a loss as to how to react. Hearing such a spontaneous and straightforward utterance, so obviously based on the boy's own direct experience, and delivered with such purity of heart, appeared to stun them, as it did, I think, most of us in the audience. After nearly three hours of talk, it took a child to silence us into a recognition of this simple but profound truth about life and death."

Some Experiences Not in Sync with LDS Doctrine

Although NDEs tend to coincide with LDS teachings, some of the experiences seem to go beyond, if not contrary to, our beliefs. Perhaps the most pronounced difference is in the belief some people hold in the principle of reincarnation. In chapter 15 it is observed that there is a persistent belief among some who have had NDEs—and with some researchers—that certain aspects of the NDE can be explained by reincarnation. That belief is soundly rejected by LDS doctrine.

As noted above, Latter-day Saints reject the metaphysical "trinity" concept—three gods in one person—as declared in the early Christian creeds. When Jesus said, "I am in the Father, and the Father in me" (John 14:11), "I and my Father are one" (John 10:30), and when he prayed for his disciples, "That they may be one, even as we are one" (John 17:22), LDS have generally interpreted these as referring to a unity of mind or purpose. Some NDErs, however, have experienced a oneness with God that appears to have gone beyond a unity of purpose. In chapter 11 you will read about **Beverly Brodsky** who had an extraordinarily

profound NDE in which she noted that the wonders of the universe were revealed to her. Moreover, she stated, "I was filled with God's knowledge, and in that precious aspect of his Beingness, I was one with him."

When we asked Beverly what she meant by that, she explained that she saw things "as if through the eyes of God. As though she were God." Although she admitted that she had still retained her individual identity, it seems this experience goes beyond the traditional LDS concept of unity with God, and Beverly is not the only one to have reported such an experience. As will be discussed in the next chapter, Latter-day Saints *do* believe that after the resurrection and the final judgment, men *may become* as God. See chapter 11 for additional insights into the nature of man's interconnection with God and the universe.

Additionally, although most who have an NDE report that their spirit body looked much like their physical body, as LDS teach, some have noted otherwise. **Sylvia,** for example, whose experience is partially recorded in chapter 15, stated that the body she had while "floating through the tunnel" was more "similar to a jelly fish . . . my eyes seemed to be straight on top of my head." Others have noted they saw spirits which appeared as flickers of light or "twinkles" (June 2002, IANDS meeting, Salt Lake City).

The Thirteenth Article of Faith notes that "God will yet reveal many great and important things pertaining to the kingdom of heaven." And NDEs suggest some of these may not exactly fit some LDS expectations. Alternatively, of course, some of the apparent discrepancies could be due to uncertainty among those who experienced an NDE in attempting to describe the undescribable—or of force-fitting a description into a predetermined belief system (see discussions in chapters 3 and 17).

Where Do We Go after Death?
The Postmortal Possibilities

In frontier America there were, of course, a variety of Christian denominations, teaching a variety of ideas regarding the possible destinations of souls after death. Most all of them agreed, however, that there were basically only two options. The "righteous" would inherit a blissful heaven; but if a person had not received the "sacraments" or "ordinances" of their faith—baptism, last rites, etc.—or if they had not accepted and confessed Jesus Christ as their personal Savior, they were destined for hell, and perhaps a fiery hell at that. And once dead there were no changes or "second chances."

Although some believed in the efficacy of "death-bed repentance," few if any Christian denominations in the 19th century believed in "an after-death-bed repentance," or the possibility of salvation for those who were not counted among the faithful believers on earth. Moreover, this was believed to be the case not only for adults, but children and infants as well. The Book of Mormon, and early LDS leaders, however, posited other more hopeful possibilities.

Alma, one of the main prophets of The Book of Mormon, declared, "Behold, it has been made known unto me, by an angel, that the spirits of *all* men, as soon as they are departed from this mortal body; yea, the spirits of all men, whether they be good or evil, are taken home to that God who gave them life" (Alma 40:11). Joseph Smith added, "The righteous and the wicked all go to the same world of spirits until the resurrection. . . . The great misery of departed spirits in the world of spirits, where they go after death, is to know that they come short of the glory that others enjoy and that they might have enjoyed themselves, and they are their own accusers" (*Teachings of the Prophet Joseph Smith,* p. 310).

To some preachers, the idea that non-believers, and even those involved in "wicked" practices, would return to God for anything other than a harsh final judgment, was blasphemous. However, the various illustrations in this book and numerous others, suggest the wisdom of reserving even partial judgments for God, and remind me of a poem I once learned:

> I dreamed death came the other night,
> and heaven's gate swung wide;
> with kindly grace an angel ushered me inside.
> And there to my astonishment stood folks I'd known
> on earth . . .
> Some I'd judged and labeled as "unfit" or of little worth,
> Indignant words rose to my lips, but never were set free,
> For every face showed stunned surprise . . .
> No one expected me!
> (Banks, 1980, p. 72)

Life Review and Total Recall: A Partial Judgment?

It's been postulated that perhaps the life review experienced by many NDErs, soon after or shortly before death, may be, or be part of a "partial judgment" process, which may help a person to understand better the rationale for his next step. Relevant to the life review, the originator of The Book of Mormon, Nephi, noted that after death, " . . . we shall have a perfect knowledge of all our guilt, and our uncleanness, and our nakedness; and the righteous shall have a perfect knowledge of their enjoyment, and their righteousness, . . ." (2 Nephi 9:14).

The time period Nephi was talking about was after the body and spirit had been reunited, but this was understood by Brigham Young, and other members generally, to be an ability of the Spirit immediately after death. For example, Orson Pratt, another apostle in Brigham Young's day, spoke of the fact that "the spirit has not lost its capacity for memory, but it is the organization of the tabernacle that prevents it from remembering." But when the spirit leaves the body and is no longer subject to its limitations and infirmities, "then is the time we shall have the most *vivid knowledge of all the past acts* of our lives during our probationary state." The spirit, Pratt said, "is a being that has capacity sufficient to retain all its past doings, whether they be good or bad." And it is the reflection of the spirit memory that produces joy, "and this *joy is a hundred fold more intense* than what the spirit is capable of perceiving or enjoying in this life (JD 2:239, 240).

George Q. Cannon, a later apostle in The Church, added that our memories will stretch back even to before we were born:

> Memory will be quickened to a wonderful extent. Every deed that we have done will be brought to our recollection. Every acquaintance made will be remembered. There will be no scenes or incidents in our lives that will be forgotten by us in the world to come. . . . men and women [will] recall not only that which pertains to this life, but our memories will stretch back to the life we had before we came here, with the associations we had with our Father and God and with those bright spirits that stand around His throne and with the righteous and holy ones." (Cannon, 1889)

Of course, life reviews are a very common part of NDEs. In his book *Lessons From The Light*, psychologist Kenneth Ring shares insights from more than half-a-dozen life reviews. Some of these are amazingly similar to the descriptions of Elders Pratt and Cannon. In this book, the life reviews of John Stirling (chapter 7) and Elizabeth Clark are described (chapter 8). Chapter 15 discusses some Less Than Pleasant (LTP) reviews. Some individuals have had LTP life reviews followed by more than pleasant events.

An Unpleasant Life Review

Barbara Rommer's book, *Blessing in Disguise*, is discussed in chapter 10. Her entire book is devoted to discussing LTP experiences. One example, provided by Barbara, is that of **Yolinda**. Portions of her experience follow (Romer, 2000, pp. 80–81):

> I went into this gray void where it felt like there was absolutely nothing at all, like I was in outer space. I was float-ing, but didn't have control and was stuck, trapped, and scared to death. Then came this sound from deep down inside me calling out: "God, God." That's when I did like a life review thing. It like zipped on, but it was more concentrated at the end, so the last years came out real clear. I saw everything that I had ever done to that day, and that it was meaningless and useless and it had brought me to that place. I felt very weak and hopeless and useless.

This is weird, but when I called out to God, a kind of light, like spiritual lightning, struck my head and went through me, and then something inside me exploded. When this happened I felt like a crackling and tingling in my mind, in my brain, and I felt tingling through my whole body and every cell became energized and alive. It was traumatizing, but it was wonderful. And the light, just like you read about, was just all knowledge, all life, all beauty, and all love. It was saying: "No you're not THAT person. THIS is who you are. I love you, totally and unconditionally." I believed that was coming from God. There was some actual voice messages and the rest was in my mind, like a knowing. I was told: "You're making this all too complicated" and that "there is nothing on earth that matters except learning to love and receive love."

Hell and Satan

LDS, like other Christians, do believe that many will go, if not directly, eventually, to an unpleasant location. As Alma went on to note:

And then shall it come to pass that the spirits of those who are righteous, are received into a state of happiness, which is called paradise; a state of rest; a state of peace, where they shall rest from all their troubles and from all care, and sorrow, etc. And then shall it come to pass, that the spirits of the wicked, yea, who are evil . . . these shall be cast out into outer darkness; there shall be weeping, and wailing, and gnashing of teeth; and this because of their own iniquity; being led captive by the will of the devil. (Alma 40:11–14)

Most Christians refer to this place of darkness and anguish as hell. Some Latter-day Saints prefer to refer to it as "spirit prison," in line with 1 Peter 3:19. However one refers to it, it is not a happy place, and many who have had NDEs have either gone there or observed souls in this dark and dreary state.

In their book, *The Eternal Journey,* sociologists Craig Lundahl and Harold Widdison provide several accounts of what they describe as the realm of bewildered spirits. One NDEer, who was dead for more than an hour following an auto accident, stated:

I remember more clearly than any other thing that has ever happened to me in my life time, every detail of every moment, what I saw and what happened during that hour I was gone from the world. I was standing some distance from this burning, turbulent, rolling mass of blue fire . . . I saw other people I had known that had died . . . We recognized each other, even though we did not speak. Their expressions were those of bewilderment and confusion. The scene was so awesome that words simply fail. There is no way to escape, no way out. You don't even try to look for one. This is the prison out of which no one can escape except by Divine Intervention. (Lundahl and Widdison, 1997, pp. 226–27)

Harriet Lee saw a similar region of the other-world inhabited by millions of miserable and unhappy occupants. She said, "They were in great confusion wringing their hands, holding them up, and tossing their bodies to and fro in fearful anguish. My guide said, These are the spirits in prison; they know the punishment that awaits them and they are in great distress by reason of their knowledge" (Lundahl and Widdison, 1997, p. 235).

Another significant footnote. While most Christian dogma and the earlier witness suggested hell as being a place of physical fire, The Book of Mormon and Latter-day Saints see this as primarily symbolic. For example, both Nephi and King Mosiah, in the Book of Mormon, describe the anguish of hell figuratively: "and the torment shall be *as* a lake of fire and brimstone" (2 Nephi 9:16; Mosiah 3:27).

On the other hand, for Latter-day Saints, the individual referred to as Satan or the Devil is very real. The Encyclopedia of Mormonism notes that in the premortal world, Lucifer rebelled and became Satan, or "the devil." A division developed among the spirits, and no spirits were neutral. There was war in heaven, and the third of the hosts who followed Lucifer were cast out. These rebellious spirits, along with Lucifer, were thrust down to the earth without physical bodies. . . . Satan and his followers are still at war with those spirits who have been born into mortality (*Encyclopedia of Mormonism*, Ludlow, p. 329).

The Book of Mormon further notes, "And because he had fallen from heaven, and had become miserable forever, he sought also the misery of all mankind" (2 Nephi 2:18).

An Extensive View of Hell

More than one NDEr has verified the reality of Satan's existence, as well. **Don Brubaker,** who is not LDS, insists that he was given a special mandate to testify of the reality of this being. Don had been rushed to the hospital with symptoms of a pending heart attack. As his doctors wheeled him into an elevator, his heart stopped, and he found himself falling feet first into what he described as a dark, damp, musty tunnel (Brubaker, 1993, p. 80). Finally he came to the realization:

> I was in Hell.
>
> The realization swept over me like an ocean wave, unstoppable though I tried desperately to dismiss it. Hell! I didn't even believe in hell! And here I was? This was it? I had only the briefest moment to react to the thought when a deep, comfortable voice echoed through the tunnel. "Have no fear my son," the voice said with a certain resounding nobility, "for I am with you. I have chosen you to write about the experience you will go through."
>
> Don wondered why he had been chosen. The voice responded, "You'll first experience hell, . . . to prove to you the reality of evil. You've only believed that there was goodness. You must see for yourself that hell is real. And then you can tell others about the awful reality of hell, and about the beautiful glory of heaven. . . . Because you represent common man. . . . People will more easily relate to and accept your story." (Brubaker, 1993, p. 81)

After this experience with God, he regained consciousness and tried to tell his physicians and nurses, but they virtually ignored him because he had suffered oxygen deprivation. He then found himself once more plunging back down the dark tunnel. He sensed the presence of a powerful being. This being informed Don that he could avoid all the pain and anguish if he would just follow him. Not only would the pain disappear, he could have anything his heart desired. Then he noted (Brubaker, 1993, pp. 109–10): "Visions of wealth appeared before my eyes, like a three dimensional movie. Diamonds, money, cars, gold, beautiful women, everything. I was overwhelmed by the vision. I could almost touch it, it seemed so real."

Don realized the tempter was Satan, who was bargaining for his soul. He struggled mightily to shake himself from these images. He said he could clearly hear the words, "Enjoy, enjoy" in one ear and in the other, "Resist, resist." He felt as though he were caught in a huge tug of war and was literally being torn apart. And one party to the battle was Satan, a being he had never believed existed. But now he knew with complete certainty that Satan did indeed exist, and was fighting for his soul.

Don then experienced a life review, but it was not pleasant (Brubaker, 1993, p. 86):

> Images appeared before my eyes, as if projected on a giant screen. I was seeing myself. All of those times in my life when

I had done something wrong were being shown back to me. As I watched I was embarrassed, and ashamed. When the long chronicle was over, I began to watch scenes of the things I had only wished for—worse things than what I had actually done!

It's interesting to note here that LDS believe we will be judged not only by our works or the things we have done, but also according to our desires (Alma 41:3). After the review, Don again heard the voice of God. The voice told him that his mission was to tell others that there is a God and that they must learn to love others, to have compassion, and to forgive. He was also told (Brubaker, 1993, p. 99):

> You will recall all of your experiences clearly, and you will write a book. You must tell others about me and about Satan. You must make them understand that there are very real choices they must make. I have chosen you for this work. You will succeed. You will be safe. I am always nearby. You are never alone.

Don noted that in his experience he saw bedraggled beings shuffling along in the "dark, damp, musty cave," blindly following each other, convinced that they were trapped in their sins and could not be saved. Don knew that if they would just look up and call upon God, they could be saved from eternal enslavement, but they resisted. They had been so blinded by Satan that they could not believe that God would or could forgive them.

Although Don was not familiar with the LDS faith, his struggle with Satan is strikingly in accordance with the words of Nephi recorded more than 2500 years earlier in The Book of Mormon:

> Wherefore, the Lord God gave unto man that he should act for himself. Wherefore, man could not act for himself save it should be that he was enticed by the one or the other. . . . Wherefore, men are free . . . to choose liberty and eternal life, through the great Mediator of all men, or to choose captivity and death, according to the captivity and power of the devil; for he seeketh that all men might be miserable like unto himself. (2 Nephi 2:16, 27).

Rescue from Hell: Positive-Negative Polarity

A smaller number of those who have NDEs report a rather hellish experience followed by a positive one, usually associated with a rescue by God. Howard Storm is a notable example. All of these modern accounts, however, are predated by the account of the ancient prophet Alma in the Book of Mormon.

Stanislav and Christina Grof, in their book, *Beyond Death—The Gates of Consciousness*, elaborate on three themes from hellish experience (Grof, 1980, p. 26). These themes are also evident in Alma's account. The themes are:

- the polarities of the hellish and heavenly experience
- the subjective sense of *eternal* torment in *finite* duration
- the use of "rebirth" imagery

Correlation between the Prophet Alma's and Howard Storm's NDE

In retelling his experience, Alma artfully highlights this positive/ negative polarity using a reflexive pyramidal poetic form known as "chiasmus." In Alma's description of his apparent NDE, which follows, Stanislav and Grof have bracketed comments with NDE elements as originally defined by Raymond Moody (Moody, 1975, pp. 21–23). The NDE elements were selected to show areas of correspondence with Alma's experience.

By way of background, Alma, who lived about 73 B.C., rejected the prophecies recorded on brass and gold plates by his ancestors. More specifically, he rejected the prophecies concerning the birth, death and resurrection of the Lord Jesus Christ. His reaction to these ancient writings and to those who believed them was to persecute those followers of Christ. He, and the "sons of Mosiah," actively fought against those who were believers. **Alma** related his story to his son Helaman, and it is recorded in the Book of Mormon:

> For I went about with the sons of Mosiah, seeking to destroy the church of God; but behold, God sent his holy angel to stop us by the way. And behold, he spake unto us, as it were the voice of thunder, and the whole earth did tremble beneath our feet; and we all fell to the earth, for the fear of the Lord came upon us.
>
> But behold, the voice said unto me: Arise, And I arose and stood up, and beheld the angel. And he said unto me: If thou wilt of thyself be destroyed, seek no more to destroy the church of God.
>
> And it came to pass that I fell to the earth; and it was for the space of three days and three nights that I could not open my mouth, neither had I the use of my limbs (Alma 36:6–10). . . .

But I was wracked with eternal torment, for my soul was harrowed up to the greatest degree and racked with all my sins. Yea, I did remember all my sins and iniquities, for which I was tormented with the pains of hell; yea, I saw that I had rebelled against my God, and that I had not kept his holy commandments [life review]. . . . Yea, and in fine so great had been my iniquities, that the very thought of coming into the presence of my God did rack my soul with inexpressible horror. Oh, thought I, that I could be banished and become extinct both soul and body, that I might not be brought to stand in the presence of my God, to be judged of my deeds (Alma 36:12–15). . . .

And it came to pass that as I was thus racked with torment, while I was harrowed up by the memory of my many sins, behold, I remembered also to have heard my father prophesy unto the people concerning the coming of one Jesus Christ, a Son of God, to atone for the sins of the world. Now, as my mind caught hold upon this thought, I cried within my heart: O Jesus, thou Son of God, have mercy on me, who am in the gall of bitterness, and am encircled about by the everlasting chains of death.

And now, behold, when I thought this, I could remember my pains no more; yea, I was harrowed up by the memory of my sins no more [feeling of peace]. And oh, what joy, and what marvelous light I did behold [the light]; yea my soul was filled with joy as exceeding as was my pain! Yea, I say unto you, my son, that there could be nothing so exquisite and so bitter as were my pains. Yea, and again I say unto you, my son, that on the other hand, there can be nothing so exquisite and sweet as was my joy. Yea, methought I saw, even as our father Lehi saw, God sitting upon his throne [Being of Light], surrounded with numberless concourses of angels [other beings], in the attitude of singing and praising God [music]; yea, and my soul did long to be there [reluctance to return]. (Alma 36:7–22)

One of the many fascinating aspects of **Howard Storm's** NDE is how closely it corresponds to Alma's experience. Howard's complete story is best described by reading his book *My Descent into Death* (Storm, 2000). Pertinent portions are given below:

Lying there, torn apart, inside and out, I knew I was lost. I would never see the world again. I was left alone to become a creature of the dark. . . .

I desperately needed someone to love me, someone to know I was alive. A ray of hope began to dawn in me, a belief that there really was something greater out there. For the first time in my adult life I wanted it to be true that Jesus loved me. I didn't know how to express what I wanted and needed, but with every bit of my last ounce of strength, I yelled out into the darkness, "Jesus, save me." I yelled that from the core of my being with all the energy I had left. I have never meant anything more strongly in my life.

Far off in the darkness I saw a pinpoint of light like the faintest star in the sky. . . . The star was rapidly getting brighter and brighter. . . . I couldn't take my eyes off it; the light was more intense and more beautiful than anything I had ever seen. . . . It wasn't just light. This was a living being, a luminous being approximately eight feet tall and surrounded by an oval of radiance. The brilliant intensity of the light penetrated my body. Ecstasy swept away the agony. Tangible hands and arms gently embraced me and lifted me up. I slowly rose up into the presence of the light and the torn pieces of my body miraculously healed before my eyes. . . . More importantly, the despair and pain were replaced by love. I had been lost and now was found; I had been dead and now was alive. . . .

I experienced love in such intensity that nothing I had ever known before was comparable. His love was greater than all human love put together. . . . Jesus *did* indeed love me. (Storm, 2000, pp. 29–31)

During Howard's NDE he also had a life review, as did Alma. Pertinent sections of Howard's experience follow:

When I was in the company of Jesus and the angels, they asked me if I would like to see my life. Unsure of what to expect, I agreed. The record of my life was their record, not my memory of my life. We watched and experienced episodes that were from the point of view of a third party. . . .

They [Jesus and the angels] insisted that I needed to see the truth of my life and learn from it. I begged them to stop it because I was so ashamed for the ways I had failed to live lovingly and because of the grief I had caused God, Jesus and the heavenly beings by my failure. The only reason I could bear to proceed with the life review was because of their love for me. No matter what we watched me do in life, they communicated their love for me, even as they expressed their disapproval for things I did.

One of the things I had done in my life was blaspheme God. . . . I was horrified at how it hurt my heavenly company when we witnessed me blaspheming God and Christ Jesus in my life review. (Storm, 2000, pp. 97, 103)

Another of the many unique messages that Joseph Smith brought to the world was that Hell is not an eternally permanent condition. Its duration is only until the final judgment and resurrection of all humankind. That marvelous message, is discussed in greater depth in the next chapter. It is also recorded in our Doctrine and Covenants in this manner:

> Brethren, shall we not go on in so great a cause? Go forward and not backward. Courage, brethren; and on, on to the victory! Let your hearts rejoice, and be exceedingly glad. Let the earth break forth into singing. Let the dead speak forth anthems of eternal praise to the King Immanuel, who hath ordained, before the world was, that which would enable us to redeem them out of their prison; *for the prisoners shall go free.*
>
> Let the mountains shout for joy, and all ye valleys cry aloud; and all ye seas and dry lands tell the wonders of your Eternal King! And ye rivers, and brooks, and rills, flow down with gladness. Let the woods and all the trees of the field praise the Lord; and ye solid rocks weep for joy! And let the eternal creations declare his name forever and ever! And again I say, how glorious is the voice we heard from heaven, proclaiming in our ears, glory, and salvation, and honor, and immortality, and eternal life; kingdoms, principalities, and powers! (D&C 128:22–23; emphasis added)

Unbaptized Infants and Children Go to Heaven

Another major departure came in Mormonism when they declared that children who died before the age of eight would not go to hell, hades or purgatory, but would be with God and Jesus in heaven, and that it was also possible for other unbaptized souls to reside there as well. The Book of Mormon made it quite clear that un-baptized children, as well as others would, in fact, return to God to stay:

> Listen to the words of Christ, your Redeemer, your Lord and your God. Behold, I came into the world not to call the righteous but sinners to repentance; the whole need no physician, but they that are sick; wherefore, little children are whole, for they are not capable of committing sin; wherefore the curse of Adam is taken from them in me, that it hath no power over them; and the law of circumcision is done away in me. . . . And their little children need no repentance, neither baptism. Behold, baptism is unto repentance to the fulfilling the commandments unto the remission of sins.
>
> But little children are alive in Christ, even from the foundation of the world . . . ; wherefore, all children are alike unto me; wherefore, I love little children with a perfect love; and they are all alike and partakers of salvation. For behold that *all little children are alive in Christ, and also all they that are without*

the law. For the power of redemption cometh on all them that have no law; wherefore, he that is not condemned, or he that is under no condemnation, cannot repent; and unto such baptism availeth nothing. (Moroni 8:11–22; emphasis added)

And in the Doctrine and Covenants, Joseph Smith reported this revelation:

> Thus came the voice of the Lord unto me, saying: All who have died without a knowledge of this gospel, who would have received it if they had been permitted to tarry, shall be heirs of the celestial kingdom of God; Also all that shall die henceforth without a knowledge of it, who would have received it with all their hearts, shall be heirs of that kingdom; For I, the Lord, will judge all men according to their works, according to the desire of their hearts. And I also beheld that all children who die before they arrive at the years of accountability are saved in the celestial kingdom of heaven. (D&C 137:7–10)

There are numerous descriptions of childhood NDEs where the Lord's love for children is clearly evident. The experience of Rocky, noted above, is a good example. These accounts are totally compatible with scriptural descriptions and with NDE memories of Christ's interaction with the innocent who die, seemingly, prematurely. The implication, of course, is that Christ accepts such into His kingdom, without the necessity of baptism.

The Ministering of Angels

Ann's NDE is related in chapter 15. Actually she had two NDEs at different times in her life. The first was as a child and was the result of leukemia. The second was later in life and was caused by spinal meningitis. In the first incident she was escorted to the other world by an angel. It is one of the more compelling stories of an angel in the NDE literature.

It is fascinating to compare Ann's story of her angel with that of the angel Moroni, as recorded by Joseph Smith. Moroni's role in Joseph Smith's account is told in some detail in chapter 1. Brief portions of each story are related here. First, let us review **Joseph Smith's** description of Moroni's appearance:

> While I was thus in the act of calling upon God, I discovered a light appearing in my room, which continued to increase until the room was lighter than at noonday, when immediately a personage appeared at my bedside, standing in the air, for his feet did not touch the floor. He had on a loose robe of

most exquisite whiteness. It was a whiteness beyond anything earthly I had ever seen; nor do I believe that any earthly thing could be made to appear so exceedingly white and brilliant. His hands were naked, and his arms also, a little above the wrist; so, also, were his feet naked, as were his legs, a little above the ankles. His head and neck were also bare. I could discover that he had no other clothing on but this robe, as it was open, so that I could see into his bosom.

Not only was his robe exceedingly white, but his whole person was glorious beyond description, and his countenance truly like lightning. The room was exceedingly light, but not so very bright as immediately around his person. When I first looked upon him, I was afraid; but the fear soon left me.

He called me by name, and said unto me that he was a messenger sent from the presence of God to me, and that his name was Moroni; that God had a work for me to do; and that my name should be had for good and evil among all nations, kindreds, and tongues, or that it should be both good and evil spoken of among all people. (Joseph Smith–History 1:30–33).

Now let us read of **Ann's** interview with the Gibsons:

"I sat up [in bed] and watched the light grow. It grew rapidly in both size and brightness. In fact the light got so bright that it seemed to me that the whole world was lit by it. I could see someone inside the light. There was this beautiful woman, and she was part of the light; in fact she glowed."

"Did the light hurt your eyes?"

"No, even though it was bright by mortal standards."

"Tell me more about the lady in the light."

"Her body was lit from inside in a way . . . it's very hard to explain what she looked like. It seemed as if she were a pure crystal filled with light. Even her robe glowed with light as if by itself. The robe was white, long-sleeved, and full length. She had a golden belt around her waist and her feet were bare. Not that she needed anything on her feet since she stood a couple of feet off the floor."

"Were you frightened by her?"

"No, just the opposite. I had never seen such kindness and gentle love on anyone's face such as I saw in this person. She called me by name and held out her hand to me. She told me to come with her—her voice was soft and gentle but . . . but it was more in my mind. Communication was easier than when you verbalize thoughts. At the time I thought of it as 'mind talk.'

"I asked her who she was and she explained that she was my guardian and had been sent to take me to a place where I could rest in peace. The love emanating from her washed over me so that I didn't hesitate to put my hand in hers."

Summary—Death and God Correlations

The topic of death has long been of major interest to the Latter-day Saints for various reasons. And as a result of this interest and earnest inquiries we believe the Lord has revealed many new insights through his prophets and others, which have been of great value to Latter-day believers.

Given this background, it is only natural that LDS members would be interested in the views provided by near-death studies. Not only do these studies provide new insights into this topic of long-standing inquiry, they also serve as another witness to the veracity of our latter-day prophets and the validity of their extraordinary doctrines.

Assuming the veracity of the various NDEs reviewed, it seems apparent that this is another tributary of ethereal knowledge flowing toward the Omega of a higher human evolutionary state as envisaged by Kenneth Ring—and as discussed in chapter 17.

When considered in the light of the restored Gospel of Jesus Christ, this, and other tributaries from various sources—as God enlightens humans as to their true nature—the attainment of Omega seems assured.

5: Near-Death-Experience Correlations with LDS Teachings on God's Plan

By David R. Larsen, MS

Not only did the new prophet and new scriptures of the Restoration provide fresh insights into God, man's relationship to God, our origins, and life after death, but, like modern NDEs, they also provided much deeper insights into this life and its purposes.

From the writings of Abraham, mentioned in the previous chapter, and other revelations, Joseph Smith learned that in our premortal existence, God our Father called a council and in that council presented a plan for his children's progression. The prophet Alma referred to this as "the great plan of happiness" (Alma 42:8). It is also referred to as "the plan of salvation" (Jarom 1:2; Alma 24:14). To quote the *Encyclopedia of Mormonism* (Ludlow, 1992, pp. 328–29):

> One purpose of the heavenly council was to allow the spirits the opportunity to accept or reject the Father's Plan of Salvation, which proposed that an earth be created whereon his spirit children could dwell, each in a physical body. Such a life would

serve as a probationary state "to see if they [would] do all things whatsoever the Lord their God shall command them." The spirits of all mankind were free to accept or reject the Father's plan, but they were also responsible for their choice. The Creation, the Fall, mortality, the Atonement, the Resurrection, and the Final Judgment were contemplated and explained in the council. The plan anticipated mistakes from inexperience and sin and provided remedies. Many spirits were foreordained to specific roles and missions during their mortal experience, conditional upon their willingness and faithfulness in the premortal sphere and their promised continued faithfulness upon the earth. The Prophet Joseph Smith explained, "Every man who has a calling to minister to the inhabitants of the world was ordained to that very purpose in the Grand Council of heaven before this world was. I suppose I was ordained to this very office in that Grand Council."

Although spoken of as a single council, there may have been multiple meetings where the gospel was taught and appointments were made. Jesus and the prophets were foreordained in the council.

Some Elements of the Plan

Although this understanding was primarily revealed and developed in the 1840's, non-Mormons who are familiar with in-depth NDEs will note many familiar words and concepts. Conversely, when Latter-day Saints hear or read about NDEs, they are often mildly surprised to find non-LDS experiencers using the same terminology. Here are three examples:

1. *A plan with a purpose.* It is not uncommon for those who have communed with divine beings to note that life on earth has a definite purpose, and whatever happens on earth is part of God's "plan" for mankind. (See discussion by Beverly Brodsky in chapter 17.)

2. *Free choice*—often referred to in LDS writings as "free agency," or simply "agency." Freedom of choice is seen by Latter-day Saints as an essential part of God's plan. If men and women were not free to choose, they could not rightly be held accountable to God for their actions, nor could they learn and progress as God intended (2 Nephi 2:27; 10:23). Many in-depth NDErs also note the importance given to "free choice." We saw agency in Don Wood's premortal account in chapter 3, where he discovered that he himself chose his malady in life, and he did so for a specific purpose. Other NDE illustrations of agency follow.

Many who experience NDEs note that they are given a choice whether or not to return to their body. And even when their return seems to have been predetermined, efforts are often made to persuade them to return rather than force them. In section 121 of the Doctrine and Covenants, Joseph Smith talks about this principle of agency and condemns coercion, or "unrighteous dominion" as a method of persuasion. He notes:

> We have learned by sad experience that it is the nature and disposition of almost all men, as soon as they get a little authority, as they suppose, they will immediately begin to exercise unrighteous dominion. Hence many are called, but few are chosen. No power or influence can or ought to be maintained by virtue of the priesthood, only by persuasion, by long-suffering, by gentleness and meekness, and by love unfeigned; By kindness, and pure knowledge, which shall greatly enlarge the soul without hypocrisy, and without guile. (D&C 121:39–42)

Susan, who had an NDE as a result of a heart attack during the birth of her twins, was guided during her experience by her aunt who had died several years before. She told of her experience at a local IANDS meeting in Salt Lake City (Gibson, 1999, pp. 79–80). A portion of her experience follows. The story illustrates the principle of choice, but choice for the right reasons.

Feelings of great peace enveloped her [as she left her body], and she noticed that her body was no longer pregnant. She felt embraced by a loving warmth, and then she saw her deceased aunt. There was a marvelous reunion, and her aunt acted as her guide during her NDE. A second lady of light appeared and said: "Consider well the choice you make."

As she studied the room she was in, she saw the health workers giving her CPR and frantically trying to resuscitate her. She also saw other spirit helpers working to assist the professional medical staff. Her aunt said: "They [the spirit helpers] are there to help facilitate your return—should you choose to return."

At one point in her NDE, Susan asked why she was born where she was—where her father could hurt her when he left her at age six by divorcing her mother. A loving voice said that such choices were made in her premortal life.

Finally, she had to choose whether or not to go back. By then she had decided she didn't want to return to the pain and problems of earth.

She was told that if she didn't go back it would hurt both the health professionals who were laboring to bring her back, and her children. Not returning would also hurt her extended family. She [chose and] returned to great pain.

3. *Preselection of missions roles and experiences.* Many NDErs, like Joseph Smith, learn they do have a specific purpose, or mission to perform in life. And often they are told they must return to earth to fulfill that mission. One remarkable example of this was shared by **Ella Jensen** in 1891 in Brigham City, Utah.

The story was well known in my family, because my mother had lived in Brigham City and was good friends with one of Ella's daughters:

When Ella was twenty she contracted an ailment that caused her to become very weak. Then finally on the morning of March 3 she began to hear beautiful music and then announced that her deceased uncle Hans Jensen "and the messengers" were

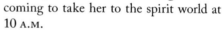

coming to take her to the spirit world at 10 A.M.

At approximately 10 A.M. Ella gave her last good-bye's and her pulse stopped. Her father then hitched up his team of horses and drove a mile and a half into town to tell President Lorenzo Snow (the fifth President of the Church) who was visiting at the time and arrange for her funeral.

President Snow expressed a desire to go with the Stake President to see the girl. It was after twelve o'clock when they arrived. After pausing by her bedside for a minute or two, President Snow decided to give her a blessing in which he said, "Dear Ella, I command you, in the name of the Lord Jesus Christ to come back and live, *your mission is not ended.* You shall yet live to perform a great mission."

He then told her parents to "be patient and wait" that "everything will be alright," and they departed. Ella remained in this condition for more than an hour after the administration, while friends came to express their sympathy and left.

Then all at once she opened her eyes, looked around the room and asked, "Where is he?"

"Who? Where is who?" they asked.

"Why brother Snow" she replied. "He called me back." She then began to relate her marvelous experiences. She noted that she was taken to a large hall, saw her grandpa, who was surprised to see her, and met other friends and relatives—some she had never met on earth, but later was able to accurately describe. She noted "Some seemed to be in family groups." She also saw many people that she did not know.

"Everybody appeared to be perfectly happy. . . . Finally I reached the end of that long room. I opened a door and went into another room filled with children. They were all arranged in perfect order, the smallest ones first, then larger ones, according to age, and size, the largest ones in the back rows all around the room. They seemed to be convened in a sort of Primary or Sunday School presided over by Aunt Eliza R. Snow. . . .

It was while I was standing listening to the children sing 'Gladly Meeting, Kindly Greeting' that I heard President Lorenzo Snow call me. He said: "Sister Ella, you must come back, as your mission is not yet finished here on earth." (Snow, 1929, pp. 884–85, 973–74)

I believe this story aptly illustrates another important LDS teaching found in Doctrine and Covenants 138:8, wherein the Lord states, "Behold, mine house is a house of order, saith the Lord God, and not a house of confusion." Order and organization are hallmarks of The Church of Jesus Christ of Latter-day Saints, and we believe are important aspects of the Lord's work both on earth as well as in heaven. Of course, music and singing are important parts of our religion as well—as exemplified by the world-renowned Mormon Tabernacle Choir.

Life Is a School

LDS leaders teach that one of Heavenly Father's ultimate objectives with this plan was to give us, His children, an opportunity to gain experience, to learn and progress, to ultimately become more like Him, so that we could enjoy the quality of life that He enjoys (2 Peter 1:2–4).

In response to Joseph Smith's prayers from Liberty Jail regarding the persecution of the saints—and the resultant physical and emotional trauma he was experiencing himself—the Lord consoled him with these words:

And if thou shouldst be cast into the pit, or into the hands of murderers, and the sentence of death passed upon thee; if thou be cast into the deep; if the billowing surge conspire against thee; if fierce winds become thine enemy; if the heavens gather blackness, and all the elements combine to hedge up the way;

99

and above all, if the very jaws of hell shall gape open the mouth wide after thee, know thou, my son, that all these things *shall give thee experience, and shall be for thy good.* The Son of Man hath descended below them all. Art thou greater than he? (D&C 122:7–8)

Later on Joseph noted, "Knowledge saves a man; and in the world of spirits no man can be exalted but by knowledge" (Smith, *History of the Church,* Vol. 6, p. 314). Later he recorded, "Whatever principle of intelligence we attain unto in this life, it will rise with us in the resurrection. And if a person gains more knowledge and intelligence in this life through his diligence and obedience than another, he will have so much the advantage in the world to come" (D&C 130:18–19). Moreover, the prophet noted, "The glory of God is intelligence, or, in other words, light and truth" (D&C 93:36). The acquisition of knowledge is seen as the key to our progress, both in this world, and in the world to come.

So, how important is the acquisition of knowledge from the NDE perspective? In Raymond Moody's "Life After Life" there is a section on the life review. He records one representative experiencer as stating:

. . . There wasn't any accusation in any of this then. When he came across times when I had been selfish, his attitude was only that I had been learning from them, too. He seemed very interested in things concerning knowledge, too. He kept on pointing out things that had to do with learning, and he did say that I was going to continue learning, and he said that even when he comes back for me . . . there will always be a quest for knowledge . . . it is a continuous process, so I got the feeling that it goes on after death. (Moody, 1975, pp. 67–68)

Increased Ability to Learn

Not only did the brethren emphasize the importance of gaining knowledge, they also noted it would be easier to acquire after death. In elaborating upon the spirit's unlimited capacity for obtaining knowledge, Orson Pratt stated:

We have spoken of the memory of spirits in the future state; the same principle will apply to many other faculties of the mind of man, as well as memory; knowledge for instance. How limited, how very limited, in its nature is the knowledge of man in this life. . . . In relation to this matter, touching the extension of our knowledge year after year, some people have thought that we should have to learn everything by study. I do not believe it; there are a great many ways of learning things without reasoning or studying them out; without obtaining them through the medium of the five senses. *Man will be endowed, after he leaves this tabernacle, with powers and faculties which he, now, has no knowledge of,* by which he may learn what is round about him. . . . I believe we shall be freed, in the next world, in a great measure, from these narrow, contracted methods of thinking. Instead of thinking in one channel, and following up one certain course of reasoning to find a certain truth, knowledge will rush in from all quarters; it will come in like the light which flows from the sun, penetrating every part, informing the spirit, and giving understanding concerning ten thousand things at the same time; and the mind will be capable of receiving and retaining all. (JD 2:242, 243, 244, 245, 246)

Roger Smith's NDE is discussed in chapter 15. A portion of his experience dealt with the acquisition of knowledge:

While I was in the Savior's presence, I was told and shown many things besides my life's review. Enormous amounts of information flowed into my mind—information that I have since forgotten. When I first arrived in the room, for example, He asked me if I had any questions. I did, and the moment the question was formulated, the answer was in my mind. It was an amazing process.

Pure knowledge seemed to pour into me from Him. The knowledge was transmitted by . . . energy. Energy flowed into me and with it was knowledge. It was as if my entire being was a receptor of knowledge. And it was knowledge that I seemed to have known before. Everything that was communicated to me made sense.

I have emphasized, in this section, the importance of knowledge for three reasons. First, it is a key element of the LDS doctrine of eternal progression. Second, this LDS emphasis and related teachings tying it to salvation and exaltation are somewhat unique within the Christian community. And finally, the importance of gaining knowledge and experience, as well as the spirit's increased capacity for learning and understanding after death, are hallmarks of in-depth NDEs. Anyone who is at all familiar with the literature on in-depth NDEs will recognize that these statements regarding the importance of knowledge, as well as the spirit's increased capacity for understanding, have been validated in numerous NDEs.

Nor will this thirst and capacity for learning end in the spirit world, echoing the testimony of the ND experiencer quoted by Moody. Brigham Young noted, "I shall not cease learning while I live, nor when I arrive in the spirit-world—but shall there learn with greater facility; and when I again receive my body, I shall learn a thousand times more in a thousand times less time; and then I do not mean to cease learning, but shall still continue my researches." (Young, JD, 1954)

Contention and Anger Management

The most important event recorded in The Book of Mormon is that of Jesus' visit to his disciples in the Americas following his crucifixion. On that occasion he taught the people his gospel, which was pretty much the same as we read in the New Testament with a few notable additions. At one point he warned them against arguing or "disputations" over the points of his doctrine, and noted:

> He that hath the spirit of contention is not of me, but is of the devil, who is the father of contention, and he stirreth up the hearts of men to contend with anger, one with another. Behold, this is not my doctrine, to stir up the hearts of men with anger, one against another; but this is my doctrine, that such things should be done away. (3 Nephi 11:30; see also Matt. 5:22)

On one occasion, at a Chaplains' conference in San Diego, I presented a class on anger management to a group of my peers from various denominations. I could tell from their comments that several did not share this perspective—seeing anger as an instrument of Satan and a deterrent to the work and spirit of God. However, there are numerous NDErs who have also sensed the antipathy between anger and the spirit of God. One was Susan, noted above. While the doctors worked on her body, she learned for herself the antipathy between anger and spirit of God.

Susan said she carried all of her earthly emotions with her during her NDE, as when she was angry with her father for not being present. On each occasion, her aunt told her to "search her heart," and reject negative feelings. She was told: "Fear [anger] and doubt will hold you back. In order to progress you must conquer them." At first, she rejected the advice, and she could feel all knowledge being withdrawn, as if she were in a lead box that blocked all knowledge. Then, as her aunt continued to help her, and she felt of the love, she was able to eliminate the anger and fear, and the knowledge she obtained returned in a rush.

It's interesting to note that we have been directed by God in scripture ninety-seven times to "fear not."

Love and Forgiveness

Almost every person that I have heard or read about who has had an in-depth NDE, and communicated with the being of light, has felt incomparable love. And if they are given any message to convey, it almost always includes the admonition to be more loving, less judgmental and more forgiving—not only of others' imperfections, but also of their own. Moverover, they note this love for others should be an active love wherein they reach out to help those in need.

David Herard, whose story is told in chapter 7, was trained as a Marine to kill the enemy. During the Vietnam conflict, he was called upon to do just that. When he sustained massive injuries in combat operations, he underwent an NDE in which he felt the enormous love of God. As Dave described it, it was all the love there was.

Today, Dave is a changed individual. He devotes much of his life to helping others. In a recent interview with Arvin Gibson he responded to Gibson in this manner:

> **"Do you now have any feeling for why you had to return to this life?"**
> David thought for a long moment, and then said: "About the only factual answer I can give you is, since my experience, I have done more for others than I ever did before. It seems that life goes well when I am helping somebody.
> "For instance, I am on a Volunteer Fire Department for our community. We are the first ones at fires and traffic accidents. We have no standing police force. I'm not sure how much I help them, but it sure helps me when I give them assistance."
> **"Do you tell injured people about your NDE?"**
> "There was only one very seriously injured young woman where it seemed proper. I was the first one at the accident. She was horribly injured and barely conscious. It was a matter of my telling her that everything would be okay—the pain would go away. I also said that if she wished to live, to tell God, and she would live. On the other hand, if God was telling her no, then it would be all right to go. She died shortly thereafter. She was eighteen years old." . . . If I can continue to help someone, then I am happy being here."
> **"Are there any last messages that you would like to leave for anyone who reads this?"**
> "Let me think a moment. . . . No matter how difficult life

is, no matter how poor or how rich you are, if you help someone else with the expectation of reward, you are not going to make it in the eternal scheme of things. If you expect to be rewarded, then don't put yourself out. On the other hand, there is a reward, but it is later down the line of eternity. And it's because of your own selfless giving."

While these concepts are pretty basic to Christianity and most other religions of the world, they are given special emphasis in the LDS faith. Consider for example the following scriptures from the Book of Mormon and Doctrine and Covenants:

"Wherefore, ye must press forward with a steadfastness in Christ, having a perfect brightness of hope, and a love of God and of all men." (2 Nephi 31:20)

"For the natural man is an enemy to God, and has been from the fall of Adam, and will be, forever and ever, unless he yields to the enticings of the Holy Spirit, and putteth off the natural man and becometh a saint through the atonement of Christ the Lord, and becometh as a child, submissive, meek, humble, patient, *full of love,* willing to submit to all things which the Lord seeth fit to inflict upon him, even as a child doth submit to his father." (Mosiah 3:19)

"Be not partial towards them in love above many others, but let thy love be for them as for thyself; and let thy love abound unto all men, and unto all who love my name." (D&C 112:11)

"Wherefore, I say unto you, that ye ought to forgive one another; for he that forgiveth not his brother his trespasses standeth condemned before the Lord; for there remaineth in him the greater sin. I, the Lord, will forgive whom I will forgive, but of you it is required to forgive all men." (D&C 64:9–10)

In his last sermon Harold B. Lee, the eleventh President of the Church, noted that many of the problems of his day were due to a lack of individual self-respect, and he counseled church members to be more forgiving of their self, as well as others, and to remember their divine origins and even to pray, "O God help me to hold a high opinion of myself" (Lee, 1974).

The LDS View of Man's Ultimate Potential

As we can see, the Latter-day Saints place great value on the importance of personal and character development, but to what end? What is

God's ultimate objective for man, according to LDS theology? Joseph Smith revealed the answer in a funeral sermon for an early convert by the name of King Follett. In that sermon he stated: "You have got to learn how to become gods yourselves." Concerning those who shall come forth in the resurrection of the just, the Doctrine and Covenants notes (D&C 76:54–60):

> They are they who are the church of the Firstborn. *They are they into whose hands the Father has given all things—*
> They are they who . . . have received of his fulness, and of his glory; . . .
> *Wherefore, as it is written, they are gods, even the sons of God—*
> Wherefore, all things are theirs, whether life or death, or things present, or things to come, *all are theirs and they are Christ's, and Christ is God's.* And they shall overcome all things.

Lorenzo Snow, the fifth President of the Church put it this way: "As man now is, God once was; As God now is, man may be" (Snow, 1901, p. 4).

Early Christian Belief

While this doctrine was considered blasphemous by most Christian ministers in Joseph Smith's day, and still is today in various Western Christian circles, it is not without parallel in the early Christian church. This ultimate objective was alluded to by Jesus (Matt. 5:48; John 17:3, 20–21) and advocated by Peter (2 Pet 1:4). And in the second century it was referred to as the doctrine of deification. Saint Irenaeus, the most important Christian theologian of the second century, taught: "If the word became a man, It was so men may become gods" (Robinson, 1991, p. 60).

This teaching, or a variation thereof, was well established and often alluded to in the Christian church up until at least the fourth century A.D. It is still an important part of the teachings of the Eastern Orthodox religion. *The Westminster Dictionary of Christian Theology*, notes, "Deification (Greek *theosis*) is for Orthodoxy the goal of every Christian." And it is the ultimate goal of the Latter-day Saints and their eternal education process and progression. But is there any evidence for this divine potential among those who have experienced the eternities and God?

NDE Hints of Man's Ultimate Potential

In the previous chapter I mentioned the experience of Beverly

Brodsky, a former agnostic born into a Jewish family. You will recall Beverly noted that at one point she felt as though she were "one with God." And she came back with the understanding that this was our ultimate potential—to become as God.

But Beverly is not the first or only person to have had such an experience. Indeed, there are several accounts of individuals who, during in-depth NDEs, have felt that they were part of something greater than themselves. Stephanie LaRue, for example, in chapter 10 described how she felt that she was "encompassed with a higher power."

Another remarkable experience was that of **Mellen-Thomas Benedict** which was described by Kenneth Ring in his book *Lessons From the Light*. In his NDE, Mellen is transported back in time through the "big bang" (see chapter 11). A brief portion of Ken's interview of Mellen follows (Ring, 1998, pp. 288–89):

> And I understood at that moment that I passed the big bang. That was the first light ever and I went *through* the big bang. . . . Suddenly I was in this void and I was aware of Everything that had ever been created. It was like I was looking out of God's eyes. *I had become God* [italics mine].
> **You had gotten back to the source of all?**
> Yes. Suddenly I wasn't me anymore. The only thing I can say, I was looking out of God's eyes. And suddenly I knew why every atom was, and I could see *everything.*
> . . . The interesting point was that I went into the Void, I came back with this understanding that God is not there. God is here [laughs pointing to himself]. That's what it is all about. So this constant search of the human race to go out and find God. . . . God gave *everything* to us, *everything* is here—this is where it's at. And what we are into now is God's exploration of God through us. People are so busy trying to become God that they ought to realize that we are already God and God is becoming us. That's what it is all about.

Multiple Heavens: A Hierarchy of Places

The Apostle Paul noted, "Eye hath not seen, nor ear heard, neither have entered into the heart of man, the things which God hath prepared for them that love him. But God hath revealed *them* unto us by his Spirit (1 Corinthians 2:9–10). And, in 1832, he revealed them once again to Joseph Smith and his associate, Sidney Rigdon, who were shown a vision in which they saw three distinct kingdoms in heaven. The highest, where God the Father and Christ dwell, was compared to the glory of the sun. It was called the Celestial Kingdom. The next glorious world, presided over by Jesus, was called the Terrestrial Kingdom, and the least glorious was called the Telestial Kingdom (D&C 76:70–85; see also 1 Cor. 15:35, 38, 40–41; 2 Cor. 12:2).

Again, to the churches of the American frontier this concept of multiple heavens was an oddity. Traditional Christianity envisioned primarily two options after death—heaven and hell. Mormon teachings about the spirit prison, paradise, and other heavens, or degrees of glory were typically seen as unbiblical and heretical, although it appears to us that the Bible does leave room for those possibilities (see also Luke 23:43; John 14:2–3).

In chapter 15 various NDEs are discussed in which the individuals saw or sensed a hierarchy of order in God's kingdoms. When asked about this apparent hierarchy in heaven, Howard Storm answered: "Yes, but everyone knows exactly where they stand, because one of the things about God's light is that only truth exists there. Nothing false can exist. So when an angel begins to feel uncomfortable in that light, there is only one place to go—the darkness."

Mormon theology, as noted, would identify three kingdoms of glory, in descending order, the Celestial, the Terrestrial and the Telestial. The darkest area, where Satan and his followers dwell, is not a kingdom but is a realm of "outer darkness" where those who fall into a category called "the Sons of Perdition" reside, and where they are cut off from God and his Son forever.

Salvation for the Dead

The previous sections suggest a very lofty potential for man, but there is one problem: the scriptures are clear that "no unclean person can enter into the kingdom of heaven" (1 Nephi 10:21). But all men are to some degree unclean, "for all have sinned and fall short" (Eccl 7:20, Rom 3:23, D&C 109:34). So no man or woman in mortality can, by their own efforts alone, merit these eternal blessings (2 Nephi 31:19).

Therefore, included in the plan of God was the means whereby all men could receive forgiveness for sin, through the love and atonement of Jesus Christ. We believe that in the premortal council Christ, the firstborn of God, offered himself as a ransom for mankind. He offered to be a human sacrifice, to pay the price of sin, for all who would repent and covenant through baptism to follow him, that by his stripes and through the shedding of his blood we might be forgiven and cleansed of our sins and thus return to live with Him and our Father in Heaven.

To Nicodemus, the Lord said, "Except a man be born of water and the Spirit he cannot enter into the kingdom of heaven" (John 3:5). Moreover, Latter-day Saints believe that when Jesus visited his disciples on this continent, he again taught the necessity of baptism (2 Nephi 31:14–21). This concept, with some variations, is broadly accepted by most major Christian churches. The big problem, however, that has not been well addressed by traditional Christians has been "what about those who have died without baptism?" In the previous chapter, we talked of those who had died as children; but what about all the other good people of the earth who died without having had an opportunity to hear about Jesus Christ or without having ever had an opportunity for baptism? Are they just lost? Not necessarily; according to LDS doctrine, their living family members (or others) can assist them in obtaining these essential ordinances.

In the LDS theology, it's all about families. We believe we lived as the family of God before coming to earth. While on earth, the family is the primary institution established by God to assist us in learning the lessons of life and passing the tests of mortality. When our time here on earth is over, Latter-day Saints believe it's possible for couples and families to live together for eternity. However, this requires couples to have been married or "sealed" together, by one having authority from Jesus Christ. These sacred ceremonies are performed in The House of The Lord—LDS temples.

But what of those family members who have not been "sealed" together for eternity? We believe that through the love and foresight of our Father in Heaven, a way has been provided whereby these ancestors will have an opportunity to learn the gospel and receive these saving and exalting ordinances. In 1 Peter 3:18–19 we read that Christ, "having been put to death in the flesh, but made alive in the spirit; . . . went and preached unto the spirits in prison." In 1918 **Joseph F. Smith,** then president of the Church, received a revelation in which he saw the righteous in Paradise being organized by Christ to continue the preaching/teaching of the gospel to those in the spirit prison:

> But behold, from among the righteous, he organized his forces and appointed messengers, clothed with power and

authority, and commissioned them to go forth and carry the light of the gospel to them that were in darkness, even to all the spirits of men; and thus was the gospel preached to the dead.

And the chosen messengers went forth to declare the acceptable day of the Lord and proclaim liberty to the captives who were bound, even unto all who would repent of their sins and receive the gospel. (D&C 138:30–31)

Therefore, we know that individuals who did not have an opportunity to learn about Jesus Christ and his gospel while in mortality will receive that opportunity in the spirit world. But before they can be released from this spirit prison, before they can be reunited and "sealed" to their family members for eternity, someone on earth must first perform the requisite acts or "ordinances" i.e. baptism and marriage, in their behalf. This is called vicarious work for the dead, or "temple work," and this is where family history or "genealogy" work becomes important. Latter-day Saints have a massive effort underway to identify, document and link the families of the earth, and more specifically, their ancestors. Then, in our holy temples faithful members of the church can be baptized and "sealed" by proxy, for and in behalf of their deceased ancestors, thereby linking their family generations together for eternity.

In addition to numerous LDS scriptures on baptism for the dead (D&C 124:29–55; 127:5–9; 128:1–25), even Paul, in attempting to convince the Corinthians of the validity of the resurrection said: "Else what shall they do which are baptized for the dead, if the dead rise not at all? why are they then baptized for the dead?" He took it for granted that his audience was already familiar with the ordinance of baptism for the dead (1 Cor 15:29).

Doctrines and Evidences

In the last few pages I have identified various doctrines and teachings related to this "work for the dead." I believe there is good evidence from various sources that these ancestors, who have accepted Jesus and his gospel, long to be liberated and sealed together as a family for eternity, and they look to their descendants here on earth to make that happen. I would now like to list these various teachings and then share a few spiritual evidences that these doctrines and practices are in fact true and desired by those who are dead but "alive in the spirit." In summary, Latter-day Saints believe:

• The gospel of Jesus Christ is being preached in the spirit

world to those who did not have an opportunity to hear it while in mortality.
- Once these spirits accept this message, they have a desire for someone on earth to be baptized in their behalf.
- Once these proxy baptisms take place and have been accepted by those in spirit prison, they are liberated from that darker domain and are then able to enter the realm of Paradise.
- Those in the spirit realm desire to have their temple work done so they can be linked and sealed to their family members, both living and dead.
- When these vicarious "sealings" take place in LDS temples, there is rejoicing in the spirit world.

I will now consider these issues in the context of NDE examples:
1. The gospel of Jesus Christ is being preached in the spirit world.

One of my favorite OBEs related to this principle is the story of **James and Frank LeSueur.** In 1898, Frank was called on a mission to England. After twenty-six months of proselyting and doing family history research on the side, James received a telegram that his brother Frank had been killed chasing outlaws.

As he met with his companions to pray for comfort or consolation he heard a voice say, "Your brother is called for a similar purpose as President Woodruff's son." He then recalled that when President Wilfred Woodruff's son was drowned, President Woodruff (third President of the Church) went into the temple and prayed to know why. He said that an angel came and stood before him and asked, "Which of all your sons would you prefer to have in charge of the missionary work of preaching the gospel to our kindred in the spirit world? President Woodruff spoke the name of his son who had drowned, and the angel disappeared. From this James understood that his brother Frank had been called to do missionary work among his kindred who had passed on.

After his return to Arizona, James went with his father to the sheep camps where his brother had been in charge at the time of his death. That night after his father had retired, he went a short distance, knelt in prayer, and asked that he might see Frank and get an idea of the work he was doing. The following is James' account of what happened next:

> Returning to the camp bed, I retired and my spirit left my body. I saw my body on the bed beside my father; I saw a person-

age standing a few feet from my spirit dressed in white and knew him to be my guardian angel. He said, "Come, go with me." We passed into space above a short distance, then out over the forest, the plains, over hills, dales, water, cities, and in an incredibly short space of time, came into a large city, which I knew to be a city where the spirits of those who had passed away were destined, awaiting preparation for the resurrection morn. . . .

We passed through the streets with people passing, and then came before us a four-story building which covered an entire block. "We will go in here," said the angel. A door opened, and a young lady beckoned us to enter. I looked at her wondering who she was, for I did not recall having seen her before. The personage accompanying me said, "This young lady is a relative of yours who, while living in mortality, was killed. She is now assisting in missionary work among your relatives who have died without a knowledge of the gospel, and these who are assembled here are relatives of yours waiting to hear the gospel preached."

I looked over the audience. I estimated there were about ten thousand present, as I compared the congregation with the assembled host at conference time in the Salt Lake Tabernacle. There was a look of expectancy upon their faces, as though they were awaiting something to begin, just like I have seen at our great conferences. Presently, speaking began and I looked toward the speaker and listened to a sermon on the first principles of the gospel, just as I had heard the missionaries give, except that when the speaker spoke on the necessity of baptism, he said that the covenant of baptism was an earthly covenant—one that should be attended to while in mortality—but that inasmuch as they had died without that opportunity, mankind in mortality could take their name and act for them; that there were temples erected upon the earth where kinsmen and friends were being baptized vicariously, the living for the dead; and that if they accepted the baptism and confirmation that was done for them, it would be as valid as though attended to by them in person while in mortality.

When the speaker had finished, he looked up at me and I saw that he was my brother, Frank. . . . By my brother's side was standing a young lady, also dressed in white, and she bowed in recognition of my visit. I looked at her very carefully and wondered who she was, when the angel said, "The young lady standing by and assisting your brother is to be his wife." Again I gazed and thought that if I ever saw her I would know her.

Then the angel said, "We will pass into other rooms." In the next room there were many thousands arranged in classes with teachers instructing them. I felt at the time as though they were preparing them with sufficient knowledge to later receive instruction like the first group who seemed so interested and eager to receive the information which was given them. Here, faithful relatives of mine who had died were the instructors, and these others, too, were relatives who had died without a knowledge of the gospel.

We then passed into a third hall where there was confusion and disorder, quarreling and loud talking, and some seemed to require force in order to control them. These, too, were relatives of a still darker age, the age known as the Dark Ages, when there was so much sin and wickedness and ignorance among the inhabitants of the earth. These people required a still more difficult training and long schooling before they could even come to the state of the second group who were willing to be taught.

After this James was returned to his father's side as he had come. He then provided an interesting verification of one of the things he had seen. He notes:

A few weeks after this manifestation, a sister Kempe came from an adjoining town and told my parents that her daughter had died a short time before, and on her deathbed told her that Frank LeSueur had come to visit her in his spirit form and asked her if she would become his wife. She had agreed to do so. Then he told her to tell her mother that she was going to die, and that after her death, her mother was to go and ask my parents for consent to have her daughter Jennie sealed to Frank. . . . When I heard of it I asked for a photo of the young lady. As soon as I saw it, I recognized the likeness of the young lady assisting my brother in the spirit world and was told she was to be his wife. The sealing was attended to, and their happy souls are now working together in the most joyous work of soul saving.

My life has been changed by these experiences, and it is my utmost desire to do all I can for the redemption of my dead and to help others at the same time. (Jensen, 1973)

James LeSueur later became a Stake President and the chairman of the building committee of the Arizona Temple.

2. Once these spirits accept this message, they have a desire for someone on earth to be baptized in their behalf.

3. Once these proxy baptisms take place and are accepted by those in spirit prison, they are liberated from that darker domain and are then able to enter the realm of Paradise.

An example of these two principles is given in the experience of

Lerona A. Wilson after her deceased parents visited her in a hospital room in the fall of 1915 (Crowther, 1967, pp. 216–17; original citation, Wilson, 1916):

> Father asked me if I would go to the temple and take up the ordinance work for our kindred dead.
>
> I said: "How can I leave my work (in my school of dress-making), and my family?"
>
> My mother spoke this time: "I had to leave my family just when I was needed the most. You can remain with your family. You will only need to spend a part of your time in the temple."
>
> Then my sister said: "I had to leave my family, too, when I was so much needed, and Lydia had to leave her little ones."
>
> These remarks made my excuse seem very weak. Father wanted me to promise him that I would do this work, and I gave him my promise that I would.
>
> "Now remember," he said, "it will require much faith. Do you think you can have faith enough?"
>
> "Father I will do all in my power," I replied, for while under that exalting influence, it seemed an easy matter to have faith. . . .
>
> Father then quoted from the scriptures giving chapter and verse, and taught me the law of baptism in greater force and beauty than I had ever heard it, and explained that this ordinance cannot be administered in the spirit world. The dead who have died without baptism must have the ordinance performed for them by the living.
>
> He alluded to our kindred, saying they were a fine people, and they had received the gospel. They were most anxious to be advancing. They need to move on with other spirits who are in like condition and give place to large numbers who are now crowding into that world.

4. Those in the spirit realm desire to have their temple work done to be linked and sealed to their family members, both living and dead.

5. Once these vicarious "sealings" take place in LDS temples, there is rejoicing in the spirit world.

A portion of **Renee Zamora's** experience is given in chapter 16. That portion which pertains to both item 3 and 4 follow:

> I knew that I would find further answers by attending the temple. . . . It became clear to me . . . that the people I had seen [during my NDE] were those who had passed on, but were confined to this earth, and who needed further work done for

them in order to progress beyond where they were. . . . Much of what I saw had symbolic meaning beyond the outward appearances of the events themselves.

Since that experience, I have become a fanatic concerning genealogy and temple work. The patience of my husband is sometimes tried as I work on genealogy. . . . The genealogical and temple work that we do is enormously important. . . . Since my experience I have been driven to locate all the people I saw that needed their temple work done. Each person is important in the sight of the Lord.

Lucinda Hecker, in chapter 6, had this to say in her interview with the Gibsons:

Arvin asked: "A while ago you said that your grandmother visited you in a dream and told you that you needed to do the genealogy research and temple work on some of your ancestors. Did that work ever get done?"

"Not for several years. I did much of the genealogical research and gave the paper work to my mother. She said that  she would do the temple work, but she kept putting it off. She said she was too busy.

"Finally, when I got my temple recommend, my parents came up and we went to the Oakland Temple and did the work for my direct family, including my grandmother. Our family was sealed, and it was marvelous. When we knelt down and they said my grandmother's name—my mother was proxy for her—we felt her spirit.

"Later, my nephew died, and he kept appearing to me in a dream. He let me know that his temple work was not complete. We did his work, and also the work for other deceased ancestors. Frequently, when I went to the temple, I could see their spirits as we did their work.

"My nephew kept appearing to me and letting me know that something was not complete on his temple work. It took some years before we found the problem and completed the work. Then he finally stopped bugging me."

Summary

From the above-noted references to teachings of The Church of Jesus Christ of Latter-day Saints and the related near-death and out-of-body experiences provided, there does seem to be a strong correlation with at least these teachings and the experiences and insights gleaned from NDEs. There could be many conjectures as to why this is. Certainly, the experiences of those NDErs who were LDS were likely influenced by their beliefs. Nevertheless, their commonalities with other non-LDS experiencers, as well as other corroborative sources suggests that their experiences and insights were real and valid. And what of those who were not members of our church who gained insights that seem to confirm LDS teachings? What is to account for these similarities?

Though there could be many answers to this, the obvious one for Latter-day Saints is that all of these teachings and NDE insights ultimately come from the same source—a kind, loving Father in Heaven and his son Jesus Christ. Moreover, this correlation suggests that they care deeply about each and every one of us, and in fact have a fantastic plan for each of us to return to them with honor to achieve our highest eternal potential.

And finally, the experiences of the many who have had NDEs, both LDS and non-LDS, appear to confirm the validity of our ninth article of faith, written by Joseph Smith, which states in part, "We believe that He [God] will yet reveal many great and important things pertaining to the Kingdom of God."

Part II

Research on NDEs

Finally, as to the motivations involved, I can only speak for those of us who spearheaded this organization [IANDS]. . . . All of us were, as a whole, generally concerned with promoting disinterested research into NDEs, furthering the professional development of the field of near-death studies, . . . and having an organization that would be helpful to people who had had NDEs as well as informative for those who were interested in the subject. We also hoped—and eventually succeeded—to stimulate interest in NDEs in other countries.

—Kenneth Ring

(Chapter 17)

6: Representative Near-Death Experiences

What Is a Representative NDE?

In a sense, there is no such thing as a "representative NDE." Although Kenneth Ring, in his book *Life at Death*, developed a method of scoring various events which frequently showed up in persons who had NDEs, it was obvious, even in Ring's early study, that there was no *fixed* pattern of events which could always be found in an NDE.

In chapter 9, which gives an overview of NDE research, Nancy Evans Bush is quoted as saying that an NDE can be triggered in different ways. In addition to a variety of triggering mechanisms, the combination of events identified by Ring and other researchers (including myself) which make up the NDE are as varied as the number of people involved.

Experiences Designed to Benefit the Involved Individual

Early in my own research, I concluded that NDEs were, to a large extent, eclectic. That is, the events which combined to constitute the NDE, as well as the triggering mechanisms, were tailored to benefit the individual involved. In the book *Fingerprints of God*, I put it this way:

> Why these differences? No one knows. Some speculate, however. My own speculation, and that of Howard Storm and Kenneth Ring, is that the Lord provides us with a glimpse of the spirit world which is suited to our needs. The Lord knows us better than we know ourselves, and if in his wisdom he decides that we should see a deceased grandparent as a young and vibrant individual, that is what we see. (Gibson, 1999, p. 101)

That is also true in frightening NDEs—designated as "Less Than Positive" (LTP) experiences by Barbara Rommer in her book *Blessing in Disguise*. In an extensive study of LTPs, she said this about what kind of NDE an individual receives:

> The cosmic forces know everything about us and know what we "need" to see, hear, or feel to break through our self-protective wall and cause us to reassess past decisions, words, thoughts, and actions. I firmly believe that we, ourselves, determine not only the type of experience we have, but also its content long before it ever occurs. A person having a brief "light" experience may only need to feel the warm fuzzies. The need of the LTP experiencer is usually more complex. William Serdahely, in an article in the *Journal of Near-Death Studies* in 1995, titled "The Individually Tailored Hypothesis stated: " . . . each NDEr receives what he or she needs during the NDE in a way that the NDEr is able to accept." (Romer, 2000, p. 30)

This, and the next two chapters, illustrate the eclectic nature of several NDEs. Lucinda, in this chapter, has never had her NDE published. Her story is representative of the diverse events and triggering mechanisms which sometimes happen to those having gone through an NDE. Bill Essex's experience is a short but life-altering type of NDE. I became aware of Bill's story when he recently contacted me.

In the two chapters which follow this one, several individuals whom I interviewed several years ago are interviewed once more. Again, the purpose here is to show the diverse nature of NDEs and also to exhibit the follow-on effects of such experiences.

At the end of this and the third chapter, I provide a brief analysis of the experiences. There, I point out certain patterns and/or unusual aspects.

Lucinda Hecker's Drowning NDE and Later Experiences: In-depth Interviews

Carol and I first met Lucinda at our home in Bountiful, Utah on March 22, 1994. She was a lovely woman with striking red hair. By way of background, Lucinda explained that her parents had divorced when she was quite young. Lucinda was a fourth-of-July baby, born in Winnemucca, Nevada in 1943. Because her mother could not afford to raise her, Lucinda and her brother went to live with their father, then in the Army and stationed at Hill Air Force Base in Utah.

While at the Air Force Base, their father met and married a wonderful lady who showed much love to Lucinda and her brother—plus a later arrival in the family, a half-sister. After the marriage of her father and step-mother, the family moved to Santa Fe Springs, California, where Lucinda grew up. She was a normal, healthy youngster, and although she was a member of the LDS Church, she knew very little of its teachings. When I asked her if she was active in the church her response was: "No, I was just a crazy teenager who never paid attention to anything."

Our interview commenced as I asked her to describe the events which precipitated the NDE. Lucinda began:

"On this particular day I was in Bountiful visiting some relatives. We were kids and no one wanted to take us swimming. It was only a few miles down the road and we decided we could handle that easily. We walked there until we came upon a sign near the pool which said, 'Swim at your own risk. No lifeguard on duty.'

"I was a darned good swimmer and thought I would have no problem with that. I did have butterflies in my stomach, for some reason, and I couldn't understand why.

" We entered the pool at the deep end and decided we were going to race across it. Everyone said, 'Lucinda, you are a good swimmer and will beat us. We aren't going to race you.'

"So I said I would do the butterfly stroke and they could swim normally. They agreed to that.

"My sister was with us but my brother wasn't. We started to swim the race, and I was right in the middle of the pool when I got cramps. I had them in both of my thighs and both of my calves.

"Remembering that when you get cramps you rub them to try and get them to relax, I did just that. It was exhausting and I would get so tired, but I kept rubbing my legs.

"Finally I reached the point where I was bobbing. My cousins and my sister were not good swimmers, and they were hanging on the side of the pool. We tried to reach each other, but it was too far. Stretching as hard as I could, I would reach out, and then I would go back to rubbing my legs.

"In a few minutes some boys swam near us. My cousins and sister called out, 'She is drowning, she is drowning.' They didn't respond.

"The guys must have thought, 'Ah, she is just a girl probably trying to make a scene so we can save her.' They thought I was making a pass at them, but I wasn't.

"As I kept going up and down in the water, I was completely exhausted. It became impossible to get air. When I reached the surface, briefly, I would try and gasp some air, then I would sink.

At the point of complete exhaustion, I inhaled water. There was no air to inhale.

"Sinking in the pool, I said to myself, 'I'm going to die.' I knew I was going to die. And at that point I just gave up. I went into, . . . it was sort of a floating slow-motion circle, like I was going to sleep."

"Then I felt a parting, I guess it was my spirit parting from my body, my eyes were still closed. When I opened my eyes I could see my body down in the water. I looked and I thought, 'That is me down there. What am I doing down there when I am up here? Oh, well!'

"Darkness surrounded me. In the distance I could see a light. Heading toward the light, I was like a homing pigeon. In a way, I knew where I was going, and yet I didn't know where I was going. My spirit was just taking me. As I got closer to the light it became brighter and brighter, and when I got near the light it was so wonderful.

"There was a beautiful sound, and I can't tell you what it was. It wasn't like singing, it wasn't like music, it was just so pleasant to my ears. It brings tears to my eyes to think of how fantastic it sounded. My body didn't hurt and I was so light weight.

"My thoughts were, 'I've got to be alive because I can hear and I can see.' Looking at my hands, I could see them.

"Heading toward what seemed to be a cloud, it was really bright. To this day, if I look at the sun it will not be quite as bright as it was up there. It was so bright it was unreal.

"Nearing what seemed like a fog, but it was not a fog, there was a familiarity which seemed to say, 'I'm on my way.'

"A voice came into my head, . . . or into my ears. Anyway, I heard it. It said, 'You have to go back.'"

Interrupting Lucinda's narrative, I asked, "Did you know the voice?"

"No, It was a man's voice. He said, 'You have to go back.' And I said in my mind, I never spoke it with my mouth, 'I don't want to go back.'

"He said, 'You have to go back.'

"I said, 'Please, please, don't make me go back!'

"Again he said, 'You have to go back.'

"In my mind I thought if I can just rush over to that spot, get a few more feet over there, I won't have to go back again. And just like that (snaps her fingers), I was back in my body. Just that fast.

"They were pulling me out of the pool and I was choking, coughing. They said, 'Are you all right?' My body was limp by the time they pulled me up. They kept asking if I was all right.

"I kept saying, 'Oh, my legs, my legs, my legs. They hurt, they hurt, they hurt.'

"I have never forgotten that experience. I didn't speak of it until I was about 40 years old, because I had never heard anything like that."

"Okay, Lucinda. You mentioned that there were other strange effects that seemed related to your NDE. Tell me about them."

"They started when I was about seventeen, in high school."

"When you were a child, were you raised in any particular religion," I asked.

"We were members of the LDS Church, but I wasn't active, and I didn't really know anything about its teachings. I was just a crazy teenager who never paid any attention to religion.

"We were living in Southern California, and I began to have dreams that seemed to come true. At first I told my mother. Her response was, 'Lucinda, you were always such a dreamer—I have never known anyone that dreams as much as you do.' So I stopped telling her most of my dreams."

"Were there other phenomena besides dreams that happened to you?"

"Yes, I could touch or handle personal items from other people, such as their keys, and I would become aware of incidents from their past. When I told them what I knew, they were mystified. They wanted to know how I did it. To me, it became sort of a game—until it became troublesome and drove me to the brink of a nervous breakdown.

"About this time, I married a man I thought I was in love with. It was a mistake, and the marriage fell apart. My life was fairly chaotic for a period of some years, and I began to get interested in my church."

"One night, when it was very peaceful and I was asleep, my grandmother came to me in a dream. She had taken care of me during my parents' divorce, and we were very close. She died when I was about seven or eight years old.

"Anyway, she appeared in my dream and said, 'Lucinda, we are waiting. All of us are waiting.'

"I asked her, 'Waiting for what?'

"She waved her hand outward toward a large group of people. Some of the faces I recognized and some of them I didn't. It wasn't necessary for her to verbally tell me what she meant, I just knew that she was speaking of the genealogical ties and associated temple work. She let me know that I was the only one that would do the work. Then she left.

"The next morning when I awakened, I thought, 'Oh Brother, I know what I have to do.' And I wasn't too keen on it.

"Based on this dream, I went to a few sessions at church to learn how to do genealogy. So I prepared all the paperwork and sent it through. Because of problems with my divorce I was not able to do the temple work for my deceased relatives, so I asked my father and mother to do it. They said they would. For some reason they kept procrastinating and the work didn't get done—except for my grandmother, a portion of whose work was performed by a friend.

"The Bishop called me into his office one night and he said, 'Lucinda, I have been plagued with dreams and visions that it is time for you to get your temple recommend.' I was so relieved and so happy. Well, I went through the classes that prepare you for the temple. The last class was so spiritual that I didn't want to leave. I was the last person to leave.

"I almost hated coming home because it was like another world. I was really on a spiritual high. Going to bed that night, I was feeling very, very, good . . . warm and comfortable. There was satisfaction in my soul, you know, deep, down inside."

"When I went to sleep, that night, I dreamt I was walking on a platform. In front of me, off the platform, it was like the sun rising. I could see the rays rising, and as I looked at the rays, my head started to hurt. I held my head and I groaned, 'Oh, my head, my head, my head.' A voice within me said, 'It will pass.' I fell to my knees and grabbed my head with both my hands and said, 'The pain!' The voice, again, said, 'It will pass.'

"As I was down on my knees, with my head in my hands, I felt a hand on my shoulder. And this person called my name. He said, 'Lucinda.' And I was in a brilliant light, and I was white and dressed in white. This person was an extremely brilliant white color, and he glowed.

"Looking into his face as I raised my head, there was such love it was sucking me in. I had never felt such love. It was as if my soul was being drawn into him. His hair was white, it came down to the back of his neck, and he was in a glowing white gown. His eyes were blue or a green color and his face was wonderful to look into. Later, I tried to write some words to describe him, but they were woefully inadequate.

"The love which emanated from him engulfed me, surrounded me, and filled my very being. It was a mesmerizing love that satiated me with joy. The happiness within me was overwhelming, and I felt at total peace. I was content, it was inspiring.

"In the midst of this immeasurable joy, he spoke to me in my mind. His words were, 'If they repent, great shall be their glory, and all that I have shall be theirs.' He led me to a small hill where there were two dirt paths. He asked if we should take the path on the left. Somehow I knew that the one on the left would lead to a destination like Sodom and Gomorrah, and I said: 'No, I don't want you to be embarrassed.' Instantly I was aware that I was wrong, and I corrected myself by saying, 'No, *I* don't want to be embarrassed.'

He repeated what he had previously told me : 'These are my children and I know what they do. If they repent, great shall be their glory, and all that I have shall be theirs.' We then took the right path down the hill.

"The next morning I woke up, enchanted by what I had seen and heard. The joy and peace were still with me, although diminished in intensity."

"How real was this experience, Lucinda?"

"You couldn't get any more real. I felt the pain in my head. I felt the joy and the love. I felt the hand on my shoulder. I heard my name. I walked with him."

"When you were on this path, you were outdoors, obviously, were there other shrubs and flowers and trees around?"

"There was grass and it was green, there was a tree and it was green."

"And how did things look?"

"Normal. Everything was clear and everything was real."

"Are you sure it was a dream?"

"I wonder about that myself sometimes. But because of the pain that I felt . . . the pain—it was so great, I wondered if . . . I don't know for sure, but I do know that it truly happened to me."

"Okay, Lucinda, are there other experiences that happened to you?"

"Well, yes, sort of."

"What were they?"

"It was auras. I saw them around people. I thought everyone saw them. But after my dream, or whatever it was, I asked someone if they could see them. When they said, no, I was surprised."

"Do you see the auras all of the time, or part of the time?"

"All of the time."

"Describe mine."

"I have been watching yours all night. It moves when you move. Earlier this evening it was white, then it became golden yellow. Now it has blue around the yellow and pink around the entire aura."

"A while ago you said that your grandmother visited you in a dream and told you that you needed to do the genealogy research and temple work on some of your ancestors. Did that work ever get done?"

125

"Not for several years. I did much of the genealogical research and gave the paper work to my mother. She said that she would do the temple work, but she kept putting it off. She said she was too busy.

"Finally, when I got my temple recommend, my parents came up and we went to the Oakland Temple and did the work for my direct family, including my grandmother. Our family was sealed, and it was marvelous. When we knelt down and they said my grandmother's name—my mother was proxy for her—we felt her spirit.

"Later, my nephew died, and he kept appearing to me in a dream. He let me know that his temple work was not complete. We did his work, and also the work for other deceased ancestors. Frequently, when I went to the temple, I could see their spirits as we did their work.

"My nephew kept appearing to me and letting me know that something was not complete on his temple work. It took some years before we found the problem and completed the work. Then he finally stopped bugging me."

"Is there anything else, Lucinda?"

"Yes, but it would fill a book. Those are the important experiences that I have had."

In April, 2004, I asked her some questions about her present situation. In addition I asked her to answer some retrospective questions. Our brief interview follows:

"Okay, Lucinda, what is your life like now?"

"Life is great. As a widow I keep busy in a variety of activities?"

"Such as?"

"Some screen play-writing, and helping others."

"How do you help others?"

"One way is by sharing some of my life's experiences, including my NDE, with them."

"Are there other ways?"

"After my NDE and the dream-like experiences, I apparently was granted some special gifts."

"What sort of gifts?"

"The gift of healing, for example. Often I can heal people who have been seriously ill. And then there is love. . . ."

"What do you mean by *love?*"

"The love that I felt during my vision of the magnificent glowing-being was insurmountable, incredible, fantastic—it was . . . there are no earthly words to describe it. And I try to pass a portion of that love on to others I meet."

"Do those experiences still feel real to you, after all the elapsed years?"

"Yes, even more so. They are as fresh in my mind as though they happened yesterday."

"So, what is your feeling about these experiences, were they a good or bad thing?"

"They were, and are, both a hardship and a blessing. In effect, I have one foot in this world and the other foot in a more spiritual world. It is hard to live this way, but it is bearable because I know what awaits me on the other side."

"Are there any messages you would like to leave for the readers of this book?"

"Yes, the one true knowledge I came away with was that we should love each other like God loves us. We are not to judge others, and we should forgive those who trespass against us."

Bill Essex's Boot-Camp NDE:
His Account and Follow-up Interview

Bill Essex first contacted me about his NDE in November 2003. He had read some of my books and felt that he wanted to get in touch with me. He forwarded a book he had written titled *The Truth, the Whole Truth, and Anything But the Truth*. It is a delightful compendium of stories from his life mingled with homespun philosophy and poetry.

Bill served in the Navy Amphibian Forces in World War II and had many wartime experiences. He was born in Harrison, Arkansas and graduated from Jasper High School in 1943. Bill is still wedded to the sweetheart he married in 1945, Ruby Parrish from Mesa, Arizona. They have three living children, ten grandchildren and nine great-grandchildren.

His early navy experience was as a signalman and quartermaster in navigation. In civilian life he was involved in a career of heavy construction machinery. During the last three years of his working life he served as a crane operator at the San Onofre Nuclear Power Plant at San Clemente, California.

As a youth and young adult, Bill was actively involved in the Methodist Church. In 1952 he joined The Church of Jesus Christ of Latter-day Saints in Pasadena, California. After joining the LDS Church, he was called to serve in many responsible positions. Having survived a bout with cancer, Bill is today living with his cherished wife in his birth-town, Harrison, Arkansas. He is a Stake Patriarch in the LDS Church.

The near-death experience of Bill happened in 1943, after he joined the Navy. It is reproduced below, largely as it is recorded by Bill in his book (Essex, 2000, pp. 53–59). Some new information has been added to the original story by Bill in recent communications:

> After joining the navy in Harrison, I traveled to Little Rock where a group of us waited for a week to fill a company with recruits. Upon boarding a train headed for Kansas City, Missouri, I became ill and ran a high fever. When the train reached Hutchinson, Kansas, they took me by ambulance to the Naval Air Station where I spent ten boring days in sick bay. Recovering sufficiently to travel, I finally boarded a slow passenger train to California. It was drafty and cold, but I finally reached San Diego where boot camp training began.
>
> On my first night in boot camp, I was assigned to "clothes line watch." I marched around a clothes line in back of our barracks from midnight to four a.m. in a light but consistent rain. The soaking from the rain wasn't exactly what I needed in my already weakened and almost sick body.
>
> The following morning we began to learn to march and do other military drills. We were each given a copy of the "Blue Jacket's Manual" with instructions to start reading certain sections. I never did figure out when we were supposed to have time to study a book. That night I began having severe pain in my shoulder and chest, I had trouble breathing and felt that I was running a temperature. I hardly slept at all because of the pain.
>
> We had been warned that if we made sick call to shirk duty we would be court-martialed. That got my attention, so I got out of bed and went right into the training routine just as if I felt well. Somehow, I made it through the day. The next night was even worse than the night before. I almost decided to turn in to sick bay that morning and take my chances, but I didn't.
>
> My day was short. About mid-morning I collapsed while drilling and was taken to sick bay. At least now I could say that I didn't turn in voluntarily. I don't recall seeing a doctor, although I may have. The Navy Medical Corpsman gave me what they called "all-purpose capsules" and diagnosed my illness as "cat fever." They also gave me a vile-tasting liquid. They thought that I might have had a reaction to the several shots I have received on the first day.
>
> So far, so good! No mention of a court-martial yet.

The next several hours, or possibly a couple of days, were quite hazy. Part of the time I was almost unaware of my surroundings or the passage of time. On the second or third night, I'm not certain which, I was delirious and kept asking for water. The corpsman on duty would bring me small paper cups of water, perhaps one or two ounces. I became impatient and yelled at him to bring me a larger container of water, not just a few drops. Instead of bringing me water he took my temperature, was alarmed and went immediately for a doctor. The doctor accompanied me into the ambulance, I was taken to the Naval Hospital in Balboa Park. Shortly thereafter my unusual experience began.

I don't know where I was taken initially, probably to an emergency unit of the main hospital complex. As the ambulance raced to the hospital, code three, strange things began to happen to me. When the vehicle negotiated sharp turns my lungs seemed to be pressed by centrifugal force to the rib cage, depending on whether the turn was right or left. The pain was unbearable, and as it reached the limit of my endurance I would suddenly experience total relief from pain and find myself somewhere in the air above the ambulance and looking down on it. Somehow it didn't seem surprising or unusual. I didn't see myself at this point, but I knew that I was inside the ambulance. This was momentary and I would immediately find myself back inside the vehicle and in intense pain. This experience repeated two or three times. I never knew when we arrived at the hospital.

My next mental awareness came as I saw my body in a basket (litter), from a position near the ceiling and in the corner of the room. Three doctors were observing and checking me. No extraordinary measures were taken to resuscitate me. They were certain that I was dead or almost so. It seemed so natural. There was no fear or personal concern. There was no physical pain.

The doctors said that there were no vital signs, at other times they were not sure. At last they decided that I would not survive until morning, if in fact, there was still a spark of life in me. A Red Cross lady was sent for to receive a dictated message to be sent immediately to my parents. The note was to inform them that I would be dead before morning and that further details would be forthcoming.

At this point I felt sadness for my parents. This was actually the only emotion I had experienced so far. Receiving a telegram in my rural home of Marble Falls, Arkansas, was complicated, to say the least. My parents had no telephone, not even electricity. The mail was delivered three times a week; in fact, my father carried the mail. The scenario that would follow went through my mind. Tomorrow morning I would be gone. The Postmaster and proprietor of the small general store would receive the telegram by phone. He would drive his old Dodge pickup the two miles to the home of my parents and deliver the message. I could see their sorrow, and their regret that they had signed for me to join the Navy—underage as I was. My body would arrive later by train and I would be buried in the local cemetery, the first member of my immediate family to reach this plateau. I still had no regrets, nor personal concern, except for them.

One of the doctors sent for a nurse and had her give me a large shot of morphine, in the event that I regained consciousness and was in pain. As soon as the morphine was injected my mental awareness ended abruptly. I was later told that this whole episode occurred on Sunday night and into Monday morning.

There was nothing but total blackness until Wednesday afternoon. I suddenly regained consciousness in an oxygen tent in the serious ward. The first person I saw was the Red Cross lady—the one who sent the telegram to my parents—when she looked in on me. Shortly thereafter I began wondering where I was, what time and what day it was. I wasn't hurting too badly when I came around, I just had difficulty in breathing and soreness in my chest.

She opened the transparent curtain slightly when she saw that I was conscious and said, "Well, hi there and welcome back. We thought we had lost you." I answered, "Yes, I know, you are the lady who sent the telegram to my parents." She looked rather surprised and replied. "Yes, I was, but how could you possibly know that? You were out cold." I proceeded to tell her what the telegram said, word for word. She looked completely shocked by now. I went on to tell her that there were doctors in the room, and a nurse came in and gave me a morphine shot, after which everything went black. She tried to trick me and asked me about all the other people in the room. I told her that the five of them were the only persons involved and she admitted that that was true.

She left to report that I was conscious and came back shortly with a doctor and a nurse. The Red Cross lady asked me if I had ever seen either of them before. I had not and I told her so. They were not in the room the night I came in. She showed great interest in my story and asked many questions. Over the next three or four days, she brought in, separately, the three doctors and the nurse who had given me the shot. Not only did I identify them, but told each of them exactly what they had said on that Sunday night. They all showed bewilderment but agreed that what I said about their conversation was correct.

The last voice I had heard was that of the nurse. When she was about to inject me, she said, "Poor little boy." I let her know that I resented being called a little boy even in my comatose condition. She admitted that she had made that comment and added sympathetically, "You looked so young and so dead." The thing that now seemed strange to me was that I recognized the doctors' faces, even though I had seen only their backs and the tops of their heads.

There was one point of the episode I didn't understand, and I asked the Red Cross lady about it. While I didn't remember arriving at the hospital, I told her that I was brought in a green Packard ambulance. She countered, "No, you're wrong about that for sure, the Navy doesn't have green Packard ambulances, they use blue Chevrolets." I told her, "I'm sure you are correct about that, but I know that I came in a green Packard." It took her three or four days to check that out, and she didn't say much more or ask many questions about my experience during that time. She came in one day and said, "You were right about the ambulance. The Navy didn't have any ambulances available close enough to get you here and they obtained a civilian ambulance, which was near the Training Center. You came in a green Packard."

That was concrete evidence enough for her. She was convinced that I had, indeed, had an extraordinary experience. She continued to visit me every day she was on duty. She wrote letters to my mother and girl friends for me, and she no longer questioned me in detail as she had previously.

At this point in my account, I would like to regress and explain my feelings and the effect this incident had upon me. I had never heard of out-of-body (OBE) or near-death experiences (NDE) at this time. I wrote to my mother while I was still in the hospital and told her about the incident, and she didn't respond at all. When I saw her again after the war I tried to tell her about it again, but her reaction was the same. No comment whatever! My first serious girl friend ridiculed my story so much that I didn't tell anyone else for several years. My wife, Ruby, was the first person, other than those involved, to give my account any credibility at all, and that was sometime after we were married.

Sometime about the mid-seventies, I ran across a book by Elizabeth Kubler Ross, a psychologist who counseled terminally ill patients. She listed many accounts of experiences far more extensive than mine. Later, Raymond Moody expanded on the works of Ross with several books on the same subject, all of which I have purchased and read. From that time on I shared my experience with carefully selected persons. (I still dreaded ridicule or disbelief). As I did so I began to find several others with similar stories. Most of their experiences, like in the books I had read, were more extensive than mine were.

How did this whole episode affect me? First of all, I am a skeptic. I'm quite sure that I would have doubted the veracity of such an account, if it would have been told to me by someone else. I'm from a fairly religious background. My own religious activities were passive at the time of this occurrence and remained so for some time afterward. This event convinced me of life beyond that of the mortal body, and while I did not become more religiously active, I found that I had little or no fear of death. This quality was of great importance when faced by extreme danger in later war-time combat situations.

I have no memory in my life, which is clearer, or more definite, or more certain. I still recall the exact words spoken and the faces of the people involved even now, more than fifty years later.

My experience was limited to the events and conversations which I have shared. I didn't see or go through a tunnel. I didn't travel toward a light. I didn't see any beings, other than those living persons mentioned. I heard no music. I leave it to you, my reader, to decide for yourself the truthfulness of the account which I have related.

I spent three months in the hospital. After about three weeks, I was released from the serious ward and was in a large facility, which had double-deck bunk beds very close together. I underwent some painful procedures during recovery. After about two months I started to feel better and began to wonder why I never got paid. Upon inquiring, the hospital staff found that—in typical military fashion—I was listed as AWOL at the training center. All of my records and issued equipment were lost.

The navy issued Bill new equipment and sent him to Oceanside, California to receive amphibious training at Camp Del Mar, a part of Camp Pendleton. After his training, he was assigned to APA 220 USS Okanogan, an attack transport. He made several combat landings on Pacific Islands, including Okinawa. He received an Honorable Discharge in 1946, and to quote Bill, "I never once regretted my decision to join or to stay in [when given the opportunity because of his medical condition], and to become a proud navy veteran, with campaign ribbons and battle stars of the big war, World War Two."

To bring Bill's story up-to-date, in the spring of 2004, I contacted him and asked for a brief commentary on how his experience has continued to affect him. Our colloquy follows:

"Bill, has the memory of your experience faded with time?"

"It has been sixty years since my near-death experience, but there are no clearer memories in my mind than that singular event. The image of it is still vivid."

"Has your NDE continued to have an impact on your life? If so, how?"

"The current effect on my life is much the same as it was in the weeks and months immediately following it. In particular, there is no fear of death. Over the past six years I have been close to death on several occasions as I battled a heart attack followed by cancer.

"The cancer was well advanced when it was discovered. Although the finding of cancer was not good news, it did not upset me terribly. My reaction was a calm one as I told the doctor to proceed with the necessary operation.

"Not long after I had surgery and 35 radiation treatments, the doctor found a spot in my mouth which appeared to be malignant. If it proved to be a malignancy the doctor was not optimistic about my options. She felt that, at most, I could prolong my life somewhat with aggressive chemotherapy. With that diagnosis facing me, I told the doctor to not consider chemotherapy as an option. To me, there seemed no point in prolonging life just to gain a few months while suffering the painful effects of chemotherapy. Again, I felt peace in making this decision.

"Shortly thereafter, the doctor called and joyfully informed me that the spot in my mouth was non-malignant. Naturally I was pleased, but not really surprised. The only real difference that finding will make in my life is that it will give me an opportunity to continue to work on numerous projects which I find fulfilling. In short, I shall continue to live life to the fullest until it is my time to be called home."

"Are there any messages you would like to leave for those who might read your story?"

"Yes, they should embrace all of the roller-coaster aspects of life—despite physical or other limitations they might have—until the end comes."

Analysis of Lucinda's and Bill's Experiences and Accounts

This is an experience that, initially brief and to the point, extends over many decades. One pattern that emerges—following the NDE during Lucinda's youth—is the follow-on effects. Many of those who have NDEs explain how their NDE led to a series of diverse epiphanies and spiritual abilities. Numerous folks, for example, explain how they can see auras. Ken Ring describes these effects thus (Ring, 1998, p. 128):

> ... it has been known for some time that having an NDE seems to accelerate the development of a whole range of psychic sensitivities. It has been found, for example, that following an NDE, there is a marked increase in reports of the incidence of such paranormal phenomena as telepathy, clairvoyance, and precognition. In addition, NDErs claim to have more instances of spontaneous OBEs [Out-of-Body Experiences] and unusual perceptions, such as seeing energy fields (or "auras") around the bodies of others.
> ... Despite the lack of careful, systematic work on the subject, there seems to be little doubt there is a strong connection between having had an NDE and the development of healing gifts afterward.

From Lucinda's description it is apparent that she was blessed—or cursed—with a full basket of paranormal effects following her NDE. This was, at times, a burden. As she expressed it: "They were, and are, both a hardship and a blessing. In effect, I have one foot in this world and the other foot in a more spiritual world. It is hard to live this way, but it is bearable because I know what awaits me on the other side."

One aspect of Lucinda's experience is singular to LDS teachings, and that is her repeated dream sequences dealing with temple work. More is written about this subject in later chapters, but suffice it to say that the concept of vicarious baptism, marriage-sealings and other familial binding ties for deceased relatives and ancestors is unique to Mormonism.

Other examples of NDEs in which sealing family ordinances "for time and eternity" are described—or implied—are discussed later. As part of that discussion, the issue of cause and effect will be explored. That is, are the peculiarities of this type of Mormon doctrine a part of the NDE because the individual is a member of that faith and the events are culturally induced, or are they provided to the individual as a matter of instructive necessity from celestial sources? Clearly, Lucinda felt that the latter was the case.

Many NDEs fall into a category similar to that of Bill; namely, short and to the point. There are several aspects of his experience, however, which make it a valuable study. First is the fact that Bill was completely unaware of NDEs at the time that he had his. As far as he knew, he was the only one who had ever had this kind of experience. This understanding was reinforced by the skeptical reaction of his mother and his girlfriend. For many years, therefore, he kept the experience to himself. As a result of his reluctance to share the experience with others, the description he finally wrote has a freshness and authenticity not always present in NDEs which have been repeatedly shared with others.

Bill's interaction with medical personnel, and their astonishment at his remarkable ability to describe what was happening to him in detail, provides an even greater feeling of authenticity. The Red Cross lady, with her repeated questioning about his observations while he was out-of-body, further emphasizes this point.

Although we do not have written statements of the Red Cross lady or other medical personnel to be able to consider this NDE as "corroborated," we do have a strident explanation by Bill about what he saw and felt during the experience. Moreover, he records those events frequently reported in the NDE literature which did *not* happen to him. His plea for the reader to decide for themselves the truthfulness of his experience is, in itself, a powerful witness.

Bill's story also gives us a picture of joyful persistence in the face of innumerable obstacles during his life. His service in World War II, as with many veterans, placed him at an early age in several desperate situations—including the illness leading to his NDE—and so, too, has his later life had its share of challenges. Most of us must ultimately be subjected to debilitating illnesses near the end of our lives. Bill's example of how to accommodate to those illnesses while still retaining the joy of life is an exemplary model for all of us.

7: Follow-up Interviews

Why Follow-ups?

In the preceding chapter, the varied nature of NDEs was explained. This chapter continues to illustrate that point. In addition, it examines the continuing life experiences of several other persons who have had NDEs, and who were initially interviewed by me more than ten years ago. Although the numbers re-interviewed are small, and therefore not useable for statistical or sociological studies, they do provide some insight about the NDE. This will be clear from reading the experiences—and the later analysis—of the selected cases.

David Herard's Vietnam Battlefield NDE and Follow-up Interview

David and I first got acquainted through his wife, Peggy. She called me in response to an advertisement I had placed in a local newspaper and told me that her husband had gone through the type of experience that my advertisement described. David was, at the time, working in Bangor, Maine, and Peggy arranged for me to call him on the phone—which I did, in March, 1991. We had a nice chat, enough to assure me that David's story about his NDE in Vietnam was worth recording. Later, when David came to Utah, I was able to record his full experience (Gibson, 1992, pp. 91–99).

David had two tours of duty in Vietnam. He was injured in the first tour when three hand grenades were remotely exploded between a group of Marines. Two of them were killed; David survived, but with substantial injuries which required treatment at a military hospital on Okinawa. After that he was sent to the States for a one-year tour of duty—which he shortened by requesting a second assignment to Vietnam. In order to return to Vietnam, he had to waive his rights for a one-year tour in the States. He arrived back in Vietnam in February, 1968, just in time for the Tet offensive. Dave was a replacement for an existing unit—at the time the units were suffering anywhere from fifty to sixty percent casualties.

A portion of my interview with Dave follows. At the time of the interview, David had only told his story to Peggy.

"In the last week of June, 1968, I was up in the hills, Hill 881-North, near Khe Sanh. While we were on the hill we were running daily search-and-destroy missions in the bush. I was holding three jobs at the time: a wireman, a radio operator, and a grunt. We were suffering a lot of casualties so we had to do extra duty.

"We went up on the hill as a fully manned infantry company, over 250 men with 81 mortars, and within thirty days we had lost between 20 and 30 percent. The last half of June we got word that we were going to evacuate the hill, just turn it over to the North Vietnam Army (NVA)—we were just going to pull out and leave it to them.

"We were told that because of the lack of helicopters 82nd Airborne was going to evacuate us off the hill. This was supposed to happen in the last day of June and the first day of July. To prepare for the evacuation we tore down all our bunkers and all our trench lines. Airborne never showed up."

"Good night, you were sort of exposed weren't you?"

"That's right. When the NVA saw us blowing up our bunkers they started dropping mortars and rockets on us daily. With our bacon hanging out like that our Commanding Officer, a Captain, was really angry and he called in helicopters. Some Chinooks came and took us off Hill 881-North and put us on Hill 681, five miles away.

"The night we landed on Hill 681, on July 6th, we ran into heavy fire-fighting. It lasted from midnight to about five a.m. We had NVA coming into the wire—it was face-to-face fighting. I usually carried fifteen magazines that hold twenty rounds apiece, six grenades, and full bandoleers for extra ammo. In the morning, after the fire-fight, I had one magazine left, with, maybe eight rounds, no grenades—everybody was in that same situation. We were all running around looking for ammo.

"Around seven o'clock, after everybody had relaxed for a while, we decided it was time to stock up on food, more ammo, and other necessities. Everybody was tired, they didn't want to do anything, so I got angry and said: 'The hell with you, I'll do it.' I started humping ammo for the people that were near me and ammo for the 81mm mortars."

"How far did you have to go to get the ammo?"

"Approximately one hundred yards. About nine o'clock I was on my ninth or tenth trip, and we started getting some 122mm rockets, 82mm mortars and small arms fire. I was tired, I was angry, and I was put out by the whole situation. When everything started coming in I said to myself: the hell with it, all they can do is kill me.

"On my last trip—I was told this later by one of the Corpsmen who attended me—when I came over the crest of the hill a 122mm rocket landed about twenty feet behind me. When it went off it picked me up and threw me twenty feet down the hill. I landed on both my knees with my head on the ground. My right arm was behind me. I was dazed, I wasn't unconscious, just dazed.

"When I looked down where my right arm was I didn't see anything. I swore, and thought: They got me, they really got me this time. I felt for my arm and pulled it out from behind me. It was all torn up. I didn't pay much attention to the rest of my body. I was looking for a Corpsman and I got up. One of the guys I knew told me to look at my legs. I did, and saw that they were in shreds and were bleeding profusely.

"I collapsed and lay there on the ground. They came over and took my flak jacket off, what was left of it, and attempted to stop the bleeding. While the Corpsman was working over me, I just . . . I had a feeling of: I'm tired, I'm going to sleep, I've had enough of this. I almost lost the will to live. I closed my eyes—the pain had just started catching up with me."

"Hadn't they given you any shots for the pain, yet?"

"While I had my eyes closed, one of the men asked the Corpsman why he didn't give me a shot of morphine. He said that he couldn't, it would just leak back out. I had shrapnel wounds in both feet, both legs, both cheeks, both arms, both hands, the back of my neck and the small of my back.

"After hearing the Corpsmen talk about me, I felt that my time was up.

"I first became aware that everything was black. Then I saw a light coming towards me, and I remember wondering why there was no pain. It felt so good. The light, at first, was like a candle. But it kept getting closer and brighter until it was a blinding light."

"Could you look straight at it?"

"No, I couldn't. I tried everything not to look at the light."

"Why was that?"

"I don't know. I wasn't afraid of it. It was extremely bright. The light finally caught up to me, and I opened my eyes, not literally, but I looked at it. And I saw a river.

"Across this river there were a lot of people waving at me. They were gesturing me to come across. They were people that I hadn't seen before, and they seemed really happy. I was getting a feeling of warmth, of happiness, of great tranquility.

"As I began to walk toward the river and the people on the other side, I felt a hand on my shoulder. I tried to turn around to see who was putting a hand on me and I . . . I couldn't move. A voice that I heard said: 'No, it's not your time, go back.' Then I was back. I opened my eyes, and this Corpsman was pounding my chest. He was screaming at me: 'Don't you dare die on me.' An hour later I was choppered off the hill."

"When you saw the river, what was the terrain like on both sides of the river?"

"On my side it was fairly white, like a brand-new coat of white paint. Closer to the river there were shades of green. The water was a shimmering blue, and I could tell it was moving. On the other side of the river it was white, but it had color also."

"Did you see shrubs and things of that sort?"

"I saw trees, bushes, flowers—vividly colored flowers."

"Were the bushes, shrubs and flowers similar to what you had seen on earth, or were they different?"

"Similar in that their growth patterns were similar, but their sizes were more robust, their colors were more vivid, and everything was very warm."

"Did you have a feeling that you knew any of the people on the other side?"

"I've often asked myself that. At the time I thought: I know those guys. But I couldn't see their faces. All I could see was their bodies. I knew they were gesturing to me but I just couldn't see their faces. I could see their hands fine, and I could see their physical makeup all right, but not their faces."

"But you had a feeling that you knew them?"

"Right. It seemed like there were people there that I knew. Maybe my team leader who was killed earlier, and maybe some of my other Vietnam buddies. But I couldn't swear to it. I knew a lot of men in Vietnam who had died, but I had no relatives who had died."

"Could you tell how they were dressed?"

"Everybody was in white. Some had robes, and some had shirts and trousers, but they were all white."

"Did it appear that there was light coming from them, or could you tell?"

"It was light behind them, but I couldn't see way beyond them. I knew that they were overjoyed to see me."

"Did you see a bridge?"

"No, I didn't. As I walked towards the river, and the people, someone stopped me. I couldn't move, my eyes were locked straight ahead looking at these people. And the voice simply said: 'Don't be afraid about not going over there. It's not your time yet.' It was a gentle voice."

"Did you have the feeling that you could walk over the water if you had wanted?"

"I never had the feeling that I was walking. It was more like . . . I was just moving. And when the hand came on my shoulder I had such an overwhelming sense of love and tranquility; everything that we, here, are looking for and have such a hard time finding, I had completely, in abundance, and I didn't want to come back to the earth."

"Why didn't you want to come back?"

"Because it felt so good there."

"Did you have any feeling of what it was you were supposed to come back for?"

"No I didn't. After I was told that it was not my time, I would have to go back, I had things to do, that was the end."

"Was it quick when you came back into your body?"

"The blink of an eye."

"When I came back I had pain in abundance, and it was instantaneous. There was no pain on the other side. I knew . . . everything worked good while I was over there. My body worked good, my hands worked good, my legs worked good. I had the feeling that I knew why things are as they are—why all the problems on the earth were as they were. It was an overwhelming feeling of knowing, but I couldn't tell you now what I knew."

"Did that feeling come over you when you felt the hand, or was it before that?"

"It was when I was going towards the people and felt really good."

"When the hand touched your shoulder, you didn't get a chance to turn around and see who it was, did you?"

"No. All I can tell you is that, as I see it, it was God's hand."

"That's what you felt?"

"Right."

"And it was just a single contact where the hand touched your shoulder?"

"Actually, after it touched my shoulder, I felt an embrace— as if I were being embraced from the back by someone. And I could see a bright light from the side."

"How did that feel?"

"When I was embraced, I felt a warmth all through me. And there was the feeling of . . . of love. As if it were all the love there is."

"Do you mean you felt that all the love in the world was there?"

"No, it was like that was all the love there was, everywhere. It was like . . . I can't explain the feeling. It's beyond words."

In April, 2004, I contacted David and Peggy in South China, Maine, where they were then living. Our telephone conversation follows:

"It has been thirteen years since our initial interview. Have they been good years for you, David?"

"As a matter of fact, yes. They have been good years."

"How about your health, how has that been?"

"Physically, I am fine. I find out, though, that I have some blockage in my carotid arteries, and I have arthritis in both knees, both hands and both elbows. Other than that, things are good."

"Are some of these physical problems due to the wounds you received in Vietnam?"

"Yes, they are due to parts of my body attempting to compensate for an arm and a leg not working right."

"Why did you move back to Maine?"

"This is home. Most of my family are older than I, and they aren't feeling well, so I figured I needed to be around them."

"How old are you now?"

"I'm fifty-nine."

"What do you do to occupy your time? Peggy mentioned that you are involved in various projects. What are they?"

"A year-and-a-half ago, my house burned down. Since then, I have been rebuilding it. As part of the project, I will build a gardening shed and a huge flower garden. Also, I will be clearing a lot of the land that I have."

"Do you ever think back on Vietnam and your near-death experience?"

"Vietnam crops up a couple of times a year, at what the government calls anniversary dates. The two serious wounds I received remind me of those times, and I tend to get ugly. I don't even recognize what I'm doing to others until someone like my wife, Peggy, reminds me."

"Is the NDE you had still as clear in your mind as it was when I first interviewed you?"

"Yes it is, especially when things aren't going well. When everything seems to be going down the toilet, the NDE is there in the back of my mind. As I reflect on it, I am able to slow down, think through my problems, and figure out solutions.

"My oldest daughter—for example, her husband is in Iraq. She is often worried about him and what might happen to him.

Without getting her too wrapped up in the mechanics of war, I try and give her reassurance while at the same time letting her know that where he is unforseen things can happen."

"Are you able to help your daughter?"

"When she wants to listen! You know, she's afraid that he's going to get hurt really bad, so I try to gently let her know that such experiences are the nature of the beast—the beast of war, that is."

"Well, Dave, you are certainly in a position to know. During our interview years ago you mentioned that you were Catholic, but you were not particularly religious in a formal sense. Is that still true?"

"Yes that is still true. In fact, people think I am funny. When they talk about God, I tell them, 'Yes, I speak to him regularly—I call his 800 number.' And I'm not kidding. When things do not go well for me, I call his 800 number. Then I can come up with solutions for my problems."

"Have you had any unusual or spiritual experiences since our last interview?"

"It's sort of like premonitions. My son-in-law—for instance, he is in the National Guard. On one occasion when we were together, I looked at him and it was as if I could see him in a uniform far away from home. Then, three months later his unit got called, and he wound up in Iraq. This kind of premonition, or foresight, or whatever it is, doesn't happen all the time, but it happens often enough to make me wonder what is going on."

"How does Peggy react to these kinds of events?"

"Oh, I don't tell anybody," and David laughed.

"Why not?" I asked.

"Well . . . it's that I don't want to get them excited. If it happens, so be it, and if it doesn't, I haven't needlessly worried them. Generally, I prefer to stay in the background."

"Do you now have any feeling for why you had to return to this life?"

David thought for a long moment, and then said:

"About the only factual answer I can give you is, since my experience, I have done more for others than I ever did before. It seems that life goes well when I am helping somebody. For instance, I am on a Volunteer Fire Department for our community. We are the first ones at fires and traffic accidents. We have no standing police force. I'm not sure how much I help them, but it sure helps me when I give them assistance."

"Do you tell injured people about your NDE?"

"There was only one very seriously injured young woman where it seemed proper. I was the first one at the accident. She was horribly injured and barely conscious. It was a matter of my telling her that everything would be okay—the pain would go away. I also said that if she wished to live, to tell God, and she would live. On the other hand, if God was telling her no, then it would be all right to go. She died shortly thereafter. She was eighteen years old."

"**What's your feeling now about death for yourself?**"

"I'm scared to death about it."

"**That's what you told me thirteen years ago, Dave. That's the strangest answer for someone who has gone through what you have. Why are you afraid?**"

"I've spent some time thinking about it. If death came quickly, that would be fine. But to leave those I love behind . . . it isn't that I don't know what's waiting for me, I do. It's life itself, though, I would fight tooth and tongue to continue with life."

"**It seems to me, Dave, that you are saying two things. One is that life is still sweet for you, and the second is that you don't fear death so much as you do getting there. Is that correct?**"

"Yes," Dave responded as he laughed. Then he said, "I'm not big on giving up. I know what's waiting for me, I'm just not in a big hurry to get there. So long as I can breathe and move, I want to be around. If I can continue to help someone, then I am happy being here."

"**Are there any last messages that you would like to leave for anyone who reads this?**"

"Let me think a moment. . . . No matter how difficult life is, no matter how poor or how rich you are, if you help someone else with the expectation of reward, you are not going to make it in the eternal scheme of things. If you expect to be rewarded, then don't put yourself out. On the other hand, there is a reward, but it is later down the line of eternity. And it's because of your own selfless giving."

John Hernandez:
A Firefighters' Group NDE and Follow-up Interviews

John called me after having read one of my books. Then, in 1996, he came to our home to be interviewed. Later, he told his story at one of our local IANDS meetings. A portion of his experience, as recounted at our meeting and later recorded in *Fingerprints of God*, is reproduced below (Gibson, 1996, pp. 128–31). In a follow up interview in 2004, John said that on the day of his first NDE (as described below), he began the day with a feeling of unease. He said it was difficult to explain, but that he was uncomfortable leaving his family on that day. He had a premonition that something untoward was about to happen, but he felt duty-bound to respond to his work commitments.

It was during a wilderness fire in 1989 that a helicopter dropped John, as a member of two 20-person Hotshot crews, onto a fire at the top of a steep mountain. The fire was burning below the crews in thick Ponderosa Pine and Oak brush. The wind was blowing the fire downhill away from the crews. The decision was made to try and construct a fire-line downhill towards the existing fire with one crew, and have the second crew follow, starting a back-fire into the main blaze.

The slope of the hill the men and women were working on was about 40 degrees. They worked their way down the steep slope, when, part way down, to their horror, the wind changed to an upward direction. The trees in front of the men and women traveling down the hill erupted into flames with explosive force.

The panic-stricken crews started to try and go back up the fire-line-trail they had built. Trees exploded and fire engulfed the immediate area, and oxygen feeding the conflagration was sucked from near the ground where the people struggled to breathe. One by one, the men and women fell to the earth, suffocating from lack of oxygen. They were reduced to crawling on their hands and knees while they attempted to get back up the hill to a safer area.

Suddenly John had the thought: "This is it. I am going to die." And with that thought in mind he found himself looking down on his body which was lying in a trench. The noise, heat and confusion from the inferno surrounding them was gone and John felt completely at peace. As he looked around, John saw other fire-fighters standing above their bodies in the air. One of John's crew members had a defective foot which he had been born with. As he came out of his body John looked at him and said: "Look, José, your foot is straight."

A bright light then appeared. John described the bright light in this manner: "The light—the fantastic light! It was brighter than the brightest light I had ever seen on earth. It was brighter than the sun shining on a field of snow. Yet I could look at it, and it didn't hurt my eyes."

Standing in the light was John's deceased great-grandfather. His great-grandfather acted as John's guide throughout his NDE. John met with others of his ancestors and had an extensive experience.

Finding himself, again, in his body, John looked around and noticed that some of the metal tools they had used to fight the fire had melted. Despite this intense heat, and the fire still raging around him, he was able to walk up the hill in some sort of protected bubble. He did not hear nor feel the turbulence around him. Upon reaching the relative safety of the hilltop the noise of the fire was again evident, and he saw other members of the crew also gathering there.

The entire happening was so profound that upon escaping from what they had supposed would be sure death, the group of saved people knelt in prayer to thank the Lord for their deliverance. All of the crew escaped, and the only visual evidence on them of what they had been through was a few singed hairs.

John said that in comparing accounts of their different episodes the men and women were astonished that they had each undergone some type of near-death experience. And this happened to a diverse ethnic and religious group of Hispanics, Caucasians and American Indians. Throughout the summer as the crew worked together they continued to discuss the miraculous adventure which they had lived through. Others of the crew confirmed, for example, that they also felt the ill effects of returning to their physical bodies. They too had met with other members of their deceased families and were given the choice of remaining where they were or of returning to earth (Gibson, 1999, pp. 128–33).

In May, 2004, I called John and explained that I wanted to interview him again. This time it would be to get an update on his life since the original visit in 1996. Most importantly, I would be interested in any new spiritual experiences he might have had.

As he recounted the recent happenings in his life, he said that in the spring of 1999 he was living at the family ranch in New Mexico with his thirteen-year-old son, James. He said:

> The day started normally with James and I saddling up our horses and riding half-a-day looking for livestock belonging to the family. We had not had any luck so we decided to eat lunch. After lunch we located ten or fifteen head, and we decided to take them to headquarters and call it a day.
>
> As is typical, we split up to gather the livestock together. Shortly after splitting up, my horse blew up with me and drove the saddle horn deep into my groin area. Unbeknown to me, this caused extensive internal bleeding. I must have been thrown off and knocked unconscious for a length of time. When I came to, James was urging me to wake up. I responded, but in a fog; I did not know where I was, who he was, or why I was lying on the ground.
>
> As my head cleared and James recalled the events to me, it became clear I was seriously hurt. While wrestling with trying to stay

conscious, my deceased Grandfather and deceased Great-grandfather appeared to me. They both took over the situation and instructed me to tell James to go for help. This I did. My grandparents agreed to split up—one stay with me and the other go with James.

It seemed like hours that James was gone, when actually it was only minutes. As James rode off my horse followed him, reins flying in all directions. I must have been to this part of the ranch hundreds of times and could count on one hand the number of people I had encountered. The same is true today; this area is a very remote area.

James said he had barely reached the main dirt road when a truck stopped with Colorado license plates. The driver had seen my horse without a rider and suspected something must be wrong.

As it turned out, the driver and his wife were a Doctor and a Nurse visiting New Mexico. They lived in Denver, Colorado.

When they returned, the doctor could tell I was near death and asked James to go with the doctor's wife to Cuba, New Mexico for help. Later, an ambulance arrived and it was determined that I needed a "flight to life" because of the extent of my injuries.

While waiting for the helicopter to arrive, a number of people from my town arrived, including members of my family. As each spoke to me, a different "deceased" member of their immediate family would come forward from a large group of deceased persons gathered around me. One interesting aspect of this situation was that I puzzled over the fact that I could see and communicate with these deceased people, but their relatives could not. It bothered me so much that I told one lady ambulance driver, who I knew, that she was rude in not embracing her father, who I also knew and who had died some years before. She dismissed my chastisement as delusion caused by my injuries.

One who did believe me was my grandmother who had come from town when the ambulance arrived. Her deceased husband was present, and I told her so. She began to cry, especially when I mentioned that he told me she would be coming to him shortly. She died three months later.

While I was in this condition and could see and communicate with people who had passed on, I saw a number of events which I understood could happen in the future. Some were distressing to me, since they involved catastrophes about which I could do nothing. One circumstance that I saw, however, was a joyous one. Another son would be born to me. At the time, I was single with no particular prospects for marriage. Subsequently, I met and married a lovely lady, and my wife and I both rejoice over the birth and life of Sebastion.

John's recovery required extensive surgery and physical therapy. Today he can walk with some difficulty. Feeling has returned to the lower portion of his legs, but not entirely to the upper portion. As we conversed, I got the same impression from John that I previously did— of a man thoroughly involved in living life to the fullest. He sounded upbeat and optimistic about the future.

John Stirling's Motorcyle-Accident NDE and Follow-up Interview

I first met John Stirling on a beautiful spring day in 1991, up Emigration Canyon, northeast of Salt Lake City. Fresh greenery was evident throughout the canyon, and the sky was a cobalt blue with puffy white cumulus clouds drifting across the heavens. It was a good day to talk about eternity (Gibson, 1992, pp. 181–90).

John invited me to sit on a chair, and he sat adjacent to me. We began our conversation sitting in the great outdoors of the Wasatch Mountains. John told me he was born in 1953 in Salt Lake City, where he was raised in a family consisting of his father, his mother, and three older sisters. He went to high school in Salt Lake City, and he went to college, for three terms, to study art. He had traveled extensively. This was his story:

"In September, 1978 my wife left me and took my son. She wouldn't let me see him for quite a long time, many months, and I was pretty miserable. Through the whole thing I didn't want a divorce, I wanted to get back together with her, but she didn't

want to get back with me. She was angry, inside, and couldn't pinpoint reasons for it. At the time my son was two years old.

"I was having a rough go of life in general. I was tired of it, pretty sick of living. I bought a motorcycle, a Yamaha 650, to have something to do at nights when I was bored or lonely because I don't watch TV. I used to drive through the canyons for diversion, to think about things, and to relax.

"One Friday, during the day, I was really agitated and nervous all day. I called my mother and told her that I didn't know where I was going, but I thought I would be leaving on a trip somewhere. I said I would talk to her when I knew where I was going. As the day went on, I had mood swings, and I was filled with a lot of confusion. I tried to figure out where I was going.

"A friend came over to visit and we talked for awhile. I thought, with him there, I would be able to determine where I was going— so I could call the airport and book a flight—if I was flying. We ended up getting on my motorcycle and going for a ride up to the cafe in Emigration Canyon.

"We spent an hour-and-a-half or so at the cafe; we had some beer, and we left and began coming down the canyon. I used to race motorcycles, so I knew pretty well what they would do under different circumstances. As we came down the canyon, we hit a washout in the road, where the water had washed out under the road, and there was a bump.

"With the combined weight of my friend and myself, and at the speed we were traveling, the bump bounced the motor-cycle off the road and into the gravel. It was about eleven-thirty at night, and as I fought for control in the dark I considered heading the motorcycle up the mountain instead of staying in the gravel. I opted to do that, to go up the mountain, so that gravity would slow us down.

"We headed up the mountain a short distance, then I saw that the mountain had been discontinued where road work had been performed. I yelled at my friend that he had to get off. We were still going fast—about fifty-five, and he wouldn't get off. I leaned back and knocked him off.

"I then hit the rock, where it had been blown away, and I thought to myself, well this is it! The right side of my body crashed into the rock where it had been, kind of, curved. The bike rolled over on top of me and stuck the rear view mirror on the top of my head—I didn't have a helmet on. Then the bike continued to tumble and ended up about two-hundred-and-fifty feet away."

"I remember the crash and the bike tumbling, then I remember lying there, for just a split second, and thinking: well, this is it, I'm leaving. I turned around and looked, and I saw a body that seemed familiar. It looked like me, but I had no emotional involvement with the body lying there.

"I then felt great relief and joy—that I was leaving, and that I didn't have to endure, any more, the pain of the divorce, or the pain of missing my child. So I immediately, without any further thinking about it, took off, because it was what I had been wishing would happen.

"I could feel an ability in my spirit body to move at great speed, and I wanted to get where I was going as quickly as possible. I was going to a place that I knew. It was the place that I had come from. I wanted to get there as quickly as possible.

"I started traveling fairly slowly, in real time, when I first started. Then, as I got farther away from earth, I traveled much faster. The stars started to look like the stars in 'Star Wars,' with a long trail, because of my speed.

"A voice came to me, as I was traveling at that high rate of speed, and . . . and I was so peaceful and comfortable. All the emotional pain that I had been feeling was gone. I looked at my hand, and I saw the shape of a hand, but . . . but it had an aura around it. It wasn't the same hand as an earthly hand. There was an energy field that defined it.

"And the voice . . . the voice asked me if I was done. And I knew the voice and it was . . ." John had difficulty continuing as he wiped away the tears. "It was a comfortable voice—a voice full of love.

"I said: 'Yes, I'm done. I don't want to go back there. I don't ever want to go back there.' The voice asked me a second time: 'Are you done?' And I said: 'Yes, I'm done. I don't want to go back.' The voice asked me a third time if I was done, and again I said that I was.

"Then the voice said: 'Well, let's look at your life.' And I saw . . . I saw my life flashed before my eyes. Everything from when I was a child up to the present time. And every emotion that I had during my life, when I saw the scene, I felt the same emotion. I could feel the reasons that I did things as I saw the scenes unfold.

"I felt very comfortable with my life as I looked at it. It was all in color and three dimensional, and it flashed in a circle as if it were a deck of cards. I felt very comfortable that I would not have to come back to earth.

"The review continued until it came to the previous Friday, when I had had my son over, on Friday night. And it . . . the review traveled all the way up to that time.

"The scene, you can call it a card that came up for me to see, or, the vision that came to my view, it . . . my eyes locked onto that night. And the life review stopped. When that Friday scene first flashed up it looked as if it was going to go by, but when my eyes locked on it, then I knew I had to come back.

"So I . . . I said yes I would come back because I knew I had to raise my son as best I could. There was no further contact with the voice after I said I would return. I came back to my body so much faster than when I left. It was almost instantaneous. I can remember reversing in space and then waking up in my body."

"That was a remarkable experience, John. Let me ask you a few questions. When you went out of your body, did you see any light or anything of that sort?"

"Not that I can recall. At that point my main concern was getting out of here as quickly as possible. I was familiar with where I was, and . . ."

"So you had a feeling that you had been there before?"

"Oh, I knew. Yes, I knew—there was no doubt in my mind. And I wanted to get out of here as quickly as possible."

"You say you knew where you were. Did you have a feeling of knowing anything else?"

"I had an internal knowledge of where I was going."

"Did you have knowledge of other things?"

"Yes. I had an expanded consciousness. It wasn't like an earthly book-type knowledge. It was a consciousness that was larger, more spiritual."

"When you heard the voice, did you see anybody, or was it just a feeling of a presence?"

"I didn't see anyone."

"You felt, though, that you knew the individual?"

"Oh, yes."

"Do you know who it was, now?"

"Well, I would say it was Jesus Christ."

"You didn't have a feeling, then, that that was the case—or did you feel, then, that it was Christ?"

"Yes, I did."

"When you communicated with him, was it vocal communication?"

"It was not a verbal type of communication. It was a communication within. There's something when you are there. . . . When you are on earth you may have all sorts of thoughts running through your mind, or all sorts of confusion in you mind, all at the same time. There, you don't feel that way. You are more at peace, and you are more sensory. Communication was within me and was given back the same way, without the spoken word.

"The life's review came as a shock. When I heard the voice say: 'Well, let's see your life,' I didn't know how it would happen. It was totally unexpected, and it was right there in my view. It was as if both the voice and I were viewing it—and both of us could feel it as well as visually see it."

"Was there judgment in the voice?"

"Not at all. It was the same feeling you would get in a heart-to-heart conversation with a loving father about anything that concerned you. Not that judgment would be involved, but that you would both view the circumstances, see the way things were, and go on from there."

"So it was a teaching experience more than a judgmental experience?"

"It wasn't judgmental. I didn't know that I was coming back so I didn't realize, at the time, that it was a teaching experience."

"You mentioned that when you saw different events from your life you could also feel the emotions associated with those events. Did you understand that the voice also felt those emotions?"

"I felt, inside, that we both felt the emotions. As I recall, the life review started when I was two or three years old. The review, starting from that time, showed all the daily events, all the people involved, as I lived through the events. There were the funny times, the sad times, and my concerns at the time—for my age.

"So that when I was five, ten, or fifteen years old, for the wisdom I had at that age, I felt the same kind of emotions as I had when I was that age. I also knew where I was at, spiritually, for that given age. That's one of the reasons I felt comfortable with my life's review. Because I felt as if I really had tried as hard as I could, in accordance with what I knew at that age."

"Some people who have had this type of life's review indicated that they also felt, when they had done something good for someone, or when they had hurt someone, the emotions of that individual. Did you feel anything like that?"

"Yes. When I was younger I was a meek and timid kid, and I didn't do many things that would create a flash-back for me—adverse things that I would feel. My father died when I was a teenager, though, and I got kind of bitter and angry. Then I did do some things to hurt other people. I saw those events and felt the effect on the people. I also felt, at the time, my own bitterness."

"When you did something to help someone, did you feel their response to that as well?"

"Yes. I could feel the joy and the happiness as well as the pain, depending upon the circumstances."

"When your father died, did you feel the pain again?"

"Yes. I felt the pain again, but it was a comfortable pain this time. It wasn't the hollow loss that it was the first time."

"Why was it more comfortable?"

"Because I was in eternity—and I knew it. And I knew that my father was there also."

"But you didn't see your father, did you?"

"No. After the experience, and I've thought much about it, I wondered why I was stopped midway to my destination. The conclusion that I came to is that if I had been allowed to go all the way, to be in the presence of the Savior, or to be greeted by my father, I would not have returned. I know that would have been true."

"As you saw the life's review unfold, did it seem as if it took a long time?"

"Not at all."

"But there were 25 years which you went through. That's a lot of years. How could you see that in such a short time?"

"Yes, it was a lot of years. But it just . . . it's hard to describe. It unfolded, it was large, it was three-dimensional, it was right in my view, I didn't have to turn my head or anything, and it just exploded right there. It was as if it were the ultimate movie—three dimensional, with feeling and color."

"All-in-all, though, you felt it was a comfortable experience?"

"Oh yes. I had worried much of my life about things that I did, that I might be doing things that would give me a failing grade in life. All the little things that I did wrong. In viewing my life, though, it was different than that viewpoint."

"You say that you saw an aura around your hand when you looked at it. Was that aura all over your body, as far as you could tell?"

"Yes."

"How did your spirit body feel when you were out of your physical body?"

"Peaceful, calm, real, existing. . . ."

"Okay, so it didn't feel like a dream?"

"No."

"Did it feel as real as any experience in this life?"

"Yes, even more real."

"Has the experience changed your feelings about death?"

"It has changed my feelings about life more than it has about death."

"In what way?"

"It's the way I feel about people, now, and life in general—that we are all part of the same plan. We are all part of the same program, in that the greatest value, for any of us, is to try and help another person in their situation. We shouldn't interfere with others negatively, nor should we hurt another person. We should not, in any way, detract from a life. Rather we should add to other people's lives."

"When you were told that you had to come back, you really didn't want to, I take it?"

"I wasn't told to come back. I saw my son come up in the life's review and I knew, when my eyes locked on him, that I had to come back. And I said I would come back. I wasn't told to—I knew I had to."

"So it was your choice to come back, not somebody else's?"

"Oh yes. I saw him and knew I had to come back. I knew that I wasn't done with this life."

"As a result of the experience, have your religious feelings changed?"

"Yes."

"In what way?"

"I was raised as a Mormon. I was raised thinking, maybe, that God loved certain individuals more than others. Or that he cared about certain individuals more than others, depending upon how they lived. I didn't find that to be true.

"I found that his love was extended to everyone, all the time, and that he understood why we are what we are, and why we are going through what we are going through. I found that we are all the same in the volume of his love. His love is not judgmental. He wouldn't think, for example, because we don't have the great amount of knowledge that he does, or the great strength that he does, that we are bad. His love is extended to everyone."

In May, 2004, I contacted John. Our conversation follows:

"John, it has been thirteen years since my interview of you. Have they been good years?"

"Yes, they have been good years."

"How is your health and that of your son?"

"The health of my son is excellent, mine is up and down."

"What do you do to occupy your time?"

"Work."

"All the time?"

"Mostly, yes."

"Well, now you have a grandchild. You must do something with them."

John laughed. "Yes, I do spend time with my son, John, his wife, Holly, and my grandchild, Kaylee."

"Do you ever think back to the motorcycle accident and the NDE you had?"

"Yes, I think about it."

"Does it still seem real, or do you now remember it as a dream or hallucination?"

"Yes, it seems real, and no, it doesn't seem like a dream or a hallucination. I've had both, and I know the difference."

"Have you had any memories of that event which might have escaped you when we spoke before?"

"Only that I popped."

"What do you mean that you popped?"

"Out the top of my head—I popped out the top of my head when I left my body."

"Do you remember getting back into your body?"

"No, that was too fast."

"In our first interview, you made a strong point that you felt you were returning home. Can you elaborate on what you meant by 'returning home'?"

"Yes, I think I can. . . . There's a longing, I think we all have, when we are on a trip. At first, as you see new faces and things, it's exciting and new. After a while, though, you become weary, and you just want to go home. It's a desire to return home to things and people you are familiar with."

"You used the word, 'longing.' Why did you use that word?"

"Because I can't imagine anyone ever having had an NDE without having a longing to return."

"That's interesting, John. The great Christian apologist, C. S. Lewis used that word to describe the epiphany he had which changed him from being an atheist to becoming *the* outstanding spokesperson for Christian belief. During the first interview, you said that you were LDS but you weren't particularly religious in a formal sense. Is that still true?"

"Well, I'm *really* religious, I just don't attend a church."

"Is religion the right word then?"

"No, I guess it's not. No . . . it wasn't the right word then. . . . Let's see—I guess the right word would be *spiritual*. Yes, I've always been spiritual. In a sense, though, I've also been religious, it's just that I've never been socially adept at attending a church."

"How does your spirituality manifest itself?"

"Prayer, fasting, and meditation. There is a saying I read years ago which expresses my feelings well: 'Prayer is when you talk to God. Meditation is when God talks to you.'"

"Have you had any other unusual spiritual or other experiences since we last spoke?"

"Yes."

"Could you describe them?"

"I've had so many, Arvin, I don't know which ones to tell you about."

"Whichever are most important to you. That's what I would be interested in."

"I brought a book with me by Roy Mills called *The Soul's Remembrance* (Mills, 1999). And, by way of background, when I was young, I was quite spiritual-religious. During that period of my life, I had dreams of having lived before—in a premortal existence. I didn't know what to do with the dreams that I had, and I didn't know what to make of them. They were quite long and extensive, and I remembered them wholly when I woke up. As the years went by, I saved the memories, but I didn't know what to do with them until I read Roy Mills' book."

"Did you write the dream experiences down?"

"No."

"In reading Roy Mills book, or in hearing him speak, which is when I bought the book, we have the same recollections."

"What are some of those recollections?"

"They are memories of flowers, of . . . of a musical garden, where he, Roy Mills, met the people with rainbows in their hands. We have that same recollection. I was a little rainbow, and he was—whatever his name was at the time. Also, the ceremony when he was assigned his mission on earth, I was there.

"At his assignment, he asked for a particular mission, and he got what he asked for. And I thought if he can ask for and get a mission, maybe I can have the same mission, too. So I asked if I could have the same mission, and I was told, no. I could have a recollection, but Roy's mission was his. I could testify of his mission, but not implement it."

"So yours was to be a support mission, not a primary mission as was his?"

"Exactly."

"Okay, John. Have you been following through with that support mission?"

"Today."

"Only today? You haven't done anything before today?"

"No. This is my time."

"Oh, I think I see. You are saying that our interview, here, has to do with part of the mission you were assigned."

"Yes."

"That's interesting—fascinating, in fact."

John laughed and we continued, **"Now your mother has passed away?"**

"Yes, and that was a spiritual experience."

"You have some sisters, I believe. How is your relationship with them?"

"Yes, I have three sisters, and our relationship is great, and it gets better every day."

"Do they know of your experience?"

"Yes."

"Do they believe it?"

"Oh, I guess as much as they can."

"How about your son?"

"He's wonderful."

"He's why you came back."

"Yes, and I thought I was an adult, then. Becoming an adult, I've found, is a life-long challenge. In that context, a scripture I rely on these days is *Come unto me and I will show you your weaknesses.* Through family and friends you have the greatest love, and you also have the opportunity to show your greatest weaknesses."

"Do you, now, have any feeling for why you returned to this life that's different than before? At that time you said that it was your son."

"Yes, it was my son. Raising my son was the highest priority in a whole pyramid of priorities. Having one choice at the time, my son, without knowing the other choices, allowed me to later come back to the rest and to grow—to learn. Without my coming back I would not have learned what I did by facing the rest of the pyramid of choices."

"Inevitably, we must go the way of all flesh. What is your feeling about death?"

"Life should be prolonged as long as possible, but passing to another world should be embraced when the time is right."

"Are there any messages you would like to leave for others who might read this?"

"Never close your mind."

Derald Evans' Exploding-Rifle NDE and Follow-up Interview

Derald Evans first came to my house in December 1990. His easy smile and soft-spoken manner quickly put me at ease. He was a tall man, and his easy movements and running clothes belied his sixty years.

Derald explained that he was an avid outdoors-man and hunter. In September, 1968, he drew through a lottery a coveted Desert Bighorn Sheep hunting tag for the San Juan area of Utah. Over a period of three days he hunted and bagged a buck on the remote Mancos Mesa. While attempting to return to his vehicle after the hunt, the weather changed from extreme hot to extreme cold, and Derald barely made it back to his truck. In a state of complete exhaustion from exposure and exertion, he had a near-death experience which is explained in detail in the book *Glimpses of Eternity* (Gibson, 1992, pp. 23–28). As part of that experience, Derald understood that he would have, in the future, responsibility for children that he presently did not have. He did not understand this portion of his experience, but through a series of unusual circumstances Derald and his wife became the principal care-givers for his daughter and a grandson. As part of that responsibility they largely raised their grandson.

In October, 1999, Derald called me to bring me up to date on his life. He explained how, in 1997, he took his grandson on an outing in a remote area of northern Utah to teach him some rudiments of firing a rifle. As they traveled in their small Geo toward their destination over desolate desert roads, Derald felt impressed to give his thirteen-year-old grandson, Steve, a driving lesson. "After all," he explained, "you never know. Some day there could be an emergency and you may have to drive for someone else." So, the grandson took over and received some elementary lessons.

Upon reaching their destination, Derald explained that he would fire the rifle a few times to sight it in, and then he would let his grandson take over. The firearm was a high-powered Magnum rifle. After firing at the target for two or three times, Derald told his grandson that he would fire one more shot, and then it would be his grandson's turn.

Derald took careful aim at the target and squeezed the trigger. As he did so, the cartridge chamber of the gun blew up. The bolt action was torn out of the rifle, with the bolt driving backward into Derald's jaw, and then into his cheek where it protruded. Surprisingly, Derald remained conscious, but he was aware of the severe nature of his wounds and he did not believe that he could survive. He told his grandson, therefore, that he would soon die, and that the grandson would have to go get help by himself. Derald was bleeding profusely from his cheek, and he expected to go unconscious momentarily.

The grandson also acted surprisingly. He said to his grandfather, "Dodah (an affectionate nickname), you are *not* going to die." With that, the thirteen-year-old boy went to the side pocket of the Geo and got a roll of cotton which he brought back and stuffed against the wound to slow the bleeding. He told his grandfather to hold it in place. Then the boy, who was large for his age, helped his grandfather as he pulled him into the passenger side of the Geo.

Derald continued to retain consciousness, although he was still convinced that he would not live. He told his grandson how to start the truck and get them started towards the nearest town. With the boy driving frantically, at times, Derald had to keep instructing him so as not to go so fast that he lost control. In the meantime, despite the cotton in his cheek, there was so much blood on the floor of the Geo that it sloshed around. Ultimately they reached a town with a hospital. The boy stalled the vehicle in the town, and Derald talked him through the procedure to restart it and to drive the remaining distance to the hospital.

Medical personnel could hardly believe that Derald could have lived through the experience. The bolt was still sticking from his cheek. The story, of course, made the headlines of local newspapers. Derald and his grandson spoke at our IANDS group in 1998 and explained what had happened. By then, Derald had undergone extensive reconstructive plastic surgery. The evidence of the horrible accident was still present, but Derald was a completely functioning person. When the rifle exploded, Derald was a bishop in a local Mormon congregation— the Grandview Ward. During his recovery the entire ward had a day of fasting and prayer for his recovery.

Today (May, 2004), he is a productive citizen and has a remarkably positive outlook about life.

To say that he is still very much an athletically oriented outdoorsman is an understatement. In a recent phone call, he indicated he was pressed for time and could only spare a moment. He was on the way to a baptism, and he had spent the morning training for a marathon run he was planning to make.

Bill English's Life Changes from NDEs

Our initial interview was in 1992, and Bill's two NDEs and extensive recovery experience are described in detail in *Echoes From Eternity* (Gibson, 1993, pp. 77–85). The story will not be repeated here. In June 2004 it seemed appropriate, in light of what others I re-interviewed had been telling me, that I check on Bill. Ours had been a continuing friendship over the years since Bill was the long-standing president of our local chapter of IANDS, but I had not really asked him about the details of his life since our early interview. In my phone call to Bill, I mentioned how the work on this book was progressing and asked if he would mind if I updated his situation. He graciously agreed; our conversation follows:

"Bill, as I recall, a few years ago you quietly announced to some of us that you were going in for a brain operation. How did that come about, and what was the result?"

"In 1998, as the result of a normal physical exam, the Doctor asked me if there were any bothering symptoms. I mentioned that I had continual ringing in my ears. He sent me to an ear, nose, and throat specialist who told me that a million things could be causing this. However, he suggested an MRI scan of my head.

"The neurologist who read the MRI called me and said that they had found a tumor which was growing into my brain stem. Whether or not it was malignant, the tumor had to be removed or pressure on the brain stem from it would prove fatal. They scheduled an early operation. They let me know that I would be in the hospital for more than three weeks, part of which would be intensive care.

"The surgery took eight-and-one-half hours. Four days later I was released from the hospital. Fortunately the tumor was non-malignant, but that, and the operation, had already done some neurological damage. I had a plate in my skull, and the right side of my face was paralyzed for one year. Now, much of the feeling has returned."

"Okay, Bill. You were also having some problems with progressive bone damage? What is that all about, and what is its status?'

"It's known as Heterotopic Ossification and it is a known complication that often accompanies spinal chord or brain trauma—and I had both in my accident. It is a progressive disease and can result in spinal instability, as it has in my case. It can be treated if caught early enough. The hospital in Seattle, where I was taken early after my accident, had a treatment plan that could have corrected it. When I was moved to Salt Lake City, however, the hospital and doctors here either ignored or did not understand the disease. In any event, it is now too late to prevent its progression."

Bill was silent and I interjected, "That sounds like a pretty grim prognosis."

He responded without bitterness with, "Yes. It's part of life."

"In your second NDE, Bill, your deceased father told you that everything would be okay. Is it okay?"

"Yes, it is, Arvin. But you have to understand that I look at life differently now than I did then. Immediately after my accident, if I had known all that I would have to face in the future, my response would have been—and was to my brother—let me die. Now I feel that life has value regardless of the circumstances. My perception of what life was all about was not based on reality.

"In a sense, I now feel that your body is mostly just a vehicle that gets you around," and Bill chuckled. I used to look at the physical body from the outside in, now I look from the inside out. The world's view of physical beauty was previously my view. Now I know how far from the truth that was. Our beauty is what's contained within us."

Our conversation ended with Bill asking how I was. Since I had just had a kidney stone removed, I briefly complained about having to go through such an ordeal. Bill was, of course, completely sympathetic, and he wished me well. As he did so, and as he had so many times in the past, I wondered about my own equanimity in comparison to the marvelous example I had just spoken with.

8: More Follow-up Interviews

Elizabeth Clark's Overdose NDE and Follow-up Interview

Elizabeth Clark first told me her story in 1993. Portions of it from the book *Echoes From Eternity*, are included below (Gibson, 1993, pp. 170–77):

"When I was fourteen years old, I got involved with drugs. On one particular day I was smoking marijuana with a boy I knew, and I accidently took a drug overdose. Without my knowledge, the marijuana had been dosed with opium. The boy and I were having a contest to see who could smoke the greater amount. He passed out, and when he did I went in the house and managed to get back to my room.

"Upon reaching my room I lay down on my bed—I was stoned. After a time I noticed that I was looking down on myself on the bed. My immediate thought was: *I'm in trouble!*

"There was no sensation of still being under the influence of the drug; my mind was clear. I knew exactly what had happened. The perspective I had was that of a fourteen-year-old, knowing I was in trouble, and I was very upset. My next thought was: *How will I ever explain this one to my parents? Mom will really be upset.*

"While in this disturbed state I found myself drawn into a tunnel and through it at a rapid rate of speed. Upon reaching the end of the tunnel I entered a room with many people in it—people sitting on chairs, and laughing at me. They were laughing because I was trying to hide. The embarrassment I felt as a fourteen-year-old—for having done what I did—was severe. Since there was no place to hide I was doing the best I could by crouching down and putting my head on my knees.

"Someone called my name, and I looked to see who it was. Everyone that had been in the room was gone, and I could see a light in the distance coming toward me. It was a very bright light. When the light got close to me He put His arms around me. And He . . ."

Elizabeth was unable to continue for a moment while her mother got some Kleenex. When she regained her composure, I asked her: "He? . . ."

"Yes. He put his arms around me and asked me if I had known that what I did was wrong. I told Him that yes, I had known it was wrong.

"The amount of remorse I had, I'd never felt before. It was remorse over what I had done. I felt so sorry; there was a deep disappointment over my previous activities. The feelings of remorse and disappointment were pure feelings that permeated my body.

"I was asked if I had known what was right and wrong—and I had. My knowledge, in the presence of Him, was that I couldn't progress from the place I had positioned myself. Knowing that I was stopped in my progression, and feeling great remorse, I asked if I could return and help others to come back to Him. There was an intense desire within me to amend for the pain and suffering that I had caused others.

"The love I felt from Him during this period was extremely intense. Love traveled from my toes to my head, filling my entire body. There are no words that can adequately describe that love. It was a fatherly type of love, and I knew that He was pleased when I acknowledged my sins and asked if I could amend for them.

"He held me in His arms the whole time, and . . . and the feelings were so intense. The love I felt was beyond belief. And while I was embraced by Him and felt of His great love, He asked me if I would help others to come back to Him. I said I would.

"We had hugged each other for a while, when I knew that I was to return—I was put back in my body, although I don't remember that event. That was the end of the experience."

Elizabeth agreed that I could ask questions of her experience. I began:

"When you first found yourself out of your body, how did you feel?"

"I felt okay, but I was concerned because of what I had done."

"Did it feel like a dream, a hallucination, or a drug-induced experience?"

"Heavens, no. It was a real experience, not like the stupor I had previously been in from the drugs. The drugs depressed my system and caused me to die. My senses during the out-of-body experience were alert and awake."

"And you could see your physical body lying there?"

"Yes. The picture of my body lying there, and the position it was in, is still vivid in my mind."

"Did you have arms?"

"Yes."

"Did you see them?"

"Yes. My feet and my hands were visible to me."

"What did your hands look like?"

"Just like my hands do now. There was a white robe that covered my arms down to my wrists. The robe started at my neck and went to my ankles—it was a pure white. There are no words to describe that kind of white."

"When you came out of the tunnel and entered the room, did you know the people that were there?"

"I'm not sure. I didn't really want to know them because of my feelings of embarrassment. They seemed to think it was funny that I was trying to hide."

"Why were you so embarrassed?"

"It was because of what I had done—and because of the marks on my robe."

"What marks?"

"The robe I was wearing was white, a pure white, but it had black spots on it."

"Where were the spots, and why did they bother you?"

"There were several of them on my left side, down to my ankle. They bothered me because I knew that they represented some of the things I had done wrong. When I bent down I was trying to hide them, and that's what the people were laughing about. There was no way I could hide them."

"How were the people dressed?"

"They were also in white."

"Could you see the people very well?"

"Yes. There was this one person in particular that I remember."

"Describe that person, if you can."

"It was a male, with dark hair, and he had pointed at me."

"How old were the people?"

"They all seemed to be . . . gosh, about . . . there didn't seem to be any age to them, except the people seemed young."

"Describe the light in the room."

"It was light like in the tunnel. It was bright, but not nearly as bright as the light that came after He called my name."

"Where did the bright light come from?"

"It was high up and distant when I first saw it. The room boundaries seemed to disappear."

"What did the light look like?"

"When it got close to me, it was brighter than the sun. The sun is yellow, but the light was white. Yet I could look at it with my eyes."

"What happened to the light?"

"It came down and stood a few inches in front of me. It was a man."

"There was a man in the light, then?"

"I didn't see a man, but I knew He was there."

"Who was He?"

"It was Jesus."

"How did you know it was Jesus?"

"I just did." Elizabeth paused for a period to control her emotions. She continued: "I don't have words for it, but I knew it was He."

"You felt Him embrace you?"

"Yes. He put His arms around me and hugged me, just as my father would. The feelings I had at that point were extremely intense. My children and my parents, for example, I love with all my heart. Yet in this life I couldn't produce a small portion of what I felt in His presence. The love was a mutual feeling between us, and it went through my whole body."

"Did you have a life's review?"

"When He asked me if I knew the things I did wrong, they were brought back to my memory with full emotion. There was a clear understanding of each wrong event, and I felt remorse. The memories were very painful."

"What was His reaction when you remembered each event?"

"There was just love coming from Him. The sorrowful feelings were coming from me."

"In a sense, then, you were your own worst judge?"

"That's true, and it was extremely painful. It was clear to me what I had done wrong, and I suffered emotional pain as the memories came to me."

"Did you ask to come back, or were you told to come back?"

"I knew that He wanted me to, and I asked if I could. It was my choice, though; I could have opted to stay."

"How did you know he wanted you to return to this life?"

"By the feeling I had."

"How did He and you communicate?"

"Through my mind. I didn't speak, and I know that He didn't speak with His mouth. It was completely through thought."

"Was it as clear as you and me talking?"

"It was clearer. There was no mistaking what either of us was saying—there was no possibility of misunderstanding."

"Do you remember what you talked about?"

"Part of what happened was taken from my memory. I remember that we were making hard, important decisions about my future life, but I can't remember what they were. I've tried, but it's as if I'm not supposed to remember everything."

"When you returned to your body, what was the next thing that you remember?"

"It was morning, and I was on my bed."

"How long do you think your experience took?"

"I don't know. I didn't really have a sense of time."

"How did you feel when you woke up?"

"I was fine, but the experience changed my life completely."

"Why did you approach me for this interview?"

"I don't know. I just felt prompted to talk to you. It was difficult, though, because I remember the problems I had after my experience, and I didn't want to relive those feelings. Initially, for example, there was a period of depression—because I felt unloved. The love with Him was so great that every other form of love seemed weak in comparison. Nobody could come close to what He gave me. It took me a long time to overcome the longing for that type of love."

Over the years, John and Liz Clark have become our good friends. As with such friends, we were generally aware of their accomplishments, joys and challenges. But we had not recently had an in-depth visit. Furthermore, as this book proceeded, I knew that the Clark family had much that they could add to the book which would help other people, so I called them and they joyously accepted our invitation for dinner in June of 2004. Both John and Liz would come as well as their oldest child, their lovely daughter, Crystal. They assured us that we would want to meet and hear from Crystal.

I had the privilege of interviewing each of them, starting with Liz. Our interview follows:

"First, Liz, it's been eleven years since our last interview. Has anything of a spiritual nature happened that we did not discuss in the previous interview?"

"Yes, there has been quite a few things that have taken place.

I had gotten very sick for a long time with a heart problem. My problem is the result of blood vessels that are too small to deliver the blood my heart needs. The doctors call it Syndrome-X, and there isn't much they can do for it except to treat me with pain killers. They put a pacemaker in me sometime ago to help my heart keep a normal rhythm. In fact, I am now on my third pacemaker."

"How old are you, Liz?"

"I'm thirty-nine, now. I was twenty-four when I had the first pacemaker put in."

"How many children do you have?"

"Four. Three of them are still at home."

"Okay, what have been your health problems?"

"At age sixteen I developed an arrhythmia. It kept getting worse, and by the time I had my second child I was in a bad way."

"Why did you keep having children?"

"I didn't know how bad it had gotten until after I had my second child. My heart would be out of rhythm for weeks at a time. The doctors told me to not have anymore children but then . . . what do doctors know?" and Liz chuckled. "Actually, I just felt like there were children to come."

"So the arrhythmia kept getting worse. What did that lead to?"

"They told me that I wouldn't make it through my fourth child. That was when I was already pregnant. It was when I was twenty-seven years old, and I was totally bedridden. I couldn't even bathe myself. I had to have help come in."

"What did they suggest that you do?"

"Well, I told them that abortion was not an option. The medical people insisted that I at least know about abortion being an option. But they understood when I continued to insist that it was not an option for me."

"Let's see, Liz. That meant, if they were right and you insisted on having the baby, there was a risk of you leaving your other three children and your husband with no mother and no wife. Were you really willing to take that risk?"

"Yes."

"Why?"

"Because I knew they were wrong."

"How did you know they were wrong?"

"There are certain things . . ." Liz struggled for words. "There are certain things you just know. I knew, for example, that there were things I needed to do here, and I wasn't done."

"That was from your first NDE?"

"Yes. There were many times . . . it was a painful situation.

My heart wouldn't work right. It wasn't getting enough blood. The vessels would have spasms, and the heart would constrict. It's like having a heart attack a lot."

"So it was painful?"

"Very painful, unbelievably painful. One evening I thought I was going to die. In a way, I was hoping I would—to relieve the pain. But in the back of my mind I knew it wouldn't happen that way."

"Then, I heard some people talking in the back of the room. That seemed strange since no one had been there. I was in my room at home, and I thought I was alone.

"Suddenly I could see people talking, men. And they noticed that I noticed. They were dressed in white robes, and they were talking among themselves until they noticed that I saw them. One of the men came over to my bed, and he gave me a kiss on the cheek and told me not to worry.

"After the kiss, I fell into the most peaceful sleep I had ever experienced. The pain was gone. It was very good. There wasn't so much pain, at least for that night.

"If I wanted to, after that, I could leave my body and the pain would go away. But I found that it was bad to do that."

"How so?"

"When I would leave, the pain would be gone—I mean all gone. But then, coming back, I had to readjust to the pain again. And it would take quite a while to again become accustomed to the amount of pain, so I decided not to do that any more."

"When you left your body, could you see it lying there?"

"No, I would go into this . . . it was a space like just before the tunnel. It was . . . I don't know how to describe it." Liz laughed. "It was a nice, very peaceful place to be. I really liked it. It was a good place."

"All right, Liz. Are those the last of the NDEs you had?"

"No, there were two more. One I don't remember very well, but I was taken to a place where there were Elders there, and I think they told me many things which I do not remember."

"Was this after you had had your baby?"

"Yes. It was about two years later."

"Was it still as the result of your heart problems?"

"Yes. But in this place where I went . . . I don't know how to describe it, other than I began to become well afterward."

"Now you used the word, *Elder;* why did you use that?"

"That's who they were. I don't know how else to describe it—they were Elders to me.

"They told me a lot of things that I don't remember. I wish . . . I wish I could."

"**And it drives you nuts.**"

"Yes it does. I knew that there were certain things I had to accomplish, and I couldn't do that being as sick as I was."

"**So you knew that you had a mission, but you were too ill to carry it out, and the Elders had something to do with making you well enough to continue with that mission. Is that correct?**

"Yes, and it was a woman who took me to the place where the Elders were."

"**Do you know her name?**"

"No. There was a glowing . . . a glowing thing in the middle. It was glowing. And I could see their eyes and . . . the words the Elders used were not audible. They communicated by thought. And I knew I wasn't done. I simply had to get better in order to get to where I needed to be."

"**You had another experience?**"

"Yes, it was in 1977, just before John's accident. On that morning I had an uneasy feeling and I pleaded with John to not go to work, to go to breakfast with me, or anything. Just avoid leaving for work. My son, also, begged him to stay home, but John refused. He said that he had promised to complete some work, and he had to go."

"While worrying about John I was lying down, when suddenly I felt . . . it was like a thousand angels touching me. They were touching . . . it was through my whole soul. At the time I didn't understand what that feeling was.

"But, within about ten or fifteen minutes, I found out that he had been injured and I needed to go to the hospital immediately. The angels were not visible to me, but I could feel them so strongly.

"They were making me stronger so that I could deal with what was about to become my reality. That was a very intense situation. It also gave me the knowledge that John was going to make it. They told me there was nothing else they could do."

"**In light of all of these experiences you have had, what have you learned?**"

"There are no accidents, everything is orchestrated. Everything has a reason."

"**What do you mean that everything has a reason?**"

"In John's accident, he was run over by an eleven-and-a-half-ton fork lift that sat on him for five minutes. By all accounts he should have been dead. I think if . . . if it's not your time, you won't die.

"**Do you have any advice to give to any readers of this story?**"

"Do not go seeking NDEs," and Liz laughed.

"Well, that for sure. But what about life itself?"

"Life is a teaching experience. We should treat everyone as kindly as possible, and we should give others love and warmth. If you think of things in the eternal perspective, there are not very many things which are so awful that you have to hurt each other to compensate for your hurt. If it's not going to matter five years from now, then don't worry about it. It's just not worth fighting about."

"Okay, Liz. Is that all?"

"Well, do you remember the first interview we had? Did I tell you about the light going through me?"

"No, you didn't."

"You were the first person I ever told anything to about my NDEs. There were several things which I didn't tell you because I was afraid . . . but I know you a whole lot better now. And I think this is important.

"In my first NDE, when Christ came and held me, afterwards he took me to another room and he showed me pictures of people who had hurt me. They had hurt me badly. And he showed me what had happened in their lives that had gotten them to that point.

"Once I saw that, I didn't hate them anymore. My anger against them was gone. Instead, I felt sorry for them. He told me that it was like *a cold*. You can give this and you can pass it on, or you can choose not to. The choice was mine.

"And it is the choice with any of us. There are a lot of people who would hurt us, but they are sick. They were infected by someone else. We have that choice, whether we pass it on or not.

"After that, there was this other experience, and I still do not know how to put it into words to establish . . . how it happened. But there was this tube of light. At the bottom . . . it was like a representation of me, it was red.

"As it came up through there, it became full of light, and it changed colors. As it came to the top, it burst forth with light. It was bright, bright, silver-white light . . . I can't describe how— but each one of those cells were me. And each one of those cells knew that they were loved and were full of joy. They burst forth with that light. And that was part of me.

"I don't know how else to describe what happened. It was interesting to try and put it into words. The entire episode was one of love. It washed away all of the anger which I had . . . anger from things that were done to me and things that I had done. Things that I had done to my sisters and brothers. It's strange—my siblings tell me I have done these things, and I have no recollection of it. It is as if they are talking about a different person. And I have to take their word for it, because they all said I did it."

"What is your feeling, now, about your religion? Are you more or less religious?"

"I'm more spiritual than I was before. It has made me stronger in my Mormon faith. When I related my experiences to my understanding of Joseph Smith and his experiences in bringing forth the Book of Mormon, it made my faith more solid."

Crystal Clark's Early Childhood NDE and Interview

"How old are you, Crystal?"

"Eighteen."

"What stage of education are you at?"

"I will be getting my associate's degree in graphics design this September. Ultimately I plan on getting a Master's Degree from BYU in Fine Arts."

"All right, Crystal. Why don't you tell me what led up to your experience."

"I was a baby, around eighteen months of age. My great-grandfather had a disease, and they put him on Thorazine. He hid the pills under the couch for some reason, I'm not sure why. Anyway, to me they looked like chocolate M & M candies, and I loved them. So, when I found them, I ate a lot of them—way too many for me.

"My parents didn't know what I had done. So, a short while later, my mom was feeding me in my high-chair and I passed out. I didn't look like I was asleep, so Mom put me in the tub and sprayed cold water on me. But I didn't wake up.

"By then, my mother said that my lips were turning blue and I wasn't breathing. She took me to the emergency room at the hospital. They pumped my stomach and did all kinds of things to me. They said that I was dead, but they kept trying.

"The thing that I have a memory of . . . I could see it happening. I was in the corner of the room, at the top in the far corner, and I was just watching all of these doctors surrounding a table. There was a little baby on it with blond hair and little ringlets. She was in her diaper, and they were pumping her stomach and there was a lot of chaos.

"My mom was there, and I could see her bawling and carrying on. Then I remember sitting on someone's lap. Someone dressed in white. I was not scared—I just knew that everything would be okay. While I sat there I continued to watch the baby."

"Did you know that the baby was you?"

"I think that I did. There was confusion at first, but . . . you know. It was mostly just my curiosity as I watched. And I thought, 'Yeah, that baby is me. . . . ' I knew that was my mom fussing about the baby, so I figured . . ."

"Could you tell what they were doing?"

"Yes, in a way. I knew that they were trying to fix it . . . trying to make it better."

"Did you think like an adult or like a little kid?"

"It was like a little child. The thing that stuck out the most was that I was sitting on somebody's lap, somebody nice, kind and loving, I wasn't afraid, . . . and I wasn't afraid of being up so high. I was up pretty high. So I was watching the doctors, watching the baby and concerned about it, concerned about my mom, you know. She was upset. Those were the things that caught my attention."

"How did you come to remember this?"

"I've always kind of had that memory. It was like when my mom told me—it must have been years ago—she was saying, 'Yes, we had to pump your stomach out.'

"I didn't remember eating the medicine, but I did remember the other things. And I would say to my mom, 'Yes, I think I remember that,' and she would say, 'No, you were little and passed out. You don't remember anything.'

"So I would ask her, 'Was I wearing my diaper when you brought me in? And was I lying on a stainless steel table with lots of doctors around—while you were crying?" She told me that, yes, that was the way it was. Also, I told her how I was sitting on someone's lap up high in the room."

"Did you know whose lap it was, Crystal?"

"I think it was an angel. That is the impression I had, and still do when I think back on it."

John W. Clark's Construction Accident NDE and Interview

"How old are you, John?"

"I'm thirty-nine."

"Tell me what led up to the experience you had."

"The accident happened in February, 1997. At the time I was a carpenter building custom homes. We were building a home in Lindon, Utah. It was a Saturday. In fact I shouldn't ordinarily have been working. Both my son and wife were trying to persuade me not to go."

"Why did they not want you to go to work."

"They had had some premonitions that something bad would happen."

"What was your reaction to their appeals?"

"I pushed it aside and didn't think any more about it, I knew I had committed to work. We were just finishing off this house and it needed to get done. My determination was to go in and complete what I said I would do."

"What was the weather like?"

"Well, for February it actually was pretty mild. My insulated bibs were on so I was warm enough."

"We picked up the forklift, and I drove it to the subdivision—less than three or four miles away, and I proceeded to work with my working partner, Andy. There was just the two of us. To finish the house, we were hanging fascia-board around the edge of the roof. Because there were just the two of us, we would move the forklift into position.

"The wood was large and cumbersome. It was ten 12-foot pieces of rough-sawn lumber, four inches thick. The height of the wood was about twelve inches. So I would have to position the forklift with my friend in the man-basket, raise him to the level of the roof, turn off the forklift, put it in park, put the emergency brake on, then climb up through the house and out a window onto the man-basket and help him lift the piece. Then we would tack it in place and I would climb back down and repeat the process for the next piece.

"Each time I moved the forklift, I would put a rock behind the tire. These construction forklifts are designed so that you can move all four tires separately, so it can do what is called *crabbing*. That way you can get it in tight spots. The forklifts weigh eleven-and-a-half tons.

"As we kept going around the house, from east to west, the incline kept getting steeper and steeper, so I would hunt for bigger rocks to stick behind the tire—these tires are like five feet tall. With no one in the driver's seat as we worked on the fascia-board, I was concerned that the lift be firmly blocked from rolling down the steep incline.

"It was about eleven o'clock in the morning, and just as I was on the third time blocking the tire, I found this big rock. I was scooting the rock into position. All of a sudden the braking mechanism gave way. My thumb was trapped between the tire and the rock. Before I could move, it was me and the forklift going down the hill. It came to rest with me squarely underneath the tire. The tire was positioned over my body, almost to my neck. I was folded over, almost in half, at the waist. It was a precarious position.

"As the forklift came down the hill, my partner was in the basket, and it hit the ground and ruptured some vertebrae in his back. He crawled out of the basket and was calling my name. I wasn't answering, and when he came around the corner he saw my leg sticking out. Then he saw that the forklift was on me, and I was having spasms—twitching like a dead cat.

"He decided that the only thing he could do was start up the forklift and drive it off of me. I remember the engine turning on, but do not remember the forklift driving off of me.

"At the time I was thirty-three years old. I had heard my wife's NDE story many times, and had attended many IANDS meetings, so I was aware of what might occur to me. It was clear to me that death was imminent, and I was conscious of that fact. It wasn't clear to me how I would prevent death, but I was determined that I wouldn't let myself die.

"In a semi-conscious, but spiritually-aware moment, I saw my wife and children. In fact, I saw their faces as clearly as if they were standing in front of me. At that point, I felt that I probably would not survive. It seems to me that my determination to stay alive kept my epiphany, or whatever it was, from progressing further than it did, and it also played a role in my survival."

"When he drove off of you, were you still conscious?"

"No. I remember being under the forklift, and of seeing the faces of my family. Also, I have a consciousness of turning my head, and seeing my body. It was from someplace outside of the physical body. And I recall looking up and seeing the underside of the forklift. But I was in such a position under the tire that I physically could not have seen the bottom of the forklift. So I was definitely out of my body. There was no panic and no pain, despite thinking that I might die."

"Did you get help?"

"My friend, Andy, first got the help of a nurse lady who lived down the hill from where we were. The ambulance got there fairly soon. I was conscious and talking to the paramedics on the ride to the hospital.

"Being under the forklift for about five minutes pushed all of the blood from my torso to my extremities. The result was that I was bleeding from my eyes, ears, nose and mouth. As my eyes began to swell, my vision decreased. This was of much concern to me."

"What did they have to do to help your health recover?"

"After one month in the hospital, I went through nine months of physical therapy. My injuries were extensive. There were eight broken vertebra in my back, multiple broken ribs, my heart was stopped, and both lungs were filled with blood except for a small upper lobe in one of my lungs with some space for breathing. The doctors told my wife there was no chance that I would live. In order to minimize pain I was put into a drug-induced coma."

"What did they do for your vertebra?"

"Nothing, I've had no surgery."

"My word, that's unusual, isn't it?"

"Yes, it is nothing short of miraculous—being able to walk out of the hospital with most of my functions restored. Of course I had several priesthood blessings, and so the Lord has had a hand in my healing."

"So what's your attitude now about all of the problems you and Liz have had?"

"To use an old cliché, if life gives you lemons, make lemonade. I don't sit and sulk about not being able to be a carpenter. My attitude is to make the most of life as it comes to you, and don't feel sorry for yourself for what might have been."

Vern G. Swanson's Account of His Deceased Wife's Appearance

My first interview of Vern Swanson was in 1993 when I visited him in Springville, Utah. At the time, he was the Director of the Springville Museum of Art. His NDE was the result of severe melancholy after the death in a traffic accident of his wife and son.

In July, 2004, my wife and I visited the Springville Museum where Carol was competing in a quilt showing. (She won a prize!) While there I visited with Vern, still the Museum Director, and arranged to talk with him some more.

It soon became apparent that Vern was the same up-beat and charismatic person that he was when I first met him. He was full of enthusiasm for his work at the museum, and he was anxious to tell me of a book he had been working on for many years and which his publisher was anxious to publish in 2006. The book will be titled *Dynasty of the Holy Grail—Mormonism's Hidden Blood Line.*

Despite his very cheerful attitude and his willingness to visit with me, I noted that Vern seemed to be somewhat in pain. When I asked him about it, he said that he had been having trouble with his kidneys, and he had just undergone a biopsy. The doctors still had to diagnose the problem and he promised to let me know how he was doing.

Later, Vern said that doctors had diagnosed his physical problem as autoimmune kidney disease. He would shortly start a regimen to minimize the damage to his kidneys. Vern said that he was completely calm when he visited with the doctor, and if he had been told that he only had a few months to live, he still would have looked on his remaining life as a blessing.

I asked Vern if he still vividly remembered the details of his NDE. His response was: "Like it was yesterday. It was a totally real event."

He summarized his view of life and death with a quote from now-deceased LDS Apostle Hugh B. Brown: "Death is not the end. It is merely putting out the lights, for the dawn has come." Later, Vern sent me the following letter reflecting back on his NDE:

> After the death of my wife, Elaine, and son, Brett, in April of 1975, my life ran on adrenalin for several weeks. My loved ones were killed in an automobile accident in Montana following a freak snowstorm. My mother and fathers-in-law made a wise decision not to have an open casket funeral because of the severity of the injuries. They saw the damaged corpses and recommended that I not look at the bodies. We decided to have one casket, not two, and have my wife and son together. So at the funeral I saw only one casket and no bodies.
>
> As I returned to Auburn University in Alabama where I was teaching, the loss began to drag me down. I understood my wife dying; after all, she had done most of the basic things that we come to earth to do. But my son hadn't done anything, and coming to grips with his death was complicated by not seeing his casket. Morbid thoughts of him moldering—or fancifully thinking that perhaps he hadn't really died after all, crowded my mind. I cried a lot, moped much more as my vigor waned. I sank deep into depression.

Then I had the experience I told you about before (Gibson, 1993, pp. 44–49). Briefly, what happened follows:

> One night, about six weeks after Elaine and our son had died, I was lying restlessly in bed. Suddenly I looked up and I saw a light. Standing there in the light was my wife.
>
> As I remember, it seems as if I were instantly out of bed—just thuung! . . . and I was up next to her. It was the most interesting situation you could imagine, because she looked exactly like Elaine, yet she didn't. It's hard to explain.
>
> My wife, the woman, the angel in front of me was so peaceful, so beautiful. There was a white light that came from within her so that she glowed. It wasn't reflected light.

I had always thought that Grace Kelly, the movie star, was the most beautiful woman in the world. Elaine, standing before me, would have put Grace Kelly to shame. She was very white with that inner glow, and she was absolutely the most beautiful person I had ever seen. To this day I can remember how she looked, and I marvel at what I saw. Elaine, in life, was a good-looking woman, working as a model during college, but her earthly body was a poor shadow, an impoverished copy, when compared with that beautiful person before me—yet it *was* Elaine.

As she stood before me I began to embrace and kiss her; I smothered her with kisses. When I touched Elaine, I was filled with joy from her warm white radiance. And she was holding my dead son, cold like clay. Three times she said, "Vern, he is dead!" I smothered them with kisses saying no, no!

Then I was awake, sitting upright in bed, bawling my eyes out. I did not know if it was dream, vision, out-of-body or visitation experience. One thing I knew was that Elaine and Brett were as tangible to me as any living person. Arvin told me that he believed it was an out-of-body epiphany because my wife and son were tactile to my touch. In addition, I remember being out of bed and embracing them.

While I don't think about this remarkable event in my life very much, every once in a while I relate it—when it seems appropriate. And when I do, the flood of images are as real as they were almost thirty years ago. I have been able to rely upon this gift during difficult times. It has definitely "been for my good," and maybe a little help for those in whom I've confided. While my health has not been great over the years, my attitude has. My faith in our Heavenly Parents, my faith in Jesus Christ, and my faith in the Restored Church has deepened because of this rare experience so many years ago.

The Objectives of Repeat Interviews

In this and the previous chapter, I deliberately set out to interview, almost at random, an unspecified number of individuals whom I had previously interviewed and recorded their NDEs. There was no predetermined agenda or list of questions for each of them, nor was there any expectation of unusual findings. It was merely a feeling that it might be useful to have a chapter in the book with a few case studies of individuals Carol and I had interviewed previously. Perhaps they could shed some additional light on the NDE.

There was some initial trepidation on my part. These were all busy people, and I feared that they might look upon this as an intrusion by that pest, Arvin Gibson. To my pleasant surprise, their response was universally positive. The greeted me with joy and enthusiasm for the project. Indeed, during the re-interview of John Stirling, he told me that our meeting again, and his being able to elaborate on his experience, was part of his mission. There was not a single person I contacted who refused to participate. As a result, I expanded the chapters devoted solely to this subject to two, and I incorporated still others in different chapters.

Over the years, several researchers have observed that those who have NDEs seem to have more difficult lives after their experiences than one would expect. No serious longitudinal studies with statistical rigor had been performed on the subject, though, so it was difficult to make generalized comments about the phenomenon—if it existed.

As I began my interviews, it soon became clear that a fairly large percentage of those I interviewed had unusually severe physical problems. There are a total of twenty individuals in various chapters of this book whom I interviewed, and with most of whom I had a long-standing and relatively close relationship. Fourteen of those twenty individuals had severe physical or other problems which beset them later in life and usually were only remotely, or not at all, related to their NDEs. Because of space limitations, I did not document all of their present problems, but they included Ann (chapter 15), Gary Gillum (chapter 16), and DeAnne Shelley (chapter 16). Thus, approximately 70 percent of those I recently interviewed or have had close contact with had unusually severe after-NDE problems. Whether that is the result simply of aging, or other random problems, or whether there is some significant effect in play, is unknown. Further, better controlled, longitudinal studies of this phenomenon would be a fruitful area of investigation.

During **Gary Gillum's** experience (Gibson, 1992, pp. 191–97), he was told what would happen if he stayed in the paradisiacal realm vs. returning to earth:

> Basically, I was given a choice to stay or to return to this life. Having prayed for some kind of experience, I sort of felt the

question and the answer. It was: "If I don't go back to earth and to my body, what am I going to miss out on?" And the answer was: "If you go back, some day you will find the truth. Also, you have a lot of experiences still to have on the earth. If you stay here, you will have at least what you now see and feel, but if you go back to your body and come here later, and if you are faithful, then you will have much more than this."

While I was in this state, I learned—I probably learned much more than this—but I learned that the important things in life are service, love, and knowledge. I also had  an inkling, because I now had an absolute knowledge that there was a life after death, that life would be more difficult for me than it otherwise would have been.

Gary's NDE, therefore, included a succinct celestial proclamation—directed at him—in response to his request to understand the options available to him. In effect, the Creator was telling him, "Okay, Gary, you have two choices, to stay or to go. If you stay you will enjoy the glory that you see here now. But you will miss out on much of what it means to live in mortality. Moreover, if you go you will find the truth which you prayed for, and if you are faithful to God's laws then you will have even more glory than what you now see. And, oh, by the way. Since you now know for sure that life continues after mortality, your mortal life will be considerably more difficult than it otherwise would have been."

Although, as pointed out, this proclamation was tailored for Gary's unique situation, much of it would be applicable to many of those whose stories were included in this and other chapters. The same is true of Liz Clark's various experiences; they were assuredly tailored for her needs, but some of the lessons she learned from them are universally applicable. And her life has had its share of problems. Similarly with John Stirling. It is left to the reader to decide how applicable these learning experiences might be to the others discussed in this book—and to all who read of them.

There was another common thread among all of those re-interviewed for this book. Here, the commonality was one hundred percent. It was that they all still felt committed to fulfilling their earthly missions. In some instances, they felt that they understood the main ingredients of their assignments, but generally they were not sure. They *were* sure that it included service and love—as listed in Gary's proclamation—but the precise nature of that service and love were as diverse as the numbers interviewed.

It is impossible to speak with Vern Swanson at his place of work without being interrupted every few minutes by people wishing to meet with him. It is true that much of what these visitors have to say deals with the Museum, but it goes further than that. Vern radiates an exuberance for life which is infectious. The same could be said of John Stirling, Liz Clark, Bill English, DeAnne Shelley, John Hernandez, Lucinda Hecker, Maxine . . . and . . .

Here, again, the commonality was unanimous. These people really are remarkable, and they reflect in their countenance and demeanor a radiance that is unmistakable.

Future Research on the Meaning of NDEs

Harold Widdison, the author of chapter 13, would not agree that any of the percentages shown in this chapter are particularly meaningful from a more rigorous sociological perceptive, and I would agree with him. He probably would acknowledge, though, that they point toward the type of longitudinal study which could develop a more reasoned and comprehensive view of another aspect of the NDE. Indeed, in his chapter he argues for increased research, using already abundant literature on NDEs, into the meaning of NDEs. He and I share that view.

This entire book, for that matter, seeks to better understand NDEs through a relatively thorough comparison with LDS teachings and doctrine. The faith of the authors of this book is sufficiently secure that their belief is already anchored in a firm foundation—the Gospel of Jesus Christ—and needs no props, NDEs or otherwise, to buttress it. Nevertheless, spiritual experiences like those documented in this book, are inspirational in and of themselves, and they can contribute to a better recognition of the widespread effect of God's love for *all* of his children.

9: An Overview of the History of NDE Research

Duane Crowther's book *Life Everlasting* was published in 1967 and has since gone through two revised editions containing many valuable additions. Crowther was the first LDS author to do a serious research study of near-death experiences recorded in the early and recent history of The Church of Jesus Christ of Latter-day Saints. He has documented well over 200 NDEs happening to Mormons, and correlated those events with LDS teachings (Crowther, 1967, 1997, 2005). The book has been extremely popular with LDS readers.

The general public became familiar with NDEs with the publication, in 1975, of Raymond Moody's book *Life After Life* (Moody, 1975), and later with George Ritchie's book *Return from Tomorrow* (Ritchie, 1978). In 1980 Kenneth Ring's book *Life at Death* was published (Ring, 1980), and in 1984 his seminal work *Heading Toward Omega* was published (Ring 1984). Dr. Ring was a professor of psychology at the University of Connecticut and a founder of the International Association for Near-Death Studies (IANDS). As a partial result of his effort, researchers all over the world began to do work in the field of NDEs and to report on their efforts.

In *Life at Death*, Dr. Ring described how, beginning in 1977, he spent thirteen months tracking down and interviewing scores of people who had come close to death. He sought out and found people who had *actually* nearly died. In some cases, his research subjects had suffered "clinical" death, that is, they had lost all vital signs such as heartbeat and respiration. In most cases, however, the men and women he interviewed had found themselves on the brink of medical death but had not, biologically speaking, quite slipped over. His aim in conducting the interviews was to find out what people experience when they are on the verge of apparent imminent death. His findings led to the identification of a series of events which most commonly might be expected in an NDE. Those findings are still used as a gauge on how complete or how typical the particular NDE being studied might be.

The early efforts by Moody, Ritchie, Sabom, Ring and others, together with the founding of the International Association for Near Death Studies (IANDS) in February 1981, at the University of Connecticut, precipitated a great deal of follow-on work by others. Initially, the work was produced by medical professionals, psychologists and sociologists—and by people who had undergone an NDE (and sometimes by a combination of both).

The International Association for Near-Death Studies (IANDS)

The formation of IANDS was an enormously important event in the worldwide spawning of serious research into near-death experiences. Those involved in IANDS' formation, and their reasons for launching such a strange venture—some at the risk of damaging their professional careers—is outlined elsewhere in this book. Among other important fruits of this early venture was the beginning of a professional journal where researchers, those having had NDEs, and other interested parties with a scientific interest, could publish articles—often with later rejoinders from their professional peers. That journal morphed into what today is the *Journal of Near-Death Studies,* published quarterly. It is edited by Bruce Greyson, Professor of Psychiatry and Director, Division of Personality Studies at the University of Virginia. Much of the success of the Journal has been due to the efforts of Dr. Greyson.

Nancy Evans Bush was the first Executive Director of IANDS, and more recently was its President. In the Fall, 1991 edition of the *Journal,* Ms. Bush wrote a retrospective article about IANDS celebrating the tenth anniversary of the *Journal* (Bush, 1991). A portion of what she wrote is reproduced below.

As for IANDS itself, the road has been no less bumpy. It may have been more rat-filled than that of the research, because whereas the work of theoretical inquiry tends to be solitary, the work of organizations involves lots of personalities and many types of constraint. That ad in the *Courant* [which attracted my attention] took me to a little windowless box, which was IANDS' home at the University, inhabited like a Hobbit hole by student volunteers. It was a one-file-cabinet operation, but what a time of excitement, with everything promising and new, and Ken Ring bouncing in every day to see how things were going. Bruce Greyson was still at the University of Michigan; Steve Straight (another of the veterans, behind the scenes) was already managing director of the journal while working on his Master's degree; Michael Sabom's *Recollections of Death* was still a year away. Within two years, the office boasted four file cabinets and had workload problems that are still troublesome.

NDE—A Misnomer

When Bush wrote her tenth-anniversary article, she was aware of the significant body of evidence resulting from ten years of research in the field of NDE studies. One troublesome issue which fell out of that evidence was the fact that the term "Near-Death Experience," coined by Raymond Moody, was a misnomer. She had this to say about it:

> In fact, it now seems that The Experience is the experience, by whatever title. What varies is the manner of its precipitation; obviously there is no single trigger. Childbirth experiences, trauma experiences, drug experiences, clinical death experiences, meditational experiences, and others share identically the pattern, the intensity, the insight, the aftereffects–all that we call the "near-death experience." Would a different name be desirable? Probably. Are we apt to find one? Probably not, if only because "near-death experience" is so widely recognized and so firmly established in public consciousness.

A Variety of Studies

A number of early researchers addressed different aspects of the NDE. Carol Zaleski, in her book *Otherworld Journeys—Accounts of Near-Death Experience in Medieval and Modern Times,* was able to describe experiences recorded by ancient writers from Plato to Pope Gregory the Great (in the sixth Century) (Zaleski, 1987). Ian Wilson, in his book *The After Death Experience—The Physics of the Non-Physical,* also traced NDEs into ancient times, citing such examples as the Tibetan's *Book of the Dead,* the *Bardo Thodol* (Wilson, 1987).

In addition to the physicians George Ritchie, Raymond Moody, and Bruce Greyson, two other physicians who collected information on their patients and those of other physicians were Maurice Rawlings and Michael Sabom. In 1979 the Bantam Edition of Rawlings' book *Beyond Death's Door* was published. Rawlings was a cardiologist, and he documented NDEs which illustrated both happy or euphoric experiences and frightening experiences. His book had chapters devoted to the subjects *Ascending to "Heaven,"* and *Descending to "Hell."* Rawlings is a Protestant Christian, and he attempted to show correlations between Biblical scriptures and the NDEs which he had documented. His book was one of the first to provide considerable detail on frightening experiences (Rawlings, 1979).

In 1982, Michael Sabom, also a cardiologist, detailed the results of his findings on 116 cases, mostly his own patients, who had NDEs. Sabom's work was especially useful since he took the trouble to document out-of-body (OBE) experiences where corroboration could be obtained. In particular, he sought to obtain data from medical professionals and other witnesses who could corroborate what the NDE claimants said they saw while they were out of their body. During periods, for example, of a medical emergency the patients' eyes are often taped shut to protect them. Where the patients were able to see the medical professionals performing specific tasks on their bodies, these actions by the medical people were later corroborated by Sabom (Sabom, 1982).

In 1990, Melvin Morse, a pediatrician, in collaboration with Perry, published his book on children's NDEs in the book *Closer to the Light*. This book was unique in that it reproduced the innocent and often matter-of-fact comments by children as they described how they went to heaven and saw Jesus (Morse, 1990).

In 1988 Phyllis Atwater's book *Coming Back To Life—The After-Effects of the Near-Death Experience* was published. In the book, Atwater detailed how, during a hemorrhaging miscarriage in 1977, she had an extensive NDE—actually three separate NDEs—which profoundly affected the rest of her life (Atwater, 1988). As a result, she set out to do research on the lasting effects of NDEs. She has written several books and articles on the subject and has frequently been a speaker at IANDS conferences.

Dr. Cherie Sutherland was a Sociologist at the University of New South Wales in Australia. In 1971, while giving birth to a son she had an NDE and, as with many such experiences, she was given a choice to stay or return to life. She chose to return to life for the sake of her two children and for her own sake. Since that experience, she began a long and extensive effort to research numerous NDEs in Australia and elsewhere. She, too, has documented frightening NDEs. Two of her best-known books are *Reborn in the Light* (Sutherland, 1995) and *Within the Light* (Sutherland, 1993).

Kimberly Clark Sharp is a clinical social worker and the founder of the local Seattle group of IANDS, one of the first and largest of the local groups in the United States. In 1970 she collapsed outside an office in Shawnee Mission, Kansas, and she had an NDE where she was encompassed by the Light. This set her on a course of finding out what such experiences were all about. She has illustrated some of the most splendid NDE cases in the literature. She wrote the book *After the Light—What I Discovered on the Other Side of Life That Can Change Your World* (Sharp, 1995).

The Nature of Early Research

By its very nature, early research consisted primarily of the gathering of anecdotal stories. This led to both one of its weaknesses and one of its strengths. The weakness came about because researchers could not fix the parameters of data that they gathered with such techniques as double-blind studies and sophisticated pretest statistical gathering methods. The strength of the anecdotal method resulted from the publishing of vast numbers of experiences with the details recorded of each event. In social science this type of early study is called an "Exploratory Study." Researchers later, therefore, studied the recorded anecdotes and performed more sophisticated work, such as searching for patterns of repeatability.

Much criticism has arisen from this method of gathering anecdotal evidence, and some of it may be justified. Kenneth Ring, for example, attempted to change research methods somewhat by introducing more statistical-gathering techniques (as in *Heading Toward Omega*). In his more recent work with blind people who have had NDEs, he deliberately sought corroborative data of the sort gathered by Sabom (Ring and Cooper, 1999).

Some of the criticism about anecdotal evidence appears misplaced, however, and reveals something of the philosophy of the criticizer. If, for a moment, it is assumed that near-death experiences are in fact spiritual events—as most of those having NDEs claim—then anecdotal events make perfect sense. Presuming that, just possibly, there is a creative higher power aware of and involved in the affairs of men, isn't it the epitome of arrogance to assume that such a higher power would craft NDEs for the convenience of researchers—instead of for the benefit of the person undergoing the NDE? As Elder Neal A. Maxwell put it in an address to a Brigham Young University audience on November 27, 1979 when he spoke of the omniscience of God: "[We] are questioning the reality of God's omniscience, as if, as some seem to believe, God were on some sort of postdoctoral fellowship" (Maxwell, 1980).

Another criticism of early NDE research was the lack of peer review. A rebuttal to this criticism might be that in those early days there were no peers—at least in the sense that there was no large group of professionals who were familiar with the NDE phenomenon. In recent years, Professor Bruce Greyson at the University of Virginia has attempted to correct this particular weakness. Greyson is the editor of the quarterly publication *Journal of Near-Death Studies* which publishes technical articles dealing with all aspects of the near-death experience. Each article is subjected to extensive review before it is accepted for publication.

Another effort to improve on the quality of near-death research has been the attempt to determine patterns from an accumulation of events described by those having had NDEs. Phyllis Atwater, for example, has done a broad study of the aftereffects of NDEs on the lives of those who lived through them (Atwater, 1988). The Sociologists Craig Lundahl and Harold Widdison did an extensive categorization of events into various subjects known to be a part of many NDEs. Their book, *The Eternal Journey*, lists such categories as: *Pre-Earth Life and Its Purposes, Earth Life and Its Purposes, The Death Transition, Death: Crossing into the World of Light, The Nature of the Spirit Body, The City of Light,* and *The Realm of Bewildered Spirits.* They catalogued numerous events from NDEs which shed light on these various subjects (Lundahl and Widdison, 1997). Widdison was a professor of medical sociology at Northern Arizona University (now retired with emeritus status), and Lundahl is chairman emeritus of the department of Social Sciences and professor emeritus of sociology and business administrations at Western New Mexico University.

A fascinating study was done by Evelyn Elsaesser Valarino, the head of the law library at the University of Geneva in Switzerland. In a five-year effort, she studied NDE accounts so as to become relatively expert in the subject. Then, she interviewed eminent personnel in diverse scientific and religious disciplines to obtain their perspectives on the NDE phenomenon. Those that she interviewed included: Kenneth Ring, the pioneer NDE researcher, Michel Lefeuvre, a professor of philosophy, Louis-Marie Vincent, a biology professor, Régis Dutheil, a professor of theoretical physics, Paul Chauchard, a neurophysiologist, and Lord Bishop Jean Vernette, advisor to the Vatican (Valarino, 1984).

In terms of more recent work, Kenneth Ring's book, *Lessons from the Light—What We Can Learn from the Near-Death Experience* illuminates his decades of research in the field (Ring, 1998). Ian Wilson, who wrote the masterful book *The After Death Experience,* said of Ring's book: "A thoroughly gripping read, this is unquestionably the most important book on the subject since Moody's *Life after Life.*" I would go further and assert that Ring is the most important single individual to advance the state of NDE knowledge. The magnitude of his contribution can be roughly measured by picking up any good book on the subject of NDE research and examining the references therein. Kenneth Ring will inevitably be a primary source.

Chapter 3 provided information on Mormon NDE researchers and other LDS professionals who contributed to the overall NDE data base. In addition, that chapter described significant findings resulting directly from the Mormon perspective. There may be room for disagreement from others with different religious backgrounds. Nevertheless, the data are presented and the reader may draw his or her conclusions concerning the validity of the findings.

Evolution of the Research Effort

Research effort, then, in the first decade or so, was primarily concerned with identifying the various elements of an NDE, determining what triggered the inception of an experience, and proposing various hypotheses to test physiological or psychological models which might explain the NDE. The effort gradually evolved to a more sophisticated type of research as most of the models based on pre-existing notions of a materialistic science failed. The principal problem with the majority of scientific explanations of the NDE in the past has been their attempt to use a material cause to describe what may, in fact, be a spiritual phenomenon. This has caused "hard science" investigators to rely on techniques that work fairly well in describing our physical universe, but seem unable to adequately explain what may be a different kind of world or universe.

A most interesting case where a model failed to account for several elements in the NDE was acknowledged by the researcher. The entire Fall, 1997 edition of the *Journal of Near-Death Studies* was devoted to an article by Karl L. R. Jansen and to the responses by other medical practitioners and researchers to his article. The title of his article was *The Ketamine Model of the Near-Death Experience: A Central Role for the N-Methyl-D-Aspartate Receptor* (Jansen, 1997). In his article, and in his follow-up response (Jansen, 1997) to the commentaries of others, Jansen argued that his Ketamine theory might explain NDEs and eliminate the need to ascribe NDEs to some spiritual out-of-body event. Most of his respondents were favorably impressed with Jansen's work. Then, just before publication of the *Journal,* Jansen forwarded a postscript which was added as the last note in the publication. A portion of his postscript is as follows:

> I am no longer as opposed to spiritual explanation of near-death phenomena as my article and this response to the commentaries on it would appear to suggest. . . .
>
> My forthcoming book *Ketamine* will consider mystical issues from quite a different perspective, and will give a much stronger voice to those who see drugs as just another door to a space, and not as actually producing that space. After 12 years of studying ketamine, I now believe that there most definitely is a soul that is independent of experience. It exists when we begin, and may persist when we end. Ketamine is a door to a place we cannot normally get to; it is definitely not evidence that such a place does not exist.

Dr. Jansen wrote his book, *Ketamine: Dreams and Realities,* and it was published in 2001. In that book he included a chapter titled: *The Metaphysical Mental Modem.* And he wrote this about Ketamine (Jansen, 2001, pp. 146, 164):

> Ketamine may be one of the substances that "re-tunes" the brain to allow awareness to enter "the quantum sea." The theory suggests that we consider reports of personal experiences of "eternity," "Infinity," and multiple universes in a new light. Perhaps we should not immediately reject an "impossible" theory after a century of the "impossible" being published in the best

physics journals. . . . One day, we may have to regard some of the reports of eternity, infinity, multiple universes, linkage with other beings, and so on, as phenomena demanding a sophisticated explanation rather than an easy dismissal as hallucinations and drug-induced psychosis, requiring no further thought.

Expansion of Research Beyond the United States

One of the goals of the IANDS organization, as explained by Kenneth Ring, was to expand the research beyond the United States. Initially, that expansion took place in Europe and Australia. The research effort followed an evolutionary path similar to that in the U.S., although it proceeded somewhat faster since it had the early research base from the United States to draw upon.

Early work by Evelyn Valerino, from Switzerland, was reported in her book, *On the Other Side of Life* (Valerino, 1984). That was followed by Cherie Sutherland, from Australia, with three books: *Transformed by the Light, Within the Light,* and *Children of the Light* (Sutherland, 1992, 1993, 1995).

Peter and Elizabeth Fenwick of England investigated over 300 near-death experiences and reported the results of their study in the book, *The Truth in the Light,* (Fenwick, 1995). As with preceding work in the United States by Kenneth Ring, Bruce Greyson, Craig Lundahl, Harold Widdison and others, the Fenwicks sought and found certain patterns or events in the NDEs which appeared to repeat themselves in a variety of experiences. The Light, for example, was a common element in most of the NDEs they studied. They also found "dark" or hellish NDEs amongst some of those who had gone through these experiences.

More recent work of importance includes the prospective study by Pim Van Lommel and several medical colleagues of ten Dutch hospitals over a period of four years (see discussion in next chapter). This was a significant study of cardiac patients and had an impact in the United States as well as Europe (Van Lommel, 2001 and 2003).

Mark Fox, a lecturer at the Joseph Chamberlain College in Birmingham, England, wrote an excellent book on his studies of the NDE phenomena. His book, entitled: *Religion, Spirituality and the Near-Death Experience,* takes the bold step of challenging different religions to compare and document their belief systems with the rich body of writings on NDEs. As noted in chapter 17, this book is a partial response to Mark Fox's challenge—even though it was well under way when I read Mark Fox's book and challenge (Fox, 2003, pp. 357–358). Other religions would do well to read Fox's book and follow through with his suggestion. Again, as with Pim Van Lommel's work, Mark Fox's effort has ricocheted from Europe to the U.S.

Research in Other Cultures

One of the first questions to arise from the growing body of NDE studies in the U.S. and in other Western countries was what of those from different cultures—particularly with a different religious background than the Christian ethic which predominates in the Western world? Do they report an abundance of NDE-type of events such as those reported in the West? Are there voluminous detailed studies such as those reported in the IANDS publication *Journal of Near-Death Studies?*

The answer is not yet. The cross-cultural work on NDEs is still in its infancy. Of course, there are, and have been for centuries, a rich tradition of religious writings from the Hindu master Patanjali, the students of Buddha and of the Bardo Thödol from the *Tibetan Book of the Dead.* Valarino, in her interviews with Ring and Dutheil for her book, *On the Other Side of Life,* reports their responses concerning these works.

> **From Ring:** There are many commonalities between what *The Tibetan Book of the Dead* and what the experiencers say happens at the moment of death. But this book, of course, goes on to talk about the various *bardos* and the various stages that people go through, which usually culminate in the process of rebirth. The NDE doesn't deal with these issues. So, there are similarities, because they both talk about the transition into death. But there is no information from the standpoint of the NDE about what happens afterward (Valarino, 1984, p. 99).

> **From Valarino to Dutheil:** Wherever we look, we find the notion of "light," which seems to be of primary importance in understanding the mystery of life. The Bible says that in the beginning there was light and the light was good. The Bardo Thödol, or *Tibetan Book of the Dead,* talks about how, for three and a half days after death, deceased persons are surrounded by a bright light, and how they must recognize this light in order to be released from the cycle of rebirth. (Valarino, 1984, p. 215)

Kundalini: The entire issue of the Spring, 1994, edition of the *Journal of Near-Death Studies* was devoted to the subject of *Kundalini.*

In the "Editor's Foreword," Bruce Greyson wrote this:

> In Eastern spiritual traditions, the biological mechanism of both individual enlightenment and evolution of the species toward higher consciousness is called kundalini, a force that can be activated under certain conditions to strengthen or purify an individual's life energy, producing a variety of mental, emotional, physical, and spiritual effects. Despite kundalini's apparent incomprehensibility in terms of Western scientific and medical paradigms, the concept has captured the interest of a significant minority of Western clinicians and researchers since Carl Jung organized a conference on the topic in 1932.

Included in that issue of the *Journal* is an article, *Kundalini and the Near-Death Experience*, by Gene Kieffer, President of the Kundalini Research Foundation. Kieffer was the person most responsible for making Gopi Krishna's works available to the Western World (Kieffer, 1994, pp. 159–176). Kieffer described, in the abstract to his article, Kundalini in this way:

> While many now believe that the near-death experience can, in some cases activate kundalini, there is still little understanding of what is meant by the arousal of this power. The awakening of kundalini actually means the reversal of the activity of the reproductive system and the activation of another chamber in the brain, which, if all goes well, can lead to enlightenment or illumination, the next stage of human evolution. One objective proof of this phenomenon is urdhava-retas, the upward flow of the sexual energy.
>
> The vast majority of the scientific community has rejected the entire concept of Kundalini. Although the same may be said—to a certain extent—about other aspects of the NDE, the Kundalini rejection is virtually complete throughout all scientific disciplines in the Western world.

An Israeli NDE

A fascinating NDE was detailed by Henry Abramovitch for the Spring 1988 edition of the *Journal of Near-Death Studies* (Abramovitch, 1988, pp. 175–184). Dr. Abramovitch, from the Sackler School of Medicine, Tel Aviv University in Israel, translated the story of **Chaim Ralbag** from Hebrew. Ralbag was originally from an ultra-orthodox community in Simon, Israel. As a youth, he was exposed to an influential text in Jewish mysticism which includes an account of the death and separation of the soul of Adam, the First Man. Another part of the orthodox tradition which Ralbag knew of, according to Abramovitch, was that "when a man's soul leaves him, it is met by all his relatives and companions from the other world, who guide it to the realm of delight and the place of torture." The soul from the dying person thus goes, after a seven-day period, to a place of peace and beauty, or pain and punishment—dependent upon the sins of the deceased.

Although raised with that religious background, Ralbag, at the time of his NDE, had lapsed into a less formal observance of orthodox Judaism. Nevertheless, his past exposure to those traditions apparently played a role in how he saw and explained his NDE. He was not aware of the Western literature describing NDEs.

His basic NDE was caused by a heart attack. The account, itself, is remarkably rich in those elements defined by Ring and others as to the constituent parts of a "typical" NDE. Representative samples from Abramovitch's paper are given below:

> As I continued to sink, the darkness around me thickened. Fear took hold of me! I was aware that the speed of my fall was accelerating. . . . But all around me was only the void. . . . I knew in another moment the impact would come. With a broken heart, I cried out, "From the depths I call to you o Lord" (Psalm 130).
>
> The echo of my cry had hardly died away when I felt the force of my fall becoming slower. The fall turned into a soft gentle landing, until I was left hanging in the dark void. . . . The darkness became less dense, its colors lighter and lighter until light returned. . . . In the same moment, I noticed that someone was lying there on the floor in a contorted position. I stopped to look at him. I was astonished and bewildered, for I knew him. . . . He was none other than myself. . . .
>
> Suddenly I realized that I was not alone. Many like me began to appear, becoming more numerous minute by minute until there was no counting them. They were all in motion, ever taking on new forms, expanding, revolving, and contracting, in their movement, merging and penetrating, passing and affecting one another. . . .
>
> I was surprised by the brilliance of a light that had no source. . . . The sound, no less than the light, amazed me. An infinity of tones mixing together in their varied and independent movement, streaming in a powerful current through vast expanse, upwards. I was light. I felt good. . . . I decided to ask the one nearest me the way there [to the light]. Through thinking

alone we understood each other. He explained to me there is no "up" or "down." There is no space and no time—no dimension and no measuring. . . .

I noticed again my hands and feet, and became like my former "self." . . . As I approached the hill, I noticed somebody was standing on the peak. . . . It was my father. A few paces behind him stood my brother, silent, smiling and looking at the two of us.

This extraordinary account, as explained by Abramovitch, illustrates particular orthodox Jewish cultural and religious influences (particularly for those skilled in the knowledge of orthodox Judaism), as well as many of the rudiments of a "deep" NDE.

Jewish Views of the Afterlife

Beverly Brodsky reviewed the book, *Jewish Views of the Afterlife*, by Simcha Paul Raphael in the Summer 1998 edition of *Journal of Near-Death Studies*. Brodsky pointed out that this is a massive (474 pages) scholarly book of Jewish thought. She notes that the book illustrates how modern Judaism differs significantly from that of previous generations. She puts it this way:

Most modern Jews are alienated from a traditional understanding of the nature of God, humankind's purpose, and life's destiny. A Gallup poll taken in 1965 . . . showed that only 17 percent of American Jews believed in life after death, compared with 78 percent of Protestants and 83 percent of Catholics. (Brodsky, 1998, p. 278)

Brodsky describes from the book, *"The Zohar* (1956), a primary Kabbalistic text, provides a clear description of the dying process and postmortem destiny of the soul. This book, only partially translated into English as of this writing, is a major source of information about the afterlife." She goes on to explain that it is virtually unknown by modern followers of Judaism. Also, it provides insight into the NDE process with the textual descriptions of how, for example, the dying person meets with family ancestral guides and Adam. She says this about the NDE (Brodsky, 1998, p. 279):

We see, then, correspondences to many elements in near-death literature: visions of the departed, a dark tunnel-like entrance, angels, a being of light, and the life review. The mystical literature reveals the feelings accompanying the journey, which are those of great joy and ecstasy at these reunions and welcome by divine beings, or of horror and pain over "sins" or errors in one's conduct during life.

Native American NDEs in North America

In the Winter, 2003, edition of the *Journal of Near-Death Studies,* Dr. Jenny Wade presents eleven historical near-death type experiences for Native Americans from North American tribes. The stories were recorded by early explorers. The stories necessarily reflect the cultures and biases of the recorders as well as those of the Native Americans. Wade wrote of these accounts (Wade, 2003, p. 101):

> What can be said about this handful of accounts spanning almost four centuries, most of a continent, and at least six different cultures? They share a number of features that are associated with the NDE markers common in industrialized countries and across multicultural studies. However, since these narratives were not gathered with the aid of today's protocols, certain areas of comparison are difficult to determine.

Wade did find some correspondence with other NDEs. Illustrative examples are (Wade, 2003, pp. 105–106):

> The radiant illumination of the spirit world appeared in over half the reports, though not in the pronounced way it does in contemporary accounts. Light was not said to glow from the natural features of the landscape, but to form a general brilliance that illuminated everything the way a celestial body does, though no source for the light was ever mentioned. . . .
>
> Most narrators specifically mentioned seeing the dead, usually meeting predeceased relatives, especially parents, but often other individuals known to them or comparative strangers. . . . These spirit beings were evidently easily recognizable so they must have closely resembled what they looked like in life.

Native American Records in Central America

To my knowledge, the literature does not include studies of NDEs among the indigenous peoples of Central and South America. What does appear to be the case—which is significantly different from the Native American situation in North America—is that there is an abundance of early records of the legends and history of these peoples. It is far beyond the scope of this book to do other than briefly mention some of the records and to touch on their substance.

Don Fernando de Alva Ixtlilxochitl was a native prince who lived near Mexico City. He was descended from the pre-Conquest rulers of Texcoco and he spoke Aztec. His history of Mexico is the earliest and most important after European contact, incorporating as it does earlier historical sources (Yorgason, Warren, Brown, 1999, pp. 11–12). His manuscripts were completed in Spanish around A.D. 1600 to A.D. 1625, after which they found their way to the Jesuit College Library of San Pedro y San Pablo in the Valley of Mexico.

The earliest known history of Guatemala is the *Títulos de Totonicapán* account written by the sixteen Lords of Totonicapán in 1554. Father Dionisio Jose Chonay translated the book from the Maya tongue into Spanish in 1834 (Yorgason, Warren, Brown, 1999, p. 42). The location of the original Totonicapán document was unknown for more than four hundred years. Then, in 1973, Robert M. Carmack, an ethnohistorian from Albany University, described how he discovered the documents in the pre-Hispanic settlement of Totonicapán. The indigenous people became his friends and, in a dramatic episode, disclosed the long-hidden leather-bound book written in the original Quiché language. They allowed Carmack to photocopy it (Yorgason, Warren, Brown, 1999, pp. 45–46). The document has since been translated into English.

The Quiché-Maya was the most powerful nation of the Guatemalan highlands in immediate preconquest times and was a branch of the Ancient Maya. With the Quiché-Maya there was the tradition of a "sacred" book, the *Popol Vuh*. Before the conquest they painted the *Popul Vuh* in hieroglyphics. It was first transcribed in the Quiché language about A.D. 1554 to A.D. 1558 by highly literate Quiché-Maya natives. It was translated into Spanish by Fray Francisco Ximénez about A.D. 1702 and has since been translated into English by Dennis Tedlock (Yorgason, Warren, Brown, 1999, pp. 48–49).

Held in common by all of these legend-histories is an accounting of the origin of the earth and cosmos, and of the subsequent branching of the ancient groups who peopled this land. Of particular emphasis is the story of the fair god of ancient Mexico and central America, *Quetzalcoatl*. This fair god was depicted symbolically on Codex and temples hieroglyphically as a feathered serpent. Some of the glyphs— such as those found at Chiapa de Corzo, Chiapas, Mexico—date to the fifth century B.C. (Yorgason, Warren, Brown, 1999, p. 134).

There are several variants to the Quetzalcoatl story. One of the more interesting ones is of a Man-God who was born about 1 B.C. Juan de Cordoba, a Spanish friar in Oaxaca, recorded an account just a few years after the coming of Cortes. A portion of the account is as follows (Yorgason, Warren, Brown, 1999, pp. 139–140):

> On the day we call Tecpatl a great light came from the northeastern sky. It glowed for four days in the sky, then lowered itself to the rock; the rock can still be seen at Tenochtitlan de Valle in Oaxaca. From the light there came a great, very powerful being, who stood on the very top of the rock and glowed like the sun in the sky. There he stood for all to see, shining day and night. Then he spoke, his voice was like thunder, booming across the valley. Our old men and women, the astronomers and astrologists, could understand him and he could understand them. He told us how to pray and fixed for us days of fast and days of feasting. He then balanced the "Book of Days" and left vowing that he would always watch down upon us his beloved people.

Although not an NDE as such experiences are usually defined, this account is remarkably similar to some NDE descriptions of the "Light" and of a "Being of Light." This story, at the time that Cortes conquered Mexico, was deeply embedded in the culture and religion of the indigenous peoples. They looked forward to Quetzalcoatl's return with power. Indeed, when Emperor Moctezuma (more popularly spelled Montezuma) heard about Cortes, a white bearded man with much power, he said: "This truly is the Quetzalcoatl we expected, he who lived with us of old in Tula" (Yorgason, Warren, Brown, 1999, p. 141).

Cortes quickly disabused the Aztecs of their confusion. He executed six thousand of them in Cholula alone.

Corroborative NDEs and Prospective Studies

Researchers next began to look for "veridical" or "corroborative" experiences—especially those where there was an out-of-body experience (OBE). A number of these kinds of situations were found, some quite spectacular, where the patient was incapacitated and could not have seen or known what was happening to his or her body. Later, the patient described the entire experience in detail—with corroboration from medical personnel and/or other witnesses. Perhaps the most famous is Kimberly Clark Sharp's account of Maria, who in her NDE saw a "tennis shoe on the ledge" (Sharp, 1995, pp. 7–14), and the most spectacular is Michael Sabom's description of Pam Reynolds who was "flatlined" on both heart and brain during a brain operation (Sabom, 1998, pp. 37–51). Sabom's account of Pam Reynolds is discussed in more detail in chapter 9.

Researchers in recent years have also begun to tackle the problem of prospective NDE research. As one would expect with a field in which events are characterized by their random and unexpected nature, anything prospective—planned for the future—is extremely difficult.

It isn't as if you could readily approach a seriously ill patient who hopes to recover with the words: "We're trying our best to make you well, Joe, but . . . That is, in case you do feel yourself dying, could you please notice the special TV screen up near the ceiling. It is out of your view as long as you are in your body, but if you do leave—I mean to say, if your essence, or spirit, or consciousness, or whatever . . . if it leaves your body, please notice the special pictures that are showing there. And, oh yes, Joe . . . I know this is hard—but if you do manage to come back, could you let the nurse know so that she can record what you remember. Try hard to remember what you saw and heard. Thanks Joe, and . . . good luck."

Despite the difficulties, this type of prospective study by Jan Holden and Bruce Greyson has been implemented. They are, of course conscious of the needs and sensitivities of the patients, so the conversation illustrated above will never take place.

More is written in chapter 10 about these prospective studies. They are very persuasive in their ability to affect medical opinion about the reality of NDEs.

This, then, is a summary of some of the research work associated with the NDE phenomenon. This cursory examination gives only a partial view of the range and scope of the work which has been, and now is, being carried out. It also shows how the work has evolved from the early days.

10: Significant Happenings in NDE Research: People, Events, and Ideas

What Is Important?

This chapter examines those events and findings that have had and will continue to have the most important impact on NDE research. The list reflects the enthusiasm of the author for particular issues when compared to others of less importance. Other researchers may create a list which emphasizes dissimilar events and findings from mine. However, since I *am* the author I reserve the right to select what I think is important. So, if you disagree with me, write a contrary book.

Raymond Moody

Any tabulation of what is important in NDE research must recognize the contribution of Raymond Moody. Because of his position as a serious scientist—a Ph.D. from the University of Virginia and an M.D. from the Medical College of Georgia—his writings and research could not be easily dismissed by other scientists. So when he wrote his bestselling book, *Life After Life*, it rapidly gained the attention of many other scientists as well as the general public (Moody, 1975). It became the impetus for a reconsideration of some of the most serious questions which religion and science had been wrestling with for centuries. Principal among those questions was, "Does human consciousness survive death?" This book seeks to shed some light on that question.

IANDS

Aside from Raymond Moody's book, *Life After Life*, the formation of the International Association for Near-Death Studies (IANDS) organization was undoubtedly the most important event concerning NDE research. Because of its importance, I sought information from someone who took part in its founding. Kenneth Ring graciously responded. His recollection of how and why IANDS was formed follows (Ring, personal communication):

In 1980, a friend of mine and a friend of Raymond Moody named John Audette was running, pretty much single-handedly, a precursor to IANDS that was officially founded in 1978 in St. Louis and was called The Association for the Scientific Study of Near-Death Phenomena. Audette was a sociologist, and it was he who helped bring a bunch of us would-be NDE researchers together with Raymond Moody for the first time in November, 1977. (Included in that group were Bruce Greyson and Mike Sabom.) In any case, by 1980, John said he wanted to be released from his administrative obligations in order to conduct an NDE research project in Peoria, where he then lived. In December of that year, he came to Storrs to ask me if I would be willing to take over ASSNDP (as we then called it) for a year so he could do his research. I agreed, but only with several conditions, which were these:

I wanted to rename the organization, and proposed its current name, The International Association for Near-Death Studies (i.e., IANDS).

I insisted on establishing a scholarly journal, which John proposed calling Anabiosis, which had been the name he used for the newsletter that ASSNDP had been publishing about three times a year.

I also wanted to establish a quarterly newsletter for members, which we decided to call Vital Signs.

I wanted to develop IANDS as a membership organization, and I also wanted to see it promote the scientific study of NDEs and encourage the involvement of scholars and other professionals in NDE studies.

Finally, I agreed to do all this only for one year. After that, John was to take over as Executive Director, and I was to return to my regular work as a professor.

John agreed to all these conditions, and together with Bruce Greyson, who was still at the University of Michigan then, the three of us became the co-founders of IANDS. This was in late

December, 1980, although the organization was incorporated as a 501.C.3 organization only on Feb. 19, 1981. That latter date should, therefore, be given as the official date of its establishment at the University of Connecticut, where it was based for years.

In any case, after John left, I assembled a group of student volunteers and some graduate students, and we were off and running. I was the first editor of *The Journal*, and edited three issues (it was published semi-annually then) before turning it over (for keeps, as it turned out), to Bruce Greyson. I also was the editor of the quarterly newsletter, *Vital Signs*. (A graduate student in English, and a good friend of mine, named Steve Straight was the associate editor of each of these periodicals.) I assumed the title of President, and pretty much ran everything like a dictator for a while, even though we eventually assembled a board of directors and an advisory board as well.

John was unable to follow through on his promise to take over the organization, so we had to search for an Executive Director to take his place. That's when Nancy Bush came into the IANDS scene and office. I resigned the presidency after that first year, and Bruce Greyson took over. At a later date I served as president for another year, and Bruce, meanwhile, had agreed to edit the journal. My own formal involvement with IANDS ceased in 1983.

Finally, as to the motivations involved, I can only speak for those of us who spearheaded this organization. There were five of us: John, Bruce, Mike Sabom, Raymond (whose role was largely honorary) and myself. All of us were, as a whole, generally concerned with promoting disinterested research into NDEs, furthering the professional development of the field of near-death studies (a term that I had proposed at a professional conference held at UCONN in 1981), and having an organization that would be helpful to people who had had NDEs as well as informative for those who were interested in the subject. We also hoped—and eventually succeeded—to stimulate interest in NDEs in other countries, which was one of the reasons we used the adjective, International, in naming our organization.

The Journal of Near-Death Studies

As noted above, the *Journal of Near-Death Studies* was spawned during the formation of IANDS. Ken Ring was the first editor, followed by Bruce Greyson in about 1982. It became a major factor in providing a professional outlet for much of the burgeoning NDE research.

Bruce Greyson, who is a Professor of Psychiatry at the University of Virginia, is still its editor. Much of the success of the Journal is due to the Herculean effort of Bruce.

Human Consciousness Beyond Death

NDE research has been struggling since its inception—after the formation of IANDS—over whether or not human consciousness survives death. Early research (Greyson, 1979) was marked by exhaustive attempts to explain the events in an NDE as a psychological or physiological phenomenon (Lundahl and Gibson, Spring 2000). As the research has advanced, a purely physical or psychological rationale has become increasingly improbable.

Interestingly, the arguments pro and con have cast the professionals of various branches of science as adversaries. A good example of this type of disputation was evidenced in the work of Pim van Lommel and colleagues who did a prospective study of patients who were resuscitated in coronary care units of ten Dutch hospitals during the period 1988 to 1992. The survivors were first interviewed within days of their experience, then again two and eight years later. 62 of 344 patients interviewed reported NDEs (Van Lommel, Van Wees, Meyers and Elfferich, 2001).

In an article entitled, "Demon Haunted Brain," in *Scientific American,* Michael Shermer, the writer of the column "Skeptic," claimed that the study by Van Lommel "delivered a blow" to the idea that the mind and the brain could separate (Shermer, 2003). Yet the researchers argued the exact opposite, and showed that conscious experience outside the body took place during a period of clinical death when the brain was flatlined.

Pim van Lommel wrote a detailed rebuttal to the article by Shermer and sent it to *Scientific American.* His rebuttal was not published by *Scientific American,* but it was picked up on the Internet and published by others. One of the sites where it was published was "Skeptical Investigations," under the title: *A Reply to Shermer: Medical Evidence for NDEs* (Van Lommel, 2003). A few selections from Van Lommel's rebuttal are reproduced:

> Only recently someone showed me the "Skeptic" article by Michael Shermer. From a well respected and, in my opinion, scientific journal like the *Scientific American* I always expect a well documented and scientific article, and I don't know how thoroughly peer-reviewed the article from Shermer was by the

editorial staff before publication. My reaction to this article by Shermer is because I am the main author of the study published in *The Lancet,* December 2001, entitled: "Near-death experience in survivors of cardiac arrest; a prospective study in the Netherlands." About what he writes about the conclusions from our study, as well as from the effect of magnetic and electrical "stimulation" of the brain, forces me to write this paper, because I disagree with his theories as well as with his conclusions. . . . There are several theories that should explain the cause and content of NDE. The physiologic explanation: the NDE is experienced as a result of anoxia in the brain, possibly also caused by release of endomorphines, or NMDA receptor blockade.

In our study all patients had a cardiac arrest, they were clinically dead, unconscious, caused by insufficient blood supply to the brain because of inadequate blood circulation, breathing, or both. If in this situation CPR is not started within 5–10 minutes, irreparable damage is done to the brain and the patient will die. According to this theory, all patients in our study should have had an NDE, they all were clinical dead due to anoxia of the brain caused by inadequate blood circulation to the brain, but only 18% reported NDE.

The psychological explanation: NDE is caused by fear of death. But in our study only a very small percentage of patients said they had been afraid the seconds preceding the cardiac arrest, it happened too suddenly to realize what occurred to them. However, 18 % of the patients reported NDE. And also the given medication made no difference. . . .

So we need a functioning brain to receive our consciousness into our waking consciousness. And as soon as the function of brain has been lost, like in clinical death or in brain death, with iso-electricity on the EEG, memories and consciousness do still exist, but the reception ability is lost. People can experience their consciousness outside their body, with the possibility of perception out and above their body, with identity, and with heightened awareness, attention, well-structured thought processes, memories and emotions. And they also can experience their consciousness in a dimension where past, present and future exist at the same moment, without time and space, and can be experienced as soon as attention has been directed to it (life review and preview), and even sometimes they come in contact with the "fields of consciousness" of deceased relatives. And later they can experience their conscious return into their body. . . .

To quote Michael Shermer: it is the job of science to solve

those puzzles with natural, rather than supernatural, explanations.

But one has to be aware of the progress of science, and to study recent literature, to know what is going on in current science. For me science is asking questions with an open mind, and not being afraid to reconsider widely accepted but scientifically not proven concepts like the concept that consciousness and memories are a product of the brain. But also we should realize that we need a functioning brain to receive our consciousness into our waking consciousness. There are still a lot of mysteries to solve, but one has not to talk about paranormal, supernatural or pseudoscience to look for scientific answers on the intriguing relation between consciousness and memories with the brain.

Physicist-Scientists vs. Physician-Scientists

Michael Shermer is a science writer who produces a regular column, "Skeptic," for *Scientific American*. As such, he and the editor-publisher and readers of the magazine tend to reject theories which are outside of a materialistic view of science.

The abbreviated dialogue described above is an excellent example of how—in recent years—many scientists stumble over some of the paradoxes of materialistic science. On the other hand, physician-scientists such as Pim van Lommel, by necessity of their profession, are thrust into realms of science which hitherto have been foreign. Consequently, they are acknowledging, and in many cases embracing, a new line of science brought about by the NDE.

It can be expected that future NDE research will reach into areas of science previously unknown or ignored. Some in the scientific community will applaud this new and exciting thought-adventure. Others will hunker down in their mind-prisons, hoping that the new intrusions will vaporize in some unknown singularity.

As a matter of interest, it has been my pleasure and privilege to become acquainted with, and in some cases close friends with, many involved in NDE research. To an individual, I have yet to find one who does not believe that human consciousness survives death. In some instances—as with Ken Ring—that belief required rethinking and overturning a previously skeptical view of consciousness survival.

Personal Interviews

Development and evolution of NDE research accelerated in large part due to the personal interviews carried out by investigators—especially those seeking discernable patterns in the experiences. By means of these interviews, and their personal nature, spiritual windows were opened on a realm previously obscured by scientific and social astigmatism. Barriers of ignorance and bias melted when faced with a plethora of heart-moving stories which appeared in the public press. Often the recounted experiences were so compelling in their sincere appeal that they literally demanded attention from both a skeptical scientific audience and an enthralled public. **Stephanie LaRue** had an experience which illustrates this point. Portions of our interview follow (Gibson, 1992, pp. 114–19):

"All of a sudden, within the blink of an eye, I left my body. It was so fast and so natural. I wasn't afraid—of course I didn't know that this was death."

"How did you know that you had left your body?" I asked.

"I turned around and saw myself in the bed."

"What did you look like?"

"I remember saying: 'That's not the real me,' and I pointed at the hospital bed. 'This is the real me; that's only a shell,' and I pointed back, again, at the hospital bed."

"Could you see your husband?"

"I could see my husband, and I could see myself. . . .

"About this time I had an experience that I'll never forget. It was an experience of complete tranquility, peacefulness, wholeness—whatever the word wholeness means; like mind, body, and soul. Also a feeling of total, total knowledge without asking.

"It's like you and me sitting here, now, and wondering how far the universe expands, or . . . just questions we have on earth about the geography of the earth, craters, or anything. This feeling I had of total knowledge was just that, I knew everything without asking. It was an incredible feeling.

"I turned around and looked at my body again, and I knew why I was there; I didn't have to ask. The only way I can relate to it is to observe that I was more alive in that realm than I am talking to you, here, now. Another way to relate to it is . . . like you and I are more awake now than when we are asleep at night. That's how much more aware I was in the other realm."

" . . . When I left my body I was encompassed with a higher power. It felt like complete wholeness, tranquility, peacefulness, . . ."

"Love?"

"Oh definitely love, definitely. It . . . there are no words in the English language to describe it. It's more than love; the word love is just the tip of the iceberg, so to speak."

"When you had that feeling, did you have any understanding about where the feeling was coming from, or what was driving it?"

"It was everything. It was an accumulation of everything that ever lived—like the trees, the flowers, every human being, animals, anything that lives or breathes, a blade of grass. It was a totality of everything. Also, when I came back into my body I knew that everything had its place, its purpose, and there was a reason for everything. Even poor children that die of cancer at a young age, somebody's life that is taken; everything has a reason. But you don't *know* that until you are on the other side."

". . .Do you feel that the experience was truly out-of-body, and that it was a real experience and not a dream or a hallucination?"

"I'd bet my life on it."

These kinds of first-hand stories, and the consequent patterns which gradually became evident to conscientious investigators, did much to advance the knowledge base of NDEs. And that effort continues to this day, particularly with regard to specialized efforts such as premortal studies and prospective investigations.

Unique Personal Accounts

Of at least equal importance to the first-hand interviews, there have been several in-depth experiences where the individuals who had the NDEs wrote complete books about their epiphanies. There are seven such stories which are my favorites. In each instance they provided new insight as to the meaning and reality of the NDE. The list of my choices and why they are my favorites, follows:

George Ritchie (Ritchie, 1978). George has to be first in this category. His book, *Return from Tomorrow*, followed shortly after Raymond Moody's book, *Life After Life*, and helped immensely in educating the public and scientific world to the NDE phenomenon. It was aided by the fact that George Ritchie was a respected M.D. and Psychiatrist who could not be easily dismissed by the scientific world.

His book introduced a number of new concepts to the world, including: a spirit separating from the physical body, the spirit traveling long distances at astonishing speeds, the spirit attempting but unable to grab a physical object, witnessing other unhappy spirits who attempted to enter another person's body, and a heavenly realm with glowing buildings and places of learning.

Howard Storm (Storm, 2000). Howard's experience is one of the more profound NDEs that I have been exposed to. Because of the experience, Howard changed from a hedonistic and atheistic professor of art to a pastor in the United Church of Christ. During his experience, Howard was attacked by evil spirits in the horrible beginning of his NDE. Crying desperately for Christ to save him, Howard was saved by angelic friends and by Jesus Christ. He described the agony and bliss which accompanied his "life's review." Of special importance was his ability to seek answers from his angelic friends about many of the questions which have plagued humans since the beginnings of early philosophic thought.

Ranelle Wallace (Wallace, 1994). Ranelle's crash in an airplane and subsequent NDE was unique, not only because of her NDE, but in the miraculous way that she and her husband escaped from the burning plane, and in their subsequent hike off the snowy mountain to safety.

Elane Durham (Durham, 1998). Elane's in-depth NDE provided much insight about the profundity of life in another realm. In addition, Elane included the descriptive account of the Priest who gave her Last Rites, thus providing some corroboration for her story.

Angie Fenimore (Fenimore, 1995). Angie's story was helpful because it not only illustrated the dual nature—frightening followed by ecstatic—characteristic of some NDEs, but it also provided an in-depth view of a less-than-positive episode during the NDE.

Cherie Sutherland (Sutherland, 1993, 1995). Sociologist Sutherland's work is important because, among other reasons, it illustrates how citizens of Australia react to NDEs. Both of her books are enlightening in that regard. She, like Ring (and Gibson) interviewed numerous people to get first-hand stories.

Phyllis Atwater. Phyllis had multiple NDEs. There were what appeared to be bizarre effects in at least one of them. As she was in the midst of this particular NDE she described what happened in this manner (Atwater, 1998, p. 46):

> Further movement on my part ceased because of what happened next. Before me there loomed two gigantic, impossible huge masses spinning at great speed, looking for all the world like cyclones. One was inverted over the other, forming an hourglass shape, but where the spouts should have touched

there was instead incredible rays of power shooting out in all directions. . . . The cyclone was crammed full of people and I had the feeling of seeing all life. The same phenomenon was happening to each and all. Past, present, and future were not separated, but, instead, interpenetrated like a multiple hologram combined with its own reflection.

When I first read this account, I feared that it was just a bad dream by Phyllis. Then I remembered the interview I had with **Forrest Hansen.** A portion of our interview follows (Gibson, 1992, pp. 76–77):

The imagery of the experience was in a blank area, just blackness. I became aware of a point of light, and the blank area was cut in half by a plane that this point of light was on. The plane looked sort of like a piece of glass, only it didn't seem to be solid. The next image, as this image grew, was the sight of two cone shapes that emanated from either side of the point of light. The apexes of the cones were located at the light and their two axes were congruent and perpendicular to the plane. The cones appeared to be constructed of light particles. . . .

. . . It occurred to me that this was more of a symbolic image than I had thought at first. The cones were . . . I knew that if I were to move forward or backward in time there was only a certain distance that I could travel within a particular instance of time. This was the construction of the cone, similar to a graph. That is, if I were to move forward one second, the farthest I could move would be this distance. The cone seemed to represent the outside perimeter of the set of experiences I could have—not necessarily that I could experience everything in the cone, but that was the limit.

The complete accounting of Forrest's experience shows even more similarities to Phyllis's experience than is evident from this brief extract. Neither Phyllis nor Forrest knew the other party, nor were they aware of the similarities of their experiences. I later told them both about those similarities.

Specialized Studies

Mindsight. The premortal birth studies by Sarah Hinze, and other aspects of a premortal life by Harold Widdison, have been discussed in chapter 3. There are a number of specialized studies which illuminate a particular aspect of the NDE. Some of these have contributed significantly to a better understanding of the how and why of these spiritual events. One of the most important studies was that carried out by Kenneth Ring on blind people who underwent NDEs (Ring and Cooper, 1999). In this investigation, Ring and Cooper interviewed and collected data on individuals with varying degrees of blindness. Also, they sought and obtained some veridical (corroborative) out-of-body experiences (OBE) of blind persons where separate verification could be made.

Ring wrote this about his findings of NDEs in the blind (Ring and Cooper, 1999, p. 186):

> What the blind experience is perhaps in some ways more astonishing even than the claim that they can see. Instead, they—like sighted persons who have had similar episodes—may have transcended brain-based consciousness altogether and, if that is so, their experiences will of necessity beggar all description or convenient labels. For these we need a new language altogether, as we need new theories from a new kind of science even to begin to comprehend them. Toward this end, the study of paradoxical and utterly anomalous experiences plays a vital role in furnishing the theorists of today the data they need to fashion the science of the twenty-first century. And that science of consciousness, like the new millennium itself, is surely already on the horizon.

Vicki Umipeg was one of the blind people in Ring's study. As a premature baby, Vicki was blind since birth due to the administration of too much oxygen. At age twenty-two she was in a serious automobile accident which precipitated her NDE. To provide a feel for the transcendent experience she had, which "beggars all description or convenient labels," a portion of her interview with Ring and Cooper follows (Ring and Cooper, 1999, pp. 25, 26):

> I knew it was me . . . I was pretty thin then. . . . And I recognized at first that it was a body, but I didn't even know that it was mine initially. Then I perceived that I was up on the ceiling, and I thought, "Well, that's kind of weird. What am I doing up here?" I thought, "Well this must be me. Am I dead? . . ." I just briefly saw this body, and . . . I knew that it was mine because I wasn't in mine. Then I was just away from it. It was that quick. . . .
> Everybody there was made of light. And I was made of light. What the light conveyed was love. There was love everywhere. It was like love came from the grass, love came from the birds, love came from the trees. . . .
> I had a feeling like I knew everything . . . and like everything

made sense. I just knew that this was where . . . this place was where I would find the answers to all the questions about life, and about the planets, and about God, and about everything.

NDEs in Children. Melvin Morse, a Seattle pediatrician, was the first to document large numbers of children who had NDEs. They first came to his attention as his patients when they described what had happened to them during a serious injury or illness. This specialized area of research is important for a number of reasons, not the least of which is the innocence that children bring to the investigator. They have not yet learned the lessons of adulthood where ego, pride and prejudice can obscure the message.

Morse had this to say about what he learned from a decade of near-death research on children (Morse, 1990, pp. 168–69):

> And how has a decade of near-death research affected me and the way I approach medicine? It has changed everything in my life, including my views on medicine, the way I see society, and even the way I deal with my family.
>
> When I began my studies eight years ago, I was in mainstream medicine. I laughingly referred to myself as a "rodent brain surgeon" who researched the effects of radiation therapy on a child's brain.
>
> I undertook near-death studies as a sideline to an already busy schedule. I was fascinated by the subject, but always felt that we would demonstrate that a particular drug or disease process was responsible for this phenomenon. When I accepted Dr. Raymond Moody's challenge to study NDEs scientifically, I felt certain that science would explain them.
>
> All these years later, I accept what the ancients knew: all men must die and death is not to be feared. There is a Light that we will all experience after death, and that Light represents joy, peace, and unconditional love.
>
> These children have taught me that we each have the ability to experience the Light and that the Light teaches us that we are each important in our own way.

One of Morse's early cases of a child who had an NDE was **Katie.** She was a nine-year old child who had fallen into a swimming pool and suffered what appeared to be non-recoverable physical damage. She shocked Moody with her later description of watching him and others of the medical team treat her—while she was in a coma. She was able to correctly describe many of the details of a highly technical resuscitation effort. Even more shocking, though, was her description of what else she saw while she was in the coma. A portion of Morse's interview of Katie follows (Morse, 1990, pp. 6–8).

> She accurately described many other details of her experience. I remember being amazed at the events she recollected. Even though her eyes had been closed and she had been profoundly comatose during the entire experience, she still "saw" what was going on.
>
> I asked her an open-ended question:
>
> **"What do you remember about being in the swimming pool?"**
>
> "Do you mean when I visited Heavenly Father?"
>
> **Whoa, I thought. "That's a good place to start. Tell me about meeting the Heavenly Father."**
>
> "I met Jesus and the Heavenly Father," she said. Maybe it was the shocked look on my face or maybe it was shyness. But that was it for the day. . . .
>
> What she told me during our next meeting changed my life. . . . Her first memory was of darkness and the feeling that she was so heavy she couldn't move. Then a tunnel opened and through that tunnel came "Elizabeth."
>
> Elizabeth was "tall and nice" with bright, golden hair. She accompanied Katie up the tunnel, where she saw her late grandfather and met several other people. Among her "new friends" were two young boys—"souls waiting to be born"—named Andy and Mark, who played with her and introduced her to many people. . . .
>
> Finally, Elizabeth—who seemed to be a guardian angel to Katie—took her to meet the Heavenly Father and Jesus. Heavenly Father asked if she wanted to go home. Katie cried. She said she wanted to stay with him. Then Jesus asked her if she wanted to see her mother again. "Yes," she replied. Then she awoke.

Frightening or Unpleasant NDEs. In general, accounts of unpleasant NDEs are less frequent than the euphoric ones. There are a number of reasons that have been advanced as explaining this difference, but they are mostly speculations. One speculation is that people are reluctant to tell the frightening stories because of the assumed negative connotation concerning cause and effect. Another supposition is that the mind blanks out the unpleasant memories.

Those who made a particular effort to find and analyze LTP experiences included the physician of internal medicine, Barbara Rommer (recently deceased), the cardiologist Maurice Rawlings (Rawlings, 1979), and Phyllis Atwater (Atwater, 1992).

Barbara Rommer advanced three possible reasons for, as she put it, "less than positive" (LTP) experiences (Rommer, 2000, p. 30): "First, it may occur in order to challenge the person to stop, look back, and reevaluate all previous choices, actions, reactions, thoughts, and words, in order to make midcourse changes in direction. Second, an LTP experience may occur if the experiencer has a Less-Than-Positive, less than loving, or fearful mindset just immediately prior to the event. Third, if one grows up with negative programming expecting hell fire and brimstone, then that is what he or she projects to the cosmos and that is what he or she will be given to experience" (Rommer, 2000, p. 26). Whatever the reason for them, there have been several studies of LTP experiences.

Rommer actually categorized LTP experiences into different types or categories. In her book, *Blessing in Disguise,* she gave several examples of the different types. A portion of one of the more frightening experiences is reproduced below (Rommer, 2000, pp. 78–79). It is similar to a couple of cases I interviewed.

Sadira, whom Rommer interviewed, was a nurse who attempted suicide by an overdose. In her words:

> I didn't care if I woke up or not. I didn't know why I was so depressed, but it was saying: "God, I'm putting it in your hands." . . .
>
> What I saw was the most hideous, horrible thing! This was no nightmare! . . . There were people screaming. It was unearthly voices, not earthly. It was horrible!
>
> These things were all over me and they were screaming. I think I was naked there, because I remember feeling very ashamed. Everything was dark. I couldn't tell where the screaming was coming from. Then I actually saw these things, like horrible human beings, like anorexics. Their teeth were all ugly and twisted. The eyes were bulging. They were bald, no hair, and weren't wearing anything. . . . There must have been at least fifty, everywhere, all around me. They were grabbing at my arms and my hair, and were screaming, pitiful screams, but not saying words. It was the type of moaning and screaming that you hear in a cancer ward, God forbid. . . .
>
> I felt judged. I felt that was my punishment. Those beings were there to punish me, but they didn't physically hurt me because I don't recall feeling pain. I just remember the pure terror! Then, slowly, the screaming started to get further away. It's like they were moving into another room to torture someone else.
>
> Naturally, as Catholics, we're taught that we aren't to take

our own lives, because that means you've lost faith in God. I can tell you this: there is no way I will ever think of attempting suicide again, or ever take that attitude. It was just so horrific! I went to hell!

An earlier effort than that of Rommer was that of Bruce Greyson and Nancy Evans Bush. They, too, identified different categories of what they called *Distressing Near-Death Experiences* (Greyson and Bush, 1992). Greyson and Bush used fewer categories than Rommer; they chose three types: the first being similar in features to the peaceful NDE, but interpreted by the experiencer as terrifying; the second involving a paradoxical experience of nothingness or of existing in a featureless void; and the third which includes "hellish" images (such as Sadira, above).

Although I did not make a special effort to find LTP or distressing experiences, in the process of interviewing different individuals who had NDEs, I did run across several who descended into a less-than-positive arena of the after-life. In point of fact, I interviewed individuals in at least three of the categories defined by Rommer or Greyson and Bush. Liz Clark's experience (chapter 8) was similar to one of Rommer's categories where it starts out LTP, but changes to ecstatic as it progresses.

Karen, who attempted suicide was an example of Greyson and Bush's second category. A brief portion of her experience follows (Gibson, 1993, pp. 133–34):

> During this period I became aware that I was conscious, but I was enveloped in total darkness. It was pitch-black all around, yet there was a feeling of movement. My conscious self assured me that I was in the form of a spiritual body.
>
> A male voice spoke to me, a different voice than the one I heard a week before. This voice said: "You have a choice. You can stay here, or you can go back. If you stay here, your punishment will be just as it is, right now. You will not have a body, you will not be able to see, touch, or have other sensations. You will only have this darkness and your thoughts, for eternity."
>
> Terrified because of the experience, and because of what I had heard, I understood that this would be my private hell. There would be no contact with other life or with the sensations of life, for eternity. Yet I would remain conscious with my thoughts in total blackness.
>
> Frantically scared, I knew immediately that I had made a terrible mistake. Telling the voice that I had made a mistake, I asked to go back, to return to life. The voice said, "All right, you may return."
>
> Suddenly I felt myself being pulled back. It's hard to explain.

There was total darkness, yet I had the feeling of movement as I was pulled back.

Next, I found myself in the hospital room, in an elevated position, looking down. I could see the doctor, I could see my roommate, I could see my body in the bed. My roommate was crying, and the doctor was explaining something to her. It was clear that they thought I was gone.

While I was watching this scene, I felt myself slowly descending. Then, suddenly, I was sucked into my body. It was fast.

Probably the most clear example of Greyson's and Bush's third category that I interviewed was that of Dee (chapter 15). Another case of this type, but somewhat different, was documented by Greyson and Bush. A portion of it follows (Greyson and Bush, 1992, p. 105). The individual had attempted suicide by hanging himself.

From the roof of the utility shed in my back yard, I jumped to the ground. Luckily for me, I had forgot the broken lawn chair that lay near the shed. My feet hit the chair and broke my fall, or my neck would have been broken. I hung in the rope and strangled. I was outside my physical body. I saw my body hanging in the rope: it looked awful. I was terrified, could see and hear, but it was different—hard to explain. Demons were all around me; I could hear them but could not see them. They chattered like blackbirds. It was as if they knew they had me, and had all eternity to drag me down into hell, to torment me. It would have been the worst kind of hell, trapped hopeless between two worlds, wandering lost and confused for all eternity.

I had to get back into my body. Oh, my God, I needed help. I ran to the house, went in through the door without opening it, cried out to my wife but she could not hear me, so I went right into her body. I could see and hear with her eyes and ears. Then I made contact, heard her say, "Oh, my God!"

Corroborative NDEs

These are experiences where the individual apparently left the body and saw or heard other mortals performing some act which could not have been physically witnessed by the one having the NDE. Later, upon recovery, the person having had the out-of-body experience is able to describe in detail what he or she saw and heard to the mortals who had performed the acts witnessed by the patient.

Corroborative experiences are especially useful in demonstrating the reality of NDEs because there seems to be no other way to explain them except as an out-of-body occurrence in some other dimension or spiritual reality. There have been a number of useful studies on corroborative NDEs, including my own (Gibson, 1999, pp. 72–82), but the most dramatic example was that of **Pam Reynolds,** described by Michael Sabom (Sabom, 1998, pp. 37–57).

Pam was thirty-five years old when she was operated on for a giant basilar artery aneurysm. The artery had ballooned out at the base of her brain and, if it burst, would result in immediate death. The operation, pioneered by Dr. Robert Spetzler, Director of Barrow Neurological Institute in Phoenix Arizona, required that Pam's body temperature be lowered to 60 degrees, her heartbeat and breathing stopped, her brain waves flattened, and the blood drained from her head. Clinically, she would be dead during the period of the operation.

The operation itself was highly technical and involved nine medical personal in the operating room—each with critical functions to take care of. A portion of Pam's NDE is reproduced as she described it:

> The next thing I recall was the sound: It was a natural D. As I listened to the sound, I felt it was pulling me out of the top of my head. The further out of my body I got, the more clear the tone became. I had the impression it was like a road, a frequency that you go on. . . . I remember seeing several things in the operating room when I was looking down. It was the most aware that I think I have been in my entire life. . . . I was metaphorically sitting on Dr. Spetzler's shoulder. It was not like normal vision. It was brighter and more focused and clearer than normal vision. . . . There was so much in the operating room that I didn't recognize, and so many people.
>
> . . . The saw thing that I hated the sound of looked like an electric toothbrush and it had a dent in it, a groove at the top where the saw appeared to go into the handle, but it didn't. . . . I heard the saw crank up. . . . It was humming at a relatively high pitch and then all of a sudden it went *Brrrrrrrr!* like that.
>
> They had cut into Pam's skull and removed the bone flap. The outermost membrane of her brain was exposed. In order to feed blood into the bypass machine, the left femoral artery and vein were prepared for use. "Someone said something about my veins and arteries being too small. I believe it was a female voice . . ."
>
> The operation reached the point where they tilted the operating table up, and drained the blood from Pam's body.

There was a sensation like being pulled, but not against your will. I was going on my own accord because I wanted to go. . . . The feeling was like going up in an elevator real fast. And there was a sensation, but it wasn't a bodily, physical sensation. It was like a tunnel but it wasn't a tunnel.

At some point very early in the tunnel vortex I became aware of my grandmother calling me. But I didn't hear her call me with my ears. . . . It was clearer hearing than with my ears. . . .

The light was incredibly bright, like sitting in the middle of a lightbulb.

Pam went on to explain how she met and was guided by her grandmother in the midst of an intensely bright light. She was guided back to her body, which "looked terrible, like a train wreck," and she was told how to reenter it.

The entire experience, as told by Pam and as reported by Dr. Sabom, is fascinating! It describes the medical emergency which developed during the operation from the perspective of both Pam and the doctors. Later, Pam was able to describe for the medical team the details of what she had seen of the operation. The details agreed remarkably with the real events as they were lived by Doctor Spetzler and his team. You are encouraged to read the complete story in Sabom's book, *Light and Death*. After you have read it, ask yourself the question: "Is there any other explanation which fits the facts other than that Pam's spiritual being was outside of her body observing the operation?"

Prospective Studies

Pim van Lommel's prospective study from the ten Netherland hospitals has already been discussed. It is likely that future NDE research will employ this technique with increasing frequency. Although the process is time-consuming, and requires careful preparation and monitoring, it can accelerate the path to Omega (see chapter 17), while at the same time improving acceptance in the scientific community.

A recently initiated study at the University of Virginia is a case in point. The study is being carried out by Bruce Greyson, M.D., and J. Paul Mounsey, M.B.B.Ch. (University of Virginia), and by Janice M. Holden, Ed.D. (University of North Texas). Bruce Greyson provided the author with this abstract of the work:

Persons reporting NDEs sometimes describe a sense of

having been out of their bodies and observing their surroundings from a visual perspective outside of and above their bodies. These out-of-body perceptions during NDEs, if accurate, may provide important information about the nature of mind/brain relationships. Research into accurate out-of-body perceptions during NDEs has been hindered by the unpredictable occurrence of these experiences, and the lack of control by investigators over the conditions at the time of the NDE.

Advances in cardiac electrophysiology now offer a unique opportunity to study these phenomena. Patients with potentially fatal cardiac illness may now have "implantable cardioverters/defibrillators" (ICDs) surgically implanted in their chests. These ICDs are electrical devices that monitor the patient's heartbeat and, if the patient should experience a cardiac arrest, the ICD would automatically detect the problem and administer an electrical shock to return the heart to normal rhythm. When these ICDs are implanted in a patient's chest, the cardiac electrophysiologist must induce a cardiac arrest under closely monitored conditions, in order to test the ICD's sensitivity and effectiveness. This induced cardiac arrest exposes the patient to the opportunity to experience an NDE under controlled circumstances.

In this study, we are investigating the accuracy of out-of-body perceptions during NDEs that occur during these induced cardiac arrests. A computer in the operating room displays randomly-selected unusual visual targets so that they are visible only from above eye level, from a visual perspective looking down upon the body of the unconscious patient. In interviews with patients before and after implantation of the ICD, we are determining the incidence of NDEs during induced cardiac arrest, and attempting to obtain evidence that patients who report NDEs can report accurate observations from an out-of-body perspective. We are also collecting data at 6-month follow-up interviews to assess the influence of such NDEs on patients' subsequent psychological and physiological outcome.

NDE vs. Non-NDE Study in a Hospital Environment

During a six-month period beginning in November 1998 and ending in May 1999, medical scientist Richard J. Bonenfant obtained information—via written questionnaires—from 56 clinical death survivors who did or did not claim to have had NDEs. Forty of the survivors (71 percent) claimed to have had NDEs while 16 persons had no memory of what happened during their emergency. The data were obtained from five health care units in New York State, including St. Peter's Hospital (Bonenfant, Spring 2004, pp. 155–94).

Bonenfant found that some of the events normally thought to be unique to those who had NDEs also were found among the non-NDE participants. However, those who claimed to have undergone NDEs were significantly more likely to report spiritual and paranormal after-effects than those in the non-NDE group.

Comparison of Bonenfant's Findings with Data from Gibson

As a part of Bonenfant's study, he developed a table showing the percentage of the NDE group which had experienced various elements often found in NDE cases. In my own research I developed a similar, though much abridged, table for the sixty-eight NDE individuals I interviewed. For comparative purposes, data from Bonenfant's study and from my earlier study (Gibson, 1993, pp. 312–15) are given below. Bonenfant's table has been condensed from his study.

Percent of NDErs Reporting NDE Elements

		Bonefont	*Gibson*
NDE Element	*N*	*%*	*%*
Feeling quiet, peaceful, secure	27	68	46
Being drawn to a bright light	24	60	60
Sensing the presence of others	21	53	55
Being in presence of being of light	21	53	
Deity for Gibson	27		
Feeling unconditionally loved	19	48	47
Transcends space and time	17	43	50
Out-of-body and seeing yourself	13	33	53
Being escorted by friendly beings	13	33	40
Seeing your life pass in review	10	25	11
Meeting deceased relatives & friends	10	25	28
Being in beautiful landscape	5	13	21
Hearing beautiful singing or music	5	13	10
Being terrified or fearful	4	10	12
Seeing buildings or cities of light	2	5	7

The fascinating aspect of this table is that the techniques for gathering the data were so dissimilar, yet the results were so close. Bonenfant, in his questionnaire, asked the participants specific questions about the different NDE elements. I did not.

In general, I interviewed each participant in as open-ended a manner as possible. Each individual was encouraged to give background material relative to his upbringing, then to tell, in as much detail as possible, his experiences. Several examples of how this was done are illustrated in various chapters of this book. Their stories were recorded, then later typed for inclusion in the book. Later, still, I made a list similar to that shown, and reviewed the details of each story to determine whether or not they included the particular element under consideration.

One other difference between Bonenfant and myself was that I determined, for several participants, that they had more than one NDE. Thus, although I interviewed 68 people, there were a total of 83 NDEs or analogous epiphanies. The percentages shown for Gibson were calculated using this total number of NDEs, rather than the total number of people.

As with Bonenfant, I included certain demographic data on each individual. In my case I determined the religion of the individuals, their ages at the time of interview and at the time of the first experience, their education, and whether they were male or female. Although I did not perform a formal statistical analysis, as did Bonenfant, there did not appear to be any significant differences in the NDEs based on these particular parameters. There did, however, seem to be a loose cause-and-effect relationship between those who had frightening (or less than pleasant) NDEs and those who did not.

The RERC Study

In the previous chapter I mentioned Mark Fox and his work. As noted there, he is a lecturer in philosophy and religious studies at Joseph Chamberlain College in Birmingham, England. In his excellent book, *Religion, Spirituality and the Near-Death Experience*, he discusses a study which came out of the archives of the Religious Experience Research Centre (RERC) at Manchester College in Oxford (now housed at University of Wales). He drew upon 6,000 accounts of religious experiences: conversion testimonies, descriptions of encounters with numinous presences, feelings of supernatural fear and horror, descriptions of answered prayers, encounters with unusual lights and many others. Fox and his fellow researchers found 91 experiences which included some of the elements originally identified by Moody, as well as other models later advanced by other NDE researchers.

Because of the difficulty of getting a clear definition of what constitutes an NDE, Fox used the terms, *Crisis Experience* (CE), and *non-Crisis Experience* (non-CE). The CE was used for subjects who had been clinically dead (as opposed to biologically dead), near death, or in some other crisis condition where there had been a threat to life, but the peak had apparently passed. Non-CE was used to describe those subjects where there was no life-threatening crisis, yet there was a range of NDE-type elements present.

Fox identified 32 CE accounts, which he analyzed; 52 non-CE accounts were also studied. The methods used were very similar to those used by Duane Crowther in his examination of a multitude of LDS religious experiences, as reported in his book, *Life Everlasting* (see chapter 2).

One conclusion that came from Fox's study—as in Crowther's study, and my own research studies, for that matter—was that there are numerous NDE elements which repeatedly occur in other types of epiphanies than an NDE. Fox said this about them:

> . . . Perhaps it is safer in future studies . . . to abandon the use of the term "near-death experience" altogether as a descriptor for a class of experiences involving the recurrence of certain key elements such as out-of-body experiences, episodes of darkness, meetings with deceased relatives and encounters with benign and comforting lights. As we have seen, such experiences can occur in a rich range of contexts, including walking, resting, meditation and simple sleep, in which the subject is seemingly in no physical danger at all. (Fox, 2003, pp. 325–26; see also Nancy Bush's comments in chapter 9 under *NDE—A Misnomer*)

In the Bonenfant-Gibson table shown above, there is no discrimination that would relate to Fox's CE and his non-CE accounts for Gibson's subjects. Since Bonenfant's data came from patients in a hospital environment who had survived some medical emergency, his data would correspond closely with the CE subjects of Fox. My data would include both those in the CE category and in the non-CE category. Since Fox's data is scattered throughout his book, I did not take the time to include it in the table. For those who wish to accomplish that chore, I encourage you to get his book and extract the information.

David B. Haight's Experience

On July 31, 2004, David B. Haight of the Quorum of Twelve Apostles of The Church of Jesus Christ of Latter-day Saints died, at age ninety-seven. He had been a member of the Quorum of the Twelve since 1976. He was the oldest of the Apostles and a marvelous and accomplished man of God—one with a special witness of the mission of the Savior. He bore testimony of that witness with power and reverence.

During World War II David Haight was a commander in the United States Navy. He received a special citation from Admiral Nimitz for his service.

In the early 1950s, David Haight was the mayor of Palo Alto, California where my wife and I lived. He was also a much respected businessman in the community. He was our Stake President, and he called me to be an Elders Quorum President when we moved to Sunnyvale, California. He and his wife, Ruby, and their children were a delightful family.

In the spring of 1988 Elder Haight had a serious operation. While recovering from that medical procedure, he was beset with terrible pain. His ordeal and the results of what he saw, felt and heard during that period were described by him in the October, 1989 Conference of the Church (Haight, 1989). His account is summarized here.

In his talk, Elder Haight described how, during the health crisis that he was going through, the pain was extreme. He prayed for his Heavenly Father to help him while his wife called the doctor. He heard the siren of the paramedic truck as he lost consciousness.

Then, he said, suddenly he was aware that all pain was gone and he found himself in a calm, peaceful setting, on a hillside. He could see two persons in the distance. He was conscious of being in a holy presence and atmosphere. He said that it was impressed on his mind, again and again, the eternal mission and exalted position of the Son of Man.

During his NDE, Elder Haight said he was shown a panoramic view of Christ's earthly ministry: His baptism, His teaching, His healing the sick and the lame, the mock trial, His crucifixion, His resurrection and ascension. Elder Haight also saw, in impressive detail, scenes of the Savior's earthly mission—confirming scriptural and eyewitness accounts.

Of the last supper, Elder Haight said: "It was so impressively portrayed to me—the overwhelming love of the Savior for each. I witnessed His thoughtful concern for significant details—the washing of the dusty feet of each Apostle, His breaking and blessing of the loaf of dark bread and blessing of the wine, then His dreadful disclosure that one would betray Him."

Elder Haight also saw the scourging of the Savior, his struggle with the cross, and the crucifixion itself. He was shown many other events associated with the betrayal, the crucifixion and the resurrection.

Finally, in his talk, Elder Haight gave powerful witness of the mission of the Savior. He said the experience gave him a more perfect knowledge of Christ's mission.

Elder Haight's NDE is of particular importance to Latter-day Saints because of his calling in the Church. The Apostles in the modern-day church, like those in the time of Peter, Paul and others of the ancient church, have a unique calling to witness that Jesus is the Christ, the son of the Living God. As Mark expressed it (Mark 8:27–30):

> And Jesus went out, and is disciples, into the towns of Caesarea Philippi: and by the way he asked his disciples, saying unto them, Whom do men say that I am?
>
> And he answered, John the Baptist: but some *say,* Elias; and others, One of the prophets.
>
> And he saith unto them, But whom say ye that I am? And Peter answereth and saith unto him, Thou art the Christ.
>
> And he charged them that they should tell no man of him.

This is an interesting passage since Christ first asked his followers who others thought he was, and then who *they* thought he was. When Peter correctly identified him as the Christ, he then instructed them not to tell others. This is because he was still early in his mission and needed time for its fulfillment before the controversy over whether he was the son of God or not be allowed to develop. He did, however, want the disciples—some of whom were to become his Apostles—to commit themselves to the knowledge that he was the Christ.

Later, after his resurrection, Christ appeared to the Twelve and spoke to Peter in this manner (John 21:15–17):

> This is now the third time that Jesus shewed himself to his disciples, after that he was risen from the dead.
>
> So when they had dined, Jesus saith to Simon Peter, Simon, *son* of Jonas, lovest thou me more than these? He saith unto

him, Yea, Lord; thou knowest that I love thee. He saith unto him, Feed my lambs.

He saith to him again the second time, Simon, *son* of Jonas, lovest thou me? He saith unto him, Yea, Lord; thou knowest that I love thee. He saith unto him, Feed my sheep.

He saith unto him the third time, Simon, *son* of Jonas, lovest thou me? Peter was grieved because he said unto him the third time, Lovest thou me? And he said unto him, Lord, thou knowest all things; thou knowest that I love thee. Jesus saith unto him, Feed my sheep.

Here, after his earthly mission was complete, Christ was instructing his Apostles how to carry on. Of utmost importance was that they continue to preach the good news of the Gospel to all of His sheep—which included all people in the then known world. And primary of all the messages to be delivered by the Apostles was that Jesus was the Christ, the Messiah, and was in absolute truth the divine son of God and the only offspring of our Heavenly Father born of the flesh; that He had drunk the bitter cup and atoned for all human sins, thus making possible the salvation of all who would repent and accept Him as Savior; that He was the first fruit of the resurrection, and that through Him, all who ever lived on this earth would be resurrected.

According to Mormon theology, that same message was delivered by the resurrected Christ to the Nephites who were followers of Christ on this, the American continent, at the time of His resurrection. Their story is told in the Book of Mormon.

In summary, David Haight's NDE, in which he was privileged to see many of the events in Christ's life, was significant to the LDS community. Like the Book of Mormon, itself, it was another witness that Jesus was who he claimed to be. And, like Peter of old, the Twelve of today continue to testify of that primal truth.

Part III

The Impact of NDEs on LDS Professionals

I can still remember the feeling I had in 1989 after reading Raymond Moody's book Life after Life *(1975). I had been raised in a conservative Mormon family and had been taught and believed the reality of life after life, as well as a premortal existence. My belief was based more on faith rather than others' experiences. Moody's book opened in me a forgotten sense of eternity that seemed to rush into me as if it had been waiting for the invite. The near-death experiences of others triggered in me past feelings of sorrows and failures, but the life reviews gave me comfort and support for my future goals and spiritual journey. The feelings of hope have not dissipated but linger as a loving friend, pressing in me a longing for more. Reading NDEs over the past 15 years has continued to swell in me a drive to better understand myself, a thirst to comprehend my spiritual environment, and a desire to be more open and caring toward others.*

—B. Grant Bishop, M.D.
(Chapter 11)

11: The Nature of God and Man

By B. Grant Bishop, M.D.

About the Author

B. Grant Bishop is a clinical professor of dermatology in the Department of Dermatology, University of Utah, School of Medicine. His first love is teaching. He has had a lifetime interest in Mormon history and doctrine, and in the spirit of the gospel of Jesus Christ. He took a year off during his medical training to teach at Brigham Young University in the Department of Religious Instruction.

In addition to his interests in medicine and religion, Dr. Bishop has had a fascination with near-death experiences. He has studied them thoroughly, both from a scientific viewpoint and from a more spiritual perspective. He is the author of the book, *The LDS Gospel of Light* (Bishop, 1998).

The Impact of NDEs on the Author

I can still remember the feeling I had in 1989 after reading Raymond Moody's book *Life after Life* (1975). I had been raised in a conservative Mormon family and had been taught and believed the reality of life after life, as well as a premortal existence. My belief was based more on faith rather than others' experiences. Moody's book opened in me a forgotten sense of eternity that seemed to rush into me as if it had been waiting for the invitation. The near-death experiences of others triggered in me past feelings of sorrows and failures, but the life reviews gave me comfort and support for my future goals and spiritual journey. The feelings of hope have not dissipated but linger as a loving friend, pressing in me a longing for more. Reading NDEs over the past 15 years has continued to swell in me a drive to better understand myself, a thirst to comprehend my spiritual environment, and a desire to be more open and caring toward others.

Nagging Questions

There have also been little gifts of insights into questions I have pondered. For example, while I was teaching theology at BYU in the early seventies the question came up in one of my classes, "If Christ was speaking to Nephi the day before he was born into the world (3 Nephi 1:9–15), how could his spirit be in his unborn body? And when does the spirit enter the body if not at quickening (16 weeks into gestation), and when does 'life' begin?" I could not answer the questions of how Christ seemed to be in two places at the same time or when the spirit enters the body, so I let the questions settle among all the other questions I wondered about.

Then, in the early nineties, I read the account of the NDE of a woman who viewed her prelife, including the conception and the development of her body. She was shown how she had the choice of when she would occupy her body. She was allowed to visit her future unborn body whenever she wanted, trying it on as she would a new set of clothing. What a wonderful experience! I had always thought in terms of one possibility—"life" began at quickening when I thought the spirit entered the body permanently, separating only at death. But maybe we had the choice to remain with our unborn body early after conception or to just get acquainted with our future self until we felt comfortable in staying, perhaps not even joining our body until the day before birth.

Beverly Brodsky—An In-Depth NDE

In 1970 Beverly Brodsky had a beautiful NDE after she was injured in a motorcycle accident. Profound insights were revealed to her about God, knowledge, suffering, light, time and space. Because of her Jewish background, she asked about the suffering of her people. She was told that there was a reason for everything that happens, no matter how horrible it appears in the physical world. She writes:

> [As] I was given the answers, my own awakening mind . . . responded, "Of course," I would think, "I already know that. How could I ever have forgotten!" . . . All that happens is for a purpose, and that purpose is already known to our eternal self.
>
> In time the questions ceased because I suddenly was filled with all the Being's wisdom. I was given more than just the answers to my questions; all knowledge unfolded to me, like the instant blooming of an infinite number of flowers all at once. I was filled with God's knowledge, and in that precious aspect of his Beingness, I was one with him. But my journey was just beginning.
>
> Now I was treated to an extraordinary voyage through the universe. Instantly we traveled to the center of stars being born, supernovas exploding, and many other glorious celestial events for which I have no name. The impression I have now of this trip is that it felt like the universe is all one grand object, woven from the same fabric. Space and time are illusions that hold us to our plane; out there all is present simultaneously. I was a passenger on a divine spaceship in which the Creator showed me the fullness and beauty of all his Creations. (Ring, 1998, p. 298)

A Different Realm of Time and Space

Beverly's NDE is not unique, not only do near-death experiencers feel time and space are suspended when in the presence of a being of light, they feel they are one with God, knowing all and having all things present before them. Compare Beverly's experience with the epiphany of Moses (described in the Book of Moses in the Pearl of Great Price) when God's glory came upon him and God told Moses: "I will show thee the workmanship of mine hands . . . [and] no man can behold all my works, except he behold all my glory." God then tells Moses that "all things are present with me, for I know them all." Moses then "beheld the world upon which he was created . . . and the ends thereof, and all the children of men which are, and which were created

229

... and there was not a particle of [the world] which he did not behold, discerning it by the spirit of God. And he beheld also the inhabitants thereof, and there was not a soul which he beheld not; and he discerned them by the Spirit of God; and their numbers were great, even numberless as the sand upon the sea shore" (Moses 1:4–6, 27–28).

One thing I realize from Moses' version and from Beverly's NDE is that God is in a dimension that I am not familiar with, a dimension without time and space, and occasionally he allows others to come into that dimension. But even more important to me is that God invited an ordinary person, like Beverly, to be a "passenger [on his] Divine spaceship." The prophets, like Moses, have always seemed beyond me, having revelations and understanding I felt I would never have. But NDEs like Beverly's brings the experiences of prophets down to my level. God does give his love and knowledge to all, even regular, struggling people.

Andy Petro's NDE

NDEs lift my spirit and teach me by touching my soul. They open a window into my own existence and help me remember that I am interconnected to the entire cosmos, just as Beverly described. Andy Petro also felt a universal connection to the cosmos during his NDE:

> Everything is going on at once, all around me . . . left, right, up, down . . . wherever I look I see my life. I can not only see it, but I can also hear, feel and experience every event [of] my life . . . past, present and future. There is no beginning! There is no end! I can see all the moments of my life all at the same time, all around me. Strange, there is no fear or judgment, it's just my life experiences as they are occurring. What incredible feelings. I can feel each and every thought, word and action all at once . . . I am in the Light! Oh, God, I am actually in the Light. I am the Light! . . . The light says, 'Andy, do not be afraid. Everything is OK.' Then the Light says, 'Andy, I love you.' . . . I am in the Light. The Light is in me. I can see me in the unending Light. But I am still 'Andy.' I'm everywhere and I am here, I can see me as a person and I can see me in the infinite, warm and loving Light. I become the Light. . . . I'm home! I feel the unbelievable warmth, love, joy and completeness of the Light! . . . I'm truly home! (Petro, Fall 97, p. 6)

A Paradox of Truth

Andy's experience seems to be compatible with what Christ told Joseph Smith: "The day shall come when you shall comprehend even

God, being quickened in him and by him. Then shall ye know that ye have seen me, that I am and that I am the true light that is in you, and that you are in me; otherwise ye could not abound" (D&C 88:49–50) Andy said, "I am in the Light. The Light is in me." Was he "quickened" by the Light and thus allowed to "comprehend even God"? It is edifying to think that through a NDE someone might have bathed in the same beautiful spirit Christ told Joseph Smith would help him comprehend and know God.

Petro's NDE is absolutely amazing! He seems to have experienced a paradox of truth, being everywhere and somewhere at the same time by having the light of God come upon him. This interconnectedness of God and man being in each other appears to teach a strange reality—truth is paradoxical, being in one place and every place at the same moment. That would support a reality of time and eternity existing simultaneously, not separately as either time or eternity. I had always thought of these two concepts as either/or. Either one is in place and time as a human, or every place and eternal as God. I had never considered that being in the glory of God meant that one could be both somewhere and everywhere at the same moment. However, both scripture and science support a reality of truth being interconnected, and a mysterious duality.

The Nature of Christ and God

God and Christ as glorified men appeared before Joseph Smith, and Joseph taught, in the famous King Follett funeral sermon that, "God himself was once as we are now . . . an exalted man" (*Teachings of the Prophet Joseph Smith*, King Follett sermon, pp. 345–47).

By contrast, Joseph was taught that Christ was, . . . in all and through all things, the light of truth; Which truth shineth. This is the light of Christ. As also he is in the sun, and the light of the sun, and the power thereof by which it was made. As also he is in the moon, and is the light of the moon, and the power thereof by which it was made; As also the light of the stars, and the power thereof by which they were made. . . . And the light which shineth, which giveth you light, is through him who enlighteneth your eyes, which is the same light that quickeneth your understanding. Which light proceedeth forth from the presence of God to fill the immensity of space—The light which is in all things, which giveth life to all things, which is the law by which all things are governed, even the power of God who sitteth upon his throne who is in the bosom of eternity, who is in the midst of all things, (D&C 88:6–13).

These scriptures teach that God has a dual nature of being somewhere and everywhere at the same time. John said, "God is light," (1 John 1:5) and God told Moses, "no man can behold all my works, except he behold all my glory" (Moses 1:5). Do people who come into the presence of beings of light comprehend God's glory and thus comprehend his works just as the prophets? Scriptures on God's light and glory, the science of light, and NDEs all support a duality of nature.

Prophets who have seen God describe him in terms of light and/or glory. The D&C states, "The glory of God is intelligence or, in other words, light and truth." In Paul's vision, he describes "a great light round about" (Acts 22:6). Steven saw "the glory of God," (Acts 7:55) and Joseph Smith, "saw a pillar of light . . . [containing] two personages, whose brightness and glory defy all description" (Joseph Smith–History 1:16–17). On another occasion, Joseph saw God and stated, "[H]is countenance shone above the brightness of the sun" (D&C 110:3). Joseph also saw the celestial kingdom and described its light in terms of blazing fire and glory. He saw the "transcendent beauty of the gates . . . like unto circling flames of fire; also the blazing throne of God, whereon was seated the Father and the Son" (Joseph Smith, 1946).

Universality of the Light

Just as light is central to prophetic visions of heavenly beings, light in some form is universal in NDEs. People who have NDEs describe seeing beings of light and even whole cities of light. George Ritchie recalled that during his NDE, Christ's light "continued to increase in intensity until it seemed to be equal to a million welders' light. I knew if I had been seeing through my human eyes instead of my spiritual body I would have been blinded" (Ritchie, 1991, p. 16).

One woman said of her NDE:

> . . . I became aware of the most powerful, radiant light, brilliant white light. It totally absorbed my consciousness. It shone through this glorious scene like the sun rising on the horizon through the veil which had suddenly opened. This magnificent light seemed to be pouring through a brilliant crystal. It seemed to radiate from the very center of consciousness I was in and to shine out in every direction through the infinite expanses of

the universe. . . . Even though the light seemed thousands and
thousands of times stronger than the brightest sunlight, it did
not bother my eyes. My only desire was to have more and more
of it and bathe in it forever. (Ring, 1984, p. 66)

The light people see during NDEs seems to be indescribable.
During her NDE one woman stated, "When I was embraced, I felt
warmth that was a feeling of love. . . . It was like that was all the love
there was, everything. It was like . . . I can't explain the feeling. It's
beyond words" (Gibson, 1992, p. 300).

Compare this description of light and love being "beyond words"
to the way the Nephites described their experience after Christ's visit.
After Christ prayed for the Nephites, the Book of Mormon says that
"the things he prayed cannot be written." It is not that they should not
be written, but that the things heard and seen were beyond words to
express. The scriptures go on to say, "The eye hath never seen neither
hath the ear heard, before, so great and marvelous things as we saw and
heard Jesus speak unto the Father; and no tongue can speak, neither
can there be written by any man, neither can the heart of men conceive
so great and marvelous things as we both saw and heard Jesus speak"
(3 Nephi 17:15–17).

The Nephites then had a vision where their children were being
tended by angels descending in the glory of God. "They saw the heavens
open, and they saw angels descending out of heaven as it were in the
midst of fire; and [angels] came down and encircled those little ones
about and they were encircled about with fire; and did minister unto
them" (3 Nephi 17:24–25).

I do not think John was writing metaphorically when he wrote,
"God is light," (I John 1:5) any more than I think it is a metaphor to
say that Jesus Christ is the Savior of the world. If God is literally light,
light would be His love, His glory, His omniscience, His omnipotence
and His omnipresence. Joseph Smith taught, "[T]hat which is of God
is light; and he that receiveth light and continueth in God, receiveth
more light; and that light groweth brighter and brighter until the
perfect day" (D&C 50:24).

The Characteristics of Light

Scriptures reveal that the light of God is a spectrum which includes
life and law. Christ is "the light which is in all things, which [gives]

life to all things, which is the law by which all things are governed, even the power of God" (D&C 88:13). God's light is the judgment by which we live. (Moroni 7:18) Light is truth, spirit and the word (D&C 84:45, 46). Light is knowledge, understanding, and the everlasting gospel (D&C 77:4, 88:11, 45:9; 2 Corinthians 4:6). Light is the power of God which is in all things (D&C 88:33), and includes mercy, compassion (D&C 88:40), and love (1 John 4:8).

The exciting thing for me is that scriptures and NDEs both support what we know about the nature of physical light. Light has a paradoxical dual nature and is expressed as a spectrum. There is an interconnectedness between subatomic particles and the fabric of the universe.

The spectrum of physical light is called the electromagnetic spectrum and includes both visual and non-visual light. All electromagnetic energy acts as if it were a wave, similar to the waves of the ocean, having crests and troughs. The length of the wave is measured from the top of one crest to the top of the next crest. The difference in wavelength creates different expressions of the electromagnetic energy.

In the range of visual electromagnetic light energy, the only difference between colors of light is the length of their waves. Likewise, the only difference between visual light and non-visual light is the length of their waves. Just outside the visual spectrum of light there are infrared waves too long for us to see, and ultraviolet light waves too short for us to see. The spectrum is continuous and infinite in both directions. It includes gamma waves and X-rays on the short side, and radio, shortwave radio and microwaves on the long side. The only thing that is different about them is their wavelength. The length of the wave determines the amount of energy produced, with the shorter waves having the greater energy. The ends of the electromagnetic spectrum are open, meaning scientists have discovered only a portion of the energy on the spectrum.

God's Light

Could it be that the energy of God's light also fits on the electromagnetic spectrum, or more accurately, is the electromagnetic spectrum a small part of the light spectrum of God? God told Joseph Smith that Christ is "in all and through all things, the light of truth" (D&C 88:6), including the physical light of the sun, stars and moon. To make it very clear what was meant, God further explained, "the light which shineth, which giveth you light, is through Him who enlighteneth your eyes, *which is the same light that quickeneth your understanding*" (D&C 88:11, italics added). This scripture says to me that the light that hits my eyeball is the same light that pierces my heart. They are variations of the same thing: the warmth that comes from the light of the sun is just a form of the loving warmth that comes from holding another person; the energy produced by an electric power plant is only a variation of the spiritual energy given and received in a priesthood blessing; the lighting of a beautiful city is but a visual expression of the compassionate light felt when a loved one is grieving; all the medical knowledge which helps heal the sick is a simple form of the atoning power of Christ which heals not only body but soul.

Duality of Light and Existence

Physical light has a paradoxical nature, having two forms: one form behaves like a wave, being diffuse without bounds; the other form behaves as a particle, being discrete. Matter also has two forms, wave and particle. These two phases of light and matter are dichotomous, having different and sometimes opposite properties, with energy constantly changing into matter and spontaneously returning back to energy. Truth is schizophrenic, showing us two sides of a harlequin, but we see her two faces as one. One side of the harlequin is matter that is particle specific to place and time, and the other side of the harlequin is energy or wave, everywhere without time.

Lehi (2 Nephi, chapter 2) blessed his son Jacob and taught him that God cannot exist unless there is opposition in all things. God exists in opposition to evil. But opposites are not necessarily all good versus all evil. There are neutral opposites, such as justice versus mercy, summer versus winter, males versus female, day versus night, and spiritual versus physical.

Joseph Smith taught of both a spiritual and physical creation, and taught that the elements are eternal and cannot be destroyed, but they change when organized or re-organized (D&C 93:33; JS, *History of the Church,* 4:575; 5:393). We are dichotomous beings. One part of us is diffuse—which gives life to our second part, our discrete physical bodies. We spend our lives trying to unite our two opposite parts for a future life in celestial glory. We seem to be trying to sneak back into the Garden of Eden and taste again of the fruit of eternal life. We do it by eating the fruit of the tree of life, which hangs there as the body and blood of Christ. But it is like mixing oil and water, yet accepting the two as one. We have eternal spirits of life and truth, housed within physical bodies of death and darkness.

Interconnectedness in the Living Cosmos

There is an interconnectedness in the cosmos we live in, just as Andrew Petro, Jr. experienced during his NDE. From a scientific viewpoint, matter seems to have life, not only because there is a wave/particle duality to nature, but also because subatomic parts have an amazing ability to be interconnected, to communicate instantaneously, as if there were no time or space separating them. Electrons come in pairs, It is possible for one electron to communicate with its paired electron instantly, even when separated by miles. Under certain conditions, a high density of electrons act like one whole, similar to a flock of birds changing directions in flight all at the same time.

One physicist, David Bohm, was so impressed with how electrons acted under certain conditions that he remarked that they actually seemed to be alive. Bohm said that "dividing the universe up into living and nonliving . . . has no meaning. Animate and inanimate matter are inseparably interwoven and life, too . . . [is spread] throughout the totality of the universe. Even a rock is in some way alive . . . for life and intelligence are present not only in all matter, but in 'energy,' 'space,' 'time,' 'the fabric of the entire universe'" (Talbot, 1991, p. 56).

Beverly Brodsky told me that during her NDE she felt a part of all creation, from large nebulae to rocks, from novas to grains of sand, and they all seemed to have life. Brigham Young said, "There is life in all matter, throughout the vast extent of all the eternities; it is in the rock, the sand, the dust, in water, air, the gases, and, in short, in every description and organization of matter, whether it be solid, liquid, or gaseous, particle operating with particle" (Brigham Young, *Journal of Discourses,* 3:277).

"Particle operating with particle!" The modern physics of light and matter reveal that we are interconnected in some way with the entire universe. In summarizing the new quantum physics, Gary Zukav wrote:

"The philosophical implication of quantum mechanics is that all the things in our universe (including us) that appear to exist independently are actually parts of one all-encompassing organic pattern, and that no parts of the pattern are ever really separate from it or from each other." (Zukav, 1980, p. 48)

Could the interconnectedness of the universe be evidence of an omnipresent God? In section 88 of the D&C we are told that the course of the heavens are fixed by law, with each planet having its own time and seasons. All these times are one with God, who seems to transcend them all. Then this strange description is given of an inter-active dance between all the heavenly bodies: "They give light to each other. . . . The earth rolls upon her wings, and the sun giveth his light by day, and the moon giveth her light by night, and the stars also give their light, as they roll upon their wings in glory, in the midst of the power of God" (D&C 88:42–46).

A Cosmic Dance

This description of a cosmic dance between celestial bodies which roll upon their wings in glory, giving light to each other, sounds more poetic than real. But the following NDEs indicate that the cosmic dance is literal. During his NDE, **Mellen-Thomas Benedict** went back in time and viewed the "big bang" creation of the universe:

> . . . I was looking out of God's eyes. . . . And suddenly I knew why every atom was, and I could see *everything*. . . . And then the experience reversed. I went back through the big bang and I understood at that point that everything since the big bang, since what they call the first word, is actually the first vibration. . . . It was like a reversal, but this time I could see everything in its energy form. And it was quite a sight to see the entire universe as we know it as an energy form, and all of it interacting, and all of it having its place and reactions and resonances. It was just an unbelievable dance that was going on. (Ring, 1998, p. 288, italics added)

Virginia Rivers had a similar NDE. She was taken back in time to the void before the creation and then saw the creation of the cosmos. She described:

> The blackness began to erupt into myriad of stars and I felt as if I were at the center of the Universe with a complete panoramic view in all directions. . . . The stars began to change shapes before my eyes. They began to dance and deliberately draw themselves into intricate designs and colors, which I had never seen before. They moved and swayed to a kind of rhythm or music with a quality

and beauty I had never heard and yet . . . remembered. A melody man could not possibly have composed, yet so totally familiar and in complete harmony with the very core of my being. As if it were the rhythm of my existence, the reason for my being. The extravagance of imagery and coloration pulsed in splendid unison with the magnificent ensemble. (Ring, 1998, p. 295)

The Paradox of Reality

Those who have had NDEs seem to have experienced the reality of the cosmos. They understand truth by interacting with it. At the beginning of the 20th century, truth was seen as out "there" beyond us. Newtonian physics had taught us that the universe seemed to run on its own, independent of us. The concept of truth was that it existed as rules and laws of nature, to be discovered and understood but not influenced. The cosmos ran like a clock, with us as observers. But the new late-20th century and early-21st century quantum physics revealed that we are not independent of our environment but an active part, even influencing how nature expresses itself. Quantum physics (and/or Quantum mechanics) deals with probabilities and uncertainty—with subatomic particles flowing and dancing with each other.

It is not only NDEs which reveal a paradoxical truth, with individuals being somewhere and everywhere at the same time; scriptures declare God as a glorified man with omni-attributes; the cosmos shows us two faces, one face structured as Newton described and the other face unstructured as Bohr imagined. Our own bodies also express a dual personality. Our brains are divided into two halves, connected through central wiring. If the connected wiring is cut, the brain acts as two independent brains. The left brain sees the world as structured with boundaries, wanting things organized with answers. The left brain is where math and language resides and where Newtonian physics was born. The right brain perceives patterns and beauty, experiencing music, poetry and art, and it is where the irrational dance of quantum physics is perceived. The occidental philosophers and scientists used the logic and reason of their left-brains, while the oriental gurus, along with poets, musicians and artists, used their right brains. Walt Whitman expressed it this way:

> The suns I see and suns I cannot see are in their place,
> The palpable is in its place and the impalpable is in its place.
> These are the thought of all men in all ages and lands, they
> are not original with me,

If they are not yours as much as mine they are nothing or
    next to nothing,
If they do not enclose everything they are next to nothing.
If they are not just as close as they are distant they are nothing.
In all people I see myself, none more and not a barleycorn less,
And the good and bad I say of myself I say of them.
And I know I am solid and sound,
To me the converging objects of the universe perpetually flow,
All are written to me, and I must get what the writing means.
(Whitman, 1855)

Intelligence and Creation

NDEs and quantum physics have helped reveal that "the converging objects of the universe perpetually flow" and that truth is a paradox with two opposite faces, and we "must get what the writing means." NDEs show the beauty of feeling the cosmos dance with itself, including us, while also allowing us to remain as individuals. If truth consists of opposites, perhaps it is the marrying of those opposites that make an eternal whole. I think we began our journey to wholeness with the birth of our spirits with an uncreated intelligence: which spirits have agency to act for themselves; which spirits are expressions of the glory of God; which spirits have shown through NDEs to be part of everything because they are the glory of God.

Man was also in the beginning with God. Intelligence, or the light of truth, was not created or made, neither indeed can be. All truth is independent in that sphere in which God has placed it, to act for itself, as all intelligence also; otherwise there is no existence. . . . The glory of God is intelligence, or, in other words, light and truth" (D&C 93:29, 30, 36).

Our spirits were then born within physical bodies that were restricted in time and place uniting the two faces of truth. We live in a foreign place to our spirits and therefore long to touch home as did those who have had NDEs. The joining of opposites continue in this life with the union of a man with a woman, who ultimately become one, and through the resurrection they are bound together for eternity. The cycle of wholeness is completed in the resurrection, with the opposites of spirit and body bound together and the opposites of man and woman married forever. "For man is spirit. The elements are eternal, and spirit and elements, inseparably connected, receive a fullness of joy" (D&C 93:33). They then are everywhere, the glory of God, but still somewhere as united individuals.

No Joy without Opposition

NDEs teach another strange doctrine about opposite truths—in order to obtain one face of truth we must experience its opposite face. Perhaps the best illustration of the value of suffering, as revealed in an NDE, is the experience of Donald Wood, who saw that he chose to live in mortality with the disease cystic fibrosis. In so doing, he was told that he would live a relatively short and very painful life, but he would learn life's lessons much quicker than those who had less-forbidding lives. Thus, as he saw it, he became a privileged participant in life's journey rather than a victim—as he believed before his experience (see the discussion of Don Wood in chapter 3).

Is that what Christ was also teaching Joseph Smith, when Joseph, aching from physical and emotional pain while in Liberty jail, pled with God for reprieve? God did not intervene, but taught Joseph that even if he suffered more than he was, "that all these things shall give thee experience, and shall be for thy good. The Son of Man hath descended below them all. Art thou greater than he?" (D&C 122:7, 8).

Lehi, in teaching his son Jacob about opposition in all things, used Adam and Eve as examples, and taught that if Adam and Eve had not transgressed, they "would have had no children; wherefore they would have remained in a state of innocence, having no joy, for they knew no misery; doing no good, for they knew no sin" (2 Nephi 2:23). No joy without misery! Doing no good without knowing sin! Eve reinforced Adam when he "blessed the name of God, for because of my transgressions my eyes are opened, and in this life I shall have joy, and again in the flesh I shall see God. And Eve, his wife, heard all these things and was glad, saying: Were it not for our transgression we never should have had seed, and never should have known good and evil, and the joy of our redemption, and eternal life which God giveth unto all the obedient" (Moses 5:10, 11).

Centered in this doctrine of learning from opposites is the life of Christ: "He that ascended up on high, as also he descended below all things, in that he comprehended all things, that he might be in all and through all things, the light of truth" (D&C 88:6). Christ comprehended all things by descending below all things, and through his death gave life not only to others but also to himself. "I lay down my life for the sheep. . . . Therefore doth my Father love me, because I lay down my life, that I might take it again" (John 10:15–17).

We also benefit from the experience of opposites when we receive eternal life, by partaking of His given physical flesh and blood. "Then Jesus said unto them, Verily, verily, I say unto you, except ye eat the flesh of the Son of man, and drink his blood, ye have no life in you. Whoso eateth my flesh, and drinketh my blood hath eternal life; and I will raise him up at the last day. For my flesh is meat indeed, and my blood is drink indeed. He that eateth my flesh, and drinketh my blood, dwelleth in me, and I in him (John 6:53–56). Christ fulfilled his own words—that "greater love hath no man that this, that a man lay down his life for his friends" (John 15:13). "Hereby perceive we the love of God, because he laid down his life for us" (1 John 3:15).

Love is central to most NDEs, which includes the greatest love of all—the spilling of all a god can give to lift up and endow us with eternal life. In Christ's given flesh and blood, eternal life is born. "In this was manifested the love of God toward us, because that God sent his only begotten Son into the world, that we might live through him. Herein is love, not that we loved God, but that he loved us, and sent his Son to be the propitiation for our sins" (1 John 4:9–10).

My Increasing Faith

As a physician, I chose my specialty of dermatology because I could "see" the problem, thinking I could help others better by identifying their disease quickly. But I quickly learned that what the eye sees is not necessarily the best way to practice the art of medicine. I learned that caring for other's problems only begins with what is obvious, and what is obvious is a window into their other problems. Patients need to tell their story regardless of whether I can see their disease or know how to treat it, even as I come into the room. Over the last thirty-five years of practicing dermatology, I have lately found myself listening to their story with more interest. Since reading NDEs, beginning in the late eighties, I find myself asking more intimate questions unrelated to their skin disease, and I have had patients tell me they have noticed the change.

The second Lecture on Faith details how prophets have seen and talked with God. In relaying their experience to others, the prophets' experiences create faith in others so they also can believe. Reading prophets' experiences has increased my own faith to not only believe in God, but to believe a part of me is not of this world. For me, NDEs also enlarge my faith that there is a God. They are edifying because they create in me a desire to be a better person. They carry an infectious spirit that shows me how to better love. They reveal a realm of beauty and light which brings hope that I once was there and can return. They show that God is not a respecter of persons because he reveals himself to ordinary people like me. NDEs expand my understanding of the nature of God and man because they support the paradox that truth is two things and not one. Most importantly, they speak louder to my spirit than to my mind, teaching me that I cannot injure another without injuring myself, because we all are one.

12: The Therapeutic Value of NDEs

By Lynn D. Johnson, Ph.D.

About the Author

Lynn Douglas Johnson was born in St. George, Utah. According to the brief biography he submitted, in his early life he acquired a reputation of being an insufferable know-it-all. He joined the Utah National Guard in 1964, and spent six years in the 19ᵗʰ Special Forces Group. From 1965 to 1967 he was a missionary for the LDS Church in Argentina. He has held numerous church positions and has taught sessions for the popular Education Week held each year at Brigham Young University.

He graduated from Dixie Junior College in St. George, from Brigham Young University, and obtained his M.S. and Ph.D. from the University of Utah in counseling psychology. When he was 29 and an almost hopeless bachelor, he was fortunate enough to marry Carol Sue Edson. They are parents of four children, none of whom have been in therapy or in jail.

Lynn is in private practice as a psychologist in Murray, Utah. He is the author of two books, *Psychotherapy in the Age of Accountability*, and *Effective Treatment of Depression*. He has also written numerous articles and chapters on psychotherapy and psychology, on leadership in business, and teaches as an adjunct professor at the University of Utah. He has taught positive psychology/peak performance classes and he currently teaches a course on problem solving to the Executive MBA students. Thus continues his reputation as an insufferable know-it-all.

A Personal Note

I am a psychotherapist: a psychologist trained in helping people overcome depression, anxiety, and compulsive behaviors. I am also trained as a marriage and family therapist, helping people resolve differences between themselves, living more peacefully together. A high school acquaintance who went into physical sciences used to mock me, saying that in his field (optometry) there were clear and definite answers, but in my field, there weren't any. He didn't really see any value in what I did.

Well, he had the advantage of me, but after many years in my career, I have decided what I do may be much more art than it is science, but that art has tremendous value. I want to briefly share with you some of the ways my study of NDEs has expanded and influenced the way I practice.

What Is Psychotherapy?

The term itself is interesting. Psyche refers to the mind, but the original meaning is soul or spirit. Therapy suggests a healing art of some kind, perhaps creating conditions in which natural healing can better be accomplished.

What could go wrong with the soul or spirit, and how would it be healed? When I started graduate school in 1970, the prevailing view was materialistic. Psyche was simply a representation of the complex of behavior and attitudes. The official doctrine was that there was no spirit, simply mental processes. Behavior could be changed, we were taught, by changing the way behavior was rewarded. Thoughts and feelings could change if behavior changed. There was, we were assured by the experts, no ghost in the machine, no psyche to energize the body.

Actually, we didn't know very much in 1970. We didn't know how much we didn't know. And paraphrasing a 19th century wit, we could have said that it wasn't what we didn't know that did us damage so much as what we knew for certain that was not so.

What if the soul or spirit can be damaged? What if psychotherapy actually is touching on things much greater than we dream of? What if there are ways the psyche can become healed? What if the materialistic view of the world (i.e., nothing exists except the material universe) is deeply and irredeemably wrong? Wouldn't it be good to know about that?

Since 1970, psychologists have been forced to take religion and spirituality much more seriously. In those days, a prominent psychologist, Al Ellis, taught his students that any belief in the supernatural or spirituality or religion was a type of mental disorder, and the therapist should attempt to convince the patient to give it up. Allen Bergin decided to test that notion, and, using data from Ellis' own clinic, Bergin showed that religious people who complained of anxiety or depression were *less* symptomatic than non-religious persons with the same symptoms. It appeared from the data from Ellis' own practice that religion played a protective role.

Since that time, the evidence has become overwhelming. Being religious, and more to the point, being involved in a community of religious persons, has a tremendously protective effect both on emotional and physical health. Both the religious and the irreligious become sick, get hurt, feel sorrow, depression, anxiety, and eventually die, but the religious suffer less.

In the mid-1990s, Al Ellis retracted what he had always taught. He said that for him there was still no god in the universe, but he had to admit that religious people appeared to have many advantages. He argued that psychotherapists must always be highly respectful of the spiritual beliefs of their patients.

It wasn't his ignorance that tripped him up, it was his certainty. He knew for sure that religion was harmful, and it turned out to be the opposite.

Allen E. Bergin received his Ph.D. in clinical psychology from Stanford University. He is a professor emeritus of psychology at Brigham Young University. In recognition of the large role which religion can and should play in psychotherapy, in 2000, Allen E. Bergin and P. Scott Richards put together a book, as editors, which provides practitioners with religious information they need to increase their competency in mental health professions. Within the context of their particular faith, chapter authors describe the therapeutic process, including conceptions of a deity, life after death, and the purpose of life (Bergin and Richards, 2000).

Finding Truth

Today, many scientists scoff at NDEs and know for sure that materialism is the only rational way to explain the universe. They are sure. They are convinced. They are wrong.

How can scientists be wrong? In this volume, Harold Widdison mentioned an example of two scientists testing results from research using a chi-square test, but misinterpreting the results. That is so very common. This life is a life of shadowlands, as C. S. Lewis put it, a place where it is very difficult for us to know anything for certain.

The paradox is that for spiritual power to operate in our lives, we must be absolutely certain. We must have unshakable faith. What I am sharing with you, I have very strong convictions of. It may well turn out that much of what I understood is actually rather different than I thought it was. Yet, what I share with you here has worked for me, worked very well, and I believe you may be the better for knowing of it.

In 1977 I was having dinner with some friends, and we discussed the recently published accounts of persons who had apparently died and returned with a variety of insights and eternal perspectives (Moody, 1975). Those perspectives spoke of a powerful reality, something that made this world seem like a shadowland of dream and fantasy. The accounts were definitive and consistent, and suggested to us that they were describing something actual.

Suddenly my friend said, somewhat heatedly, "I resent these near-death stories!" Wonderingly, I asked him to elaborate. "All my life," he continued, "I have attended church, and these stories do more for my religious faith than anything I ever got from church."

This reminded me of a quote by a favorite writer, B. H. Roberts. He said:

> Now, the third point; the one about men being constantly under the inspiration of the Holy Spirit; so constantly under his inspiration that all they say or do is an inspiration from God, that all their answers to questions are in the nature of revelation.
>
> Is there anything in the Mormon doctrine that makes it

necessary to believe that of men, even high officials in the Church? No, there is not. We know that they do not always speak under the direct inspiration of the Holy Spirit; for some men high in authority, aye, Apostles, have preached discourses for which they were finally excommunicated from the Church. They were not inspired in those instances, were they? Evidently not . . .

What mere automatons we would be if we found truth machine-made and limited, that is to say, finite, instead of being, as we now find it, *infinite, illusive, and attainable only as we beat it out on the anvil of our own experience?* (Roberts, 1912, pp. 521–22, 529; emphasis added)

This observation made sense to me as I thought how hard it is to beat truth out on the anvils of our own experience, and how much I had struggled myself. It has never been a simple matter for me to believe anything; I have to ponder it, wonder about it, roll it over and over in my mind, and test it against my own experience. I thought that the NDEs reported were helpful to me, given my tendency to over-analyze and question everything. I appreciated them, and wondered what I might be able to learn from them.

Years later I was talking with another friend, and he asked me as a psychologist what I thought about people who could dream about the future and it came true. I said I didn't think anything about it because I had never met someone like that. "You have now," he said.

He then related a very detailed dream that had very literally saved the life of his wife during a crisis brought on by an ectopic pregnancy. Had he not had the dream, had he not acted immediately when it began to come true, without a doubt his wife would have died. I was dumbfounded.

I had to re-evaluate my own thinking. I was too caught up in a materialistic view of the world, and to hear of such a powerful experience made me open my mind.

Interviewing Those Who Had NDEs

In 1984, I approached my friend, Ted Packard, a professor at the University of Utah. I suggested we do a small study on Near Death Experiences. I thought we could interview a few people who had experienced them and perhaps write a paper on what we learned. He found some unused research funds, and we designed a study. The very next day, as soon as I had committed to this study, one of my patients told me of a near-death experience he had at the age of nineteen. In seven years of practice, no one had ever mentioned such a thing. Within two months, two patients had. We easily found around thirty people, and interviewed them. We found them to be amazingly normal (I think we expected people who were strange, weird, and perhaps wearing crystals and turbans). Over and over, these people talked about what a powerful and positive experience the NDE was, and how it had helped their lives. Over and over again, they said what a wonderful thing it was to die.

It was not a personal transformation so much that I was seeking as simply to satisfy my own curiosity. But this did end up changing me in many ways. I always felt I was a pretty good member of the LDS Church, but I found much growth from my NDE interviews. My anxiety about death diminished. When you listen to thirty people in a row tell you that death is the most wonderful thing you can ever imagine, it has an effect. It did on me. I saw death as an interesting step forward, rather than a terrifying leap into the unknown.

My materialistic view also decreased. Life was now seen by me as primarily a spiritual experience, and I began to believe that we could influence such things as weather and illness through prayer. You should probably read that sentence with a certain amount of charity. It is not that I was unfamiliar with teachings that we influence such things. I thought I believed it, but it seemed more like something I was supposed to believe. I had a nagging doubt. That doubt receded and dwindled in the light of growing faith. I now have no doubt whatsoever that we can influence many things simply by an exercise of faith and prayer, things like illness, weather, and things as silly as simply finding lost objects.

My NDE interviews helped me be less interested in material objects. I had never been particular about my possessions, like cars and houses, but I became much less interested. Other people having more than I seemed of less and less importance. Me having more than others did bother me, and in small ways I tried to increase my giving.

Spirituality was now seen by me in a much broader way, and I became willing to grant that people from many religious traditions might have very common spiritual experiences. I was more inclusive, more accepting of many points of view. My supervisors had scoffed at spiritual things. I accepted them with appreciation and support. When a patient, Nancy, wondered whether her soul was leaving her body at night and traveling around, I was open-minded enough to help her design experiments to determine whether she could actually leave her body or whether she was just hallucinating. I believe now that I can improve how I conduct psychotherapy through my own personal prayer and listening carefully to my own heart. I believe prayers are generally answered through "coincidences" that seem to come just at the right time. God's hand, I am now convinced, can be just inches from my own hand at any time, and that divine help comes at precisely the right time.

Certain things I learned from the NDEs began to change how I conducted my psychotherapy. All my professional career I have wanted to be a short-term therapist. I wanted to help people in the quickest and deepest way possible, and I have always been quite active. My therapy is much more of a give-and-take than my psychoanalytic supervisors would have approved of. I was taught to listen patiently and intervene only occasionally. My own style was different. I would share my thoughts and ideas much more openly and readily. I believed I could directly influence another person's experience of who they were, right then, during the session. When I met many NDE experiencers, that was bound to leak out in my work.

So I began to mention to people what I had learned about NDEs when it seemed appropriate. I never asked people to believe, but I would share what had happened to me. I pointed out that it was perfectly fine to disbelieve these stories, but they were interesting experiences. I openly talked about their influence on me and how that seemed to help my own mental health. Most of the time it was not an issue, but when a patient talked about the death of a child, about fear of death, and about the meaning of life, I tended to share more of my own thoughts, and they seemed to be helpful and comforting.

That has continued to this day. I would suppose a week doesn't go by without my work being influenced once, twice, three times or even more by what NDEs have taught me.

Therapeutic Value

Boyd K. Packer is well known for saying that proper doctrine, properly understood, will change behavior more than the study of behavior will change behavior. If NDEs are a genuine glimpse into the life beyond, then logically a clear understanding of the features and truths of NDEs should have a positive impact on behavior.

That is true in my case. I believe I have become more patient, more open-minded and accepting, and more faithful as I have learned and understood. I learned from my NDE friends that the world is a spiritual experience, and the physical is simply a means by which that spiritual growth takes place. So I see things through the lens of spirit.

As I see things differently, my psychotherapy must necessarily change. If my eyes perceive spiritual issues, then my response to a client must necessarily change. In this chapter, I want to give you some concepts of how it has changed.

Death and Meaning

Therapists must face death over and over, because one of the things that brings people to see us is their loss of a loved one or the approach of their own death from a progressive and incurable illness. I have spent many hours wrestling with the questions of what life means and how to accept tragedy and loss.

Is life fundamentally fair? Or is life unfair? To put it more boldly, at times we suspect that life is not only unfair, but actually malignant. It seems as if God has taken a personal dislike toward innocent people. One of my old professors asks me how I can believe in God when there is so much pain, suffering, and unfairness in the world. "How can you believe in a God that would let such things happen?" he asks indignantly. "Wouldn't such a god be a monster?"

C. S. Lewis himself, in his book *A Grief Observed* (1961; 2001), went through such an episode. Lewis had become a Christian early in his college career, and for the rest of his life he was a firm and effective apologist (meaning, a person who argues in favor of something) for Christianity.

He was content with his status as an old bachelor—but when he was about 60, he found love. He married, and for three years was tremendously happy. Then his wife, Joy, had a recurrence of cancer and died. After she died, he turned to God for comfort. There was none, and he could not understand why God had forsaken him. He pleaded for some word of peace, of acceptance, for some sign that Joy still had him in mind.

The silence was deafening. For a time, he wondered whether he had misunderstood God's nature. He could not doubt the existence of God. That had been clear too many times, in too many ways. But, he wondered, what if God is not as loving as I had supposed? He entertained the concept that God may take pleasure in our pain. Could it be that God was not loving, but even malicious?

As he finally came to terms with Joy's loss, as he finally felt some peace in his soul, he was able once again to receive answers to prayers. Again, he felt the flow of inspiration from God. Lewis was a tremendously thoughtful person, and he recognized that his own anger and grief at his wife's death had made him incapable of hearing God's soft voice. God was there all the time, but God would not shout above Lewis' own anger and pain.

It is vital, Joseph Smith taught, to understand the true nature of God. How are we to understand times of trial and tribulation? My experience with NDErs has given me a new view of this that I have used many times to help clients. There is a plan for each one of us. Each of us is capable of great things. Because of the accounts of my NDE friends, I have come to believe that God is vitally interested in each of us, and that He wishes to speak to us. But we must become quiet and respectful if we are to hear. If we don't hear, God is still speaking, but our own anger, grief, or even desperation may make it impossible for us to hear.

I came to see the wisdom in that. As a psychologist, I well recognize that whatever is reinforced is repeated. If I feel desperate and God speaks to me, I am comforted. But what if I find that communication so transcendental that I long for it again? Perhaps I will, albeit not consciously, work myself up into a desperate state and expect God to speak again. Wouldn't that raise a terrible risk that I am coercing God into speaking to me? Wouldn't I find myself more and more desperate?

What loving Father could reward such behavior? I recognized that God's respect for our own agency, and his vital concern for our eternal welfare make it extremely unwise for Him to somehow shout through the noise of our own internal dialog. A loving God would never do such a thing.

So it is vital, when someone is in pain, to help that person first quiet the internal dialog, and to open the mind to some new possibility. There must be a pausing of the shouts of injustice, an opening of the ears. How to do this?

Understanding Suffering

Certain accounts from my NDE friends have been especially useful in the practice of psychotherapy. These accounts, that I will relate shortly, helped me to have a new and more empowering view of the environmental stresses that seem to cause various mental illnesses.

The traditional view of mental illness involves an unfortunate combination of innate vulnerabilities plus some kind of environmental stress. For example, if someone is born with a tendency to be low on the neurotransmitter *seratonin* (neurotransmitters are the messengers of the brain, the chemicals that the brain uses to pass on information), and if that person grows up in a family characterized by chaos and violence, then that person is more likely to be a violent person. A sibling born with a greater supply of seratonin is not so much at risk. A low-seratonin person growing up in an atmosphere of peace and appreciation is not at risk. It is an unfortunate combination that triggers the mental illness. Ironically, a high-seratonin person in a chaotic family comes out of it relatively unscarred.

This model, called the *stress-diathesis* model, obviously shifts all responsibility for one's condition onto environment and genes, things that one cannot control. Where is personal agency? Accountability? How can one say God is just when "A" is born with great genes and a beneficial homelife, and "B" carries a load of bad genetics plus a cruel and neglectful childhood?

Cassandra Musgraves was accidentally drowned while water skiing. She explained her experience to me by saying, "When I died, I didn't meet Jesus, I met Melchizedek. I don't know if you know who that is, but I can tell you, if you have met Melchizedek, you don't need to meet anyone else." I told her that within my Church, Melchizedek is certainly a person of great importance. She said that he was a loving, forgiving, understanding person who helped her learn from her life.

One important learning, Cassandra said, was to help her heal her relationship with her mother. She had a very antagonistic relationship. She viewed her mother as very negative and critical of her, as never having shown love. During her NDE, she learned that she had specifically chosen that mother-daughter relationship before she had been born. She suggested that her mother had agreed to be critical and judgmental so that Cassandra could develop the kind of inner strength and independence that she wanted to develop during her life. Her mother had actually been cooperating with what Cassandra had requested!

Elane Durham had a difficult childhood, and during her near-death experience, and before she was LDS, she was asked whether she would like to see herself before she was born. She told me that question jolted her; she had never considered that possibility. She was shown herself in front of a large screen, something like a mirror, but in it were projected possibilities for her life. She decided she would learn as rapidly as possible, so she selected a family in which she knew for certain that she would experience much emotional pain.

Don Wood suffered from Cystic Fibrosis. Every breath he took was painful. When he was 37 years old, he experienced an NDE, and during that experience he asked why it was that he had to suffer so much pain throughout his life. He was told, "You chose the pain you would suffer." He was amazed and quickly was shown himself being told, before he had been born, that there were two ways to learn on earth, fast and slow, and the fast way always involves pain. The person talking to him explained that cystic fibrosis was a disease that caused much pain, so those who selected that disease did learn much faster. Then Don saw that he volunteered to take on that disease.

As I reflected on Don, Elane, and Cassandra, I came to see that there was justice in the apparent injustice of inequality. Those whom we might say were cursed were actually being blessed by a more accelerated course of earthly learning. I recognized that such learning would rise with us in the resurrection, and would have to confer upon us great advantage.

So how to use that? Isn't it disrespectful for me to insist that my patients accept an extra-doctrinal vision? After all, there is no official doctrine I am aware of that says that each person's trials are chosen by that individual. Jesus does tell us that a problem might exist so as to allow God's healing grace to be made manifest. But to assert that is always true, isn't that improper?

Using Premortal Choice Respectfully

Of course it is. My own opinion, based in part on these three accounts, is only an opinion. I am out of line to teach it as a doctrine.

But Albert Einstein gives us a key. It is the *thought experiment.* Einstein imagined how the universe would look if he could ride on a beam of light. His thought experiment lead him to a true understanding of the nature of light, gravity, and time.

I can ask people to do a thought experiment. I can ask a patient who has clearly suffered from significant pain in life, "Would you be willing to do a small experiment? Pretend, if you will, that somehow we knew for sure (and we don't!) that you had actually chosen to have this pain, so as to learn something during your life. I am not saying you did, only that you imagine, as if you *had* chosen that severe trial. What do you suppose you might have wanted to learn by it?"

In this way, I can engage a person in a dialog about the redemptive power of suffering, about the transcendental aspects of seeing suffering as a useful learning experience. I cannot change their suffering, but I can help them to see their suffering in a way that changes their relationship with it.

None of this is unique to NDEs. People have always been able to see suffering as something that brings out good qualities. Those who suffered through Nazi concentration camps sometimes realized they were learning a great deal from that horror. Many pilots imprisoned in viciously brutal conditions in North Vietnam during that conflict found their POW time to be the most powerful and important experience of their lives. But perhaps I didn't have the depth of understanding to see that. Perhaps I needed a more direct lesson. Perhaps I could learn it only through my friends' courageous sharing of their learning.

Respecting Freedom of Choice

Some LDS people ask, "Why aren't people told to join the LDS church when they return?" Through my friendship with NDE experiencers, I gained a greater appreciation for the principle of individual agency. Several times this has been made clear to me.

Which church, asked Howard Storm, is the best church? The answer he was given is that the best church is the church that helps you get closest to God. Elane Durham, during her NDE, asked which version of the Bible was the best for her to study. She was told that the King James is the version that her spiritual guide preferred, but he added that things had been taken out, put in, and mistranslated. Then he added that he preferred to call that book "A history of God's dealings with a people" and said, "There are other words of God on the earth, other histories of God dealing with people, and if you look for them, you will find them." He didn't tell her to do so, simply promised that if she wished to find them, she would.

When Don Wood was about to join God, he saw a vision of his

son asking him, "Daddy, what are you doing?" Don repeated, "What *am* I doing?" God replied to him, "What do you want to do?" What a profound question! What do I want to do? That is the key. God scrupulously honors our own freedom to choose. Whether we choose good or ill, we are respected in our right to make the choice.

This translates into a greater respect in psychotherapy for individual choice and a greater scrupulousness at honoring that individual choice. I have a good friend who demanded exact obedience from his children, and he cut them off from the family if they opposed him. While most of his children were obedient, one was disfellowshipped from the family, much to the emotional pain of the rest of the family. The individual cut off from the family was a good and kind person and lived a temple-recommend-worthy life. It was just that the child didn't follow the idiosyncratic family rules. When a second adult in the family came to the point of being cut off from the family, a Church crisis followed.

This man, this father who cut off his own offspring, was eventually disfellowshipped from the Church himself, and I believe the core problem that has alienated him from God's kingdom was his own conviction that the rightness of his beliefs justified requiring exact obedience and robbing his children of their own freedom to act. He thought he was free to demand complete obedience.

But what was God's question? "What do you want to do?" Don was not told what he must do, but was given a choice. What did Don want? That is what is of interest to God.

Such a respect for agency is helpful in counseling. I have a patient whose wife became rebellious and began to stray from Church activity. She rebelled against advice from their bishop, and accused church authorities of being insensitive and abusive. My patient prayed long hours that his wife would want to be reconciled to him and save their marriage. He wondered during his counseling with me why God didn't answer that prayer.

My talks with Don had given me a deeper understanding of agency. It is entirely understandable that we want to pray for people to change their behavior, but there is a problem with that prayer. I suggested to my patient that if a prayer like that were answered, it would be like black magic. It would be forcing someone in a direction she didn't want to go. Certainly, God could not support black magic!

He then suddenly remembered how he had talked to a close relative who is in the quorum of the twelve. This apostle had encouraged him to come and visit, and asked him to open up. My patient finally admitted his marriage was in trouble, and how he was praying that his wife would return to her vows. The Elder told him, "The longer I am in this Church, the more impressed I am with the vital role of free agency in our lives."

As he recalled this, my patient then felt a great sense of peace. His relative in the Twelve and his counselor were telling him the same message. He recognized he had to let this woman do as she wished to do. It became clear to him that he was out of line in trying to force her to return to her marriage. Her life was hers to do with as she wished. His duty was to honor her choice, not to try to force her to abandon it.

Freedom of choice—or agency! We should not be praying prayers that would require the Father to abrogate that principle, yet we do it all the time. "Make them come back to the Church, make him quit smoking, make her love me."

So when it seems appropriate, and when I can do it respectfully, I share that concept. Occasionally, patients have countered with the example of Alma the Younger from the Book of Mormon. This is a hard example to deal with; all I can say is that perhaps he gave his permission prior to his earth life for that event to occur. I do know it seldom does occur! In all my life, I have never known a person who was sinning and was chastised by an angel. It may well occur, but I don't seem to hear of it.

Another Psychologist's View

Fortuitously, during the preparation of this chapter for inclusion in the book, an article appeared in the *Journal of Near-Death Studies* which showed that I was not alone in recognizing the therapeutic value of NDEs. John McDonagh, Ph.D. is a licensed clinical psychologist in private practice in New York. In the article Dr. McDonagh described how—after reading Moody's description of how those who had NDEs, after suicide attempts, rejected suicide as an option—he decided to expose some of his patients to that information. He reasoned that, although such information would not be as pronounced as in an NDE, it could have a similar palliative effect.

What happened to two of his patients was explained by Dr. McDonagh as follows (McDonagh, Summer 2004, pp. 270–71):

> What I took from this [descriptions by Moody and William James about changes in behavior] was that whatever the NDE

survivors learned during the NDE "worked" insofar as their behavior changed permanently: they did not attempt suicide again. That is what I wanted for my client: to learn that suicide was not an option. . . . I reasoned, if my client were exposed to the accounts given by Moody's patients, she could learn vicariously. The input would change her belief system in a way that traditional cognitive therapy had not been able to do.

. . . In the weeks that followed, there was more psychological movement than there had been in many months. It was as if the desperation option of suicide no longer existed for her, so she would have to focus more energy on her remaining options. I cannot say that this intervention resulted in the total remission of her depression, but I can say that she was no longer suicidal.

Encouraged by the positive effect of introducing NDE-related material on suicide, I did the same with another client and witnessed virtually the same result. Even though this second client was not planning suicide, he frequently fantasized about dying and sometimes pictured himself committing suicide.

. . . My use of NDE material in psychotherapy sessions has evolved to the point that when clients begin to express suicidal ideation, I ask them what they think happens after death.

. . . I then discuss with them that there are a number of NDE survivors who have come back with very interesting reports, and that it might benefit them to listen to what they have to say.

Degradation and Redemption

I want to close this chapter with an essay I wrote that incorporates some of the insights I have received from studying NDEs and how a therapist might use them in psychotherapy.

St. Paul explains love (*agape*) in 1 Corinthians 13, verses 4–7. He describes love as "patient and kind, it is not jealous or conceited or proud; love is not ill-mannered or selfish or irritable; love does not keep a record of wrongs; love is not happy with evil but is happy with the truth. Love never gives up; and its faith, hope, and patience never fail." (Today's English Version).

Greeks could describe various kinds of love. While Paul says *agape* is the key to salvation, *eros* is what we more often think of with our word "love." We find a poignant contrast to Paul's inspired description of love in Joni Mitchell's album reflecting her understanding of love, *Court and Spark*. In arguably the greatest pop music album ever made, Mitchell describes a love affair she began after breaking up with Graham Nash:

"You've had lots of lovely women, now you turn your gaze to me,
weighing the beauty and the imperfections, to see if I'm worthy.
"Like the church, like a cop, like a mother, you want me to
be truthful.
"Sometimes you turn it on me like a weapon, though, and
I need your approval."

The Apostle Paul would tell Mitchell that this is not love, for love
would not keep a record of wrongs. It would not be happy with evil,
and most of all, love is not selfish. What is this that drags out of a
person secrets and then uses them against the person?

Jane is a 28-year-old single woman. For years, she had been
nominally Mormon and technically a virgin. When she was 25, she
met a professional man, John, an attorney who was 11 years her senior.
John was immediately infatuated with Jane and turned his considerable
charm her way, turning his eye on her after having had many lovely
women in his life. She was smitten, fell for his charm, and soon they
were having sexual intercourse.

She now believed she had finally found true love, and that this man
was the one she would marry. She committed herself to him through
sex to a greater degree than she had any other man. To her family's
horror, she moved in with him.

But it was not enough for John. He began to encourage, and eventually demand and require a variety of sex practices she found objectionable
and distasteful. She began to feel degraded. John reinforced this by introducing a new element into their relationship, verbal degradation. "You
put yourself here, it is your fault we did these things. No one else will
have you now; I love you much more than any other man could," which
implied that she had degraded herself irredeemably, that it was her fault,
that it would now color every part of her life, and it was unchangeable.

Now she entered into a phase of the relationship characterized by
false promise of redemption. When we give much to something, we are
loathe to give it up. If I sink $2,000 into a car's transmission, I am
more likely to keep investing in that car to keep it running. We call
this "sunk costs." She had experienced "sunk costs" in the relationship,
and having given so much, the only road to redemption seemed to be
to somehow get back to the Garden of Eden where she thought she
was early in the relationship. In her imagined version of the Garden of
Eden, she could change John so that he would again treat her with the
intense infatuation he once did.

Throughout this phase, though, John continued to degrade her, always staying one step ahead of her attempts at redemption. At one point he let her know that he had, earlier in that day, had sex with another woman in the same bed where they now slept together. Somehow he was able to convince Jane that it was her fault that he had done that!

A period of oscillation followed. They would separate, he would become seductively charming for a brief time, and she would return. He then degraded her, and the process began again. The pattern was clear: She would become desperate, separate from him; he would then charm her, she would return, and he would degrade her further.

She finally sought the help of a therapist. Her goal was a simple one: how could she redeem the relationship? How could she return to the Garden of Eden they had once shared?

After discussing the pros and cons of continuing to seek a new beginning, Jane finally decides that her only hope for safety lies in abandoning John's false promises. But how can she turn her back on Eden, how can she not look back?

The thought occurs to the therapist that perhaps all idolatry involves some form of degradation. In ancient Israel, Baal worship involved group sex with different partners in groves of trees, clearly a degradation and betrayal of the marriage covenant. The worship of Moloch involved an ultimate degradation of casting one's own child into a flaming furnace. The evil genius behind that degradation sought to alienate one from God and convince one that now there was no turning back, that it was now too late for redemption.

Jane's relationship with John was idolatry, so redemption was always an empty promise—like a rich meal in a dream—always just out of reach.

Can redemption ever be out of reach? Some Book of Mormon prophets teach that as long as one is alive, one may be redeemed, even from murders (see Alma 24). However, Alma teaches that " . . . this life is the time for men to prepare to meet God; yea, behold the day of this life is the day for men to perform their labors" (Alma 34:32). Alma adds that "if we do not improve our time while in this life, then cometh the night of darkness wherein there can be no labor performed" (v. 33). Today, we know more of the gospel than Alma was allowed to know, and we recognize that repentance leads to the remission of sins upon condition of faith and a proxy baptism.

One of the individuals whose experience is related in this volume, Howard Storm, might question Alma's pessimism about salvation after death. While Howard went into hell, he recalled early religious instruction, he remembered how to pray. He did pray, and his prayer was answered. His inspiring story affirms our modern understanding that salvation can come to those who repent, even if they repent after death.

But his NDE account has another aspect, something that helped Jane escape from John's degradation. So the therapist asked Jane if she would listen to a simple story, one that might shed light on John's need to degrade her. The therapist briefly told of Storm's descent into hell, the demonic spirits there who buffeted him, both physically and emotionally degrading him, and how through reaching up through prayer he escaped. Storm had to give up his old ideas (such as, "prayer is for weaklings, it doesn't work") and abandon his old life ("I am strong enough to handle anything").

Storm's story helped Jane. It was a model of redemption, but only a redemption through the proper channels. "Sunk costs" cannot be redeemed. They must be given away.

The therapist used a Twelve Step model to help Jane. In Step One, addicts affirm, "We came to see that we were powerless over alcohol, and that our lives had become unmanageable." She admitted that John was like a drug or alcohol to her, that she was powerless over John (she couldn't redeem him), and that her life had become unmanageable. Step Two says, "We came to believe that there was a Higher Power in the universe that could restore us to sanity, and asked for his help." The therapist asked her if she could believe that there might be a higher power than John, a power that cared enough about her to restore her to sanity.

She embraced the fact that she was lost. With the therapist's encouragement, she embraced the thing she most feared, the thing she fought against. She said, "I am a loser." She then paradoxically smiled with relief. She said she agreed that her life had become unmanageable. She did still believe in God, and wanted to believe that He could restore her to sanity.

She agreed that only by committing herself to God could she expect a redemption, that such a redemption seemed impossible (and was impossible, given her constraints that it had to involve John admitting that she had value and that he was wrong). This need for John to change is a form of trying to practice Satanism, a taking away of John's agency. John must be free to follow his own path. Jane was given an assignment to find sponsors, just as she would if she were to attend a 12-Step program. Her possible sponsors included her parents' bishop and her own parents.

She returned to her roots and reached out to church authorities to help her break the destructive cycle. Redemption came.

Requisite Disclosure

I do not think that every therapist should study NDEs. In fact, it might be that often they would do a person more harm that good, in terms of incorporating them into a helping relationship. There is too much temptation to try to "prove" something from them, and such efforts to prove are always wrong—inherently disrespecting, as they do, freedom to choose.

Perhaps I ended up studying them because I was weaker and less faithful than others, and I needed additional insights. Perhaps they came because I was more caught up in a materialistic view of the world. Not a view of acquiring, but a view that God was far, far away, and not particularly interested in me. That view suggested that material explanations of behavior were sufficient, that understanding stimulus-response, reinforcement, and biochemistry, we could understand all that was of value about human behavior.

My association with NDE experiencers changed my views. I came to see the world as fundamentally a spiritual place. I came to see God as vitally involved. And I came be deeply believe that truth is, indeed, attainable, as we beat it out on the anvils of our own experience.

We live in phenomenal times. I am constantly thrilled to be alive at this time. In my career, spiritual issues have gone from peripheral to core. In the society, the reality of the spiritual has become much more widely accepted. (In a *Simpsons* episode, the dog, Santa's Little Helper, dies and heads toward the light, when he is resuscitated. Such a scene would have made no sense in the 1960s.) In a recent book, one of the outstanding psychologists of my generation, Marty Seligman (2002), has summarized all that we know about what helps people to be happy. In the book, *Authentic Happiness*, he approves of people believing in spiritual things and attending church, even though he himself has been an atheist all his career. In the last chapter, he begins to struggle with his own atheism, and while that struggle is far from satisfying to me, it speaks to a process going on, a process I have seen in others (Seligman, 2002). Many researchers in NDEs started out as materialists determined to find no ghost in the machine, and ended up believing that the machine itself is a kind of ghost, and the only real thing in it is the soul. Now Seligman, studying happiness, feels the gentle tap of God's finger on his shoulder. He doesn't want to turn and see, but finds himself being drawn. Happiness, joy, fulfillment are what God wants us to study, and Seligman is doing God's own work. His reward is that he begins to be uncertain about what he has always "known for sure."

I do believe strongly that God will speak to all people, in whatever way they can hear, if they will simply turn to Him. For me, study of the NDE was a way to turn to God and hear His voice. For others, they do not need such assistance. Wisdom doesn't come from walking the same path I walked, but in seeking wisdom. It will come in the proper way, suited for you, measured and tailored for your own make-up. It will come.

13: The Need for Proper Research Methods and Techniques: An LDS Sociologist Views the NDE

By Harold A. Widdison, Ph.D

About the Author

Harold A. Widdison was born in Salt Lake City in 1935. His family moved to Helena, Montana in 1947, where Harold graduated from Helena High School in 1953. Two weeks after graduation, at the age of 17, he was called to serve a mission for The Church of Jesus Christ of Latter-day Saints in what was then the West Central States Mission. Harold enrolled at BYU after his release and graduated in 1959 with a Bachelors Degree in Sociology. In 1961 he received a Masters Degree in Business Management also at BYU.

Harold received his Ph.D. in 1972 in Medical Sociology at Western Reserve University in Cleveland, Ohio. While working on his degree, he taught at Cleveland State University and at the University of Pennsylvania at Edinboro, then called Edinboro State University. Harold taught for a couple of years at Eastern Illinois

University before moving to Northern Arizona University in Flagstaff, Arizona where, over a 31-year period, he taught 22,000 students before retiring in 2003.

Harold has written numerous articles for scholarly publications and co-authored a book on the Near-Death Experience, *The Eternal Journey*, (Lundahl and Widdison, 1997). Over a lifetime of active participation in The Church of Jesus Christ of Latter-day Saints, Harold has held numerous ecclesiastical and teaching positions.

Background

As a young child, I often heard members of my family speak of unusual events that they or other members of the family had experienced. There was no element of the mysterious to these experiences; they were considered to be "spiritual manifestations." And during Fast and Testimony Meetings it was not unusual for people to share experiences they had with departed loved ones. Early in my teaching career at Northern Arizona University, I created and taught one of the first courses on death, grief and bereavement offered on a university campus. As I was preparing materials for the course, I came across accounts of individuals who believed they had died but had later revived. What they reported struck a very familiar chord within me. The Near-Death Experience, or NDE as it came to be called, confirmed what I had first heard at family reunions and at church and supported my understanding of LDS doctrine.

My Introduction to NDEs

The first book I discovered on this subject was Duane Crowther's *Life Everlasting* (1967), followed by Raymond Moody's *Life After Life* (1975), George Ritchie's *Return From Tomorrow* (1978), Kenneth Ring's *Life At Death* (1980), Michael Sabom's *Recollections of Death* (1982), and Melvin Morse's *Closer to the Light* (1990). I gradually accumulated an extensive library (over 350 books and several thousand articles) and became somewhat of an expert on the subject of Near Death Experiences.

The summer of 1982 I accepted an offer to teach a seminar at Western New Mexico University on *Coping with Crisis: Death and Terminal Illness*. While there, I met Craig Lundahl, who taught at Western New Mexico University and was a fellow member of the LDS

Church. Craig happened to be compiling a book on near-death research readings and asked me to write the introductory chapter. The book, *A Collection of Near-Death Research Readings: Scientific inquiries into the experiences of persons near physical death*, was published by Nelson Hall (Lundahl, 1982). My contribution was entitled *Near-Death Experiences and the Unscientific Scientist*. Some of the contents of that chapter are included in this chapter, and it is surprising to me at how little has changed since I wrote the original some twenty-five years ago.

When I first graduated from university, computers were just beginning to make an impact on the scientific community. They rapidly became faster and more efficient and able to handle larger and more complex problems. For example, at the United States Atomic Energy Commission (AEC) in Washington, D.C. we had a 10,000 channel analyzer that filled the whole side of our lab. It approximated the size of 10 four-drawer-filing cabinets. But when I left the AEC five years later, its equivalent was sitting on my desk and was no more than two feet by three. It was not many more years before personal computers could handle many thousands of times more data than the model I had on my desk at the Atomic Energy Commission in 1966, and you can now carry them around in a briefcase.

Cost-Benefit Studies

My job at the AEC was to help evaluate the need for additional scientists with expertise in various aspects of atomic energy or subatomic matter. The Cold War with the Russians was intense at that time, and many felt the survival of the West and the entire free world was at risk. The computer was seen as having the potential to be a very powerful tool in that war. While Congress had allocated massive amounts of money to the AEC, funds were not unlimited, so I and a few others were assigned to try and figure out the most efficient and effective places to concentrate funds and personnel so as to get the most benefit over both the long and short run. This is known as "Cost Benefit Analysis." We looked over every program being conducted at the AEC and broke them down into their basic components. Then we identified the benefits derived from each component.

One program we evaluated was nuclear medicine, and one of its goals was the curing of cancer and the prolongation of human life. In order to determine the benefits of this program, it became necessary to determine the worth of a human life. We quickly discovered major problems in making such an analysis because we realized that human life has many meanings. For example, how could the life of a noted neurosurgeon be equated to that of a child with severe mental impairments, or the life of an 80-year-old senile woman to that of a young mother? Yet it would be our responsibility to select the factors that determine the value of a human life. How does one choose or weight one factor over another when it comes to the value of a human life? I was most uncomfortable using quantitative weights for this purpose.

Sociology—Areas of Study and Limitations

At the time I started work at the AEC I was a rank empiricist, very impressed with the ever-increasing potential of the computer. In graduate school, some sociology graduate students did their dissertation research qualitatively, that is, by noncomputer-assisted means, and others quantitatively. The quantitative method involved collecting large samples of data and reducing them to binary bits which the computer could work with in generating massive amounts of statistical information very quickly.

Those of us who went the quantitative route were able to complete our research, impress our professors, and achieve our degrees more quickly, sometimes years sooner, than our colleagues who chose the qualitative route. But trying to quantify the worth of a human life caused me to stop and reflect about the value of reducing intangibles to numbers.

When I left the AEC to go back to school to study for a Ph.D. in Sociology, there were three major theoretical areas in that field. *Conflict Theory* sees the world and everything in it as in conflict, or potential conflict over scarce and shrinking pools of resources—specifically prestige, wealth and power. *Functionalism* sees society as an integrated whole and attempts to identify all of its components, the role each plays in human affairs, and when changes occur how those changes impact on the whole and on what specific part(s). The third theoretical field is *Symbolic Interactionism* (S/I), which tries to understand the meanings of objects and actions.

Since I was specializing in medical sociology, I found the theoretical approach of symbolic interactionism to be the most useful in my research. For example, what cues do individuals use to define themselves as sick? Next, what should they do to address their illness—self medicate or turn to expert or quasi-medical professionals? If they decide to seek help, who will they turn to? To understand what an individual will do in a given situation, I discovered that one must first learn how the individual defines the situation. Just because a physician sees a situation as critical and recommends specific actions, there is no guarantee the patient will do what the physician recommends. I discovered that many physicians assume that patients understand and agree with what they are told. However, in many cases, this is far from the truth. The reality of any situation, if there is such a thing, has nothing to do with how the patient/individual will actually act. It is how the situation is defined, and its relevance for the person doing the defining that is critical.

As a Symbolic Interactionist, I am interested in *meanings*. No object has intrinsic meaning in and of itself. Objects are labeled and assigned meanings by their observers. Where do these meanings come from? Determining or discovering meanings is one of the chief tasks of the S/I investigator. We know that, from the earliest days in children's lives, they are systematically taught such things as the names of body parts and other objects such as tables, chairs, blankets, bottles, etc. More importantly, they are taught what can or cannot be done to or with those items—their *meanings*. For example, what is a rock? Depending on the observer's perspective, that is, his or her meaning system, a rock could be viewed as a potential danger (as in the hand of a small child in front of a mirror), as something to be admired for its perceived rarity, as material with the potential for being turned into a piece of art, or perhaps as a construction material, or as an object to be removed from a garden because it is a nuisance.

As a sociologist, I try to understand the meanings assigned to various experiences/behaviors and how these meanings impact on the experiencers' behaviors. My task is not to determine which set of meanings is correct (if there is a "correct" meaning), but to try and understand what the implications of those meanings are for further interpersonal behaviors. Depending on the cultural background of the experiencer, the experience will be evaluated using the linguistic tools the individual has learned relating to a specific context and the individual's personal experiences. If the person is blind, for example, that individual cannot speak in terms of color, nor can the deaf in terms of sound. They must use terms they have available to describe their experience. For the researcher involved in NDE studies, it becomes extremely important that he/she understand these limitations on those being queried about their NDEs.

The words in our vocabulary represent a complex set of meanings that help us to make sense of our environment and to communicate that sense to others. As a result, the linguistic tools provided us by our culture may either assist in sharing meanings or become a significant encumbrance, particularly when we do not share common meanings for specific events or objects with those of a different culture. One problem for many individuals who have had an NDE is that there is nothing they can refer to that correctly describes or explains various aspects of their experience. They do their best, but their best is often inadequate and frustrating.

Cultural Effects

I have had long discussions with colleagues from the Department of Anthropology at Northern Arizona University (NAU) about the reality of the Near-Death Experience. They point to accounts coming from people living in isolated areas who have had NDE-like experiences which they describe in terms that clearly reflect their cultures. These descriptions necessarily vary significantly from culture to culture. This, they claim, documents the fact that NDEs are culturally specific and cannot be used as evidence that some aspect of the being survives physical death. I have been asked, "If the accounts are truly glimpses into another world, why don't all the observers report seeing the same things? For example, a Navajo might report seeing a Great Chief, a Catholic report seeing Jesus, and a Hindu report seeing a Death Messenger coming to take him away. Therefore, an examination of near-death accounts gives credence to the concept that the afterlife is a mirror image of, and hence the product of, the culture of the individual."

According to most sociologists and anthropologists, an individual's near-death experience results from his culturally-induced expectations. But if you examine a wide variety of accounts to see what they have in common, there are a lot of common factors. Skeptics point only to the differences and make no attempt to account for the commonalities. It could be that individuals from many different cultures are seeing the same event, but in trying to share it with others are restricted by the linguistic tools they possess. Therefore, the various accounts would inevitably be very different from one another. For example, the Being of Light could be described as Buddha to a Buddhist, Allah to a Muslim, and Jesus to a Christian. In most of the accounts I have read, the Being of Light does not announce his identity; the near-death experiencer makes the assumption that it could only be the Supreme Being, so differing linguistic tools could make common experiences sound very dissimilar.

Vicki Umipeg was born prematurely. Her eyesight was destroyed when she was placed in an overly oxygenated tank, so she has never seen light. During her near-death experience, her sight was restored and she saw with her eyes for the first time. We know that color is wavelengths of light that are reflected from objects in differing intensities, but she had never seen color so she did not know what to make of it, let alone describe it. If her description had talked of "green" grass or "blue" skies, I would have immediately suspected the validity of her account. But she didn't. And with no prior experience with sight, she had a very difficult time describing her experience and explaining what it was like to see. Therefore, her account is very different in some ways from other NDE descriptions even within her same culture (Ring and Cooper, 1990, pp. 41–59).

So prior experiences, and the linguistic tools we have to work with, can help individuals to share their NDE. But—and this is a serious qualification—our limited ability to express the unexplainable can also distort it when there are not words adequate or equal to describing the experience.

Science and Religion

In 1975, Raymond Moody published his book *Life After Life*, purporting to document cases of individuals who had been declared clinically dead but who had revived and, subsequently, reported some very unusual yet remarkably similar experiences. Within weeks of publication, the book had become a best-seller and the subject of significant controversy both to scientists and to the general public. The fact that the book stimulated discussion was not surprising, but the unscientific reaction generated within the scientific community was.

The emotional reaction of many scientists to Moody's book was reminiscent of the conflict which took place before science was liberated from the domination of religion in the Middle Ages. The persecutions of Galileo and Michelangelo, because their ideas conflicted with Catholic theology, are classic examples of the way scientific advancement was inhibited by a dogmatic theological perspective. It took hundreds of years before science, as it is known in the western world, came into its own.

Today, science has become totally independent of any religion. Not only that, but many scientists tend to believe that science and religion are incompatible and mutually exclusive. Because Near-Death Experiences suggest that something survives the death of the body— which is a religious construct—physical scientists have deemed such experiences as inappropriate for scientific investigation. While it is true that many individuals do interpret their experience within a religious framework, near-death research does not necessitate a theological orientation. Indeed, the area could be better explored from a scientific, non-theological perspective.

By definition, science must not be precommitted to any particular theory or theories so that it can maintain an objective posture and thereby be in a relatively unbiased position to explain why things are the way they are. Scientists claim to believe that anything and everything can, and indeed should, be subjected to rigorous scientific inquiry. Concepts, including pet theories that at first appear to have great explanatory utility, may actually be inadequate and even misleading.

Examples of incorrect ideas that at one time were assumed to be true include the flatness of the earth, the movement of celestial bodies around the earth, and the pooling of "bad" blood within the circulatory system. Scientists also claim to believe that nothing is so small or so trivial that it should be taken for granted and that the true significance of pure research may not be readily apparent. For example, Anton van Leeuwenhoek first observed microbes in 1676, but nearly 200 years passed before Louis Pasteur and Robert Koch discovered the connection between microbes and disease.

Although claiming and attempting to be objective, scientists are not immune to the influences of their respective cultures. The cultural setting in which a particular scientist functions affects the areas which will be researched, the topics selected within these areas, and even the tools and techniques that will be employed in the research. The history of science reveals the extent to which scientific investigation has been subject to cultural influences, yet many contemporary scientists appear to be unaware of the degree to which their own research efforts may also be affected.

Partly due to the historic struggle with religionists who sought to proscribe what could or could not be allowed to be studied or taught, scientists tend to view anything that even remotely hints of religion— and assuredly Near-Death Experiences fall in this arena—as not an appropriate area of research. Near-Death Experiences suggest that something survives the physical death of the body, and therefore people must have spirits or souls, and spirits/souls have historically belonged to the domain of religion.

Physical scientists "know" that life ends at the time of biological death and that nothing survives other than an individual's creations, his historical impact, and other individuals' memories. Chemists and physicists suggest that the cells of the brain become excited as an individual approaches death and that, in this excited state, information stored there is recalled. They explain that the brain stores information in the form of electrical impulses and, when the brain begins to die, these impulses are released and the individual experiences hallucinations based on memories of persons, actions, and thoughts stored in the brain. These scientists do not, however, attempt to explain why this trauma-induced excitement produces such consistent reactions in individuals widely separated by time, space, culture, age, and philosophical/theological orientation.

Enigmas of Science

More significantly, neither are they able to explain why or how individuals are able to report events and information they knew nothing about. Examples of this include meeting friends and relatives during their Near-Death Experience who they had not even known had died. More revealing are the cases of children who met siblings who had died before the children were born and about whose existence they had never been told. There is no way these experiences could have been created by electrical impulses stored in the dying brain because they had never been stored there in the first place.

Medical science's objections to the accounts of Near-Death Experiences seem to revolve largely around the issue of when the reactions reported as Near-Death Experiences actually occurred. Until fairly recently, it was assumed that death occurred when the heart and lungs stopped functioning, because that is when the body begins to deteriorate. (For an in-depth overview of this process, see Sherwin B. Nuland's book, *How We Die,* 1995.) However, medical scientists have learned to keep the body from deteriorating during resuscitation attempts. Medical doctors now tend to draw a major distinction between clinical death, which is reversible, and irreversible death.

Clinical death refers to the period of time when the heart and lungs are not operative but other organs are still functioning. Some medical scientists today reason that Near-Death Experiences are produced by the process associated with the death of the brain, clinical death, and are not, therefore, glimpses into an afterlife. Physicians may not deny that the individual who reported a Near-Death Experience is sincere or that his experience was real to the experiencer. However, they are very likely to assert that the individual mis-perceived the source of the experience, which they claim results from reactions to severe pain, drugs, oxygen deprivation, brain disease, high temperatures, etc., or that the individual came far enough out of his anesthetic that he was able to hear what was happening around him.

In light of the refusal of many in the physical and medical sciences to empirically investigate the near-death experience, consider the words of Albert Einstein, "It is possible there exists human emanations which are still unknown to us. Do you not remember how electrical currents and 'unseen waves' were laughed at? The knowledge about man is still in its infancy."

This observation is just as applicable today as it was in Einstein's day, which was not so many years ago. The more we begin to understand about the human body, the more we realize we are only beginning to scratch the surface of understanding. The brain is indeed physical, but the mind is not, and the interplay between the two is just beginning to be studied.

It is distinctly unscientific to engage in research with a closed mind and, worse, to refuse even to conduct research because you already "know" the results. Scientists must move beyond the historic fight with religion and apply their scientific expertise to studying near-death phenomena to see if they are real or not, and if the soul/spirit survives death.

The Rush to Legitimacy

Various researchers I have encountered assert that there is no scientific evidence that anything exists after death. While being interviewed on a news spot on *MSNBC*, Dr. Nuland, the author of the previously mentioned book, *How We Die*, was asked about my book. In a very authoritative tone of voice and demeanor he said, "The book is totally dependent on anecdotal accounts and is lacking scientific rigor." And that was that.

There are always competing hypotheses regarding unexplained phenomena, of which death is one. When Dr. Nuland stated his belief that the essence of the individual ceases totally at death, he stated as fact an unproven hypothesis. The survival of the spirit after death is an equally valid hypothesis, but also scientifically unproven. Intensive study of death is going to have to be done before either theory is proved, and the difficulty is that at this point in time there are no viable methods for making such studies. But supporters of the Near-Death Experience hope to validate their position, partly because of assertions from people such as Dr. Nuland that NDE research is totally based on anecdotal accounts which are not proof. Therefore, a number of NDE researchers have lately rushed into the scientific arena totally unprepared both methodologically and statistically, and are doing more damage than good.

Problems Associated With NDE Research

Some individuals claiming to be researchers seem to believe that the mere collection of cases—and especially large numbers of cases—is somehow proof of the validity of the Near-Death Experience. If large numbers of people believing something to be true makes it true, we would have all fallen off the edge of the earth by now.

There is nothing wrong in collecting numerous cases; it is how you go about analyzing them that is critical. For example, a well-known writer in the field of Near-Death Experiences introduces virtually all books and lectures written by that author by stating that they represent well over 3,000 individuals interviewed by the author. Unfortunately, the author-"researcher" does not inform the reader where the accounts came from, how they were gathered, or how they were analyzed. Speaking very authoritatively and referring frequently to the many years the author has spent collecting cases, and the fact that the author has had three NDEs, seems enough to legitimize the author-researcher's claims. Some individuals are impressed with large sample sizes, but it is not the numbers of NDEs that make a legitimate case. Rather, it is how they were collected, analyzed, and presented.

Representiveness of the Data

One of my favorite memories is a picture from 1948 of president-elect Harry S. Truman, holding up a newspaper with the huge headline, *"Dewey Defeats Truman!"* What had happened was that the now-defunct magazine, *The Literary Digest,* had included in one of its issues a questionnaire that readers could fill out and return concerning who they were going to vote for in the upcoming election. Many thousands of its subscribers tore out the questionnaire and mailed it to the magazine indicating that they were overwhelmingly going to vote for Dewey. But the thing the editors failed to take into account was the fact that the subscribers to their magazine were not a representative sample of the voting public. The readers of *The Literary Digest* tended to be upper-class Republicans, so the "survey" oversampled the Republicans and undersampled the Democrats.

When doing research on NDEs, a researcher quickly discovers that many individuals who have had an NDE refuse to be interviewed about it. This could be for any number of reasons. It is therefore methodologically dangerous to assume that any given sample is representative of all NDEs. It could be that those who agree to be interviewed are in some critical way different from those who refuse to participate. It is very tempting to generalize from the sample one has studied (regardless of its size) to all NDErs as a number of researchers have done, but further research could reveal that what they assumed to be the case is not so.

When I left the AEC, my colleagues congratulated me for receiving an NDEA Fellowship. But when they heard I was going to do my Ph.D. in Sociology, they were generally astounded. They would say, "Harold, you have too good a mind to waste on something as trivial as Sociology. Change your area of study and go into one of the *real* sciences." I was not long at Western Reserve University before I found that some of the sociologists there were smarting from this widespread negative assessment of Sociology and were trying to address it by resorting to analytic techniques used in the "hard" sciences (such as physics, biology, chemistry, and medicine), utilizing statistical methods and the computer.

In order to do this, data has to be reduced to numbers. While this can be problematic even in physics or chemistry, it is extremely problematic in Sociology. Sociologists study human behaviors, attitudes, feelings, motives, and beliefs. To reduce any of these intangibles to something that can be punched into a computer, it is necessary to figure out a way to turn them into numbers or a series of numbers.

Quantifying something as elusive as love, for instance, initially seemed feasible to sociologists. After all, love is a common-enough phenomenon. Hasn't everyone experienced it at some time in their life? But it was not long before it became obvious that love is not a single thing, but a very complex set of radically diverging emotions that are never static. In the process of trying to quantify love, a questionnaire was developed. In it, the respondent could indicate that they Strongly Disagreed, Disagreed, Had No Opinion, Agreed With, or Strongly Agreed with various statements. Numbers were assigned to the responses, which were then analyzed. If the scale measured anything, and that was seriously debatable, the higher the score the more a respondent supposedly demonstrated love. It was clear to me that something that was intrinsically very meaningful had been turned into something that I was not sure measured anything.

While there is a strong debate in Sociology over the advantages of qualitative versus quantitative research methods, this debate has yet to surface in NDE research. This is partly due to the fact that many researchers in this field do not understand the limitations of most statistical procedures and thus tend to use them inappropriately. But some NDE researchers do feel the need to introduce an aura of scientific objectivity into NDE research, and the usage of statistics would be a significant step. Certainly, the inclusion of statistical tables does seem to assure that research will be accepted for publication in professional journals and that the readers and reviewers of the research materials will be duly impressed.

Examples of the Improper Use of Statistics

At the 2002 International Association for Near Death Studies (IANDS) conference in Seattle, several individuals made a presentation in reference to gays and the Near-Death Experience. As part of their study, they asked gay individuals two questions about the impact of their NDE on their sexual identity:

1. Did sexual identity come into play during your NDE?
2. After the NDE, did the Near-Death Experience change your sexual identity in any way or change the way you feel about your sexual identity?

Since none of the respondents found their sexual proclivities condemned, it was assumed that being gay was not a negative. The researchers, a psychologist by the name of Dr. Liz Dale and Dr. Jeff Long, a physician, had created a number of tables showing the distribution of their 21 respondents' responses to the two questions and several other variables. The data was put into two-by-two tables and analyzed for statistical significance. The statistic they were using was chi-square, which is a descriptive statistic, and appropriate for the type of data (ordinal) they were analyzing.

However, when Drs. Dale and Long interpreted the chi-square statistic that was generated, they interpreted it incorrectly. They were talking about the strength of the relationship between the variables shown in the various tables. But chi-square only lets the researcher know what the probability is that the numbers as shown in the table could have happened by chance. It does not say anything about the type of relationship or what it means. The larger the value of chi-square, the less likely the pattern observed could have happened by chance. But they were interpreting the large values of chi-square as showing a strong causal relationship. They were using chi-square as if it was somehow equivalent to a Correlation Coefficient. I tried to explain that they needed to compute the ordinal equivalent of the correlation coefficient, which was Gamma, but they did not understand that what they had done was wrong.

One of the presenters attempted to justify their faulty methods by stating that other researchers had done the same thing and that their results had been published in respected journals. But because some other study uses the wrong tools and has been published in a prominent journal does not make the results accurate or scientifically acceptable. This study was subsequently published by Emerald Ink Publishing Company as *Crossing Over & Coming Back* (2000).

Not too much later, I was reading a copy of the *Journal of Near-Death Studies*. In it was a report submitted by an Italian nurse, Laura

Cunico, entitled *Knowledge and Attitudes of Hospital Nurses in Italy Related to Near-Death Experiences* (Cunico, Laura, Fall, 2001). I am always intrigued with studies done internationally. (I thought it impressive that she was actually able to get 476 nurses to complete a complex questionnaire!) I discovered her research was a replication study utilizing a questionnaire created by Nina Thornburg in 1988 to study the knowledge and attitudes of registered nurses in Intensive or Cardiac Care Units concerning the Near-Death Phenomena.

Dr. Cunico's study was intended to contrast the results of a cross cultural study of Italian nurses with those collected by Thornburg and other researchers, but when I examined her findings, I discovered that she had used the wrong statistics to analyze her data. Unlike the study of gays where the researchers did not understand the limits of the statistic they were using, Cunico used inappropriate statistical tools to analyze her data. Virtually all of the data she collected was ordinal at best. Her questionnaire was comprised of several scales which consisted of items where the respondent was asked how they felt about each item. They had five choices: *Strongly Agree, Agree, Don't Know, Disagree, and Strongly Disagree.* The researcher then assigned a numeral value to each category and added up the numbers for the various items as marked. But the problem is that you do not know what it means when a respondent agrees with a statement. If you look at two respondents, one who marked *Strongly Agree* and the other *Agree,* all you know for sure is that their responses differ. To assign a value of 4 to *Agree* and 5 to *Strongly Agree* implies that a known and measurable difference exists between each item. But the actual distance between the two possible responses is unknown. All you know is that one response is more positive than the other—an ordinal quality. The distance could be very narrow—almost identical—or extremely wide. To be able to interpret the statistics she used, you would have to know the exact distance between each response.

Thornburg also created a list of items which the respondents could check indicating how they felt about the different items. Each item that was checked was given a value of one and then totaled up. There were 29 items in the list that was supposed to measure the attitude of the respondent toward NDEs. But it was very possible that there were one or two items in the list that were significantly more important than all the other 27 combined. However, until you evaluate the relative contribution of each and every item included in the scale, you have no idea what any item included in the scale really means.

I looked up Thornburg's original report and discovered that she had two major objectives. The first was to create an instrument that could be used to study attitudes as to NDEs, and the second was to see how well the instrument worked. It is what is called an exploratory study. As I looked over the questionnaire, I thought it was crude and could use a significant overhaul, but the real problem I discovered was that all of the statistics Thornburg used were inappropriate. All the statistics required interval-level data, and hers was only ordinal. Since all her conclusions were based on an inappropriately used statistic, they were not justified.

What is really sad about this example is that a number of other researchers used her questionnaire and the statistical procedures she used. In 1989, Drs. Walker and Russell surveyed 326 psychologists. In 1992, Bechtel, Chen, Pierce and Walker surveyed 2,722 clergy. Then in 1994, More surveyed 143 staff physicians. Finally, in 2001, Ketzenberger and Keim surveyed 50 college students. Replication studies can be very informative in discovering similarities and differences across groups, cultures, and the influence of time, but in this case, all the time and effort expended in doing the research, and the space taken up reporting it in professional publications, was a complete waste. I initially thought it might be profitable to go back to each study and reevaluate the data using the appropriate statistical tools but, in the intervening 16 years since the instrument was created, a lot has happened to make the instrument totally inadequate today.

In the cases cited above, Drs. Dale and Long used an appropriate statistic but used it incorrectly in drawing their conclusions. In the second series of studies, the researchers used totally inappropriate statistical tools. The desire to collect data on the NDE systematically and to then analyze it using statistical techniques is a positive step, but it will work only if the researcher understands correct statistical procedures and the limitations associated with the type of data being collected. Data improperly collected, analyzed, and presented will raise serious questions of legitimacy and scholarship and cannot help the public image of NDE researchers.

The Interactive Effect

Unlike the physical sciences, where experimentation will not alter the makeup and composition of an object, research in the social and behavioral sciences can alter in significant ways the end product being sought. In the physical sciences when you heat an object, it is the heat that produces observed changes, not the object's awareness of the heat. Unfortunately, this is not the case in social settings. Human subjects are very much aware of their social environment, and this awareness will impact their behaviors. Being interviewed is not a routine procedure for most people. They tend to look for cues (both consciously and subconsciously) for what they should do or say. They try to second-guess the interviewer as to what he/she is looking for so they can respond in what they perceive to be an appropriate way. A raised eyebrow, a slight leaning towards the interviewee, the wording of questions—each can encourage specific responses and discourage others. The interview situation itself becomes a variable in the equation affecting respondents' responses and behaviors.

A structured questionnaire itself provides information that suggests information/ideas/categories to the respondent that was not reported in the narrative of the respondent's experience but is now incorporated into it. For example, on their Near-Death Experience Research Foundation (NDERF) web site, the Longs request that participants do two things. First they are asked to report their experience in a narrative form. Then they are asked to respond to a series of questions regarding their NDE. One item in the questionnaire is, "Did you see a tunnel?" I have noted that no tunnel is mentioned in the narrative segment of a number of respondents. But in the questionnaire segment, one is.

Two things could be happening. The first is that the question triggers memories of going through a tunnel. The other is that because a tunnel was mentioned, the experience is reinterpreted to include a tunnel. If a tunnel is supposed to be part of the Near-Death Experience, a huge valley is reinterpreted to be a tunnel, or a respondent says that he or she went through a "tunnel-like" area. Neither response is a valid "yes" to the question about going through a tunnel. It is not clear whether the questionnaire helps to round out the experience or distorts the reporting of the experience. Researchers must be very careful of their potential impact on what the respondent says and as accurately as possible record the experience in the words of the respondent and not put it in their own words.

I have a colleague who thinks he knows what respondents are trying to say and fills in their accounts with what he considers to be better wording. When respondents read over what my colleague has written some will say either, "No! That is not exactly what happened during my experience!" Or, "Yes, but you said it much better." In an attempt to add what he calls "a more human touch" to several accounts I had collected, he rewrote them. The accounts were from my mother, my aunt, and my grandmother. When he was finished, I could hardly recognize them.

I have recorded many accounts on tape with the individuals' permission. Many of my respondents, during the telling of their experience, want me to affirm that what they are telling me is true/correct/acceptable. Not wanting to distort their experience, I respond, "This is your experience! I want to hear what you experienced! We will chat about it once you have finished." As I listen to them trying to find the words to recount a deeply personal and emotional experience, the temptation is great to comment or sympathize with them. But to do so would have the effect of interjecting myself into the experience in some way.

The interactive impact can and does distort both the telling and recording of an account and could reflect just as much the biases of the interviewer as it could the actual experience. From the experiencers' perspective, it is often very frustrating trying to share an experience which has no referent—but they do their best even if they fail in the attempt. One additional factor I have discovered that impacts on what ultimately gets written up and shared with others is that the experiencer may want to edit her/his account to come across better. They will delete things they think are not significant and also add qualifiers that reflect more what happened *after* the experience.

From the Experience to Its Interpretation and Meaning

Invariably, near-death experiencers yearn to know what their experience means for themselves, their family, and even for all of society. As they contemplate the meaning of their experience, some share it with people they respect or who they think might help them understand the meaning better. The reactions they receive might either encourage the sharing of their experience with more people or cause them to refuse to speak of it again. Whether they have shared their experience with others or not, experiencers begin to create a context in which the experience makes sense to them. I have no problem with the experience as originally reported by the experiencer.

Where problems can and do arise is when the experiencer attempts to interpret and explain its meaning to others. This is where their cultural and personal beliefs, or suggestions by others as to their experience's true meaning—often provided by professed occult experts—may distort the experience. Some see the experience as an affirmation of their beliefs in reincarnation. Others see it as a sign that they have a mission to go out and proclaim their vision of the future of mankind. Still others see their experience as a sign from God that they have been called to form some new ministry or to reform existing ministries. Many become more sensitive to the needs of others, and some tend to become dogmatic.

At various IANDS conferences I have attended, sometimes one or more individuals who, after hearing someone's report of their NDE, will reject it outright because it does not correspond to theirs in every particular. As I stated previously, I have no problem with the experience as originally reported. It is the interpretation, the attempt to explain it to others, the recounting of it over and over with embellishments and "minor" changes, where many problems arise. Non-near-death experiencers tend to look to NDErs as having a first-hand grasp of the meaning of life and death and look to them for guidance since they have experienced death and returned tell about it. This role as an expert on death might affect the perceived self-importance of a near-death experiencer to the point where the story is padded and enhanced almost beyond recognition.

In addition, some NDErs may have agendas that are designed less to inform, help and inspire than to insure their own financial gain. At least two prominent speakers/authors have so promoted their own NDEs, and the meaning associated with their experiences, that they have become full-fledged advertising and commercial enterprises. Any resemblance of their current account of their NDEs to that of the original accounts is almost coincidental. Their stories have morphed into what most satisfies or awes the unsuspecting audience, and thus maximizes the profitability of their enterprise. Despite the historical variation in their stories, they continue to attract substantial followings at their "conferences," and they do enormous harm to the majority of legitimate researchers and others involved in serious NDE studies.

Different Impacts of Being Transformed by the Near-Death Experience

One thing about the Near-Death Experience that fascinates me as a sociologist is how the experience impacts on the experiencer. The impact can be so traumatic that it disrupts relationships, forces a few individuals into clinics for psychiatric evaluations, and causes others to retreat into themselves. To the best of my knowledge, these cases are the exception rather than the rule, but they are significant.

To start with, most NDEs are not the type reported by Elane Durham (Durham, 1998) or Howard Storm (Storm, 2000) which are examples of in-depth experiences. Generally, the experiencers sense that something very unusual has or is happening to them. The experience of some goes only to the point where they hear medical personnel saying something like, "We are losing him." Others feel themselves leaving the body. Still others find themselves suspended above the scene, watching with some curiosity people working feverishly on a body below them which they are shocked to realize is theirs. People who have this type of experience no longer have any fear of death because they now know that the essence of the individual survives death. They are still concerned about the dying process, that it could be lengthy and extremely painful, but they know that the transition from life to death is not painful because when they "died" the pain and suffering stopped and was replaced by a sense of total freedom and peace.

But for the deeper experiences, other significant transformations take place. Melvin Morse in Oregon (Morse, 1992), and Cherie Sutherland in Australia (Sutherland, 1992), were so taken by the impact of NDEs on the people they interviewed that they each wrote books focusing on the impact that the NDE had on the experiencer. Melvin Morse's book was entitled *Transformed By The Light*, and Cherie Sutherland's, *Reborn In The Light*.

For those individuals who left their bodies and traveled to a different sphere of existence where they met deceased loved ones, the transformation they demonstrated was dramatic. They not only lost any fear they might have had about death, but they learned that death was just a door to another realm and the reuniting with deceased loved ones.

Individuals such as Don Wood (chapter 3), Elane Durham (chapter 16), Angie Fennimore (1995), and Joyce Brown (1997) discovered that their difficult earth lives were not punishments as they had supposed. Don found out, much to his surprise, that he was the architect of his earthly life and that he had volunteered to have his life one of suffering. He then shifted from thinking he was a victim to searching for ways he could reach out to others. Elane, Angie, and Joyce had been severely abused but learned that they were not worthless flotsam on the sea of life after all. Instead, they were beloved daughters of God. Their entire perspectives of the world and themselves changed.

The preface of this book, and chapters 7 and 8, give examples of people who were first interviewed by Gibson thirteen years ago. In recent follow-up interviews, he was able to document some engrossing impacts which became a part of their life's adventure. These events, in some cases, were startling in their apparent other-worldly causes.

Those who meet the Being of Light experience the greatest transformations. They become, literally, new and very different persons. Being in the light, feeling unconditional and total love for the first time in their lives, changes them socially and psychologically.

A number of persons I interviewed said that they came back with greatly enhanced psychic abilities. One woman said,

> I did not ask for these abilities, and at times I do not know if they are a gift or a curse. You see, I can understand what those in my immediate vicinity are thinking. I have never liked gossip. At times, my ability to know what people are thinking is a lot like gossip. When I am in groups, I have to make a concerted effort not to listen. At times, I have been prompted by the spirit to share things with people who are seriously troubled. I not only hear their thoughts and pleadings, I am sometimes given information that can help them. But I do so only under spiritual direction. I am not a psychic or medium and do not feel it appropriate to use my abilities for profit. At a number of national meetings of the International Association for Near-Death Studies (IANDS), I have encountered a number of individuals who have become professional psychics following their NDEs. While I do not want to judge them, I just do not feel that what they are doing is right.

An older man told me that after his NDE he could see auras radiating out from people. He pointed to a man and said, "I can see a black area in his aura, just over his right shoulder. That indicates to me that his shoulder is bothering him." We walked over to the man and the NDEr asked him, "Are you having problems with your right shoulder?"

The man looked at him with surprise and said, rubbing his shoulder, "Why yes! How did you know?' My associate explained briefly that following his NDE he had been given the ability to see auras. I do not know if the man understood or believed him, but he did let his shoulder be massaged and within seconds reported that it was relieved of all pain. It was not long before my friend was surrounded with people pointing out areas of their bodies that were troubling them. He later told me that he could develop a lucrative business if he chose, but that he felt he should not sell his gifts for money.

The changes manifested by NDErs are most interesting. Some NDErs come back with the electromagnetic and chemical composition of their bodies so altered that they cannot wear watches because they will stop working. Some changes are unique to a specific experiencer, but other changes are shared by a number of experiencers. The greatest shared transformation is how they view their lives on earth. One NDEr described it as a wake-up call. Where before the frantic search for wealth, esteem, power and possessions had driven his life, now it is interpersonal relationships. He and other NDErs are more concerned about the feelings and well-being of others. They want to make the world a little better in whatever way they can. They discover, as Howard Storm did during his life review, that it is not what impresses others on earth that is significant on the other side, but how you reach out and help others. All one's earthly possessions mean nothing in and of themselves, but only if they are used unselfishly to help people to improve their lives.

For those who were told that they had to return to earth life even though they didn't want to, the general reason given was because they had not yet completed their missions and that there were important things they needed to do before they could stay. What that mission was was crystal clear during their experience, but once back in their physical bodies all the specifics were blocked from their memories. For the most part, the only thing they knew for sure was that there was something very important they needed to do. However, there are exceptions (see John Stirling, chapter 7).

Some, like Howard Storm, George Ritchie, and Ned Dougherty, came back as new men. Their quest for power, wealth, and the admiration of men was replaced with a burning desire to serve. Their countenances changed perceptively; they now radiate a totally different demeanor and disposition than they did before, and many peoples' lives have been helped and blessed because of them.

The Impact of Misuse of NDE Information

While many of the transformations are permanent, it would appear that even the most profound experience can fade if used inappropriately. As indicated with the two sorry cases mentioned earlier, there are, unfortunately, live examples of such misuse.

It would seem that the sharing of an NDE would have kept the experience alive and crystal clear for those who experienced them. But how it is received during its sharing with others seems to impact both on the teller and on subsequent retelling. Where the actual NDE may have been intended to refocus the individual's behaviors, perceptions and attitudes, and did initially, over time its original purpose (consciously and unconsciously) may become lost.

While claiming that writing books, giving presentations, appearing on radio and television etc., is to help others, there is a danger that the fringe benefits may become the primary focus and the helping secondary. The individuals become famous and sought after by the media. As their fame spreads and their wealth increases, alterations to their self-perceptions may occur. The real message they received during their NDE may be in danger of becoming less and less significant. It would be very interesting to do a longitudinal study (a study that runs over an extended period of time) to see what distinguishes those whose transformations were relatively permanent from those who are not (see chapters 7 and 8).

Interesting Findings

As a sociologist I find the following aspects of the NDE particularly intriguing:

1. That an NDE typically negates the experiencer's fear of death.

2. That the experience has dramatic consequences for the experiencer's self-image.

3. That the experience has significant consequences for and on the individual's interpersonal relationships.

4. That the experience can alter the electro/chemical/magnetic

composition of the experiencer's body.

5. That the experience can change the individual's attitudes, values, and goals.

It would be very informative to collect data from close associates of experiencers to determine what it is about these individuals that actually changed and what seems to be associated with the permanency of the changes. It could be the social environment in which individuals live and how supportive those around them are. There is no guarantee that significant NDE-related changes will occur but, if they do, why and how would be a fascinating research project.

NDEs and Research Efforts

Being challenged by physical science to prove that NDEs are evidence of something surviving death, NDE researchers have taken up the gauntlet and are urgently trying to prove that something indeed does. Covered elsewhere in this book (chapter 10) are attempts to create situations where the spirit/soul can see something while out of the body which is verifiable and not visible to anybody else. But to those who have already made up their minds, this will prove nothing.

I personally do not feel the urgency to prove anything to other sociologists or to my colleagues about doing research on NDEs. I feel it is important to be able to determine my own research agenda and not let other people determine what and how I study something. Instead, I accept the fact that the NDE exists because of its universitality and that it appears to be a significant aspect of the human condition. So, now, what can we learn about it?

Fruitful Areas for Future Research

Rather than come up with a theory to use in directing research efforts, I feel it is more fruitful to go to the data and see what it tells us about the phenomenon in question—the NDE. This is called grounded theory, in that it is grounded in the thing one is trying to explain. The researcher starts by collecting everything he/she can about NDEs and then analyzes the data to look for categories that seem to distinguish it. As more cases/data come in, the data is evaluated to see if a category exists for various characteristics. When new information is discovered, new categories are added. The researcher continues collecting cases/ data until no new categories are discovered. The categories are then examined to see what they reveal about whatever is being studied. To a large extent, this book is an example of such grounded research theory.

Raymond Moody, when he first wrote about the NDE, created categories that he used to describe what NDErs experienced. As grounded theory it was a crude and incomplete attempt—as he readily admitted. One general category he listed was going into a dark tunnel. If you look at the original segment that related to tunnels in his book, *Life After Life* (1975), the tunnel was only one of a number of descriptive words. Others included were a cave, a well, a trough, an enclosure, a funnel, a vacuum, a void, a sewer, a valley, and a cylinder.

Because Moody labeled this category "The Dark Tunnel," subsequent writers and researchers reduced the entire category to the "dark tunnel." As the mention of going through a tunnel came up only occasionally in my interviews, I decided to see what NDErs reported experiencing from the time they left their bodies until they entered the light. I identified 1,000 NDErs who met the criterion of leaving their bodies and traveling to the light. Only 26 percent of the adults even mentioned the word tunnel, and a significant number of them used qualifiers such as tunnel-like. Of those who mentioned a tunnel, the majority describe it as dark, but a significant number described the tunnel as a tunnel of light. Others described it as displaying a wide variety of colors, and some even noted that it twinkled like a gaily decorated Christmas tree.

Those NDErs I studied who mentioned a tunnel also described the various ways they entered the tunnel, what happened to them while they were in the tunnel, the movement of the tunnel, the shape of the tunnel, and how they exited the tunnel. I discovered that it was rare for a child to mention a tunnel. Most of them were suddenly in the light. This was also reported by Melvin Morse in his book, *Closer to The Light* (Morse, 1990).

Allan Kellehear, in his book *Experiences Near Death*, tended to differentiate between Western NDEs and non-Western NDEs by the reference to the tunnel (Kellehear, 1996). Non-western-NDEs do not see a tunnel according to Kellehear (Kellehear, 1996). Because he did not have access to the large data base I did, he was not aware that the tunnel is not a part of most western NDEs either.

Just this one general category of the NDE, the transition from life to the light, is proving to be more complex than has been treated in the NDE literature. Further research could possibly show how this segment of the experience impacted the experiencer. I suspect that all other aspects of the NDE would prove to be just as interesting and informative and complex.

While each NDE is unique, each also has qualities which are shared by other experiencers. It would be useful and informative to:

1. **Identify the qualities that are shared and by what groups, especially of the in-depth experiences** (where the individuals enters another sphere, meets deceased loved ones, meets the being of light, has a life review).

2. **Take the qualities of NDEs that are shared and see how they fit various cultural and religious traditions.** In the case of Latter-day Saints, it would mean taking the qualities identified of the NDE and see how well they fit LDS theology. It would be better to go this route than to take LDS theology and see how well it fits. I think there would be a lower probability of forcing a fit. To a degree, Robert Fillerup in his presentation at the Sunstone Symposium titled, *Early Mormon Visions and Near Death Experiences,* attempted to do the latter, i.e. show how well LDS theology and the NDE mesh (Fillerup, 1990). To a major extent, this book moves in the direction of filling this gap for the LDS religion (chapters 4–5 and 15). It would be useful to have corollary works from other religions.

3. **Study how the NDE impacts specific beliefs** (see chapter 16). I have discovered that, in some cases, the NDE results in individuals becoming alienated from organized religion because what they see happening during church services does not match the peace and harmony experienced during their NDE, i.e. too much emphasis on the collection, petty comments, and noise during services, etc. On the other hand, other people had their faith confirmed and became very active in their churches. In what key ways did the two differ?

4. **Study to what extent the NDE had a positive impact on the human condition.** Literally millions of people have had an NDE of some degree, and this could be impacting others around them. Kenneth Ring felt that the NDE might be a precursor of what mankind could become. See his book, *Heading Toward Omega* (Ring, 1984; see also chapter 17).

In making numerous presentations, I have been surprised to discover that a significant number of the people in the audience were willing to believe that NDErs did meet a Being of Light who was the source of truth, love and peace. However, it went against their grain to be told that some experiencers met a Being of Darkness—evil personified. Barbara Rommer looked at negative NDEs and discovered that they served as a wake-up call to those who had them and ended up being *Blessings in Disguise,* the title of her book (Rommer, 2000). Identifying the differences in the experiences and their impact on the experiencer could be a very fruitful area of research. How does the negative NDE differ from the more positive? Or do many or all NDEs start off negatively and end up positively but this is not reported because, perhaps, the respondent represses the negative aspects? (See chapters 10 and 15.)

Conclusion

In conclusion, I was asked by Arvin Gibson to comment on how my research on NDEs impacted on my professional career. The answer is that it did have an impact—a positive one. Because I was teaching courses on Death, Grief and Bereavement anyway, the NDE was seen as a legitimate outgrowth of these courses. The publishing of my book, *The Eternal Journey,* (Lundahl and Widdison, 1997) was also seen as a plus in my annual review at Northern Arizona University.

Where I did encounter significant problems was because of my membership in the LDS Church. My colleagues knew that I was a member of the LDS church, and when my application for promotion to full professor came before the Promotion and Tenure Committee, two individuals in all seriousness asked, "Is it possible for a Mormon to be a good sociologist?" This evidently impacted on the Committee because I was turned down that year and my promotion was held up for two years. When I was working on my Ph.D. in Cleveland Ohio, the reverse question was asked by members of the Cleveland Second Ward, "Can a sociologist be a good member of the Church?"

As to the Near-Death Experience and LDS theology, I personally and professionally do not see any significant conflicts. Some critics have equated the life review with the final judgment and objected to the report that no matter what the individual had done, he or she did not feel a reduction in love or acceptance from the Being of Light. But God *is* love, and what else would you expect from Him? My belief is that the Life Review and the Day of Judgment are not the same. In specific cases, especially when the individual interjects his or her own interpretation as to what happened during the NDE, significant differences between that experience and LDS theology do occur.

In final analysis, a person cannot rely on an NDE as a substitute for scripture study, prayer, and active involvement in the church for a personal testimony. And it is we who must develop and sustain a relationship with the Lord, not the other way around. Remember, the most important message of the NDE experience is that we are loved unconditionally and are to love our fellow beings, His children, in the same way.

I would be greatly surprised but delighted if it turned out to be possible to prove scientifically that something can exist beyond the physical body. For true skeptics, no amount of evidence will convince them. On the other hand, several avowed skeptics who I know personally did change their views, but it was because they had NDEs themselves and not because of all the evidence. There are millions of modern-day *Lazareths* who have been to the other side and returned to share what they saw and did there. This vast body of cases is a gold mine of information where a lot of "good" research awaits.

14: The Life-Changing Aspects of Teaching about NDEs

By Sandra L. Cherry, MS

About the Author

Sandra was born and raised in Northern California. She received her Bachelor degree at age 49 and Master degree at age 55, thus proving that women can do anything. She has been married 36 inspiring years to Bert L. Cherry—which shows that men can survive anything. They have two children, five grandchildren and two dogs.

Sandra received her M.S. in Psychology from Brigham Young University. She received a Teacher Education Certificate—Elementary, and a Bachelor of Arts degree from Sierra Nevada College. She obtained an Associate of Arts degree in Humanities from Lake Tahoe Community College.

Sandra has taught courses in psychology and near-death experiences at Brigham Young University and Utah Valley State College. She began teaching in 1997 and has continued to this date.

Sandra is a member of the Board of Directors of the Utah chapter of the International Association for Near-Death Studies (IANDS), and is Vice President of Research in that chapter.

She was a convert to the LDS Church and has been an active member for thirty years. Currently she has a calling as a temple worker in the Provo Utah Temple.

The Near-Death Experience (NDE) and the life-changing after-effects on an experiencer are well documented (Ring). The NDE leaves such an impression on NDErs that they typically feel they are profoundly changed by the event. As a psychology instructor, I have an abiding interest in understanding the complex individual and how an event can change not only the behavior and personality of an individual but also his most deeply held beliefs. I have also found, in my research on NDEs, the powerful effect learning, studying and listening to NDErs has on the student.

Studies by Ken Ring and others indicate that the effects of exposure to NDEs and related materials can mirror the life-changing effects seen amongst NDErs (Ring). This phenomenon intrigued me, and it led to my thesis project. In that project, I studied students at Brigham Young University (BYU) taking a course on NDEs, and also the after-effects it had on them (Cherry, 1998). Since that time, I have had the privilege of teaching a course on NDEs at a secular college, as well as introducing the subject to my students at BYU. This chapter will address the development of a course on NDEs, the effects of studying NDEs on the students, and comparing these effects to findings in previous studies.

Course Development

The first challenge in teaching a course on NDEs is to determine what the focus and intent of the course will be. The NDE can be studied from many perspectives: physiological, theological, scientific, psychological, mystical, anthropological, etc. The college or discipline under which the course is being taught will most likely determine the focus and intent of the course. The following are some examples of ways to approach the course curricula and focus.

In 1995 I was privileged to assist Kenneth Ring, a Ph.D. at the University of Connecticut, on a research project he was conducting. At that time, I learned about the courses he had taught in the previous years on NDEs. Dr. Ring was a Professor of Psychology, and the focus of his course reflected the various fields of interest within this discipline. The topics covered were history of research into death-related phenomena; out-of-body experiences; NDEs as related to mystical experiences, suicide, and childhood onset; after-effects; psychic phenomena; interpretation of the experience; evolutionary implications; and life after death. The course included various audio and video tapes featuring accounts of NDEs, NDErs telling first-hand of their experience, and guest lecturers on related topics.

Students were assigned two books as texts; they also were given a list of reading materials from which they were to choose two other books to complete for the course. They were to keep a log of their personal reactions to the material presented in class and their readings. A ten-page term paper on a related subject also was required. Grading for the course was evaluated from the log kept by the students and from the term paper. The format of the class was open and allowed for discussion, exploration and interpretation. At the end of the semester, Dr. Ring administered a short survey to the students regarding their subjective reaction to the course which will be reviewed in detail later in this chapter.

The following example of a NDE course is one where the focus and intent was from many disciplines. While researching my thesis as an undergraduate at Brigham Young University in 1997, I was invited to co-teach an honors course on NDEs by one of the professors on my thesis committee. This provided me with an unusual opportunity to be a part of a *multi-disciplinary course* designed to expose the students to the various explanations for NDEs from the fields of neurophysiology, pharmacology, psychology, anthropology, as well as religious explanations. The course was designed to study the NDE and encounters with death and the spirit world within the context of Latter-day Saint doctrine. Approximately one-half of the course was focused on the biological processes of death and possible medical explanations for the NDE. Professor Brent Top, Dean of Religious Education, and David Busath, M.D., Professor of Zoology, taught the course with an extensive list of professors from many other disciplines as guest lecturers. The list of guest lecturers also included NDErs, researchers, and authors with expertise in NDEs.

Students were assigned two books as texts and also given a list of reading materials. They were assigned to choose a book to read and then to write a book report on it. There were also numerous copies of articles from books and journals provided at weekly readings. Quizzes, take-home assignments, a seven-to-ten-page personal essay on NDE concepts learned, and two mid-terms and a final exam were the basis for grading. Obviously, the focus of the course was broad and very comprehensive. Because this course was an honors class, the curriculum was very advanced and demanded a great commitment on the part of each student. Classes had a formal and structured format and were mostly lectures with time for questions. The same short survey administered in Ring's study also was administered to these students regarding their subjective reactions to the course, which also will be reviewed in detail later in this chapter.

From these examples of NDE courses, it is obvious the curricula diverged in some areas, yet there are elements that are common in these courses. These classes provided the students with a sound definition and understanding of the elements of the NDE. They were given opportunities to explore the cultural and religious differences found in the interpretation of the NDE. The courses also looked at possible biological, psychological and spiritual explanations for the phenomena. Students were immersed in the actual phenomena through lectures, extensive reading material and first-hand accounts of the various NDEs.

Course Texts

In developing an NDE course, the second challenge is to find reading material from an academic textbook on NDEs. Limited information on the NDE can be found in academic texts on "death and dying" as a subtitle in a chapter, but thus far there is not an academic text on the subject of NDEs so it has been necessary to use many different books written by experiencers, researchers, and academic journals. For example, the required readings for Ring's courses were *Life After Life,* by Raymond Moody (1976), and *Heading Toward Omega* by Kenneth Ring (1985). For Top and Busath's course the textbooks were *Beyond Death's Door,* by Brent and Wendy Top (1993), and *Dying to Live* by Susan Blackmore (1993). These books were excellent for the focus and intent of the courses. In the course I taught, the required text on NDEs was *Lessons From the Light,* by Kenneth Ring (1998). This book, I believe, is the most comprehensive textbook available on the subject of NDEs, as it covers the scientific efforts to validate the experiences and also cites rich first-hand-experience accounts to support the subjects addressed. Other books I have recommended in my courses are asterisked on the reference pages. The *Journal of Near-Death Studies* is also a great resource, especially for research projects, and can be found at www.iands.org.

Course Effects on Students

As a university instructor in psychology, it has been my personal endeavor to introduce the NDE to students within an academic format with an emphasis on behavioral, personality and cognitive effects of the experience. I have done this in both courses on NDEs as well as other psychology courses wherever appropriate (and it seems most psych courses are appropriate for the subject at some phase). As part of the course on NDEs, they are submerged in the NDE as a paranormal event and the possibilities that the NDE brings to understanding the meaning of life. They are also introduced to the limitations of science in verifying the experience as viewed, felt, understood and expressed by the NDEr. The most powerful element in the course is for the student to hear firsthand the experience from the NDEr. Along with the reading of personal documentation of NDErs, the student begins to absorb the depth of this phenomenon and its power to affect the lives of the experiencer as well as his own.

Inviting NDErs into the classroom to share their firsthand experiences provides the students with a profound understanding and insight into this phenomenon. They are able to formulate questions that bring them to appreciate the limitations of studying the NDE in a scientific arena while being convinced of the reality of the event as viewed by the NDEr. As the students personally witness the experiencer telling her/his story, they themselves become caught up in the evolutionary impact of the experience and discover they are also changed. The possibility of change in a student due to the direct impact of studying the NDE and listening first hand to those who have experienced this phenomenon is the most pronounced influence from these courses.

Dr. Ring was a pioneer in teaching the NDE phenomenon in an academic setting. According to Ring, one of the most rewarding aspects of teaching such a course is the effect it has on the students. But he was to find the course affected a particular kind of student in a very surprising and rewarding way. Here is an example of such a case:

For the past ten years, I have been teaching a course on the near-death experience at my university. Every semester thirty-five to forty young undergraduates arrive at my classroom on the first day of the new term, usually somewhat nervous about taking such an offbeat course but generally enthusiastic and curious about the topic that has already excited their interest. Normally there is one person—and ordinarily no more than one—among these students who comes to the class with a markedly different orientation, and an advantage over his or her peers. This is the student, though I will only learn later, who has already had an NDE. He or she is there for quite different reasons, and several weeks or even most of the semester may pass before the other students and I learn that there has been an experiencer all along in our midst. But by the time the semester is over, however, we have usually been privy to the story of that student's own NDE who becomes for that day the real teacher in the class. (Ring, 1998)

The fact that a student is comfortable enough to tell his/her story in a public setting is remarkable, as many NDErs are reluctant to share such a personal story. Some have felt the pain of rejection when they have attempted to share their experience. Students who have told their stories about loved ones, friends, or their own experiences with death provide an insight for others to learn and also give great validation to the student that they are not viewed as being off-the-wall. This is an indication that the environment created by such a class encourages students to explore many issues fundamental to their most basic beliefs, values, and fears.

Students Who Had NDEs

An example of one of these unique events occurred during a psychology course I taught several years ago. I had invited an NDEr to tell his story as part of the curriculum on phenomenological theory. I noticed one of my students, a man in his mid 30s, was deeply moved by the account given by our guest speaker. When the students were invited to ask questions, this student had some profound questions that gave the rest us pause to wonder if he had had an NDE. After class he revealed to the guest speaker and I that he had had an NDE and had always been reticent to talk about the experience. I could sense that he was touched by what he had heard and wanted to share with the class his NDE, and he said he would.

Greg Hyde was a successful businessman with an aggressive achieving nature. His business success was interrupted when he was overcome with a manic-depressive episode brought on by bipolar illness. After a serious automobile accident, he began treatment for the illness. The alternating mood swings between the highs of the manic state and the lows of the semi-awake medicated depression were devastating to him. Finally, in a fit of depression, he ingested four times the legal limit of Depacote in an attempt to commit suicide.

The immediate result was to land him in the emergency room of a hospital in Salt Lake City. There he underwent many tests and procedures in an effort to save his life. During one of the procedures, his left lung was penetrated, thus complicating the rescue attempt. He was in a coma for 96 hours, during which time his brain scan was flat. Medical opinion was that even if he awoke from the coma he would suffer severe brain deterioration.

During this period, Greg had his near-death experience. His first memory during this period was of being out of his body. The following is an account of his NDE:

> "The most I remember was that I was out of my body. I was watching all of my relatives talking to me, in my face all the time, but I couldn't talk back . . . I tried and tried, but I couldn't talk back. It was really frustrating.
>
> "I could see all of them, but I couldn't recognize who was who. I just remember . . . what I remember the most was in this really dark room; or at least it seemed dark, and there were these aliens—young alien people.
>
> "All of a sudden it like this great WHOOSH! I just sat there and I couldn't speak, but I looked around and I remember Dad saying something like, 'He's alive, he's alive,' and he ran out of the room. Then I hurt. The pain was everywhere, [especially in] the tracheal tube. I thought maybe I had stuck a knife in my side.
>
> "I was gone then. I was actually visited by Grandpa Don . . . Then Grandma Clark [both deceased].
>
> "Grandpa Don was the same way he was in the hospital when I saw him on his death bed. He was just smiling . . . Also, I saw Sarah and Don in temple clothes [deceased relatives]. They were together and we talked. She gave me a lot of good reasons to live. . . .

"I did see—this is where people don't believe me, but I became a little baby again. I wasn't an adult. I became a little baby in Jesus' arms. He just held me like that. We just talked. He just talked to me. I would say that for ninety hours of the ninety-six hours I was out, I was with Jesus.

"My family asked me what he looked like. I said the hardest thing for me to describe would be Jesus. He is glorified . . . He had a red robe on, and had kind of reddish hair. That is the closest . . . he didn't have a beard.

"I talked to God, too, for just a short time. He didn't have a lot of time.

"I was told the degree I would have had there, and I wasn't satisfied with it. There are three degrees of glory, and there are three degrees within each degree. I was told what degree I would be in, and I wasn't going to be a son of perdition. I didn't see Satan. He was the only one I didn't see. I saw a lot of evil spirits . . . on my journey, in the darkness. Lots, pulling at me, tugging, screaming and hollering, and hooting and drinking and playing. Just like Vegas, except you turn off the lights. Just like it—Babylon. . . .

"All those aliens I saw . . . they were actually human people, but they looked like aliens.

"Later on, I was kind of in the hospital room for, probably, the first two days. I could hear the Goodman music. They played the CD over and it was beautiful. . . . Then I would zoom off. I went upstairs to Heavenly Father. I became a baby again and set in the arms of Jesus, literally. Also, I saw Layne Sayers, who is Chad's sister, who died in an automobile accident in a head-on collision.

"The other thing is that I met my children up there. I have more kids. I knew they were my children and they need to come down."

Greg states that during his recovery period, he had other experiences. For example:

"I had several angels visit—while I was there in bed. Several angels visited and administered to my needs for respiratory healing and strengthening my lungs. Also for guidance through the veil.

"One morning I was visited by the three Goodman children [who were killed in a car accident in December, 1996]. They were all talking to me, each individual: David, Peter, and LeeAnn. They were helping me fight for life by [tapping into] the greatest power from on high. I also felt three ladies, whom I didn't recognize, who had had lung problems, lung failures, working my deep breaths."

As one can deduce from Greg's account of his NDE, it was extremely personal, and he perceived it as sacred. Gregory was very emotional, and each member of the class was deeply touched as we felt the magnitude of what had been witnessed to our spirits. In fact, it is this phenomenon of truth revealed in the personal testimony of the NDE to the listener that seems impossible to fully communicate, for it is impoverished by the limitations of language. But it is a spiritual charge that causes the students to feel and understand the truthfulness of these experiences. Gregory was also affected by his telling of his NDE, for in the testifying of his experience he became a witness of its power to speak to the hearts of others.

I invited Gregory to attend a meeting of the International Association of Near Death Studies—Salt Lake Chapter (IANDS-SLC) to hear and meet others who had had an NDE. He was invited to be a guest speaker at the following meeting. He told me the experience of feeling accepted and free to share his NDE was the beginning of a new life for him. Since that time, Greg has gone on to realize many truths he was given in his NDE and to integrate this new understanding into his life. Gregory is presently working toward getting a graduate degree in psychology so he can help those who share his illness.

During another class, I was privileged to meet a remarkable young woman, **Sage Volkman,** who also turned out to be an NDEr. She was taking my class in Psychology on Personality Theory at Utah Valley State College. When she entered the classroom I, like all others in the room, knew she was different. The most obvious difference was the fact that she was a burn survivor who had sustained numerous scars. But the most powerful impression was her countenance—she was so kindly in manner, even under such scrutiny.

As I began to learn about her, I became very aware that she had a special gift of love and openness. I introduced the topic of NDEs early in my course and soon learned privately from Sage that she had experienced an NDE, so it seemed natural to invite her to be an NDE guest speaker for the class near the end of the course. She was a bit nervous to speak in front of her peers on such a personal subject, but she agreed and even invited her brother and friends to come on the special day. The following is Sage's story:

> "I will start at the beginning. When I was a little child, my parents were hippies. They tried every drug there was available in

those years. At the age of about 3, I asked my parents who God and Jesus were (I was a pretty precocious child). They said if I really wanted to know, they would find a church where we could go and find the answers. My mom had been baptized Catholic as a child, but my father did not have a background in any religion. We went to different churches but my dad was drawn to the Mormon Church. After two years of visits from the missionaries, my family decided to be baptized. I was very disappointed because I was only five years old and couldn't be baptized, but my eight-year-old brother, Avery, and my parents, were baptized in 1986.

"It was a week later when my dad took Avery and I on a fishing trip. I was a tomboy and loved to go with them. Besides, I got out of school. Fishing is best really early in the morning, so Avery and dad left me asleep in the camper while they went fishing nearby. Dad came back to check on me frequently. While they were fishing, Avery heard the dog bark and turned to see the camper engulfed in smoke and flames. He and dad ran to the camper, where dad rushed in to find me but was unable to locate where I was. He was overcome by the smoke and flames and had to leave. He entered a second time, knowing that if he couldn't find me he would have to watch his little girl die. This time he found me. The sleeping bag had melted to my body, and I was not breathing. Dad sustained second-degree burns on his hand and face while saving my life. Dad carried me out and gave me mouth-to-mouth resuscitation until I started to breathe. Avery felt a prompting that they should move away from the burning camper, and within seconds of them moving me the camper blew up. If we have not moved, we would all surely have been engulfed in flames by the explosion. I was in a coma by this time and remember none of these events.

"By this time people from the camp had called for help, and I was taken to a hospital. I had received second- and third-degree burns over seventy percent of my body. I was so horribly burned that when they were moving me, Avery saw the gurney and asked, 'What was that?' and my parents said, 'That was Sage.' They soon had to move me to the Shriners Hospital Burn Center for Children in Texas. Without any reluctance, my family packed up and moved from Albuquerque, New Mexico, to Texas to be near me. During that time, my parents were told over and over by the doctors that I wouldn't make it, but not once did they give up hope. I was in a coma for six weeks. When I finally opened my eyes, my parents were thrilled. They were remarkable, as they never questioned their new faith, never asked why, or tried to blame God. Instead, they were sustained by their faith in Heavenly Father and the LDS Church. The wonderful members of the stake in Texas were always there for them and performed endless acts of kindness.

"During the following years, I underwent 78 surgeries. It has been hard and painful, but I have been sustained by my faith in Jesus Christ.

"This is the part I want most to share with you. When I came out of the coma, my parents asked me where I was during all that time. I told them that I had had a nightmare and I was in darkness. I could see these eyes glaring at me, and I was scared. I remembered that in Primary they had taught me that if I was ever afraid, all I had to do was pray to my Heavenly Father, and He would help me. So I started to pray, and soon the darkness became a gray, and then I was in a place where it was filled with light. The light was brighter than anything here, but it did not hurt my eyes. I knew that I was not dreaming any more and I felt such peace.

"There before me were two angels standing on either side of a platform that led to a stairway. These stairs led to a throne where Jesus was sitting. I began to climb them, and I felt Jesus beckoning to me to come to Him. I climbed up on His lap where He held me and loved me. We did not need to talk because everything we wanted to say was communicated telepathically. I felt His love, and it filled me with indescribable joy. He comforted me, and I told Him I never wanted to leave. He said He knew, but that I needed to come back. I told Him that it would be too painful. He told me He knew, but He loves me and would always be there for me. I felt so safe and in total peace. I said, 'Okay.'

"Next thing I knew I woke up in a hospital bed. The whole time lapse could have been a minute of earthly time, and yet I know I was with Him the whole six weeks while He loved and comforted me.

"This experience has given me a deep and abiding faith in how much we are loved. I have had many trials, both physically and emotionally, but I have overcome them through believing in the constant love of my Savior. Once, after I was home from the hospital, I was looking out the window at the trees and wondering when my hands would grow back, like the branches of the trees that always grew new limbs. I asked my mom when would my hands grow back. She said that was one of the saddest days of her life when she had to tell me I would never grow hands. I have my little stubs, and they serve me well, but at that time I could only try to realize they would never be like my hands used to be.

"The doctors told my parents I would never walk. Well, I would not let that stop me. I was going to walk, and I continued to work toward that goal until it became a reality. I know that people are jealous of my beautiful hair, because they always look at me (laughing by class members). And my brother, Avery, says I get all the attention, and he is jealous. (Avery hugs her and says it's true.) I tell people my nickname is 'crispy critter' (more laughing).

"Life is good, and I live each day with a sense of humor. I am happy, and people wonder how I can be with all that I have gone through. I tell them you have two ways to see the world—you can see it as a good place with wonderful people to love and be loved by, or you can see everything as a problem and always feel anger in your heart. I choose to be happy."

Many of the students were visibly touched, and some were crying as Sage finished her story. She asked them if they had any questions. A young man named Peter, who was over 6'4" and viewed as a strong, masculine character by his peers, stood up and with a voice filled with emotion said, "Sage, I want you to know that from this day forward I am a different person. Your life story and incredible example have changed something inside of me, and I will never be the same. Because of you I will be a better person. Thank you from the bottom of my heart."

The entire class burst into applause! It was a poignant moment.

These are two examples of how hearing the NDEr tell his/her story creates an atmosphere for a paradigm shift. A paradigm shift does not occur due to a conscious effort in the majority of instances. Rather, a profound shift in attitude seems to be a spontaneous response to the cognitive or external environment. The listener has a new perception of the values and beliefs that direct her/his life. It is very extraordinary for an event to consistently create an atmosphere in which many persons have a paradigm shift, but that repeatedly seemed to be the case in these courses where students were exposed to an NDEr and her/his story.

Kenneth Ring observed this same kind of change amongst many of his students and decided to take an informal self-report survey following his NDE courses. As can be seen from the results of these surveys, persons exposed to an NDEr frequently do have a paradigm shift that influences their deeply-held beliefs and values.

Results of Surveys on Changes in Attitudes and Beliefs

Dr. Ring, along with myself and other instructors, were impressed by the changes we witnessed in our students during our courses on

NDEs. In an attempt to measure these changes, we administered Ring's (1996) brief questionnaire at the conclusion of our courses. The survey items were taken from a past survey evaluating attitude changes amongst NDErs (Ring, 1984). In administering this survey, we were aware of the vast limitations of the self-report method, especially without a precourse survey for comparison or a follow-up to determine the lasting effects. Also, the computation of results by percentage without a statistical analysis was less than scientific. Nevertheless, the results gave a glimpse of the possibility that exposure to the NDE can make a profound difference in people's lives.

As noted in an earlier discussion, the development of course curriculum reflects many different approaches to the phenomenon of the near-death experience. The courses in the table below reflect this diversity in NDE course structure as well as courses in psychology that expose the students to only one NDE or, in one case, to no NDE content in the curriculum. It is also worthy to note that these courses were taught by different instructors with different approaches to the scientific, spiritual, religious and personal meaning of the NDE. Also included in the table are the results of a survey given to members of IANDS who are self-selected by virtue of their interest in NDEs and with varied exposure to NDEs. These diverse environments exposed survey participants to a variety of contexts along with exposure to the NDE. Thus, the possibility of the survey results showing a common element of change amongst these groups is phenomenal.

The surveys given at Brigham Young University (BYU), Utah Valley State College (UVSC) and International Association of Near-Death Studies (IANDS) included questions regarding demographics, sex, age, religious affiliation, education and occupation. There were no significant correlations found in Sex, Age, Education or Occupation. The results did indicate a large majority of these participants were members of The Church of Jesus Christ of Latter-day Saints, which was interesting due to the fact the only non-secular institution was BYU. And yet, religious affiliation does not reflect the individual's activity level or religious/spiritual beliefs. This finding could be a variable in interpreting the survey results, as will be discussed in the conclusion.

The following table indicates the percent of students for each course (or IANDS members) reporting changes in attitudes and beliefs on eight different items. Here is a sample of a survey question and the choice of responses:

I believe the near-death experiences to be authentic

Strongly Decreased	Decreased	No Change	Increased	Strongly Increased
1	2	3	4	5

Explanation of the Column Headings
in the Following Charts (*Uconn 1, etc.*)

1—Represents results of survey developed by Ring (1996) and *administered to students in NDE course.*

2—IANDS: SLC: International Association of Near-Death Studies: Salt Lake Chapter. These are the results of the survey, first used by Ring (1996), administered to IANDS:SLC members, which represents the one group highly exposed to NDEs that were not students enrolled in a university.

3—Psychology 3460—Personality Theory students who were exposed to one guest NDE speaker.

4—Psychology 111H—Intro to Psychology students were not exposed to NDEs during the course curriculum.

NDE-Course Effects on Students

Percent of Students Reporting Changes in Attitudes and Beliefs After Exposure to NDEs:

	UConn 1 Spring '93 (N=28)	UConn 1 Fall '93 (N=28)	MSU 1 Fall '93 (N=45)	BYU 1 Fall '98 (N=32)
1. Belief in Authenticity of NDE:				
Increased	**96**	**90**	**96**	**72**
Decreased	0	0	2	3
No Change	4	10	2	25
2. Fear of Death:				
Increased	0	4	0	3
Decreased	**71**	**60**	**71**	**66**
No Change	29	36	29	31
3. View of Death:				
More Positive	**82**	**90**	**82**	**59**
Less Positive	0	0	0	3
No Change	18	10	24	63

4. Belief in Life After Death:

Increased	**82**	**90**	**76**	**34**
Decreased	0	0	0	3
No Change	18	10	24	63

5. Openness to Reincarnation:

Increased	54	29	38	6
Decreased	4	7	9	31
No Change	43	64	53	63

6. Spiritual Orientation:

Increased	**61**	**57**	**64**	44
Decreased	0	0	2	0
No Change	39	43	33	**56**

7. Belief in God:

Increased	29	29	36	25
Decreased	0	4	2	0
Other Change	43	**54**	27	—
No Change	29	14	36	**75**

8. Belief in Purposefulness of Life:

Increased	**68**	**79**	**58**	**50**
Decreased	4	0	2	0
No Change	29	21	40	50
9. Exposure to NDEs:	**High**	**High**	**High**	**High**

Percent of Students Reporting Changes in Attitudes and Beliefs After Exposure to NDEs, Continued:

	UVSC 1	IANDS 2	UVSC 3	BYU 4
	Fall '01	Fall '99	Winter '02	Fall '98
	(N=16)	(N=44)	(N=31)	(N=36)
1. Belief in Authenticity of NDE:				
Increased	**100**	**93**	**81**	14
Decreased	0	0	3	8
No Change	0	7	16	**78**
2. Fear of Death:				
Increased	0	2	0	6
Decreased	**75**	**82**	45	11
No Change	25	16	**55**	**83**
3. View of Death:				
More Positive	**88**	**82**	**55**	14

Less Positive	6	5	3	6
No Change	6	14	42	**80**
4. Belief in Life After Death:				
Increased	**56**	**89**	**65**	25
Decreased	0	2	0	0
No Change	44	9	35	**75**
5. Openness to Reincarnation:				
Increased	6	34	0	0
Decreased	31	39	29	14
No Change	**63**	27	**71**	**86**
6. Spiritual Orientation:				
Increased	**81**	**89**	**55**	25
Decreased	0	2	0	6
No Change	19	9	45	**69**
7. Belief in God:				
Increased	**56**	**77**	45	19
Decreased	0	2	0	0
Other Change	—	—	—	—
No Change	44	21	**55**	**81**
8. Belief in Purposefulness of Life:				
Increased	**69**	**96**	45	30
Decreased	0	2	0	3
No Change	31	2	**55**	**67**
9. Exposure to NDEs:	**High**	**High**	**Low**	**None**

Observations about the Surveys

The results of these brief surveys supported the hypothesis that many students would experience significant changes in attitudes and beliefs after exposure to NDEs. It was expected that the IANDS members would show a high percentage of attitude change due to their high interest in NDEs, but the percent of change reported in all courses where the NDE was the focus was most impressive. Even the UVSC students in the psychology course (Winter '02) who were only exposed to one NDE, serves as a comparison group to determine whether significant attitude changes could be expected to be the norm in college courses involving NDEs. The course survey results for this class show the largest percent of "no change" in all items. Comparing these results to the course results of students exposed to more NDEs implies that the NDE exposure could be an altering factor. This is an exciting possibility and hopefully will lead to more rigorous research in the possible effects of exposure to NDEs.

Another area of interest is the LDS population taking the BYU course on NDEs. It could be assumed that persons with a deeply religious or spiritual orientation already rooted in a strong belief in the continuation of life after death would hold strong beliefs that would not be affected by exposure to NDEs. This is supported by the results that indicate they were the least affected in the areas of *Belief in Life After Death, Spiritual Orientation, and Belief in God.* And yet the results also show a 66 percent decrease in *Fear of Death,* a 59 percent more positive *View of Death* and a 50 percent increase in *Belief in Purposefulness of Life.* This could be an indication that exposure to the NDE supports and increases the belief system of religiously oriented individuals in unique areas related to one's mortality.

The participants of the NDE course taught at UVSC and IANDS (both secular organizations) indicate a predominately LDS affiliation, but unlike the BYU (fall 1998) students, they report over a 50 percent change in values and beliefs in most areas.

Why do these LDS participants indicate stronger changes than the LDS students at a non-secular religious institution? As indicated earlier, the individual's level of activity and strength of religious/spiritual beliefs are not always reflected in one's religious affiliation. In fact, my experience in teaching at UVSC has led me to believe a significant number of these young people are searching for answers to many of the issues in this survey. Unlike the students at BYU who are presumed to already have a deep commitment to their religion and to be actively engaged in their church in order to attend BYU, the UVSC students and IANDS members have no such criteria for acceptance into the organization. Therefore, it seems a forgone assumption that those affiliated with the LDS faith but not especially actively engaged in church-school attendance or systematic learning of doctrine would experience the most profound changes in attitudes concerning the items of this survey.

The implications of being able to create an atmosphere where a person's beliefs and values are profoundly affected is an important goal of psychology. Therapy is the most common method used to help clients change behavior, cognitive patterns, and hopefully to permanently change deeply held beliefs and values in a positive direction. These results support the possibility that exposure to NDEs can create an atmosphere for such a paradigm shift. Further quantitative research on the effects of exposure to NDEs conducted with a control group could provide further evidence of a valid change in beliefs and attitudes. Also, the importance of qualitative research in future studies should be considered as an alternative research method that might give greater understanding of the effects of NDEs on others.

Since the NDE is a subjective event whose meaning is embodied in the language of the experience, then an alternate way to examine the experience and its impact on the non-NDEr could be to use a descriptive analysis of the participant's experience. An example of a participant's description of the effect of taking the BYU '98 NDE course is evident in the following statement provided by a student:

"The most important thing that I have learned is that death is life, just in another state. Much of the fear is gone. It makes me realize that this life is really important. I feel that because of this class I am at a higher consciousness than before. I see life in a different way. It's made me feel more passionate about living, and I almost think of death as a reward for living."

This example clearly does reflect the quantitative results obtained from the course survey. And yet the survey could not capture the subjective meaning of these life-changing repercussions reported by the above participant. This is only one example of the many anecdotal comments by students that illustrate changes in their attitudes and beliefs that were not evident in the quantitative data.

In closing, I would like to encourage instructors to include the NDE as a part of their curriculum in both religious and secular institutions. In doing so, I believe they will expose their students to a possible value shift that can positively and significantly affect their lives.

The following statement by Professor Lawman (1995) emphasizes the importance of influencing university students in ways other than merely academic skills: "The quality of our teaching is best evaluated not simply in terms of what our students learn, but in terms of the probability that all students will be changed for the better—often in personal ways that go far beyond course content." (Lawman, 1995, p. 10)

Whether it be in a classroom, a community, or among neighbors, family, friends or intimate loved ones, we can further the insight learned from the NDE by exposing others to such a remarkable phenomenon.

Part IV

Comparisons, Religious Effects, and the Future

I haven't shared this experience with many people. It is too sacred to me. But whenever I have shared it, I have always told people that the experience has taught me that God is willing to reach out and talk with us. I'm nobody special . . . nobody knows my name—but I do know that God knows my name. And that he was willing to reach out and talk with me. If he would talk to somebody like me, then he would do it for anybody.

That was a realization that profoundly influenced my joining the Church. God didn't just talk to Joseph Smith, a farm boy in New York. He talked to me too. And he would talk to anybody, it seems to me, if he would talk to somebody like me.

—Joe Swick
(Chapter 16)

15: NDEs that Add Insights to Mormon Theology: A Comparison with Key Elements of LDS Theology

Chapters 4 and 5, in Part 1 of this book, describe in some detail the teachings, and to a certain extent, the origin and history, of The Church of Jesus Christ of Latter-day Saints. They draw from other chapters in the book, as well as other sources, to show areas of correlation—or non-correlation—of the teachings with NDE accounts. The emphasis there (in Part I of the book) is on the doctrinal data rather than the NDEs. As such, the NDE examples in Part 1 are sparse and given solely as reinforcement of the main theological message being discussed.

On the other hand, in this Part IV of the book, a more complete NDE exhibit of particular LDS teachings is given, and in this latter portion, the NDE is emphasized rather than the particular LDS teaching and its scriptural origins. This technique was adopted so that each area could get relatively complete exposure within a limited space. It has the advantage of full coverage of the subject, but the disadvantage of some duplication.

What follows will be an examination of different events, repeatedly found in NDEs, to determine their correspondence or lack of same with different LDS teachings. The resulting display will not be comprehensive, for to do so would fill several volumes. Nevertheless, it will show points of agreement or disagreement with some primary LDS teachings.

The reader is encouraged to make his/her own judgment as to the validity of the illustrated comparisons. In making those judgments, the reader should bear in mind that the majority of the referenced LDS materials were published in the early to mid 1800s.

As noted earlier in this book, the resultant work will be the product of the authors, with all of their biases and prejudices intact. Undoubtedly there may be areas—both in the NDE selections and in the LDS references—where others may disagree with our comparisons and analyses.

The Light

The Light is one of the most frequently mentioned aspects of those having had an in-depth NDE. My own research showed that sixty percent of those I interviewed described some aspect of The Light. Words failed many of those being interviewed as they struggled to explain the magnificence and otherworldly brilliance of something which was visual, yet incorporated features which were beyond a mere visible electromagnetic frequency. See chapters 4, 10, and 11 for LDS teachings on The Light.

In 1970, after her twenty-second birthday, **Kimberly Clark Sharp** was in a waiting line at the Kansas State Department of Motor Vehicles, when she collapsed. Her NDE is described in detail in her book, *After the Light* (Sharp, 1995, pp. 17–28). A portion of her experience is reproduced below:

> Suddenly, an enormous explosion erupted beneath me, an explosion of light rolling out to the farthest limits of my vision. I was in the center of the Light. It blew away everything, including the fog. It reached the ends of the universe, which I could see, and doubled back on itself in endless layers. I was watching eternity unfold.
>
> The light was brighter than hundreds of suns, but it did not hurt my eyes. I had never seen anything as luminous or as golden as this Light, and I immediately understood it was entirely composed of love, all directed at me. This wonderful, vibrant love was very personal, as you might describe secular love, but also sacred. The only words I could formulate in the midst of this incredible Light were from my childhood: "Honey home." It was something I used to say when we had been on an outing and I began to spot the familiar landmarks of our neighborhood.
>
> Though I had never seen God, I recognized this light as the Light of God. But even the word God seemed too small to describe the magnificence of that presence. I was with my Creator, in holy communication with that presence. The Light was directed at me and through me; it surrounded me and pierced me. It existed just for me.

In 1965, **Lois Clark** and her husband took the children Christmas shopping. When the car ran out of gas, her husband parked the car alongside the road and went for gas. As Lois and the children sat there waiting for him, a drunken driver hit them, knocking their car into the median. The children were relatively unhurt, but Lois was thrown from the car and it rolled backwards over her prostrate body. A portion of our interview follows (Gibson, 1992, pp. 48–40):

> "I didn't hear anything else for awhile—and I'm floating up here—and I'm looking down at this woman on a table, and . . . and I realize it's me. There were all these people working around the table, and there was this form lying there.
>
> "I thought, What's going on? and all of a sudden I saw this bright light. I've never seen anything like it as long as I've lived, since. It was just beautiful. So I started walking towards this light to see what was beyond it, but . . . but every time I started to take a step towards it I was told, 'No, go back.'
>
> "I didn't want to go back to all that pain. But finally I went back, I guess, because I kept hearing the doctors say, 'Okay, okay, she's starting to get stabled out.'"
>
> "**. . . When you saw this light, did you see anything dark ahead of time?**"
>
> "The only dark I saw was to the side. I saw that light and wanted to go towards it, that's all my mind would hold."
>
> "**What did the light look like?**"
>
> "It was kind of a . . . a yellow, mellow, bright, white light."
>
> "**Was it hard to look at?**"
>
> "Yes. It was so bright to begin with that I had to, sort of, look down, then up, and then blink my eyes down again."
>
> "**Did you feel as if it was real, or a dream?**"
>
> "At the time that I was in the place to see the light I thought it was real. The whole thing—oh, there was the light, and there seemed to be soft, soft, soft . . . you couldn't really hear it, you more felt this music. It . . . it was soft, and immaculately beautiful. There was, I guess there's no way to really describe it, there was a feeling of peace, beauty, love, and . . . it just felt like this is what I want. This is the ultimate. You're so at peace within your whole being that you just seem to float, like. . . ."

The Plan: Everything Has a Purpose

Many of those who have NDEs return with an understanding that *everything* that happens in this life does so, in the broadest sense, for a purpose. Several of those I interviewed made it clear that this was the case. Indeed, I used to have good-natured debates with Don Wood (chapter 3) where he would insist that "there are no accidents," and I would take the opposite position.

Implicit in this understanding of purpose is that there is some preordained plan which governs much of what happens in our life and in the known universe. Some who have had NDEs actually use the word "Plan" to define what they saw and heard in their experience.

The existence of a premortal plan and the fundamental part it plays in LDS doctrine is described in chapter 5. Our knowledge of this plan as premortals is also discussed.

Ranelle Wallace had a premonition of disaster before she and her husband crashed and burned in a light airplane. Her in-depth experience is described in the book, *The Burning Within*. A brief extraction from her story follows (Wallace, 1994, p. 109):

> The younger spirits, the ones who hadn't been to earth, were then called away. They seemed younger only because they hadn't gained the experiences of earth life yet. We all looked the same age, somewhere in our twenties. After they were gone, the rest of us spoke on a higher level, sharing things we could not share with the others. Life on earth does something to us. It strips away a naivete, an innocence, and infuses our eternal selves with maturity and wisdom. With the others gone, we could now bare all of our lessons and experiences from earth. We looked forward to the future in a way we hadn't before, knowing better what the whole *plan* entailed.

Jayne's experience was told at an IANDS conference and later recorded by Carol Zaleski in her book, *Otherworld Journeys*. It occurred when she was young. An extract from her story follows (Zaleski, 1987, p. 125):

> It was a dynamic light, not like a spotlight. It was an incredible energy—a light you wouldn't believe. I almost floated in it. It was feeding my consciousness feelings of unconditional love, complete safety, and complete, total perfection . . . It just POWED into you. My consciousness was going out, getting larger and taking in more; I expanded, and more and more came in. It was such rapture, such bliss. And then, a piece of knowledge came in: it was that I was immortal, indestructible. I cannot be hurt, cannot be lost. We don't have anything to worry about. And that the world is perfect; everything that happens is

part of a perfect *plan*. I don't understand this part now, but I still know it's true. . . . Later, when I was saying the Lord's prayer, and I got to the part that says "thine is the kingdom, and the power, and the glory," I thought that nothing could describe this experience any better. It was pure power and glory.

The question might reasonably be asked, if God has a plan, what about the holocaust? Either that was included in the plan, and if so, why? Or, it was not included in the plan, in which case, why did God let it happen?

In **Howard Storm's** extensive NDE he asked those questions of his angel "friends." In response, he was taken back in time and witnessed the horror of the Jews being destroyed. He also saw angels greeting them as they rose from their destroyed bodies, and he felt of God's anguish over the obscenity which was the Holocaust. His account of what they told him is repeated, in part, here (Storm, 2000, pp. 110–11):

> I asked how could God allow this to happen. They told me this was not God's will. This was an abomination to God. God wants this never to happen again. This was an abomination to God.
> . . . They told me that God was very unhappy with the course of human history and was going to intervene to change the world. God had watched us sink to depths of depravity and cruelty at the very time that God was giving us the instruments to make the world a godlier world. God had intervened in the world many times before, but this time God was going to change the course of human events.

Love

Portions of an interview conducted by Dr. Ring (Ring, 1984, pp. 39–40) with the anthropology professor, **Patrick Gallagher,** are intriguing. He had been an agnostic prior to his NDE. His experience occurred after an automobile accident in which he was thrown from his car and sustained massive injuries, including a skull fracture. He was comatose and close to death when he arrived at the hospital:

> I also felt and saw of course that everyone was in a state of absolute compassion to everything else. . . . It seemed, too, that love was the major axiom that everyone automatically followed. This produced a phenomenal feeling of emotion to me, again, in the free sense that the flight did earlier, because it made me feel that . . . there was nothing but love. . . . it just seemed like the real thing, just to feel this sense of total love in every direction.

David Herard was first interviewed by me in 1991. Then, in 2004, I called him and interviewed him again. David was severely injured twice during his double tour of duty in Vietnam. He had an NDE as a result of his second injury. His story is told chapter 7 of this book. A portion of our interview illustrates what David had to say about the love he found during his NDE:

> **"When the hand touched your shoulder, you didn't get a chance to turn around and see who it was, did you?"**
>
> "No. All I can tell you is that, as I see it, it was God's hand."
>
> **"That's what you felt?"**
>
> "Right."
>
> **"And it was just a single contact where the hand touched your shoulder?"**
>
> "Actually, after it touched my shoulder, I felt an embrace— as if I were being embraced from the back by someone. And I could see a bright light from the side."
>
> **"How did that feel?"**
>
> "When I was embraced, I felt a warmth all through me. And there was the feeling of . . . of love. As if it were all the love there is."
>
> **"Do you mean you felt that all the love in the world was there?"**
>
> "No, it was like that was all the love there was, everywhere. It was like . . . I can't explain the feeling. It's beyond words."

Life's Review

A life's review is not all that common among those who have NDEs. Of sixty-eight people I interviewed for the two books, *Glimpses of Eternity* and *Echoes From Eternity,* only 10.8 percent of those who had NDEs also had life reviews. For those who did have a life's review, the experience was profound. Their memories of the review were clear, even many years later, and it shaped much of the rest of their life. During their reviews, they saw and felt the emotions of the events as if they were real time. Usually, they relived the emotions that they had felt when they had undergone the experiences—as well as the emotions and feelings of those they had interacted with.

Barbara, interviewed by Dr. Ring, had her NDE after a spinal fusion operation (Ring, 1984, pp. 105–7). As a child, she was raised in a middle-class family. She was severely punished when she violated particular family rules, such as wetting the bed as a very young child.

Following her operation, she wet the bed and immediately went into an NDE. There, she had a "Life's Review."

... Then I was able to see my whole life unwinding from that perspective of this poor neurotic little girl who was, you know, not really coming from the same place all the other little kids were coming from. I was a very, very lonely child. I was watching this whole childhood unfold and realizing that my head was in the wrong place and I was able to refocus so that I had a better understanding of the rejection I had felt. All that rejection was in my own head. It wasn't everybody else rejecting me. Everyone else was just coming from their own problems and hangups. All of that stuff that had been layered on me was because my vision of what was going on was really screwed up. . . .

Did you actually see these scenes like images, or were you just aware of this?

Okay, this is very, very hard to explain . . . what I was really sensing was that I had layers and layers and layers of this stuff. Like the domino effect, the sudden realization from the beginning was just going through and everything was shifting. Like each electron was jumping into another orbit. It was like a healing. . . .

The whole overall effect was that I had relived my life with a much healthier attitude that had healed me. And by the time I got to the end I had the first sense of wanting to live, of wanting to turn around and struggle again in that bed.

John Stirling had a remarkable life's review midst the stars. Due to a motorcycle accident during a devastating despondency, he had an unusual NDE. His story is told in chapter 7. Pertinent portions of our interview follow:

"The life's review came as a shock. When I heard the voice say: 'Well, let's see your life,' I didn't know how it would happen. It was totally unexpected, and it was right there in my view. It was as if both the voice and I were viewing it—and both of us could feel it as well as visually see it."

"Was there judgment in the voice?"

"Not at all. It was the same feeling you would get in a heart-to-heart conversation with a loving father about anything that concerned you. Not that judgment would be involved, but that you would both view the circumstances, see the way things were, and go on from there."

"So it was a teaching experience more than a judgmental experience?"

"It wasn't judgmental. I didn't know that I was coming back

so I didn't realize, at the time, that it was a teaching experience."

"You mentioned that when you saw different events from your life you could also feel the emotions associated with those events. Did you understand that the voice also felt those emotions?"

"I felt, inside, that we both felt the emotions. As I recall, the life review started when I was two or three years old. The review, starting from that time, showed all the daily events, all the people involved, as I lived through the events. There were the funny times, the sad times, and my concerns at the time—for my age.

"So that when I was five, ten, or fifteen years old, for the wisdom I had at that age, I felt the same kind of emotions as I had when I was that age. I also knew where I was at, spiritually, for that given age. That's one of the reasons I felt comfortable with my life's review. Because I felt as if I really had tried as hard as I could, in accordance with what I knew at that age."

"Some people who have had this type of life's review indicated that they also felt, when they had done something good for someone, or when they had hurt someone, the emotions of that individual. Did you feel anything like that?"

"Yes. When I was younger I was a meek and timid kid, and I didn't do many things that would create a flash-back for me— adverse things that I would feel. My father died when I was a teenager, though, and I got kind of bitter and angry. Then I did do some things to hurt other people. I saw those events and felt the effect on the people. I also felt, at the time, my own bitterness."

"When you did something to help someone, did you feel their response to that as well?"

"Yes. I could feel the joy and the happiness as well as the pain, depending upon the circumstances."

At fourteen years of age, **Elizabeth Clark** had an extensive NDE as a result of an overdose. Her resulting experience was diverse, and apparently tailored to her needs at the time. Portions of her NDE dealt with the means by which she was brought to an acknowledgment of her transgressions, but in a spirit of love. Her story is told in chapter 8. The pertinent portions of our interview—dealing with judgment—follows:

"When you came out of the tunnel and entered the room, did you know the people that were there?"

"I'm not sure. I didn't really want to know them because of my feelings of embarrassment. They seemed to think it was funny that I was trying to hide."

"Why were you so embarrassed?"

"It was because of what I had done—and because of the

marks on my robe."

"What marks?"

"The robe I was wearing was white, a pure white, but it had black spots on it."

"Where were the spots, and why did they bother you?"

"There were several of them on my left side, down to my ankle. They bothered me because I knew that they represented some of the things I had done wrong. When I bent down I was trying to hide them, and that's what the people were laughing about. There was no way I could hide them."

". . .You felt Him embrace you?"

"Yes. He put His arms around me and hugged me, just as my father would. The feelings I had at that point were extremely intense. My children and my parents, for example, I love with all my heart. Yet in this life I couldn't produce a small portion of what I felt in His presence. The love was a mutual feeling between us, and it went through my whole body."

"Did you have a life's review?"

"When He asked me if I knew the things I did wrong, they were brought back to my memory with full emotion. There was a clear understanding of each wrong event, and I felt remorse. The memories were very painful."

"What was His reaction when you remembered each event?"

"There was just love coming from Him. The sorrowful feelings were coming from me."

"In a sense, then, you were your own worst judge?"

"That's true, and it was extremely painful. It was clear to me what I had done wrong, and I suffered emotional pain as the memories came to me."

Families and Genealogy

Chapter 16 provides a portion of **Renee Zamora's** experience. Her experience, as detailed more completely in *Echoes From Eternity* (Gibson, 1993, pp. 207–14), was unique in that she was told to refer to a particular LDS scriptural reference. In addition, she saw an individual during her NDE whom she identified as Satan. The pertinent portion is reproduced:

> Not only did I know who the man was, but I understood that I should read the 138th Section of the Doctrine and Covenants in order to understand my

experience. Also, I knew that I would find further answers by attending the temple.

Many of the answers came in the temple, and some of them are too sacred to discuss here. It became clear to me, though, that the people I had seen were those who had passed on, but were confined to this earth, and who needed further work done for them in order to progress beyond where they were. I also understood why Satan was there, why he knew me, and how privileged I was to see what I did. Much of what I saw had symbolic meaning beyond the outward appearances of the events themselves.

Since that experience, I have become a fanatic concerning genealogy and temple work. The patience of my husband is sometimes tried as I work on genealogy.

As a final thought, Renee said:

The genealogical and temple work that we do is enormously important. We should work diligently to find those people who are not necessarily on our direct genealogical line, and we should perform the work so that their temple ordinances can be done. Since my experience I have been driven to locate all the people I saw that needed their temple work done. Each person is important in the sight of the Lord.

Stella's story, as told to Dr. Ring (Ring, 1984, pp. 110–14), was remarkable in a number of ways. **Stella** was raised in the deep south of the United States as a fundamentalist believing Christian. Her parents saw to it that she adhered to the strictures of her religious upbringing. When she was eight years old, a friend told her—to her amazement and dismay—that she was adopted. When confronted by Stella as she sobbed out the accusation, her parents confessed that she was adopted. They refused to tell her anything about her birth parents.

After this discovery Stella struggled for many years over her "identity." On one occasion prior to her NDE she had a vision in which she saw some strange characters. Much later she determined that they were Hebrew characters whose translation meant "Beyond the Vanishing Point."

During her NDE Stella encountered a being of light. Dr. Ring asked her:

"Did this being communicate with you?"

"Yes . . . [that] there was a purpose to my being sent back here and the purpose had to do with bringing knowledge, particular knowledge. One, of the experience and that there is life after this on a much greater level. . . . We're so much more. That we have the ability and capacity to know."

While communicating telepathically with this being of light she was told—much to her surprise—that she was Jewish. As she described it:

> You ready for this? He told me [that I was Jewish]. . . . This was part of what I had to do, part of a process to be able to do what I will ultimately come to do. This was something that was a blockage that I didn't know anything about. But it definitely was a key to understanding. It has great meaning to me. There wasn't anybody who could have told me that.

So, without telling her adoptive family, she started a search for her biological roots. She knew where she had been born so she started there, with no success. It was as if she didn't exist. Despondent, she walked on a nearby beach. She uttered what amounted to a silent prayer which was: "Okay, I'm trying to do what you said to do and it can't be done by what I'd consider to be normal means. The paperwork's not there, so if this is what you want done, you're going to have to help."

Stella went back to town, and was at a table in a restaurant when two policemen walked in. She thought to herself, "I bet there's a clue."

Dr. Ring describes how Stella summoned her courage and told one of the policemen that she was looking for someone and wondered if he could help. The policeman referred her to a couple who had run a local newspaper, and they, in turn sent her to a local judge. The judge was astonished when she approached him.

> It was like turning back the clock when he saw my face. . . . [He] took one look at me and, after [seeing me], he put me in touch with my grandfather who had retired and moved down to Florida.

Ring recounts what happened next in this manner:

> She goes on to describe a very dramatic meeting with her grandfather in which he showed her the family album and other memorabilia and confirmed for her *another* fact that had been conveyed to her by the being of light—that she did indeed have a brother. She subsequently spent some time with him and his family in Texas as well. She was also finally able to meet briefly with her own biological mother, but that visit, unfortunately, was not pleasant. . . .
>
> Stella's life changed remarkably after those experiences. She became a very successful woman in all respects. She was planning to write a book titled *Beyond the Vanishing Point.*

There are numerous instances in the literature where deceased relatives helped one of their kin having an NDE. **Bill English's** experience is just one among many (Gibson, 1999, p. 78):

> As I walked along the path in the meadow I came to a stone archway. It seemed almost as if I were called, or drawn, to the archway. I walked through it and entered a courtyard where I saw my father. He was dressed all in white, and he was bathed in sort of an iridescent white light.
>
> We approached each other, and I remember telling him that I was feeling lost and confused. I realized at that point that I was either in the process of dying, or I had already died. My confusion centered on my earthly life. I was feeling a great loss because of my children, and I was sharing that feeling with my father. Additionally, I wasn't sure that I wanted to live in the paralyzed state that the doctors said I would live in.
>
> My father said to me: "You aren't going to be lost or confused any longer. Everything will be fine. It's not time for you to be here, now, but when it is I will be here." Then he embraced me— there was an enormous outpouring of peace—and he took me back to the archway. As I entered the archway, I had the feeling that everything would be okay. That's the last thing I remember until I came out of the coma.

Knowledge

In the Spring of 1993, **Roger Smith** came to our house to be interviewed (Gibson, 1993, pp. 215–21). His NDE was the result of a crash in his Volkswagen during a wintery day in 1968. He had a detailed life's review, and he saw and communicated with the Savior. Portions of his experience follows:

> While I was in the Savior's presence, I was told and shown many things besides my life's review. Enormous amounts of information flowed into my mind—information that I have since forgotten. When I first arrived in the room, for example, He asked me if I had any questions. I did, and the moment the question was formulated, the answer was in my mind. It was an amazing process.
>
> Pure knowledge seemed to pour into me from Him. The knowledge was transmitted by . . . energy. Energy flowed into me and with it was knowledge. It was as if my entire being was a receptor of knowledge. And it was knowledge that I seemed to have known before. Everything that was communicated to me made sense.
>
> Just before He asked me the last question, I was told firmly, but in a loving way, that much of what I had seen and heard I would not

remember if I came back. He let me know that some of the things that would be taken from me I would again be allowed to remember, as they were needed to help me in some part of my future life.

One of the many extraordinary experiences which Ken Ring documented was that of **Virginia Rivers**. She explained how, in 1986, she lost consciousness when she could no longer breathe due to pneumonia. Her NDE followed. A small portion of the pertinent events is reproduced below (Ring, 1998, pp. 295–96):

> The farther forward I was propelled, the more knowledge I received. My mind felt like a sponge, growing and expanding in size with each addition. The knowledge came in single words and in whole idea blocks. I just seemed to be able to understand everything as it was being soaked up or absorbed. . . . I remember thinking, "I knew that, I know I did. Where has it all been?"
>
> . . . He told me many things of which I have little or no recollection. I only remember that we spoke, or rather, he inspired and I learned. It seemed then that the exchange lasted for hours or eons and now it seems that eons passed in only moments. I remember only two things from that exchange. First, God told me there were only two things that we could bring back with us when we died . . . LOVE and KNOWLEDGE. . . . So I was to learn as much about both as possible.

Premortal Life

Undoubtedly, the most explicit and in-depth experience of an individual preparing to enter this life was that of **Don Wood**. The pertinent portion of the experience is recreated in chapter 3. A more complete account is given in the book, *Echoes From Eternity* (Gibson, 1993, pp. 117–31).

Maxine's interview is recorded in its entirety in chapter 16. During her experience she saw herself in a premortal environment, getting ready to come to earth. What was especially interesting about Maxine's story was how closely it resembled the experience of Julie, whom I had interviewed in 1992. Pertinent portions of **Julie's** story follows (Gibson, 1993, pp. 54–55):

> Sitting on the sofa, I leaned my head back and closed my eyes. I could hear the TV in the background and was aware of the presence of my Dad. And then . . . I don't know how to describe this. Suddenly I had a remembrance—that's all I can tell you—

just a remembrance. I could see it as a scene, yet it was a memory of something that had happened before.

I was in a long white dress, and I came through some large double doors, wooden and beautifully carved, into a large room. Chairs were arranged auditorium style on either side of the room. The chairs were empty when I came in. I went down a center aisle to . . . it's so hard to describe this.

The room was like an amphitheater; it was slanted down. At the front of the room there was something that looked to be a table or an altar. As I looked at the front of the room I saw three men dressed in white.

I knew where I was supposed to sit, and I came down the center aisle and sat on the left side, in toward the middle of the seats. All the chairs were padded, and they were hooked together.

I remember looking at my hands on my lap, and. . . . It wasn't as though I were watching a movie, it was a memory as though I were feeling it while I was in that body. And my mind, being nineteen years old, questioned some of the things I saw. Yet it was *I*, and the thing that surprised me was my composure. I had the same personality that I had in this life—except it was significantly more mature; much more dignified and self assured than the nineteen-year-old that I was.

Looking at my hands, I wondered why they seemed so small. Then I remember thinking: *It is going to be so strange to go to earth and forget home. I can't comprehend that. I understand exactly what I'm getting into and what I have to do. But I cannot comprehend forgetting home. Please let me remember this experience and this room.*

When the double doors to the room would close, I knew that I would not remember what was behind those two doors—a veil would be placed over my mind. But I wanted to remember this room, and I studied it very carefully. That's what I remember.

The three men at the front of the room, I understood to be in complete control of when I was to go through. When my time came I would know it, and I would move down the aisle and go through the white curtains that were across the front.

The three men were reverently whispering, but I didn't pay any attention to what they were saying. I was studying the room—I did not want to forget it. Drapes were over the windows, and the ceiling was very tall.

It seemed strange to be getting ready to go to earth. And when I thought about earth, it was as if I could see through the walls of the room and see the earth suspended out in space. I was not afraid, I just didn't want to forget.

Then . . . it was as if a bolt of electricity went through my body. Just like that—a snap of the fingers. It was a jolt, and I felt my body jerk with the electricity. And I realized that I was on the sofa. My Dad was there and the TV was still on. I didn't know how long the experience had been. I was astonished.

Kevin R. Williams documented sixty-two NDEs which he considered to be especially profound. Kevin had been studying the various spiritual phenomenon since his grandparents taught him about them in Sunday School lessons when he was a child in the Nazarene Church. He maintains a website about NDEs entitled: "Near-Death Experiences and the Afterlife," at www.near-death.com.

One of the stories that Kevin documented in his book, *Nothing Better Than Death*, is of **David Oakford,** who had an NDE as a result of a self-inflicted overdose. Portions of his experience follow (Williams, 2002, p. 34):

> All of a sudden, I saw my parents on earth before I was born. I saw how they came to be together and watched them have my brother and sister before me. . . . I picked [my parents] to help them on their path as well as to achieve my learning.
>
> I saw my soul go to my mother and go inside of her. I saw myself being born from an observer standpoint as well as having the actual experience.

Reincarnation?

Mormon theology rejects the principle of reincarnation. The book, *Fingerprints of God*, presented arguments against reincarnation (Gibson, 1999, pp. 225–29). In that discussion, some of the reasons for belief in reincarnation by some researchers and some who had NDEs were outlined. It was noted, for example, that those having undergone an NDE often felt that they had always lived and would continue to live forever. A natural outgrowth of this feeling was the assumption that they must have lived many lives in their premortal existence. On the other hand, LDS philosophy teaches that, indeed, they did live forever in a previous premortal state, but not in successive physical lives.

Most accounts by those having had NDEs relate reincarnation to this feeling of having always lived. It is rare that they even allude to first-hand knowledge of the details of any previous lives. A more complete discussion of the LDS theology on this subject is advanced in chapter 4.

There are, however, a few accounts where those having had NDEs declare with some certainty that they became aware of previous incarnations. Three such incidents follow (Wells, Fall 1993, p. 30). Each of these cases were extracted by Wells from previous accounts of Ken Ring.

1. "It is a matter of personal knowledge from what the Being with whom I spoke during my NDE told me about my older son, that he had had 14 incarnations in female physical bodies previous to the life he has just had."

2. "My whole life went before me of things I have done and haven't done, but not just of this one lifetime, but of all the lifetimes. I know for a fact there is reincarnation. This is an absolute. I was shown all those lives and how I had overcome some of the things I had done in other lives. There was still some things to be corrected."

3. "I had a lot of questions, and I wanted to know what they [light beings she encountered in her NDE] were doing—why are you just kind of milling around here? And someone stepped forward . . . it wasn't just one . . . I got information from a number of them . . . that they were all waiting for reincarnation."

Opposition: Pain and Joy

Barbara Rommer documented an NDE by **Wilson** who had a multidimensional life's review. Portions of his record of the experience follow (Rommer, 2000, p. 12):

> The life review was multidimensional. I felt it. I felt the pain and also the joy. You don't get one without the other. I could see the whole thing and it was so totally mindboggling that something like that could happen in microseconds. Your sense of time and space is so distorted.

Theresa was a young woman whom Carol and I interviewed in 1994. **Theresa** told us that she never completed high school, and most of her conversation reflected that lack of education. She did not claim any affiliation with organized religion, but she seemed spiritually affected. When I asked particular questions about her experience, Theresa became a different person. The manner in which she dictated the thoughts which I recorded was simply amazing, and I had to listen to the tape again to assure myself that I had heard it correctly the first time. A portion of our interview is repeated below (Gibson, 1999, pp. 172–75):

> **"Did you see anything during your experience of a negative nature?"**
> "No, because there is no such thing as negative."

"What do you mean?"

"Negative is a concept that we have developed to describe things that work against our preconceived notions. Everything is both—negative and positive—and they both create energy. It works for you or it doesn't. It works for God or against Him. But they both serve a divine purpose."

"Did you see anything that worked against God?"

"Yes. Even that was of a divine nature, though. It enters a person as ego—a driving force of self, to please oneself."

"How did you see that?"

"It came in the form of an angered spirit. I couldn't imagine him being so angry, but he was."

"What was happening to him, and why was he angry?"

"He was isolated within himself. The energy emanated by him created his own world, almost a separate planet. When I saw him I also heard laughter. It was a hideous type of laughter."

". . . Do you have any special messages for anyone who might read your story?"

"Yes. I want to talk a little about fear. Fear is a blessing."

"How so?

"Fear is the key to unfolding what is within us. If we didn't have fear there would be nothing to propel us into the next adventure or experience. Without fear we would not be alert to the full measure of the experiences we pass through. Those experiences are vital for our growth. Tears and grief are what carve the opening for us to have joy and love. If we didn't have a cavity carved by fear, pain, and grief, we wouldn't be able to fully appreciate the love and joy that are within our reach.

"The key to growth in the future is to love ourselves and to extend that love to others. The interconnectedness of all living beings, and the love we feel for all life, are gifts from God. The Lord made it possible for us to love as we should, but we often deny ourselves that privilege. When we grieve, we should know that we are grieving tears of precious love—a love for the connectedness of all humans."

Satan, Demons, and Hell

In chapter 10, several researchers and individuals who have had Less than Pleasant (LTP) experiences were highlighted. From that discussion, and from other material in this book, it is clear that LTP events are as varied and common as the more ecstatic epiphanies. And, as with the euphoric experiences, their variety appears to be tailored to the needs of the individual. A few examples will illustrate the point.

Barbara Rommer wrote of **Anthony** who, during a resuscitation, was stuck by an infected needle and contracted HIV. In a period of despondency, Anthony took a quantity of sleeping pills in order to commit suicide (Rommer, 2000, p. 44):

> Then I heard a voice and I knew it was God. It was weird. The voice wasn't real authoritative, but it was sort of peaceful and calm. He said to me: "If this is what you're going to do, then this is where you're going to be." I perceived it as being in hell, even though I didn't see any little devils or pitchforks or flames. It was terrifying, being suspended in darkness with annoying sounds.... God was showing me that if you commit suicide, then you'll go to hell. God gave me the choice to either give up or fight.

Dee was interviewed by Carol and me in 1992. She had been in an abusive marriage which deteriorated to the point where Dee's emotional well-being was in serious jeopardy. She had stayed in the marriage longer than she should for her children. Her terrifying NDE happened one evening when she left her body. Portions of our interview follow (Gibson, 1992, pp. 150–57):

> "The next thing I knew was . . . there was something behind me, and I was afraid. I felt this 'awful presence'—and I knew that it was after me. I looked back and I saw that my string, which I was hooked to, was getting tight. I was afraid, and I was thinking: What is this thing behind me? I started to circle, because I knew I had to get back to the house.
>
> "The thing was coming after me fast, and I had the feeling it could kill me. I was moving through the tops of the trees, and I was thinking that I couldn't break my string, and I had to get back quick. Then . . ." Dee's hands were visibly shaking as she tried to continue with the story.
>
> "This . . . this thing, this awful, this terrifying thing—I could feel it on me. It was pushing me away from the house, and I could see the string getting tighter. I was sure I was going to die. I was frantic for Sara, frantic over the idea that if I died she would be stuck with my husband. I felt I had to get back, but the thing kept trying to push me away from the house.
>
> "Every time I would circle and try to get back to the house the thing would come up behind and push me. I knew I was going to die. I could feel the tug at my string. I was being chased by something that was the personification of 'evil.' And it wanted me. It wanted to destroy me. I was terrified and I was crying, and I remember thinking: Oh God, help me, help me God. I got all my strength to go as fast as I could—I could

actually feel this thing on the back of my neck.

"The next thing I can remember was: SLAM! I was in my body and I was screaming. My husband and my daughter woke up, and I was screaming and shaking. My husband said: 'What's the matter with you? You were only having a dream.' I told him: 'That was no dream. Something was trying to kill me.'"

"How real did it seem, Dee?"

"The evil spirit experience was horribly real. Look, I' m shaking just thinking about it. I know that if that thing had been able to push me away so that my string broke it would have killed me. I believe that these two incidents happened, maybe as a warning, a signal, or something, so that I would get out."

"What did you feel that the presence was?"

"I thought that it was the Devil, or a spirit that was trying to get my body. That' s what I thought. I' ve always had a healthy fear of evil spirits. As soon as I felt this presence behind me I knew that this was ugly, this was terror, this was the worst . . . it was the most ugly, the most horrible thing that I had ever encountered. It was going to get me—it was going to destroy me—it was after my body.

"I knew that if it broke my string I would be dead. It kept pushing me away from the house; it was trying to get me as far as it could from my body. It wanted my string to break. The most important thing in my mind was to get back to my body, so I wouldn' t leave my daughter.

"The terror was awful. I could feel myself wanting to scream. I was flailing my arms, grasping for something to pull me back, but there was nothing to hold onto. I was fighting to go back, and I flailed my arms to try and get the thing away from me. It was the most horrible experience I had ever had. Even today, when I think about it I am terror-stricken. Look at my hands!" Dee's hands continued to shake as she remembered the experience.

A portion of **Renee Zamora's** experience is given in chapter 16. A part of the experience not repeated there concerned her spiritual visit to a park-like area where she saw many deceased people who were related to each other—and none of whom could see her. In addition, she saw another individual who repulsed her. Our interview of that portion of her NDE follows:

During each of these trips to the park and to the picnic area near the tree, I was still exasperated by the fact that no one could see me. Finally, on one trip to that area, I looked at the man whose relationship I didn't know. He looked back at me—he could see me—and I felt an impact in my heart that was indescribable. It was as if some physical object violently hit me. Instantly, upon receiving this jolt, I wanted to remove myself from the proximity of the man who could see me. I wondered who he was, but I knew that I wanted to be as far away from him as possible. The thought came into my mind: *He knows me.* And I didn't want him to know me.

Repelled by the man who knew me, I looked at the people around him. They seemed to be oblivious to what was going on. The unpleasant man was able to see me, and my side of existence, but the others could not. They could only see themselves and the park area.

It was sometime after recovery from her NDE that Renee understood who the man was. She identified him as Satan. Renee asked for and received a blessing from her bishopric to remove all possible evil influence from her experience. As noted in her picture, today she is a lovely, active church lady, grateful for Christ in her life.

Encounters with Deity

Angie Fenimore's in-depth NDE resulted from her attempt at suicide. As a result of a chaotic youthful circumstance and other difficult life experiences, she overdosed on prescription drugs to relieve her chronic depressive state. She got some solace as a child in various Protestant and LDS churches. Her complete story is told in her book: *Beyond the Darkness.* A portion of her story follows (Fenimore, 1995, pp. 99–101):

Then I heard a voice of awesome power, not loud but crashing over me like a booming wave of sound; a voice that encompassed such ferocious anger that with one word it could destroy the universe, and that also encompassed such potent and unwavering love that, like the sun, it could coax life from the earth. I cowered at its force and at its excruciating words: "Is this what you really want?" . . .

From the light I felt love directed toward me as an individual, and I was baffled by it. I had never felt deserving of God's love. . . . I had grossly underestimated my importance and the nature of my origin—I am literally the spirit offspring of God.

I even looked like Him. I was surprised that He really had a body with arms and legs and features like mine, . . . As I studied the features of God, I marveled to see that what I had learned in church and from the Scriptures, which I had assumed was figurative or symbolic, was apparently literally true. We are actually, physically created in His image. This realization was staggering.

George Ritchie's amazing account is known by thousands of people. At one point in his experience, he became aware that he was in the presence of the Savior. That portion of his story has fascinated me for years since it is so similar to what my own father saw in his NDE (see below). A portion of George's story follows (Ritchie, 1978, pp. 48–49):

> I stared in astonishment as the brightness increased, coming from nowhere, seeming to shine everywhere at once. . . . It was impossibly bright: it was like a million welders' lamps all blazing at once. And right in the middle of my amazement came a prosaic thought probably born of some biology lecture back at the university: "I'm glad I don't have physical eyes at this moment," I thought. "This light would destroy the retina in a tenth of a second."
>
> No, I corrected myself, not the light.
>
> He.
>
> He would be too bright to look at. For now I saw that it was not light but a Man who had entered the room, or rather, a Man made out of light, though this seemed no more possible to my mind that the incredible intensity of the brightness that made up His form.
>
> The instant I perceived Him, a command formed itself in my mind. "Stand up!" the words came from inside me, yet that had an authority my mere thoughts had never had. I got to my feet, and as I did came the stupendous certainty: "You are in the presence of *the Son of God.*"
>
> . . . This Person was power itself, older than time and yet more modern than anyone I had ever met.
>
> Above all, with that same mysterious inner certainty, I knew that this Man loved me. Far more even than power, what emanated from this Presence was unconditional love. An astonishing love. A love beyond my wildest imagining.

My father, Marshall Stuart Gibson, only told his story a few times in his life. Fortunately, my mother—who was a witness to all of the trauma that occurred with his massive heart attack, and later, his miraculous recovery following a blessing—recorded major portions of his NDE. From those portions, plus my memory of his explanation of what happened, I pieced together his story. It is told in its entirety in the book: *In Search of Angels.* The pertinent portions follow

(Gibson, 1990, pp. 110–11):

"I somehow knew that I was to stay with Daniel, and I sort of wished myself to stay with him; all of a sudden we arrived in this new world.

"Anyway, as we walked along the path, I noticed a profusion of flowers and trees. They were of a wider variety, and they had many more colors than on earth—or maybe it was that I could see more colors than on earth, I'm not sure. We continued walking for a while and I noticed someone on the path ahead of us."

"But I thought you said you wished yourself wherever you wanted to go. Why were you walking?"

"I knew I must stay with Daniel, and he was now walking, so I walked too. As we got closer to the individual on the path, I could see and feel that he was a magnificent person. I felt overwhelmed as I looked at him. He was bathed in light. Daniel asked if I knew who that was, and I answered yes. It was Jesus Christ.

"When we got close to the Savior, I felt a tremendous love emanating from him. It's hard to describe, but you could feel it all around him. And I felt a similar enormous love for him. I fell at his feet—not because I thought about it, but because I couldn't stand. I felt an overpowering urge to fall at his feet and worship him. I stayed there for some moments with this wonderful feeling, when . . ."

My Dad stopped for a period, and looked emotionally drained.

"Go on Dad, what happened next?"

"As I knelt there at the feet of this marvelous being I became conscious of my past life being reviewed for me. It seemed to occur in a short period, and I felt the Savior's love during the entire process. That love was . . . well, it was everywhere. And it was as if we could communicate with each other without speaking. After a period the Savior reached down and I knew I should stand. As soon as I stood, he left."

A Being of Light

One of the strangest experiences was that of **Forrest Hansen,** whom I interviewed in 1991. Forrest had several NDEs as a result of an allergic intolerance for certain chemical fumes. When I interviewed him, he characterized himself as an agnostic Humanist. This was true, even though he experienced several intense experiences out of his body. A portion of our interview follows (Gibson, 1992, pp. 75, 78):

"The next thing that happened was that I was aware of something moving into my range of vision. This was a being, or an image of a being, constructed completely of light. It was not focused enough to make out distinct details, but it was obviously a human-type image.

"Upon confronting this image, I recall vividly the ideas exchanged between me and it. The specific exchange didn't seem spoken, but was understood. The image asked, 'Do you want to terminate your physical existence?' I recall pausing long enough to consider it and I said, 'No, I can't do that yet.' That was the end of the experience—I woke up."

"When you said that you couldn't do that yet, at the time, did you have any emotional feelings about why you said that?"

"No. At the time I felt that it was a physical consideration, that I couldn't do that yet. It seemed to me that the image was asking if I wanted to terminate my physical existence and become a mental entity like it was. And it just occurred to me that I couldn't do that yet—I wasn't to a point that I could do that in my development."

"So you felt that there were other things that you had to do for your development to proceed?"

"Yes, but . . . it even occurred to me that it wasn't something that I was going to be able to do in my lifetime."

"Tell me what you remember about the appearance of the image."

"When I say constructed of light, I also mean that it was semi-transparent and had depth. The light seemed to be particles of light, of which there were an innumerable quantity.

"These experiences have affected the way I think and live in every way; partly because I think of them a lot and have analyzed and researched them to death. The resulting conclusions, and the philosophy I've developed from those conclusions, have had a profound effect on my personal character."

"In what sense was your personal character changed?"

"I used to be. . . ." Forrest laughed with a somewhat embarrassed demeanor. "I was a less than desirable character—I don't think I am anymore."

"Why did these experiences change the way you dealt with others or whatever it is that you say profoundly changed?"

"The philosophy is pretty involved. If I were to say something about being near death, just that in itself, would affect your attitude. It's like anything else—if you lose something, you learn to appreciate it."

"That's true. What is your attitude about death? Is it different from before?"

"Ever since I was young I haven't had any belief in an after-life. I still don't, so in that sense my attitude hasn't changed. And . . . and at the same time I carry a belief that there might . . . that is, there could be. . . ."

"That sounds like a contradiction."

"Well, it isn't, in the sense that . . . a lot of people who have had near-death experiences look on it as an after-death experience. I don't, so I don't see it as a reinforcement of that belief. I try to keep an open mind, though, and I realize there are a lot of things that people don't know yet. So I have to leave some possibility that there may be. . . . I don't see it as proof though."

"Do you think the experiences were related to your background, or to your culture, or to how you were raised, or were they independent of those effects?"

"They were related to issues and ideas that I was thinking about—that most people think about."

"How do you know what most people think about?"

"Well I would think that anybody who was dying, and was aware that they were dying, would have some thoughts about death. As to the content of the experiences being related to anything I was familiar with, no they weren't. They were new ideas."

Different Levels in the Spirit World

Another of the profound NDEs which Kevin R. Williams documented in this book, *Nothing Better Than Death,* was that of **Dr. Rene Turner**. It occurred in 1982 in Newcastle, Australia when a car crashed into her car and caused extensive neurological injuries. She met her grandfather and was led by guides to a beautiful place. A small portion of her experience follows:

We wandered in this beautiful place for what seemed an eternity. We discussed my life. We discussed religion. We discussed secrets of the soul that as humans we must forget, lest we'd never be able to thrive on earth. All the while I was in awe. Some things were just as I always dreamed an afterlife would be. Some things I was just plain wrong and I remember thinking, "Wow!" Where were my other loved ones? When could I see my other grandparents who had passed? In time—they were on a different plane. When my transition was complete I could choose to go to other levels when I was ready. (Williams, 2002, p. 42)

In May 1992, **Susan** had a caesarean section in order to deliver twins. Shortly thereafter she had a heart attack and an NDE (Gibson, 1999, p. 70):

> At first Susan didn't know that she was dead. When she realized that she was dead, Susan told her aunt-guide that she needed a blessing. The aunt said: "That is being taken care of." Looking at her body, Susan saw three spirit men about to give her a blessing. Her father was not one of the men and Susan felt anger that he was not there. Her aunt told her, "He can't be here right now, Susy, but don't worry, he's okay." (He had committed suicide when Susan was fifteen.)

None of the individuals Carol and I interviewed told us that they were in heaven during their out-of-body experience. Most felt that they were in some wonderful spiritual realm, but it wasn't heaven. **Howard Storm** characterized it "as way out in the suburbs." Two others told us that they were at a spiritual "way station." Many felt that if they had proceeded into the other world and not come back they would have found an even more marvelous place.

One of the questions asked Howard Storm after his experience was:

> **"There seems to be a hierarchy of order in the whole creative process, like an organization—is that true?"** Howard's answer was:
> Yes, but everyone knows exactly where they stand, because one of the things about God's light is that only truth exists there. Nothing false can exist. So, when an angel begins to feel uncomfortable in that light, there is only one place to go—the darkness.

A Beautiful City of Light

My father, in his NDE, was transported to a "City of Light." In fact, he entered one of the buildings where a meeting was being held. In that meeting, among others, were Peter, James and John, Apostles of Jesus Christ during his mortal ministry. Dad described the city as one of immeasurable beauty in which the streets were paved with what appeared to be gold, and the buildings shone with their own brilliance.

George Ritchie, in his in-depth NDE, also described a City of Light. He described it and its occupants in this manner (Ritchie, 1978, pp. 72–73):

> And then I saw, infinitely far off, far too distant to be visible with any kind of sight I knew of . . . a city. A glowing, seemingly endless city, bright enough to be seen over all the unimaginable

distance between. The brightness seemed to shine from the very walls and streets of this place, and from beings which I could now discern moving about within it. In fact, the city and everything in it seemed to be made of light, even as the Figure at my side was made of light.

... Could these radiant beings, I wondered, amazed, be those who have indeed kept Jesus the focus of their lives? Was I seeing at last ones who had looked for Him in everything? Looked so well and so closely that they had been changed into His very likeness?

... Even as I asked the question, two of the bright figures seemed to detach themselves from the city and start toward us, hurling themselves across that infinity with the speed of light.

But as fast as they came toward us, we drew away still faster. ... I knew that my imperfect sight could not now sustain more than an instant's glimpse of this real, this ultimate heaven. He had shown me all He could; now we were speeding far away.

Choice as Part of the Plan

Ned Dougherty was a real-estate broker for twenty-six years and the owner of two high profile, successful nightclubs. By his own admission, he was an alcoholic and dedicated to the fast life. He became a changed man through two deep spiritual experiences. The first was an NDE precipitated by a fight with another individual. Following his experiences, Ned changed his life. He became a board member of IANDS and set about to create a nonprofit organization dedicated to building a more spiritual life. He also wrote the book *Fast Lane to Heaven*, which described his epiphanies.

Ned's first experience occurred in July, 1984. A portion of his story follows (Dougherty, 2001, pp. 28–29):

> I wanted to know more about my origin as a spiritual being. God revealed to me that I had been created as a spiritual being at the beginning of the creation of the universe to inhabit the universe on a spiritual level and to exist in spiritual schools of learning in preparation for further growth and understanding. Part of this experience for myself and for all other spiritual beings is the necessity to be born into a physical body and to become part of the human experience. It was God's plan to enable the spiritual beings of the universe to grow in His image and likeness through the spiritual journey in the universe, but it was also part of God's pan to create a physical world as a place of learning and growth.
>
> God gave each of us an intellect, memory, and free will to

enter upon our learning experience in the universe. Part of our mission as spiritual beings included taking form as humans and learning from our journey in the physical world before returning to spiritual world through the process we know as death.

When I asked **Theresa** if she had any final thoughts about her NDE, she said:

> "Just know that life is not a series of circumstances; each of us are given the privilege of creating our life. We even create our own troubles; it's really amusing."
> **"Do you mean create, or do you mean choose?"**
> "We chose before we came here certain big events. But all the roads in between, we create." (Gibson, 1999, pp. 174–75)

Spirits Seen in Different Forms

One of the surprises which resulted from my interviews of people who, during their NDEs had seen spirit beings, was the variation in the form of those they saw. For the most part, deceased relatives were seen as glowing individuals in the prime of life. Their clothes also varied, some appearing in white, glowing garments, and others dressed as though in earth clothes as they were last seen alive. There was also variation in how some individuals who had NDEs saw themselves. Not all bothered to look at themselves, but to those who did, the results seemed to confirm that they saw themselves—and others—in forms that made them most comfortable. One lady I interviewed was able to see and feel her deceased husband's restored limb during her NDE.

In **John Stirling's** voyage to the stars he saw his hand. He said of it (Stirling, chapter 7):

> A voice came to me, as I was traveling at that high rate of speed, and . . . and I was so peaceful and comfortable. All the emotional pain that I had been feeling was gone. I looked at my hand, and I saw the shape of a hand, but . . . but it had an aura around it. It wasn't the same hand as an earthly hand. There was an energy field that defined it.

Vern Swanson's NDE was triggered by extreme grief from the death in an automobile accident of his wife and son. Vern, who was at Auburn University in Alabama as an Assistant Professor of Art History at the time, was unable to assuage his grief. A portion of his experience follows (Gibson, 1993, pp. 46–47):

> One night, about six months after Elaine and our son had

died, I was lying restlessly in bed. Suddenly I looked up and I saw a light. Standing there in the light was my wife.

As I remember, it seems as if I were instantly out of bed—just thuung! . . . and I was up next to her. It was the most interesting situation you could imagine, because she looked exactly like Elaine, yet she didn't. It's hard to explain.

My wife, the woman, the angel in front of me was so peaceful, so beautiful. There was a light that came from within her so that she glowed. It wasn't reflected light; it was almost as if there were a bright candle inside of her.

I had always thought that Grace Kelly, the movie star, was the most beautiful woman in the world. Elaine, standing before me, would have put Grace Kelly to shame. She was very white with that inner glow, and she was absolutely the most beautiful person I had ever seen. To this day I can remember how she looked, and I marvel at what I saw. Elaine, in life, was a good-looking woman, working as a model during college, but her earthly body was a poor shadow, an impoverished copy, when compared with that beautiful person before me—yet it *was* Elaine.

As she stood before me I began to embrace and kiss her; I smothered her with kisses. When I touched Elaine, I was filled with joy from her white radiance—not a cold white, but a warm white.

One of the most inspirational descriptions of an angel that I heard was that of **Ann,** who as a child had leukemia. Her NDE was a result of the leukemia. She returned from the NDE cured of the disease. Indeed, her story affected me sufficiently that I had the cover of *Glimpses of Eternity* include a picture of Ann's angel painted by Florence Susan Comish. A portion of my interview with Ann follows (Gibson, 1992, p. 53):

"I sat up [in bed] and watched the light grow. It grew rapidly in both size and brightness. In fact, the light got so bright that it seemed to me that the whole world was lit by it. I could see someone inside the light. There was this beautiful woman, and she was part of the light; in fact, she glowed."

"Did the light hurt your eyes?"

"No, even though it was bright by mortal standards."

"Tell me more about the lady in the light."

"Her body was lit from inside in a way . . . it's very hard to explain what she looked like. It seemed as if she were a pure crystal filled with light. Even her robe glowed with light as if by itself. The robe was white, long-sleeved, and full length. She had a golden belt around her waist and her feet were bare. Not that she needed anything on her feet since she stood a couple of feet off the floor."

"Were you frightened by her?"

"No, just the opposite. I had never seen such kindness and gentle love on anyone's face such as I saw in this person. She called me by name and held out her hand to me. She told me to come with her—her voice was soft and gentle but . . . but it was more in my mind. Communication was easier than when you verbalize thoughts. At the time I thought of it as 'mind talk.'

"I asked her who she was and she explained that she was my guardian and had been sent to take me to a place where I could rest in peace. The love emanating from her washed over me so that I didn't hesitate to put my hand in hers.

"As soon as I was standing beside her we moved through a short darkness to a beautiful, even brighter, light. And then I saw . . . there was this astonishingly beautiful world before me. It was like nothing else I have since seen on earth. Somehow I knew, inside of me, that the earth had been left behind. I had no idea where I was, and I didn't care. I felt a deep, profound peace . . . no, it was more than that. It was a world of peace and love.

"The new world looked sort of like the world I had left behind, but it was also very different. Everything glowed from the inside with its own light. The colors were beyond anything on earth—they were more vibrant, brilliant, and intense. And there were colors I had never seen before—don't ask me what they were. There were shrubs, trees and flowers, some of which I had seen on earth, like evergreens, and others which I hadn't seen before, and I haven't seen since. They were beautiful, beautiful.

"I asked my guardian why she took me to this place. She said that I needed the rest because life had become too hard for me to live.

"There was also grass all around, and a little hill with sand at the base in a sort of play area where several other children were playing. My guardian took me to the area and left without my knowing it. I immediately joined the children in play. There were toys in the sand and we built castles and roads and played with the toys. I was totally immersed in this new world of love, peace and play."

"Did you stay with the children very long?"

"It seemed long in one sense; in another, it seemed timeless.

I felt thoroughly refreshed, enlivened and spiritually rejuvenated. I was filled with a zest for life. It is impossible to explain what it felt like to be lighter than air, with no pain, and totally at peace with everyone and everything around. I simply accepted my existence in the new world and lived.

"When my guardian returned, I thought we were going to another part of this fascinating and wonderful world. Calling to me, she gently took me by the hand and said that I had to leave. When we started back the way we came, I realized that we were returning to the earth, and I asked her why I had to go back. She told me it was time to return, and it would be easier for me to live on the earth now.

"We came back through the darkness, as before, with the surrounding light making a sort of tunnel through it. The peace followed me and I was content. We emerged back in my bedroom. My guardian smiled at me, and suddenly I was back in bed without the slightest idea of how I got there."

Sylvia was a seventeen-year-old student and atheist living in Italy when she had her NDE. It resulted from a motor scooter accident with a car. Sylvia was thrown from the scooter and her unprotected head hit the pavement. A portion of our interview follows (Gibson, 1999, pp. 58, 61):

The . . . essence . . . of me was there, but my body that was floating through the tunnel in that moment was not my body as I had known it until that point in life. I was floating upward in the tunnel toward what I believed would be the other end of it, and the best analogy I can use to describe the form of my body is that I was similar to a jellyfish. My direction was head first, and my eyes seemed to be straight on top of my head, because I was looking at things from up there.

My impression was that I had a head, and eyes on the cusp of it. Also, I seemed to have a neck and ears—I'll tell you later about the ears, because there was this music which I could hear. From the neck down, though, it was like a very gentle medusa— or a very gentle octopus. There seemed to be many appendices on me which were mellifluously floating. The manner in which I moved upward was by the shrink-and-stretch movement of these appendices and maybe partially of my neck—similar to the movement of jellyfish. There were no arms and legs, just these gently moving appendices. . . .

The instant I said no, my body . . . my jellyfish body . . . it resumed the shape of my usual human physical body and, in a fraction of a second, the tunnel became like the narrow tube of a vacuum cleaner. Immediately, I felt sucked very rapidly backwards. As I was being sucked, derriere first, I remember seeing my long hair being blown in the direction opposite that from which I was being sucked. My two arms and my two legs were in an outstretched position, as though reaching out, in front of me. And I remember thinking, 'Wow, what an over-reaction to my saying no.' In my estimation it took no more than about one-and-one-half seconds to be propelled from near the membrane of light back to the sidewalk.

In his extensive NDE, **Howard Storm** called them his friends—those angels and spirit beings who, with Jesus, loved him back to spiritual health. Some of what he experienced he explained in this way (Storm, 2000, pp. 33–34):

Then Jesus called out in a musical tone to some of the luminous entities radiating from the great centre. Several came and circled around us. The radiance emanating from their luminous being contained exquisite colours of a range and intensity far exceeding anything I had experienced before. They were composed of many colours that I had not seen before. It was like looking at the iridescence in the deep brilliance of a diamond. The words we have are simply not adequate to express their beauty. The emanations from those beings didn't resemble light as we experience it. When you look into a bright light, the intensity hurts your eyes. The luminous beings were far brighter than a powerful searchlight, yet I could look at them with no sense of discomfort. In fact, their radiance penetrated me; I could feel it inside me and through me, and it made me feel wonderful. It was ecstasy. These were saints and angels. . . .

Everything I thought, they knew immediately. It was in this way we conversed.

"You're upset. What can we do to help you?"

"I don't belong here."

"You *do* belong here."

"This is right. It's all been for this moment."

"We can appear to you in our human form if you wish, or in any form you want so you will be comfortable with us."

". . . No. Please don't change anything for me. You're more beautiful than anything I've ever seen."

Other Events and Examples

This chapter could have been extended almost indefinitely with other NDE events, and with examples showing those events. Many who have had NDEs, for example, speak of visiting glowing cities with magnificent libraries and other structures whose purpose is to teach and advance those living there. My own father, as noted above, visited such a city in his NDE.

Many individuals heard and felt music with a tonal beauty that was indescribable in earthly terms. Some related the music they heard to an inherent sense of mathematics.

Travel to distant places in the universe at velocities exceeding the speed of light is not uncommon. Just thinking or desiring to be at a distant place seems sufficient to transport individuals to these places.

Time is totally different from what we experience on earth. It is almost as if time is non-existent in the otherworldly realm. Furthermore, as with wishing to be at a given location places you there, so, also, wishing to be in a different time takes you either to the past or to the future according to your desires. In the case of the future, individuals are often shown alternative futures depending upon how people behave.

As noted in chapter 11, there is a whole category of NDEs—some derivatives of suicide attempts—which deal with less than pleasant (LTP) experiences. Numerous examples of these theophanies are given in the cited references.

The problem is that there is insufficient room to accommodate all of the examples which could be illustrated. Nevertheless, to the extent that it is practical, all of those itemized above are compared with LDS doctrine in chapters 4 and 5 and in other chapters of this book.

16: The Religious Impact of Some NDEs: Individuals Who Became Mormons as a Result of NDEs

Interesting Conversion Cases

A key tenet of LDS belief is that each individual is entitled to personal revelation concerning issues of importance to the individual. Indeed, each person has a responsibility to seek revelation from God concerning the truth of the Book of Mormon and the Church. Prayers of supplication pertinent to the individual's needs are an important part of the process for obtaining personal revelation.

During the period when I was interviewing people who had undergone NDEs, it became evident that many of them enjoyed remarkable examples of personal revelation. There were two individuals who had previously undergone NDEs, and one who had not, which were especially dramatic in their outcome, and remarkably similar in process.

The two NDE cases came to my attention in response to an advertisement I placed in the newspaper. Both individuals called me within a few days of placing the advertisement, and, uncommonly, they both were located at Brigham Young University. They both agreed to an interview date on the same day. Neither of them were aware of or knew the other person.

As a young man, **Gary Gillum** was attending St. John's College in Kansas, studying to be a Lutheran minister. He was fairly far along in his studies, but he was plagued by a question which had not been answered to his satisfaction. He wondered about the Lutheran doctrine that there was only heaven and hell, and if you weren't baptized you were consigned to hell. He prayed to know the truth concerning this issue.

During Christmas vacation, he made a trip to his home in California. While on his way back with a friend, traveling in the friend's car, they had a head-on collision with another automobile. Both Gary and his friend were critically injured. While in the hospital, Gary had a fairly extensive NDE. During the NDE he was bathed in the light and love that often accompanies an NDE, and he was given a choice to stay or return. Gary understood that if he returned he would find the truth that he had prayed for, and he saw a vision of his future that he did not understand. The vision was of a spired building with people inside dressed in white involved in a strange ceremony. He chose to return.

Some six years later, following his recovery, after Gary completed his studies at St. John's College, he began dating a girl, Lyn, who was LDS. She asked him if he would like to have the LDS missionaries teach him about the Mormon religion. Gary agreed, since he believed it would make him a better Lutheran minister. As the missionaries began their lessons, Gary noted that from a scriptural point of view there was no contest. Gary could read the scriptures in the original Hebrew and Greek, whereas the twenty-year-old missionaries struggled with the English translations. He was curious, though, about the strength of their conviction and what they called a "testimony" of the truth of what they were telling him. So, when they asked him to pray about the truth of the Book of Mormon and of their teachings, he agreed.

To Gary's astonishment, when he began his prayer, he was again bathed in the light that he had previously encountered during his NDE. It was a personal testimony to him that he had found the truth that he had prayed about. Two years later, after joining the Church and marrying Lyn, while they traveled to Manti, Utah, to be sealed in the temple, he recognized the temple as the vision of the spired building he had seen during his NDE. Inside, during the ceremony, he also recalled the same view from his vision of the people dressed in white (Gibson, 1992, pp. 191–97).

Joe Swick had his NDE as a nine-year-old child. He was crossing a street with a bicycle when he was hit by a car. During his NDE, he left his body and traveled through a black space to a beautiful bright light. The light was filled with love, and it communicated to him that there was still much that he had to live for. Then he found himself back in his body, with paramedics working over him.

When Joe was fifteen years old, he began to investigate the Mormon Church. He listened to the missionaries because he saw how the Church had helped his father. As the missionaries continued through the normal course of lessons, Joe decided he could not believe the significant role played by Joseph Smith. He seemed to Joe so obviously fraudulent that he concluded he would terminate the discussions on their next visit.

When the missionaries arrived, therefore, he proceeded to tell them that he was no longer interested. When asked why by the senior missionary present, Joe told him that he did not believe that Joseph Smith was a prophet, and he was convinced the Book of Mormon was bogus. The missionary then asked Joe if he *really* wanted to know if it was true. Joe was about to tell him no, when something inside of him impelled him to say, "Yes, of course I would like to know if it is true." The missionary then asked Joe if he would join the missionary in serious prayer to find out the truth, and Joe agreed.

The missionary and Joe retired to a separate room and both began their silent prayers. During their prayer the missionary interrupted Joe and said: "That feeling you are now getting is the Holy Ghost, and if you will ask for the truth, it will be revealed." Joe was surprised that the missionary knew that he was feeling anything, and he closed his eyes again and continued with his prayer. In Joe's own words, this is what happened next:

> At that point it was as though the walls fell away from my room, and the floor fell from beneath me. I was just there. And it was that same intensely bright light. There was that same powerful feeling of love that I had known when I was hit by the car.
>
> It was more than viewing the light. It was like being totally enveloped. And it was reassuring me—again not with an audible voice—but it was speaking very powerfully to my heart, that the step I was about to take, I needed to do; that it was important for me to do that.
>
> I don't know how long that continued, but after a while it was done. I became aware of my surroundings. The missionary was still praying beside me. Then he opened his eyes, and we went into the other room. He never asked me what I experienced, and I don't know what he saw or felt. But that was my experience.
>
> The other two missionaries were sitting at the kitchen table.

They looked up, and I told them I was going to join the Church. I thought they were going to fall out of their seats. (Gibson, 1992, pp. 197–202)

Joe Swick, with tears streaming down his face, said this about his experience:

I haven't shared this experience with many people. It is too sacred to me. But whenever I have shared it, I have always told people that the experience has taught me that God is willing to reach out and talk with us. I'm nobody special, I don't have a . . . all I do is translate languages. Nobody knows my name—but I do know that God knows my name. And that he was willing to reach out and talk with me. If he would talk to somebody like me, then he would do it for anybody.

That was a realization that profoundly influenced my joining the Church. God didn't just talk to Joseph Smith, a farm boy in New York. He talked to me too. And he would talk to anybody, it seems to me, if he would talk to somebody like me.

Jack Wait—A Friend from High School

My interviews with Gary Gillum and Joe Swick occurred in 1992. It was a few years after that when I interviewed **Jack Wait**. Jack had been a friend and high school colleague from my youth in Willows, California. He lived a few miles outside Willows on a farm, and he commuted by bus to the school. Because, when he was not in school he was on his farm, we were friends but not close ones. The total high school student body may have consisted of, at most, three hundred young people, and everyone was acquainted with nearly everyone else. My sister and I were the only Mormons in the entire school.

Some years after I married Carol, I heard that Jack had joined the Mormon Church. The young lady that he married was LDS, so I assumed that she had persuaded him to join. We saw each other from time to time over the years at high school reunions, but we never talked further about his joining the Church. On one occasion, I gave Jack one of my books on near-death experiences and dismissed it from my mind.

About five years ago, I received a phone call at my home in Kaysville, Utah, from Jack. He said that he and his wife, Pat, were visiting relatives in Salt Lake City and would like to get together with us. We invited them to dinner at our home. During dinner, Jack seemed somewhat anxious and ill at ease, and soon after dinner he said that he needed to tell me how he came to join the Mormon Church. Readily agreeing, I tried to put him at ease by mentioning that I just thought he had been influenced by his first wife—she died many years ago, and he later married his current lovely wife, Pat.

Jack, and his first wife, Jean Brown, were married in 1951 in Sacramento, California. Jack and Jean had both graduated from Sacramento State College, and they began their careers by teaching school. They decided, however, that in order to improve their teaching opportunities they needed to do graduate work. New York City seemed the opportune place to go since Jack could attend New York University and Jean could attend The Julliard School of Music. Jack ultimately obtained his Ph.D., and Jean gave a spring recital in Carnegie Hall.

It was in New York City that they found comfort in the Mormon Church. After arriving in New York they felt lonely, and Jean said, "I'm going to find the Church—I know we'll find friends there." And friends they did find, in abundance. Jean often played her violin, and Jack sang in the choir, ultimately becoming Choir President even though he was not a member of the Church. They had a marvelous home teacher, Max McBeth, who visited them regularly and became a close friend. As they finished their first year of studies, Jack described his feelings in this manner:

> Jean said her prayers at bedtime each night. She didn't ask me to pray. There was no pressure put on me to join the Church on her part. Finally Max asked me if I said my prayers, and I said *no!* He gently suggested that if I would, it probably would help me to get some answers to some of my hidden questions about God and Jesus. It was a thought that I finally embraced, and I asked Jean to help me pray, as I really didn't know how to do it.

In the spring of 1954, both Jean and Jack were immersed in work and studies. Jean had a contract to play in the Music Circus orchestra in Sacramento and had to report by May 20th. Jack, on the other hand had work and study commitments which would keep him in New York through June 30th. He was desolate over the prospect of spending five weeks in New York City alone. He described what happened next in this way:

I began to pray with much more earnestness and asked the Lord to help me work out my consternation. One night in early May, I prayed with much more concern and asked the Lord to let me know what to do about the Church. "Is it true?" I asked. "Should I join? What will my family think? What will my colleagues think?"

As the time drew near for Jean to leave, I prayed more earnestly for answers. One night I was worried about being left alone in New York City for so long a time, and I asked for strength to calm my fears. Sleep finally came.

It seemed just a few minutes later, and I was awake—sitting up in bed with this bright light all around me. Wondering what the light was, I got up and looked out the window to see if it was lightning and a storm—but it was clear and calm.

A calmness came over me, and "the voice" said, "Don't worry, you are on the right path. Follow your feelings and do what is right. I will not lead you astray, and you will be fine here on your own. You know what you should do, so do it!"

The next morning Jack told Jean that he was going to be baptized into the Church. When he and Jean went to Sacramento for the summer, Jack had second thoughts. Upon returning to New York City in the fall, however, with the help of Max he decided to go ahead, and he was baptized by Max in 1955 in New York City.

As Jack told me this story, he was overcome with emotion, and often he had difficulty continuing. His story, like Joe Swick's, was a very personal one, and in both cases emotion levels were high.

It was May, 2004, that **Maxine Zawodniak** came to our house to be interviewed. Her interview follows:

"My name is Maxine Zawodniak. My maiden name was Metcalf."

"Tell me something of the background that led to your experience."

"It was the little town of Richfield, Idaho, where I was born. We had a few milk cows, chickens and other things to sustain life. I was born April 6, 1929, just six months before the major crash and depression in America.

"Somewhere, deep down inside of me, I always felt that I was a stranger here. I had no idea why I felt so lonely even when I was around a crowd.

"It must have been late October, just before the first snowfall, when I first recalled the experience. I was around four years of age.

"My brothers and sisters had gone to school. I was sent out in the yard to play. Often, I entertained myself by playing 'pretend.' That is why it didn't seem unusual to me as I looked toward the hills of the Sun Valley area, and I felt that I had seen them sometime in the past from a different perspective. As I stared at the hills, a vision opened in my mind.

"In the vision, I saw a group of boys and girls in a circle, as if they were sitting on the ground. I don't know how many there were, but it appeared to be a rather large group of, maybe, twenty-five or thirty. It seemed as though we were learning something—like in a school.

"Suddenly from behind me, and over my right shoulder, I could feel my name being called. It wasn't like a verbal sound, it was just that *I knew*. It was me being called, I'm not even sure of the name I was called, but I knew it was me. As I turned and looked for where the sound was coming from, I saw a slender, tall man standing there."

"What did he look like, Maxine?"

"As I said, he was tall and thin. He was wearing a robe, of sorts, that was nondescript. It wasn't particularly bright or anything. Looking at him, though, I knew that I was supposed to leave the group of children. Mentally, I asked him if it was my time to go. He indicated that it was. Turning back to the group, I saw the face of a boy who appeared to be sad. He mentally asked me if it was my time to go. I said, 'Yes, but I'll be seeing you.'

"For a period of time—I don't know how long—I remembered nothing. Then the vision returned and I was again with the tall man, and we were floating over those hills that I had been looking at when the vision commenced.

"The tall man and I were conversing as we floated along until suddenly we stopped. Looking down, I saw a farmhouse, a barnyard with a fence, and a canal behind the house. As we paused, I asked my guide, 'Is this where I am going to live?'

"He said, 'yes.'"

"'Will I be the only child?'" I asked."

"No, you will be one of many."

"Will I be happy there?"

"If you want to be."

"The vision faded and I was back standing in the snow and looking at the hills. Later, I told my mother what I had seen."

349

"Was that the end of your vision, Maxine?"

"It was the end of that one. A few years later my Aunt Delia got sick with cancer. One day, when she was terribly ill, I asked her if she was sick. She said that she was, and I tried to make her feel better by fanning her. At the funeral, my mother lifted me to see her in the coffin. She looked awful, and I was frightened—especially when my brothers teased me by saying that Aunt Delia would come and get me.

"Terrified, I crawled into bed with my parents. Later, I saw a small light up in the corner of the room. It seemed to be getting larger, and I was mesmerized as I watched. It was like looking into a beam of a flashlight backwards. There was movement in the light, way off in the distance. It was bright, but it didn't hurt my eyes. Then I could see the flowing of what looked like a long white dress. And I could see a small person coming down the beam of light. It was a beautiful woman, and suddenly I knew that it was Aunt Delia. Even though I had never seen her young and beautiful with dark hair, I knew who it was.

"Since I was still horrified that Aunt Delia would 'come to get me,' as my brothers claimed, I cried, 'Oh, don't get me.'

"She spoke my name. 'Maxine, do you think I would hurt you?'

"Then she asked me, 'Do you remember what a nice girl you were and fanned me in the yard when I was so sick?'

"When I told her yes, she said, 'Do you think I would ever hurt you?' Finally, I felt at peace and fell asleep. The next morning I told my mother that Aunt Delia had come and talked to me."

"Was that the end of your visions, Maxine?" I asked.

"Yes."

"Please tell me then, what led to your joining the Mormon Church?"

"When I was twenty-seven, I had been searching for a long time to find a church I could be happy with. At the time I was working for Yellow Page Advertising, and every time we would list a church, I asked them to send me more information. As a result, I had many brochures that I had studied about different churches and religions. Also, I had visited numerous churches and asked them questions about their beliefs—particularly about where I came from. None of them answered my questions to my satisfaction, so I just kept searching."

"Why did you care about where you came from?"

"Because of the experience I had when I was young. I knew

that the real me came from someplace before I was born."

"Were you living alone while you were making this search?"

"No, I was married and had a little boy. I wanted to raise him to believe in God."

"How old was your son?"

"He was five."

"Was your husband also interested in a church?"

"No. Unfortunately, he didn't believe there was a God. Later, I divorced him over other issues."

"So you set out to find a church in order to know where you came from. That's a strange way to look for a church. Presumably that was the focus of your search because of your youthful experience. Is that true?"

"Yes."

"Where did you think you came from?"

"In terms of telling you exactly where, I didn't know. But I *did* know that I came from some place that wasn't of this earth. It was clear from my experience that this was true, and I knew it. So when I talked to different ministers and pastors, I always asked them where I came from. They would look at me rather strangely, and . . . and they would ask me something like, 'You mean you are this age, and you don't know that you came from your mother and father?'

"My response to them was, of course I knew that. But I also knew that I was a spirit or in some other form before I came to this earth. They then would ask why I believed that, and I would tell them of my recollection of the experience I had."

"How many churches did you investigate in that way?"

"Well, that's hard to know exactly. Actually, my girl friend and I started looking when we were still in grammar school in Modesto, California. We went to the Baptist Church, the Catholic Church, the Church of God, and a few others. And they were okay, you know . . . especially for young kids. But they still didn't have the answer to what I was looking for."

"How did you finally find what you were looking for?"

"My niece came out to visit me in California. She was from Utah, and I knew that she was a Mormon. There were also other Mormons in my extended family, but I didn't know anything about their religion. When she came to my house, she saw all the information I had on different churches and she asked me about them.

"I told her that I was trying to get information about differ- ent religions—how they started, what they believed and . . . and I said that the first question I asked every one of them was, where did I come from? and none of them could answer my question.

"She said, 'Well you've studied all of those churches. Why don't you go to church with me?'

"So I went to church with my niece, and by the next week I had a couple of missionaries from the Mormon Church knocking on my door. We made an appointment for the next week and they started seeing me."

"How did that go?"

"There were three or four questions I had in my mind, and I had decided that if they didn't answer them correctly I was going to continue my search elsewhere. The first question I asked was, 'Where did God come from?' They flipped to someplace in the scriptures where it said, in effect, he has always been.

"The next question I asked was, 'Where did I come from?' They proceeded to draw a picture that showed me high in the picture, from which they said I came to earth and got an earthly mother and father. At that point I said, 'Whoa, wait a minute. . . . I think I can tell you about that.'

"My comment seemed to startle them, but I then told them of my youthful vision in which I saw myself as a premortal being. They remarked that what I saw was unusual since most people are not aware of their premortal existence."

"Okay, Maxine. How did their discussion after that proceed? Did they carry you through a series of lessons, and if so, how long did it take?"

"Yes, they taught me the basic beliefs of the Church, and it didn't take long. It all made sense to me. When they got to Joseph Smith, I didn't have any problem believing in a modern-day prophet. In fact, during my search for a church I used to ask, 'If they had prophets in ancient times to tell people what to do, why don't we have any now?'"

"How long was it before you were baptized?"

"About a month."

"Your son was five years old when you were baptized. Did your husband object?" Maxine laughed and said:

"When I continued to study churches, he said that he didn't care what I did about religion so long as I didn't join one of the weird ones, such as the Catholics or the Mormons. When I finally said I was going to join the Mormon Church, he didn't say anything, but he didn't listen to any of the discussions, either."

"Do you remember your baptism date?"

"It was February 8, 1957."

"What impact has all of these experiences had on your life?"
"The impact is that I know where I came from, and I know that there are other people there who have not been born yet.

Elane Durham

In her extensive NDE, **Elane Durham** was told that in time she would find "a New People" with the same spirit she felt during her NDE. When the LDS missionaries called on her fifteen years later, she recognized the Spirit. A small portion of what she wrote about that experience is taken from her book *I Stand All Amazed* (Durham, 1998, p. 138):

> Something else was happening to me, though. Once again, just as I had before my spirit had popped out of my body back in Chicago, I was feeling a heightened sense of spiritual awareness. As I had listened and asked questions of the young elders, my own spirit had been touched. And the more I conversed with and told God of my feelings, and the more I read from the scriptures, the more my own spirit grew. That afternoon as I spoke with God I came to a realization. I knew I was going to be a part of this church so what did it matter when I joined it?
>
> If after joining, things didn't turn out like I truly felt they would, I could always leave and go back to what I had been doing—settling for services in various churches while never really having a place to call home. In my heart, however, I knew that wouldn't happen. I had felt a special spirit that I'd not felt for almost fifteen years, and I really wanted to explore and grow with it. . . .
>
> And when [the baptismal service] was over, I knew that I had found my "new people," as the angel had told me I would "within fifteen to twenty years," and I had joined them of my own choice and accord.

A Remarkable Healing

One of the more dramatic experiences I have encountered is that of **DeAnne Anderson Shelley**. My first meeting with DeAnne and her husband Fred was in the spring of 1970 when I was bishop of the San Jose 12th Ward. As I became familiar with Fred and DeAnne, they told a remarkable story.

Fred and DeAnne were living in Vacaville, California, in January, 1964 when DeAnne was diagnosed with multiple sclerosis. Since, in

1961, she had contracted Bulbar Polio and was partially paralyzed from that disease for a time, this particular illness rapidly became extremely serious. DeAnne deteriorated to the point where she became blind, and in June, 1964, after being in the hospital for five months, her physician, Dr. Parkinson, notified Fred that she couldn't live through the night.

Dr. Parkinson, who happened to be LDS, left the hospital and went home for the night. As he was getting ready for bed he felt impressed to go back to the hospital and give DeAnne a blessing. Although neither Fred nor DeAnne were LDS, they had been asking Dr. Parkinson about his religion, and they had begun to study it. Fred readily agreed to a blessing by Dr. Parkinson and his companion. After giving the blessing, Dr. Parkinson returned home for the night.

The next day, when Fred and Dr. Parkinson visited DeAnne, at five in the morning, she was alive but crying. When they asked her why

she was crying, she said it was because she felt so awful, and because she had been in this beautiful place where all pain had left her, and where she could see again. She saw her deceased father in this place of brightness. He was dressed in a glowing white robe with a sash, and he looked wonderful. She seemed to know that she had to come back, and she communicated that to her father. She didn't want to return, but knew that she had to.

Gradually, DeAnne recovered sufficiently so that in September 1964 she was able to leave the hospital. Her sight returned, but she still had multiple sclerosis, and her limbs were atrophied to the point that she could only get around in a wheel chair, or with difficulty, with braces and a walker. She and Fred joined the LDS Church and looked forward to the time that they could go to the Oakland Temple and be sealed as husband and wife for eternity.

In February, 1965, Dr. Parkinson felt that DeAnne was well enough that she and Fred could go to the Oakland Temple. He accompanied her, along with many from the Vacaville Ward. DeAnne was wheeled in on her wheel chair. During a part of the ceremony she began to feel strange, as if electricity were flowing through her and forcing her to vibrate. Her friend, Maxine, noticed the problem and signaled that something was wrong. They stopped the ceremony and Dr. Parkinson wheeled her into the lobby where she lay on a couch while he examined her. He found nothing wrong except for a slightly elevated pulse. DeAnne tried to explain that it seemed as though feeling had returned to her legs and she could walk, but Dr. Parkinson put her in the chair, and they returned to the room where the ceremony was resumed.

They reached the point in the service where a few couples were invited to come up front. DeAnne stood up from her wheelchair and walked to the front of the room. Fred joined her, with tears streaming down his face, as he and DeAnne stood together unaided for the first time in more than a year. DeAnne left the temple without the use of the wheelchair or braces. Later, when her legs were measured, all atrophy had disappeared. As a result of witnessing what had happened to DeAnne, many of the health-care professionals who had worked with her joined the LDS Church. Some years later I met Dr. Parkinson and heard him explain how there was no medical explanation for what happened to DeAnne.

As of the date of this book, DeAnne is still as vigorous and vital as ever. Fred was killed in an airplane crash, and DeAnne later married a marvelous man, Melvyn Shelley. In 2002 DeAnne became ill and her kidneys began to fail. She asked for a priesthood blessing, and shortly after receiving it she recovered her health. In 2004 Melvyn died from an illness. Despite losing two husbands and suffering through numerous illnesses, DeAnne continues to live an exuberant life of service. Needless to say, she has complete faith in the power of Deity to heal, when it is His will.

Revelation and the Power of God: Why the LDS Church?

None of these people knew each other. Yet their true accounts were remarkably similar. Most of them sought me out when they became aware of my research on NDEs. Do I think that their finding me was a chance occurrence? No, I do not. There were too many reasons why they should not have found me. In the case of both Gary Gillum and Joe Swick, the advertisement I placed in the newspaper was a small one with no particular urgency associated with it; yet Joe and Gary called me within a short time of each other, and both felt an urgency to meet with me. Indeed, Joe got tied up at home and was late for our appointment. He lived a couple of miles from campus and he had no transportation to reach me—so he ran all the way. Just as I was about to leave, Joe came puffing in. We held the interview in my car. Similarly with Jack, he sought me out because of the urgency he felt about telling his story.

In each of their experiences, the individuals learned through personal revelation the truth of what they were looking for. This, then, is the strength of The Church of Jesus Christ of Latter-day Saints. As stated by President James E. Faust in the Sunday morning session of General Conference in October, 2000: "The great strength of this Church comes from our collective and individual testimonies, born of our own trials and faithfulness." It is the testimony, through personal revelation, of millions of members who proclaim a certain knowledge of revealed truths. These are ethereal truths bestowed by Deity for the personal benefit of the individual.

Elder Joseph B. Wirthlin, of the Quorum of Twelve Apostles, put it this way in the October, 2000 Conference: "For Latter-day Saints, a testimony is the assurance of the reality, truth, and goodness of God, of the teachings and atonement of Jesus Christ, and of the divine calling of latter-day prophets. . . . It is knowledge buttressed by divine personal confirmation by the Holy Ghost."

When the prophet Joseph Smith saw the Father and the Son in the Sacred Grove in the spring of 1820, he was told that he should join none of the churches which were situated in the New York area where he was living at the time. A major reason for this prohibition by the Lord was that "they draw near to me with their lips, but their hearts are far from me, they teach for doctrines the commandments of men, having a form of godliness, but they deny the power thereof" (Joseph Smith–History 1:19). Knowledge buttressed by divine personal confirmation by the Holy Ghost is a form of that power. So, also, is the healing influence of prayers and priesthood blessings.

This chapter could have been expanded many times with other illustrative stories. Books have been written by individuals who joined the LDS Church as a direct result of a spiritual experience.

By reason of the location of those I interviewed—Salt Lake City and environs—most of those were already members of the LDS Church when they had their experience. Out of sixty-eight people interviewed, fifty-seven percent were LDS at the time of their experience, and seventy-four percent of those expressed a feeling of coming back to mortality with a strong sense of mission. Sixty-seven percent of the non-LDS also had a strong sense of mission (Gibson, 1993, pp. 312, 315).

Those who were LDS often expressed specificity about their mission. This was true, for instance, of **Lucinda Hecker,** whose story was detailed in chapter 6.

Renee Zamora was an LDS member who contracted the Epstein-Barr virus and was improperly treated in the hospital with an antibiotic. The treatment precipitated her NDE. A portion of our interview follows (Gibson, 1993, pp. 213–14):

> For a long time I wondered about this experience, and why it happened to me. It seemed real, yet I couldn't explain it. During my release from the hospital, though, something happened to convince me that it was real.

Previously, Renee had explained that at one point during her NDE she had traveled through walls in the hospital, and had entered a room with a frail old man with oxygen-assisted breathing. The room was some distance from her own room and was not visible from her bed. She continued with her narrative:

> They put me in a wheelchair to take me to the hospital entrance. At one point, while they went to get something, they parked me in the wheelchair at the doorway next to my room. Knowing I was just outside the room where I saw the frail old man in bed with the oxygen tube in his nose, I leaned around the corner and looked in. It was the same man—I saw and recognized him. From where I was lying in my room it would have been impossible for me to have seen him.
>
> I knew that I would find further answers by attending the temple. . . . It became clear to me . . . that the people I had seen [during my NDE] were those who had passed on, but were confined to this earth, and who needed further work done for them in order to progress beyond where they were. . . . Much of what I saw had symbolic meaning beyond the outward appearances of the events themselves.
>
> Since that experience, I have become a fanatic concerning genealogy and temple work. The patience of my husband is sometimes tried as I work on genealogy. . . . The genealogical and temple work that we do is enormously important. . . . Since my experience I have been driven to locate all the people I saw that needed their temple work done. Each person is important in the sight of the Lord.

Not all Latter-day Saints who have NDEs become more religious. In some cases, they become more "spiritual," but less oriented to the formal aspects of their religion. This is also true of many non-LDS people who have extensive NDEs. **John Stirling** responded to my question in this way in chapter 7 of this book:

> **"During the first interview, you said that you were LDS but you weren't particularly religious in a formal sense. Is that still true?"**
>
> "Well, I'm *really* religious, I just don't attend a church."
>
> **"Is religion the right word then?"**
>
> "No, I guess it's not. No . . . it wasn't the right word then. . . . Let's see—I guess the right word would be *spiritual.* Yes, I've always been spiritual. In a sense, though, I've also been religious, it's just that I've never been socially adept at attending a church."

Stephanie LaRue was raised in the Catholic faith. Carol and I interviewed her in 1991 (Gibson, 1992, pp. 118–19). Her NDE occurred as a result of a difficult hysterectomy in 1980 at the University of Utah Medical Center. I questioned her about how her NDE had affected her religious beliefs. Her response is given in this portion of our interview:

> **"Has your experience changed your feeling about religion?"**
>
> "In terms of formal religion, not particularly, but it has made me more spiritual. I consider myself deeply spiritual, but not necessarily religious."
>
> **"Do you have any evidence of this increased spirituality?"**
>
> "Yes, sometimes I have experiences where I will see a light, like an aura around somebody, and I know, somehow, that the person is important to me."

Which Is the Best Religion?
The Religion that Brings You Closest to God

The preceding stories and discussion of those who became members of The Church of Jesus Christ of Latter-day Saints after their NDEs is not to suggest that the LDS Church is the sole recipient of individuals who received personal revelation from their NDEs. Indeed, several of those I interviewed enjoyed NDEs, or other epiphanies, which led them to other churches. **Howard Storm,** for example, in his extensive NDE, changed from being an atheistic professor of art to a pastor of the United Church of

Christ. He was led to that vocation as a direct result of the angelic teachers—and the Lord Jesus Christ—who instructed him so effectively.

In his book, *My Descent Into Death,* Howard describes what happened while undergoing his deep NDE. He asked a number of questions, and his angelic friends provided answers (Storm, 2000, pp. 129–31). Two of the most interesting questions and answers were as follows:

> Question: Which is the best religion?
> I was expecting them to answer with something like Methodist, or Presbyterian, or Catholic, or some denomination. They answered, "The religion that brings you closest to God."
> Question: Why did [Jesus] not do something spectacular to prove it to everyone?
> God wants us to choose God freely without coercion. God doesn't threaten or need to force our belief. God wants our love and trust, for love alone. God doesn't want slaves in mindless obedience. God wants us to choose God freely. Behavior that looks religious but is devoid of genuine love is abhorrent to God. God loves an honest agnostic more than a religious hypocrite.

These answers seem most appropriate to me. They coincide with my understanding of LDS doctrine, and they are also harmonious with my own research into near-death experiences. In the book, *Fingerprints of God,* I put it this way (Gibson, 1999, p. 188):

God Doesn't Abrogate Man's Freedom of Choice

One of the questions frequently asked me, especially by Latter-day Saints, is: "When people have these experiences, why doesn't the Lord tell them to join The Church of Jesus Christ of Latter-day Saints—after all, it is His Church, isn't it?"

My response to that question is, yes it is His Church, but if he told people to join it, then he would be abrogating their freedom of choice. The follow-on question to that answer is: "But that's what the Lord did when Joseph Smith asked the question. Why shouldn't he do as he did with the Prophet?"

And that's just the point. Joseph *was* the Prophet, and his mission was to restore the pristine church. Those who have NDEs are participants of a singular experience for *their* benefit. If everyone who lived were told by God what church they should join then there would be no freedom of choice. God inspires, entreats and occasionally grants a marvelous vision or experience to fortunate individuals, but He never *forces* His will on anyone.

17: How Close Is Omega?

Mormons and NDEs

By now, in this book, the reader should recognize that Latter-day Saints feel at home with the NDE. In chapter 2, Duane Crowther described his experience in seeking out inspirational stories, from the large body of family histories kept by the saints, for his book *Life Everlasting*. Many of the accounts he collected fell in the category of what has become known as a near-death experience. He also explained some of the reasons for LDS attraction to NDEs and hypothesized several reasons why Mormons apparently have and record more "beyond the veil" experiences than do others who are not Mormon.

Basically, the NDE plays an ethereal tune whose harmony touches the very soul of a Latter-day Saint. It is a familiar melody, and it vibrates with the truths from an eternal home. The chords of the NDE tune blend with the long-familiar chords of the restored gospel, and the resultant melodious strain is like hearing again, after a long absence, the magnificence of Beethoven's *Ode to Joy*.

Common Elements or Stages of the NDE

In his book, *Life After Life*, Raymond Moody identified fifteen elements which are frequently found in an in-depth NDE. He noted that it is rare that all elements would be present in any given NDE—although he found two NDEs which were very close to identical to his "ideal" model. Taken collectively, it was not uncommon to find various of the elements present (Moody, 1975, pp. 21–25).

Kenneth Ring, in his book, *Life at Death,* also found that there were five common stages that represented what he called the "core experience." As with Moody, those stages were frequent enough, and independent enough of external factors (such as gender, sex, age, race, religion, and culture) to form a coherent pattern (Ring, 1980, 39–66).

In chapter 10 of this book, a more-recent study by Richard Bonenfant included 37 different elements which can be found in NDEs. In his study of 56 clinical-death survivors, he traced the number and percentage of those who included some of these elements. As a matter of interest, I compared those in Bonenfant's study with my own percentages of 68 subjects I interviewed.

As with Moody and Ring, neither Bonenfant's study nor mine showed any strong cultural, religious, or other predilection on any given element. For example, on Bonenfant's study, his element of *Feeling quiet, peaceful, secure* was true whatever the background or religious disposition of those having the NDE. Similarly, *Seeing your life pass in review* was true independent of other external cultural or religious factors.

Despite the apparent independence of NDEs from most cultural, religious and other effects, the issue of cultural and religious influence keeps reappearing in the literature. There is no question that some cultural and religious parallels can be detected in various NDEs. Examples are given throughout this book.

When Raymond Moody asked the question (concerning NDEs he had recorded), "Did all these people profess a religion before their experience? If so, aren't the experiences shaped by their religious beliefs and backgrounds?" Moody responded with: "They seem to be to some extent. As mentioned earlier, though the description of the being of light is invariable, the identity ascribed to it varies, apparently as a function of the religious background of the individual" (Moody, 1975, p. 140).

A reductionist theory of the NDE has been formulated which posits that most of what one sees and feels during the experience derives from a last-grasp of what one was exposed to during mortality. This particular theory—as well as many others—founders on the shoals of corroborative NDEs. The multiplying evidence of the reality of out-of-body consciousness, as illustrated throughout this book, points with increasing strength to survival after death. As now seems likely, prospective and other research projects being planned and carried out will require a serious scientific examination of consciousness beyond death.

Why the Many Parallels between NDEs and LDS Theology?

That being true, it still leaves open the question, "Why do certain cultural and religious effects keep finding their way into so many NDEs? And that question is particularly pertinent to this book where an attempt is made to compare many commonly found NDE elements to the numerous doctrinal parallels of LDS theology (see chapters 4, 5 and 15).

In studying the various chapters of this book where examples are given and where comparisons are drawn, readers are encouraged to draw their own conclusions about the validity of the claimed similarities. It may be useful, for instance, to carefully read Joseph Smith's history of his various visions and make your own comparison with many of the NDE cases illustrated in other chapters.

But, back to the question at hand. chapter 3 addresses the question in this manner, "If one grants the possibility that the NDE data gathered by the researcher may be supportive of LDS theological positions because they are reflective of ultimate truth given by God, then the answer is simple. The data correlates with LDS doctrine because both the data and LDS doctrine correspond to the same source of all truth. Such truth becomes almost binding if the data from other, non-LDS investigators, also correlates well with that of the LDS investigators." Again, readers are encouraged to draw their own conclusions regarding this correspondence.

What of Omega?

In his book, *Heading Toward Omega,* Kenneth Ring said this about Omega (Ring, 1984, pp. 252, 254, 255):

> Omega, then, represents an end, as death itself seems to be the end of life. It is in this sense that a well-known journal in the field of thanatology is called *Omega.* Omega means death.
>
> But it also means something else, just as the word "end" similarly has a double meaning. "End" can obviously signify either finality or a goal, and it is Omega as an end *point* that has special meaning to us here. In this sense, Omega stands for the aim of human evolution, the ultimate destination toward which humanity is inexorably bound.
>
> . . . But, of course, the point is not simply that many millions will know the NDE for themselves but also *how the NDE will transform them afterward.* We have already examined in depth

how people's lives and consciousness are affected by NDEs and what values come to guide their behavior. Now, to begin to appreciate the planetary impact of these changes, we must imagine these same effects occurring in millions of lives throughout the world, regardless of race, religion, nationality or culture.

Yet it is not just NDErs whom we have to visualize on this collective level but also *all* persons who have undergone a similar transformative experience as a result of a deep spiritual awakening. Remember that it has already been established . . . that the NDE is only *one* of a family of related transcendental experiences, and that it appears that most such experiences, however they are brought about, lead to transformations similar to those documented for NDErs. . . . NDErs themselves, then, should probably be regarded as one distinct stream feeding into a larger river, with many tributaries, of spiritually transformative experiences.

From this perspective we are now finally able to discern the larger meanings of NDEs. May it be that NDErs—and others who have had similar awakenings—*collectively represent an evolutionary thrust toward higher consciousness for humanity at large?* Could it be that the NDE itself is an evolutionary mechanism that has the effect of jump-stepping individuals into the next stage of human development by unlocking spiritual potentials previously dormant?

Ken goes on to suggest that we, indeed, may be closing on Omega as transcendental awareness spreads. In the year 2000, Ken wrote this:

> My views have changed quite drastically in some respects since I published *Heading Toward Omega.* In particular, I have foresworn my previous hypothesis about NDEs leading to "Omega" or anywhere else. I no longer think, and haven't for years now, that NDErs are part of a vanguard of folks leading us to the glory of higher consciousness. I won't deny that NDEs themselves can be transformative experiences for those who undergo them, but I do not think that such changes will spread like a kind of wildfire of consciousness to affect all of humanity.
>
> . . . I was in my mid-40s when I wrote *Heading Toward Omega,* and there is a lot in that book that I still stand by and am proud of. But my evolutionary speculations about NDEs leading toward Omega now seem to me to be the equivalent of my "youthful indiscretion." I am much older now, and I no longer glow with roseate optimism about humanity's future.
>
> I still believe in NDEs, though. They are the real thing, whatever else might be said. (Ring, Summer 2000, pp. 226–27)

In private conversation on ths issue, Ken jokingly confessed that now, instead of suffering from youthful indiscretion, he may be suffering from aged senility.

Other Evidence in Support of the Omega Theory

One cannot read the chapters in this book provided by those having different professions without acknowledging the impact that the NDE has had, at least on those who wrote the chapters. It is clear that their exposure to the NDE—although not as participants in these types of other-worldly experiences—was profound in its influence on them professionally, and personally. It is almost as if, as Ken Ring once put it, they were infected with the NDE virus. This effect was strikingly illustrated in Sandra Cherry's teaching experience as described in chapter 14.

Beverly Brodsky is a delightful lady who favored the Salt Lake chapter of IANDS with a visit in July, 2004. Carol and I were privileged to be her host.

For those of you who are not familiar with Beverly's story, as a young adult she had a life-threatening motorcycle accident in which many of the bones in her skull were fractured, and she sustained numerous other serious injuries as well. Her resultant NDE was featured in Ken Ring's book, *Lessons from the Light*. He commented that her experience was perhaps the most profound NDE he had encountered in his years of research.

During her visit, Beverly granted me the favor of a brief interview. During the interview we discussed, among other things, Ken Ring's concept of Omega. Our interview follows:

"Who are you?"
"I'm Beverly Brodsky."
"What are you doing here?"
"I'm here to speak to the Utah IANDS group."
"They tell me you are writing a book. What's the title?"
"My working title is *Round Trip: Wisdom From Beyond Death.*"
"What's the book about?"
"It's about my research as well as my personal near-death experience. The book's thesis is that the near-death experience tells us everything we need to know about living. Then I draw parallels to other types of experiences, and the big shift that is going through our culture to incorporate the possibility

that consciousness is primary—and that life continues beyond death."

"You said that your book is about living. I thought the near-death experience was about death."

"No. The near-death experience really teaches us about *living*. Because if we understand what it is that we *are* . . . who we *are*, and our true nature, then we understand better how to live. In that manner we can then enjoy and cherish the opportunities we have in life. Things are so fleeting in this physical realm."

"They are, indeed, fleeting. What got you started on this project?"

"My involvement with IANDS. I have been a support group leader, and as a chapter leader, for fifteen years. Actually, what precipitated my interest was when I read Dr. Kenneth Ring's book, *Life at Death*, which I read a few years after it came out in 1980. Also, I read Raymond Moody's *Life After Life*, and I realized that I wasn't the only one in the world who had this type of experience. Through Dr. Ring's book, though, I became aware that there were people who were studying this, and groups that were sharing information and talking about it. And I had had eighteen years of silence."

"Why silence?"

"Because when I had my experience you could be locked up for talking about it. Also, so many people told me it was a hallucination, when I knew it wasn't. It was too precious to share and have people write it off. It would have been like 'casting your pearls before swine.' I just knew it was true, yet there was nothing I could do with it."

"How did you know it wasn't a hallucination?"

"The main reason is that it changed my entire philosophy about life. It took away my fear of death. For a period of time I saw things as they truly are. And I permanently changed my core beliefs about the meaning of life, why we are all here, and who I am. As for hallucinations, I have experienced things with medication, and child-birth labor, where I felt that I was hallucinating, and that was more like an unreal dream. When you consider it afterwards, you understand that you were hallucinating, and it wasn't real. Also, you certainly wouldn't reorient your entire philosophy of life based on a hallucination."

"What was your philosophy of life before you had the NDE?"

"Well, I had been raised in a non-observant conservative Jewish background. But I actually rejected that, and at one time I was an atheist. There couldn't be a God, I believed, because of the Holocaust, and because of a lot of horrible things going on in the world. I was even a Marxist at one point. At the time of my experience, I would characterize myself more as an agnostic. I felt that maybe there was something, but I wasn't sure. I had tried meditating and things like that, but I didn't *believe*. You know, I didn't believe in God. Religions, I thought, were not true.

"After the experience, though, it was so undeniable. It was something that was so real, and so *clear.* And I was so alive in that place, it was something I could never, ever doubt. That was the real world, this is the hallucination. In reality nothing is a hallucination; we are here for purposes, but *that* was undeniably real. So, it is not a matter of belief with me, I *know* that there is a God, a higher power. There is *purpose* to our existence here. And we are loved. Life is not a random, chance event.

"It is a beautiful school that we are going through. We are learning the lessons of love and knowledge and service, and to perform them within the boundaries of the challenges which we have. But anyhow, I just *knew* it.

"It was an ineffable experience. In fact, Dr. Ring and Leon Rhodes encouraged me to write my experience down. It was difficult to write because of this ineffability. The perfection there made it almost impossible to use the English language to attempt to describe it—to express something so profound."

"How far along are you in your book?"

"I'm in about the first third. It will probably be a full year before it is complete."

"Is it easy writing?"

"When I sit down and put my mind to it, it does come out pretty easy. It's just that I haven't done this for a long time. It's a matter of getting into the rhythm of it."

"You speak very well, Beverly. You speak most emphatically, as if you have a certitude that one rarely sees in life. How can you be that sure of anything?"

"Well, this is the one thing that I am sure of. It's the nature of the experience, and the quality of being in a place of which this is a reflection. The body that we have, and the physical world—this is a reflection of our true home."

"What do you mean by our true home?"

"My belief is that we are a part of this realm of love and light. And there is this feeling I had, of being one with God—the God who created everything. But what is there is in its fullness and magnificence. Here, we are in these limited physical bodies, and we have these brains which are filters and dampers of our limitless consciousness. In that realm, our consciousness perceives all knowledge, and we can understand all knowledge very simply. Here, we struggle to master little parts of that knowledge.

"It is as if our brains are not capable of the mastery we have in that realm. It might be likened to a slice of bread, or a sliver, or . . . a crumb of bread compared to perceiving the entire loaf. The scope and magnificence of that realm is beyond . . . I can't even imagine it, even though I remember that it happened."

"Was it worth your motorcycle accident and all of the physical problems that it has brought to you?"

Beverly laughed. "Oh yes. Much as I hate pain, and I'm a real baby with pain, I would do it again if I had to lose all four limbs just to be a part of that ethereal journey and share in the magnificence of that realm of love and light and knowledge. It was the most tremendous gift to my soul. To have been in the presence of the being of light, and to know . . ." Beverly shed some tears, "I'm getting emotional because I'm going through a grieving process. But to know that we are so loved, in perfection—regardless of our imperfection. We are loved *perfectly*.

"We are immortal and eternal. The things that look so terrible here . . . and death is a classic one that looks awful and tragic and horrible, yet it is a wonderful, a beautiful experience."

"Would you recommend, then, that people go out and have a motorcycle accident so that they can have a beautiful experience like this?"

Beverly chuckled, "No, and as a matter of fact, Ken Ring, who is one of my mentors, in his book, *Lessons from the Light,* talks about there being a benign virus, if you read about NDEs, think about them, and immerse yourself in the literature. You do not have to die or be hurt, in order to get the lessons and to understand. The reason for that, I think, is because we are all from this same source. We are all waves in the cosmic ocean. We are all part of each other and of the wholeness. So, this kind of information resonates. You don't have to have an NDE to receive at least a portion of that peace and love found there—if someone is ready to receive the information."

"Beverly, I agree with you, and I argue with Ken Ring, that his initial assessment that we were on the march towards Omega, and that civilization would benefit from these kinds of experiences that open up a knowledge that they previously did not have. Since he first wrote that in about 1984, he apparently has had second thoughts on the Omega journey. I still believe that he was right in his initial supposition, and one can learn from reading and hearing of these experiences. Most importantly, we can feel of the love which you reflect without having to go through an NDE."

"Yes, I agree with you, Arvin. I understand that it has been discouraging, because in the course of all those years Ken has put into this work, or even in the course of a lifetime, progress may seem slow. In the case of Martin Luther King, for example, he spoke of peace and tolerance, and I remember watching him on TV and laughing and saying, 'We will never get there,' when in fact, we only take these baby steps. For a shift in civilization, when we are taking baby steps, it is slow. My perspective, though, is that I look at the cup as half-full. There is still so much to be done, and the news certainly does not inform us of our progress.

"But I know that many people are going through this transformation in which they are awakening to their true nature. If we can help one person in that journey, there is a Jewish aphorism which says, 'If you can save one person it is like saving the whole world.' It is a very personal thing for people to understand this. If someone is not ready, he can read all the books in the world and it won't register. But many people are ready. In fact, I think there has been a shift in our civilization. I think that this is the biggest news of the twenty-first century—which I believe will come to be recognized as the century of consciousness. News of life after death is turning upside down a lot of the old theories about the materialistic-reductionistic views of creation, life, and the universe we live in. The resistance comes, I believe, from those who still follow the materialistic views of science. Most people, it seems to me, are open to a more spiritual understanding of reality."

"I agree, Beverly, and I don't want to take too much from your book. The way you speak cries out for you to put some of these thoughts into print. Bearing that in mind, are there any last thoughts you would like to leave if anybody reads what we have just talked about?"

"Yes. We are beings from this infinite realm, and whatever we have done—or whatever we are suffering or going through—there are lessons at every level. And we are okay! Sometimes it doesn't seem like that, but we are such radiant beings of light—each one of us—we are like sparkling diamonds. Every thing and every one, and the whole of creation, is *beautiful*. This is the vision where I saw the love and light in every thing and in every part of God's creation. My true life's goal is to get back to the point where I can see that again. I don't know whether that will happen, but I know that this marvelous beauty that I saw is *true*. We are from God, and we are made in that image, which is an image of tremendous beauty and love and perfection."

Mormon Contributions toward the March to Omega

Referring back to Ken Ring's comments in *Heading for Omega,* he said that "the NDE is only one of a family of related transcendental experiences," and that "NDErs themselves, then, should probably be regarded as one distinct stream feeding into a larger river, with many tributaries, of spiritually transformative experiences."

If one accepts that premise—and I do—then the body of religious transcendental experiences also becomes part of the march to Omega. In his book, *Religion, Spirituality and the Near-Death Experience,* Mark Fox said this:

> . . . Perhaps a discernible common core can be found across a *range* of religious experiences, including NDEs, and not just within and between the testimonies of NDErs themselves. Surely, the existence of such a core would be a tremendous and potentially hugely significant discovery in itself. The attempt to compare a range of testimonies to different types of religious experience in search of such a core would also require a number of skills which would mark out theologians as particularly suited to the challenge, not least because of their sensitivity to phenomenological approaches to testimony and their knowledge of the wide variety of religious experiences which exist.
>
> . . . The stakes are indeed high, for the NDE continues to offer, for many, the possibility of proving the existence of the human soul, the possibility of that soul's immortality, the possibility of learning what lies beyond the grave, the potential for adjudicating between competing religious truth-claims, and last, but by no means least, the need to deal with a growing number of sometimes confused NDErs. . . . In attempting to build a bridge between religion and the NDE, it is also my keen hope that the current study may offer a way for theological and religious differences among the pioneering NDE researchers to be themselves bridged. (Fox, 2003, pp. 349, 358)

Although many NDE researchers, and to a large extent many religionists, would doubt that the NDE or similar epiphanies would *prove* the existence and survival of the soul beyond the grave, it could provide powerful evidence for such a premise. Most theologians would probably argue that faith is still a primary prerequisite for belief in survival of the soul, and no amount of evidence could replace it.

It is interesting that Fox proposes exactly the type of prospective and corroborative NDE research which Bruce Greyson and Jan

Holden have initiated. The study will be performed at the University of Virginia Medical Center (see chapter 10 under *Prospective Studies*). Fox based his recommendations for this type of research on an idea generated by Paul Badham in 1997 (Fox, 2003, p. 73).

This Book as a Tributary

As one of the tributaries of spiritually transforming experiences, this book contributes to the river of knowledge flowing from the tributaries. As noted in the Preface, the book is about Near-Death Experiences (NDEs) and how they relate to the doctrine and teachings of The Church of Jesus Christ of Latter-day Saints. Those doctrines, for example, speak of the glory of God as it is reflected in an all-embracing light and love.

The book concerns the many-faceted aspects of the NDE, and how they do or do not correlate with LDS teachings. The book considers research findings which have accumulated from various scientific disciplines over the last thirty years or so. Thus, it not only gives a Mormon perspective of NDEs, but it does so with an updated view of NDE findings.

The book illustrates primary findings—including some of the controversies and uncertainties still remaining—and it speculates on the future course of research in the NDE realm. Most important, it compares NDE related events with LDS teachings and scriptures. These controversies and comparisons are located in various chapters throughout the book, with special emphasis on chapters 4, 5, and 15.

Perhaps the most influential group in obscuring the enormous value of publicizing and researching the NDE were the materialistic scientists who denied the reality of anything which fell outside of Einstein's relativity theories, together with Planck's quantum theory and Heisenberg's uncertainty principle.

Those so-called "hard science" boundaries are gradually crumbling under the onslaught of the multiple tributaries heading toward Omega. To the Mormons, the obfuscating scientific boundaries merely meant that the saints simply kept their sacred histories within a different boundary; namely, that of the family. That boundary has been opened as LDS authors have discovered and published hundreds, perhaps thousands, of LDS NDEs and other life-after-death accounts. Their writings have, in effect, served to recognize within Mormondom a different type of sacred document, one that recognizes the reality and truth of these religious experiences and treats them with the respect they deserve. The present book provides insight into the impact of NDEs on different portions of the LDS community. Some joined the Church as a result of NDEs. Other professionals altered the manner in which they conducted their work.

Other LDS Correlations with Near-Death Experiences

That the NDE had, and is having, a significant impact is undeniable. In general, the impact has been to reinforce the truth of what Mormons already believe. As Dave Larsen shows in chapters 4 and 5, the correspondence of various elements of the NDE with LDS theology is remarkable by any measure.

Especially pertinent to Mormons is the strong correlation of NDEs with survival of the family beyond death. When those having NDEs describe different members of their deceased families greeting them and helping them, and when numerous NDErs speak with wonder of returning "home," it speaks to the most sacred of ordinances performed in LDS temples where family members are sealed to each other "for time and eternity." The concept of returning home, and even the growing cache of NDE descriptions of a premortal existence where choices were presented to the individual prior to birth, again point the average Latter-day Saint to the temple and to their understanding of creation theology.

Equally important are the NDE accounts of encounters with beings of light, or of being embraced, comforted and taught by *the* being of light. One cannot read Joseph Smith's story or that of the three witnesses to the Book of Mormon—Martin Harris, Oliver Cowdery and David Whitmer—without seeing the amazing similarities. And the multitude of angel stories in the NDE literature cannot help but call to mind Moroni's and other ancient prophets' visits to Joseph Smith and his colleagues.

To deny that NDErs were in the presence of and saw Deity during their epiphany would be, for Mormons, to deny the very foundations of their religion. Even the manner of these visitations rings true to Mormons. Those NDErs who were in the presence of Deity often say that they were somehow changed or they couldn't have been able to stay in that glory. Mormon theology teaches that to be in the presence of Deity and live we must be changed.

The light—and the peace and love which accompanies it—spoken of by so many who had NDEs that it has become a primary indicator of an NDE is also a primary indicator of Mormon doctrine. Dave Larsen in chapter 4 and Grant Bishop in chapter 11 have written extensively about it. What that light is, how it interacts between God and Man, and what role it plays in the creative process is covered more completely in LDS scriptures than in any other religious cannon. To read of the light in the 88th Section of the Doctrine and Covenants is to read of God's relationship with *all* things, which were created by Deity.

Let me quote from a person who had a profound and in-depth NDE:

> So, it is not a matter of belief with me, I *know* that there is a God, a higher power. There is *purpose* to our existence here. And we are loved. Life is not a random, chance event.
>
> It is a beautiful school that we are going through. We are learning the lessons of love and knowledge and service. And to perform them within the boundaries of the challenges which we have. But anyhow, I just *knew* it.

If one were to write a succinct statement as to what it is that Mormons believe, that is as good a summary of LDS theology as most Mormons could write. It was not written by a Mormon. You have probably already recognized it from Beverly Brodsky's commentary at the first of this chapter. Those are *her* words, not mine. Now in defense of Beverly, I must confess that this was a unique selection by me from a plethora of profound statements she recorded. Also, there are no doubt other religions which could lay claim to that statement as being representative of their beliefs.

To further the LDS claims, though, let me note that fundamental to LDS belief, and as discussed by Dave Larsen in chapter 5, there was a God-formulated plan—before the universe and world were created—that laid out what is known by the Latter-day Saints as *The Plan of Happiness,* or *The Plan of Salvation.* That plan provided that a physical world would be created upon which we would obtain physical bodies and be tested in a school of mortality. A Savior, or Messiah, would atone for all sin committed by humans, and upon their repentance His atonement would make possible their return to God's presence.

Many NDErs speak of returning from their experiences with

a sense of mission. That too, is part of the Plan, as is the fact that much of what we knew of our missions prior to this life would be blocked by a veil of forgetfulness—so that free choice might be really free.

Another key element frequently found in NDE literature is the feeling that they are being fed by a limitless fount of knowledge—knowledge that they previously knew. Numerous examples of this awakening to an immense store of knowledge are given throughout the book. As is pointed out in chapter 4, LDS scriptures amply describe the realm of knowledge where we previously lived. Those scriptures teach that increased knowledge in mortality will be of advantage to the individual in immortality.

Less-than-pleasant (LTP) experiences, where individuals are exposed to the terror and distress of evil beings set on their destruction, have been reported in this book. LDS scriptures cover this aspect of The Plan of Happiness, and of the need for "opposition in all things," as it is described in the Book of Mormon. The idea that there is no time, as we know it, in the other realm is also discussed.

Some Deviations

So, are there some deviations of NDEs with LDS doctrine? Yes there are, again, as discussed in chapter 4. Perhaps the most obvious deviation is the belief by some NDErs and some researchers that reincarnation provides answers to certain elements of the NDE. This is simply rejected by LDS theology as not being a part of the overall Plan of Happiness.

Another deviation may be some of the NDE descriptions of the form of the spirit body or that of luminous angels. While most accounts indicate that the disembodied spirit—or the angelic visitor—resembles its human form, some do not (see Howard Storm's account of his experience with his friends; Storm, 2000, p. 34). LDS teachings speak of spiritual, angelic or resurrected bodies being in the form or image of a glorified God. The only divergence from this teaching is when speaking of evil beings, who may be in any number of demonic images.

There are probably some other minor deviations from LDS theology, but these are the two which seem most evident. In the book, *Fingerprints of God*, I provided some arguments against the principle of reincarnation (Gibson, 1999, pp. 222–29), and they will not be repeated here. Dave Larsen provides some speculative ideas on reasons for both of these NDE differences from LDS teachings.

So, What of the Future?

What, indeed? That question is addressed from several different perspectives by some of the contributors to this book. As is obvious from their responses, there is no simple answer for a knowledge domain as complex as NDEs. We are attempting to understand a subject which generally defies understanding. The rules of materialistic science do not readily apply.

The dilemma, then, is how to create a model, or a scientifically acceptable hypothesis, which can explain some of the strange happenings reported by those having undergone an NDE. As Nancy Evans Bush observed, "In fact, it now seems that the Experience is the experience, by whatever title. What varies is the manner of its precipitation; obviously there is no single trigger."

The problem is made even more complex than Nancy's explanation since there is no single set of events which are consistently duplicated in an "NDE." One person may describe passing through a "tunnel," while another sees no tunnel, but instead comes to a "river" beyond which there is no return. One individual may have a euphoric encounter with the Light and relive much of his or her morality in a "life's review," while another will enter a black void filled with demonic beings set upon destroying the person having the NDE.

Why the enormity of such differences, while at the same time often repeating many rudiments of the NDE? It is almost as if each NDE is tailored to the needs of the individual having the experience—and perhaps it is.

One of the purposes of this book is to present an up-to-date view of the near-death research effort, and to make that view broad enough to reveal many of the disciplines now being applied in the field. A corollary objective is to illustrate for the scientific community that the growing knowledge base from NDE research can no longer be dismissed as a passing New Age fantasy. One of the difficulties of this corollary objective is that those having NDEs often report after-effect phenomena which defy the rationality of materialistic science.

It is not uncommon, for example, for those having had an NDE to report strange electrical effects associated with their emotional state. Battery-powered wrist watches do not work, and street or room lights extinguish when the individuals walk near them. Persons having had NDEs often tell how they can sense or dream of future events which later happen. They can look at some people and sense areas of disease or injury. Some have the gift of healing.

These paranormal experiences are frequently found in the NDE community, and to say that they are difficult to explain is an understatement. Researchers, therefore, must exercise extreme care in attempting to document what seems, at first glance, to be merely an overly active imagination. It is particularly helpful, in such cases, to obtain corroboration from others who witness some of the particulars of the strange happenings. Again, the Mormon view detailed in previous chapters may shed some light on these dilemmas. These, then, are just some of the difficulties facing researchers working to better understand NDEs.

Future Research

This chapter also takes a peek into the future and attempts to project where research might be headed. This is a highly speculative area, since the future is, by definition, unknown. Nevertheless, there are some interesting trends already appearing in the research community. These trends could be the dimly marked trails which become the information highways of tomorrow.

One very positive attribute falling out of the March to Omega is the impetus it has given to new and expanding research thrusts. Reading Harold Widdison's plea in chapter 13 to examine different cultural and religious groups, and their reactions to the NDE, for example, is almost identical to the same plea made by Mark Fox in his book, *Religion, Spirituality and the Near-Death Experience* (described above). This book which you are reading is, in fact, a partial response to those pleas.

Similarly, the request by Fox for more corroborative research and prospective studies—where the investigators lay out a plan to document portions of medical emergencies *before* the events occur—is almost identical to the work being carried out by Bruce Greyson and Jan Holden (see chapter 10 under *Prospective Studies*).

Harold Widdison wrote, in chapter 13, of the value of longitudinal studies. These are studies where a number of those who have had NDEs are selected, by some set of criteria, for a continued evaluation over a preselected period of time. The evaluation could consist of any number of interesting parameters. For example, it could seek to answer the question, "Does an NDE predispose the subject toward a more difficult life than one would expect the "normal" non-experiencing individual to have?"

As a part of the research for this book I selected, somewhat randomly, fourteen of the sixty-eight NDE subjects I originally interviewed about thirteen years ago. In addition, I tracked the lives of six other individuals I had not previously interviewed, and I included them in the book. Without any particular agenda, I proceeded to interview these twenty people. The surprising results are given in chapter 8 under *The Objectives of Repeat Interviews*. Basically I found that about 70 percent of those interviewed had severe physical or other problems which beset them later in life. On the other hand, 100 percent still had a positive attitude about life, and all of them still remembered their NDEs as if they had happened yesterday.

When I asked Bill English how he could still have such a positive view of life despite the extremely difficult physical problems he had been subject to, he responded: "Now, [after my experiences], I feel that life has value regardless of the circumstances. My [previous] perception of what life was all about was not based on reality."

Although the control parameters—or rather, the lack of same—the sample size, and the duration of the brief longitudinal review which I performed were insufficient to draw any meaningful conclusions, it did reveal possible future directions for such studies. They could add much to our understanding of NDEs.

Undoubtedly there are numerous diverse research paths and destinations which are not yet perceived. The very nature of research is to uncover new areas of study as information points to still unanswered questions. And, as with other scientific fields, knowledge adds to knowledge in an exponential fashion. The resultant explosion of knowledge will inevitably accelerate our journey to Omega. This could well turn out to be, as Beverly put it, "the century of consciousness." Then Ken Ring would have to admit that his original assessment was correct: we will reach Omega.

Conclusions

Any first-order conclusion must reflect the achievements of Mormons in contributing to the overall NDE research effort, and in aiding the quest for Omega. So, without totally abandoning humility, I ask the reader to consider the evidence in this book for the proposition that Mormons have contributed substantially to a better understanding of the NDE phenomenon and to the quest for Omega. In point of fact, I would suggest that the LDS effort is almost unique in the magnitude of effort by any particular religious group.

Next in order of importance must be the answer to the questions, "Do the observed elements in an NDE compare well with Mormon theology and doctrine?" and, "Are there significant deviations?" Both of these questions are discussed in some detail in the above material. Both should be considered by the reader in light of the exhibited evidence. Briefly, the answer to the first question is a resounding yes, and the answer to the second is a qualified yes.

The question of whether we will ever reach Omega is another issue which needs a conclusion. If the NDE is the sole contribution to the quest, then the answer is probably, no. If, however, as Ring originally proposed, and as Mark Fox and Beverly Brodsky stipulate, the combined streams of knowledge from other tributaries of knowledge join in the contribution, then Omega can surely be reached. A basic belief of Mormonism is that the earth will be restored to its paradisaical glory when Christ comes again.

A corollary conclusion comes out of the evidence presented from both streams of knowledge—the NDE and Mormon theology. And that conclusion is the most important of all conclusions. It is that, taken together, there is overwhelming evidence for, as Beverly put it:

> We are a part of this realm of love and light. And there is this feeling I had, of being one with God—the God who created everything. But what is there is in its fullness, and magnificence. Here, we are in these limited physical bodies, and we have these brains which are filters and dampers of our limitless consciousness. In that realm our consciousness perceives all knowledge, and we can understand all knowledge very simply. Here, we struggle to master little parts of that knowledge.

In other words, there is a Creator of this universe and everything associated with it. We are part of that creation, and our consciousness will survive death. In that other realm of glory and light and love, if we so choose, we shall dwell with God, sharing in His light and glory. For that is part of the Plan of Happiness—to raise righteous humans to the level of Godhood and in the process add to the glory of God.

All living humans, good, bad or indifferent, will live again in a resurrected body, for Job was right after all: "Though after my skin worms destroy this body, yet in my flesh shall I see God" (Job 19:26).

Just as in ancient Israel the temple was the focal point and most holy of all religious activities carried out by the children of Israel, so too is that true of Mormonism. It is in the temple that the deepest epistemological truths are revealed, and the sacred binding ordinances tying this world to the celestial sphere are carried out. Here, the real meaning of familial "roots" becomes evident. "'Til death do us part" is replaced by "for time and eternity."

Chapter 1 describes the experience of Joseph Smith and Oliver Cowdery in their vision of Jesus Christ as he appeared to them in the Kirtland, Ohio Temple in 1836. In that vision the Lord told them "I have accepted this house, and my name shall be here; and I will manifest myself to my people in mercy in this house." Ancient prophets also appeared to Joseph and Oliver, including Elijah who said: "Behold, the time has fully come which was spoken of by the mouth of Malachi—testifying that he [Elijah] should be sent, before the great and dreadful day of the Lord to come—to turn the hearts of the fathers to the children, and the children to the fathers, lest the whole earth be smitten with a curse."

A portion of Renee Zamora's NDE is given in chapter 16. There she describes how she saw many individuals "who needed further work done for them in order to progress beyond where they were." In chapter 5 Dave Larsen describes the function of genealogical-temple work in tying families together. The correlation between the NDE participants' recognition of "home" and the Mormon temple ordinances which bind us, if we choose, to that home is explained.

Some major conclusions originate with this uniquely LDS doctrine. Moreover, many of the precepts stemming from the doctrine are found in the experiences described by those having NDEs. The major conclusions are actually a part of the *Plan of Happiness* mentioned above. They are:

1. We lived prior to this life, forever, first as Intelligences, then as spirit children of God.

2. As created sons and daughters of God, we left our heavenly home to be tested in a physical environment and with physical bodies. Here we forget much of what we knew in our premortal state in order that we might have freedom of choice.

3. Death is merely closing one door and opening another. We will return home to an environment largely of our choosing.

4. The glory we obtain after this life will depend upon how well we kept God's laws and whether or not we repented of our sins, accepted the atonement of Jesus Christ, and embraced Him as our Savior.

5. Families formed on earth have an opportunity to be bound together forever. That opportunity will be open to all who have ever lived on this earth. The sealing ordinances take place under God-authorized priesthood authority, either in live ceremonies for the living, or vicarious ceremonies for the deceased—in temples dedicated to the Lord.

6. All who have ever lived on earth ultimately will be resurrected with physical bodies, never to die again.

Omega Found?

To a Latter-day Saint, Alpha and Omega has special meaning, as given in the scriptures:

> Thus saith the Lord your God, even Jesus Christ, the Great I AM, Alpha and Omega, the beginning and the end, the same which looked upon the wide expanse of eternity, and all the seraphic hosts of heaven, before the world was made;
> The same which knoweth all things, for all things are present before mine eyes;
> I am the same which spake and the world was made, and all things came by me.
> I am the same which have taken the Zion of Enoch into mine own bosom; and verily, I say, even as many as have believed in my name, for I am Christ, and in mine own name, by the virtue of the blood which I have spilt, have I pleaded before the Father for them. (D&C 38:1–4)

In the sense, then, that we find Jesus Christ, repent of our sins, are baptized in His Name by those having authority, and accept him as our savior, then we have found Alpha and Omega. Referring back to Ken Ring's definition of Omega:

> "End" can obviously signify either finality or a goal, and it is Omega as an end *point* that has special meaning to us here. In this sense, Omega stands for the aim of human evolution,

the ultimate destination toward which humanity is inexorably bound.

Even here, Omega is harmonious with the definition from the LDS scriptures—if one accepts the concept of a Messiah, Jesus Christ, who atoned for all human sins. Under such terms, the ultimate goal for all humanity would be to return to that God who created them, redeemed and cleansed from sin by his grace and atoning sacrifice.

As to how near we are to Omega in the scriptural sense, we read:

> Behold, verily I say unto you, that these are the words of the Lord your God. Wherefore, labor ye, labor ye in my vineyard for the last time—for the last time call upon the inhabitants of the earth. For in my own good time will I come upon the earth in judgment, and my people shall be redeemed and shall reign with me on earth. For the great Millennium, of which I have spoken by the mouth of my servants, shall come. (D&C 43:27–30)

We also read, "Therefore, the keys of this dispensation are committed into your hands; and by this ye may know that the great and dreadful day of the Lord is near, even at the doors" (D&C 110:16).

So, where does all this leave us with regard to finding and reaching Omega? It would appear that there are many paths leading toward Omega, just as Ring, Fox, and Brodsky stated. In an earthly sense progress may seem slow, but given enough "baby steps," as Beverly phrased it, the end result is inevitable. Moreover, in God's time, the end probably *is* near.

Thus, dear readers, be of good cheer. Of a certainty we are spiritual children of our Father in Heaven, bound together in a joyous march to Omega. Though temporarily housed in a pain-susceptible physical body, we are part of a cosmic dance created by God so that we may, if we choose, join in His glory and in His creations. There our happiness will be complete in an extended family linked for eternity with the celestial chains of Godly power. And, sharing in that power, we shall add new pirouettes to the cosmic dance through our own God-endowed creativity.

References

Latter-day Saint Scriptures

The Book of Mormon—Another Testament of Jesus Christ. Salt Lake City: The Church of Jesus Christ of Latter-day Saints, 1989.

The Doctrine and Covenants [D&C]. Salt Lake City: The Church of Jesus Christ of Latter-day Saints, 1989.

The Holy Bible (Authorized King James Version). Salt Lake City: The Church of Jesus Christ of Latter-day Saints, 1979.

The Pearl of Great Price [P of GP]. Salt Lake City: The Church of Jesus Christ of Latter-day Saints, 1989.

Other Latter-day Saint Writings

Barrett, Ivan J. *Joseph Smith and the Restoration.* Provo, Utah: Brigham Young University Press, 1973.

Bishop, M. Guy. "To Overcome the 'Last Enemy': Early Mormon Perceptions of Death," *BYU Studies* 26, no. 3 (Summer 1986): 64–65.

Bishop, Michael Guy. *Henry William Bigler, Soldier, Gold Miner, Missionary, Chronicler, 1815–1900.* Logan, Utah: Utah State University Press, 1998.

Cannon, George Q. *Desert Weekly* 38 (April 7, 1889): 677. Published in Salt Lake City by The Church of Jesus Christ of Latter-day Saints.

Cannon, George Q. *Deseret Weekly* 51 (November 2, 1895): 803.

Givens, Terry L. *By the Hand of Mormon: The American Scripture that Launched a New World Religion.* Oxford: Oxford University Press, 2002.

Keller, Carol S. (Original documents), Keller, Lewis C. and Keller, Allen M. (Typing). Sketch of the Life of Thomas Crowther, *Anderson Family Stories.* North Richland Hills, Texas, July 1998, p. 39.

Lee, Harold B. *Stand ye in holy places.* Salt Lake City: Deseret Book Co., 1974., p. 6.

Ludlow, Daniel H., Editor. *Encyclopedia of Mormonism,* 4 Volumes. New York, Macmillan Publishing Company, 1992.

Maxwell, Neal A. "Patience." *Ensign,* October 1980.

Haight, David B. Sacrament—and the Sacrifice. *Ensign,* November 1989, pp. 59–60.

Reynolds, Noel B. (Edited by), *Book of Mormon authorship revisited: The evidence for ancient origins.* Provo, Utah: Foundation for Ancient Research and Mormon Studies, 1997, Skousen, Royal, chapter 4.

Roberts, B. H. *Defense of the Faith and the Saints.* Volume 1. Salt Lake City: Deseret News, 1912.

Robinson, Stephen E. *Are Mormons Christians?* Salt Lake City: Bookcraft, 1991.

Snow, LeRoi C. Raised from the dead. *Improvement Era,* Volume 32, Numbers 11 and 12. Salt Lake City, The Church of Jesus Christ of Latter-day Saints, 1929.

Smith, Joseph F. "The Second Death," Oneida Stake Conference, January 20, 1895, Franklin, Idaho. *Collected Discourses* 1886–1898, vol. 4.

Smith, Joseph, Jr. King Follett sermon. *Teachings of the Prophet Joseph Smith* [TPJS]. Salt Lake City: Deseret Book Company, 1976, pp. 345–47.

Smith, Joseph, Jr., *Teachings of the Prophet Joseph Smith, 1843–1844.* Salt Lake City, Deseret Book Company, 1976.

Smith, Joseph, Jr.; edited by Roberts, B. H. *History of the Church of Jesus Christ of Latter-day Saints.* Salt Lake City, Utah: Deseret Book Company, 7 Volumes, 2:380, 1946.

Snow, Lorenzo. "As God Is, Man May Be." *History of the Church of Jesus Christ of Latter-day Saints,* July 20, 1901, p. 4.

Top, Brent L. *The life before.* Salt Lake City, Utah: Bookcraft, 1988.

Young, Brigham and other authors. *Journal of Discourses* [JD], Volumes 1–26. Salt Lake City, Utah: The Church of Jesus Christ of Latter-day Saints.

Young, Brigham, *Discourses of Brigham Young* selected by Widtsoe, John A. *Journal of Discourses,* Volume VIII, p. 10. Salt Lake City: Deseret Book Co., 1954], 248.

Wilson, Lerona A. "My Testimony Concerning Temple Work." *Relief Society Magazine,* Vol. III, No. 2, p. 82, February, 1916.

Other Writings

Banks, Hal N., Ph.D., "An Introduction to Psychic Studies," Anchorage Community College, Anchorage, Alaska 1980.

Bergin, Allen E. and Richards, P. Scott. *Handbook of psychotherapy and religious diversity.* Washington, D.C.: American Psychological Association, 2000.

Eyre, Richard. *Life before life.* Shadow Mountain, 2000.

Lewis, C.S. *A grief observed.* San Francisco: Harper Row, 2001 (first published in 1961).

Nuland, Sherwin B. *How we die: Reflections on life's final chapter.* New York: Knopf Publishing Group, 1995.

Seligman, Martin E. P. *Authentic happiness—Using the new positive psychology to realize your potential for lasting fulfillment.* Free Press, 2002.

Talbot, Michael. *The holographic universe.* New York: Harper Collins, 1991.

Whitman, Walt. *Whitman, Poetry and prose, leaves of grass.* New York: The Library of America, 1855, pp. 43, 45, 46.

Zukav, Gary. *The dancing Wu Li masters.* New York: Bantam Books, 1980.

Near-Death Literature

Abramovitch, Henry. "An Israeli account of a near-death experience: A case study of cultural dissonance." *Journal of Near-Death Studies,* 6(3), 1988, 175–84.

Atwater, P.M.H. "Is there a Hell? Surprising observations about the near-death experience." *Journal of Near-Death Studies,* 10, 1992, 149–60.

Atwater, P. M. H. *Coming back to life: The after-effects of near-death experience.* New York: Dodd and Mead, 1988.

Brown, Joyce H. *Heavenly answers for earthly challenges: How to be certain you enjoy the other side when you get there.* Pasadena, CA: Jemstar Press, 1997.

Bishop, B. Grant. *The LDS gospel of light.* Salt Lake City, Utah: Origin Book Sales, 1998.

Bishop, B. Grant. "Book review: Fingerprints of God: Evidences from near-death studies, scientific research on creation, and Mormon theology," by Arvin Gibson. *Journal of Near-Death Studies,* 21(1), Fall 2002, 35–41.

Bonenfant, Richard J. "A comparative study of near-death experience and non-near-death experience outcomes in 56 survivors of clinical death," *Journal of Near-Death Studies,* 22(3), Spring 2004, 155–78.

Brodsky, Beverly A. "Book review: Jewish views of the afterlife," by Simcha Paull Raphael. *Journal of Near-Death Studies,* 16(4), Summer 1998.

Brubaker, Don. *Absent from the body: One man's clinical death, a journey through Heaven and Hell.* Peninsula Publishing, 1996.

Bush, Nancy Evans. "Guest Editorial: Is ten years a life review?" *Journal of Near-Death Studies,* 10(1), 1991, 6–8.

Christensen, Kevin. "'Nigh unto Death': NDE Research and the Book of Mormon." *Journal of Book of Mormon Studies,* Volume 2 Number 1, Spring 1993. Provo, Utah: Foundation for Ancient Research and Mormon Studies.

Crowther, Duane S. *Prophecy—Key to the future.* Salt Lake City: Bookcraft, Inc., 1962.

Crowther, Duane S. *The prophecies of Joseph Smith: Over 400 prophecies by and about Joseph Smith, and their fulfillment.* Salt Lake City: Bookcraft, Inc., 1963.

Crowther, Duane S. *Gifts of the Spirit.* Salt Lake City: Bookcraft, Inc., 1964.

Crowther, Duane S. *Prophets and Prophecies of the Old Testament.* Salt Lake City: Deseret Book Company, 1965.

Crowther, Duane S. *Life everlasting.* Salt Lake City, Utah: Deseret Book Company, 1967.

Crowther, Duane S. *Inspired prophetic warnings: Book of Mormon prophecies about America's future.* Bountiful, Utah: Horizon Publishers and Distributors, Inc., 1987.

Crowther, Duane S. *Life everlasting: A definitive study of life after death.* Bountiful, Utah: Horizon Publishers & Distributors, Inc., 1997.

Cunico, Laura. "Knowledge and attitudes of hospital nurses in Italy related to near-death experiences," *Journal of Near-Death Studies,* 20(1), Fall 2001, 37–50.

Dougherty, Ned. *Fast lane to heaven: Celestial encounters that changed my life.* Charlottesville, Virginia: Hampton Roads Publishing, 2003.

Durham, Elane. *I stand all amazed: Love and healing from higher realms.* Orem, Utah: Granite Publishing and Distribution, 1998.

Ellwood, Gracia Fay. "Religious experience, religious world-views, and near-death studies." *Journal of Near-Death Studies,* 19(1), Fall 2000, 5–21.

Essex, Bill. *The truth the whole truth and anything but the truth.* Harrison, Arkansas: Books Galore, 2001.

Fenimore, Angie. *Beyond the darkness: My near-death journey to the edge of hell and back.* New York: Bantam, 1995.

Fenwick, Peter and Elizabeth. *The truth in the light—An investigation of over 300 near-death experiences.* New York: Berkley Publishing Group, 1995.

Fillerup, Robert. "Early Mormon Visions and Near-death Experiences." Paper delivered at *Sunstone Symposium 90,* Salt Lake City, August 22, 1990.

Fox, Mark. *Religion, spirituality and the near-death experience.* London and NY: Routeledge, Taylor & Francis Group, 2003.

Gallup, George, Jr., *Adventures in immortality.* New York, NY: McGraw-Hill, 1982.

Gibson, Arvin S. *In search of angels: Finding joy midst the bramble bushes.* Bountiful, Utah: Horizon Publishers and Distributors, Inc., 1990.

Gibson, Arvin S. *Glimpses of eternity: New near-death experiences examined.* Bountiful, Utah: Horizon Publishers and Distributors, Inc., 1992.

Gibson, Arvin S. *Echoes from eternity: New near-death experiences examined.* Bountiful, Utah: Horizon Publishers and Distributors, Inc., 1993.

Gibson, Arvin S. *Fingerprints of God: Evidences from near-death studies, scientific research on creation, and Mormon theology.* Bountiful, Utah: Horizon Publishers and Distributors, Inc., 1999.

Greyson, Bruce. "The Investigation of Near-Death Experiences." *Journal of Indian Psychology,* 2:7–11, 1979.

Greyson, Bruce and Bush, Nancy Evans. "Distressing Near-Death Experiences." *Psychiatry,* Volume 55, February, 1992.

Grof, Stanislav and Christina. *Beyond death: The gates of consciousness.* New York, Thamses and Hudson, 1980.

Hinze, Sarah. *Coming from the light: Spiritual accounts of life before life.* New York, London, Toronto, Sidney, Tokyo: Pocket Books, 1994, 1997.

Jansen, K.L.R. "The ketamine model of the near-death experience: A central role for the N-Methyl-D-Aspartate Receptor." *Journal of Near-Death Studies,* 16, 1997 and *Journal of the American Society for Psychical Research,* 72, 1978.

Jansen, K.L.R. "Response to commentaries on "The ketamine model of the near-death experience." *Journal of Near-Death Studies,* 16, 1997.

Jansen, Karl. *Ketamine: Dreams and realities.* Sarasota, Florida: Multidisciplinary Association for Psychedelic Studies (MAPS), 2001.

Jensen, Margie C. *When faith writes the story.* Salt Lake City: Bookcraft, Inc., 1973.

Kieffer, Gene. Kundalini and the near-death experience. *Journal of Near-Death Studies,* 12(3), 1994.

Kellehear, Allan. *Experiences near death.* New York: Oxford University Press, 1996.

Kübler-Ross, Elisabeth. *On death and dying.* London: Tavistock, 1969.

LaFleur, Philip D., Livingstone, Kevin, and Schaalje, Bruce. "Book Review: Fingerprints of God: Evidences from near-death studies, scientific research on creation, and Mormon theology, by Arvin S. Gibson," *FARMS Review of books,* 13(1), 2001, 73–85.

Lundahl, Craig R. *A collection of near-death research readings.* Chicago: Nelson Hall, Inc., 1982.

Lundahl, C. R. and H. A. Widdison. "The Mormon Explanation of Near-death Experiences," *Anabiosis—Journal of Near-Death Studies* 3, no. 1 (1983), 97–106.

Lundahl, Craig R. "Angels in near-death experiences," *Journal of Near-Death Studies,* 11(1), Fall 1992, 49–56.

Lundahl, Craig R. "Near-death visions of unborn children: Indications of a pre-earth life," *Journal of Near-Death Studies,* 11(2), Winter 1992, 123–28.

Lundahl, Craig R. "The near-death experience: A theoretical summarization," *Journal of Near-Death Studies,* 12(2), Winter 1993, 105–18.

Lundahl, Craig R. and Arvin S. Gibson. "Near-death Studies and Modern Physics," *Journal of Near-Death Studies* 18, no. 3 (Spring 2000), 143–79.

Lundahl, Craig R. "A comparison of other world perceptions by near-death experiencers and by the Marian visionaries of Medjugorje," *Journal of Near-Death Studies,* 19(1), Fall 2000, 45–52.

Lundahl, Craig R. "Prophetic revelations in near-death experiences," *Journal of Near-Death Studies,* 19(4), Summer 2001, 233–39.

Lundahl, Craig R. and Widdison, Harold A. "Social positions in the city of light," *Journal of Near-Death Studies,* 11(4), Summer 1993, 231–38.

Lundahl, Craig R. and Widdison, Harold A. "The physical environment in the city of light," *Journal of Near-Death Studies,* 11(4), Summer 1993, 239–46.

Lundahl, Craig R. and Widdison, Harold A. *The eternal journey: How near-death experiences illuminate our earthly lives.* New York: Warner Books, Inc., 1997.

McDonogh, John M. "Introducing near-death research findings into Psychotherapy," *Journal of Near-Death Studies,* 22(4), Summer 2004, 269–73.

Mills, Roy. *The Soul's remembrance: Earth is not our home.* Seattle: Onjinjinkta Publishing, 1999.

Moody, Raymond A. *Life after life: The investigation of a phenomenon—survival of bodily death.* New York: Bantam, 1975.

Moody, Raymond A., Jr. *Reflections on life after life.* New York: Bantam, 1978.

Moody, Raymond A., Jr. *The light beyond: New explorations by the author of Life after Life.* New York: Bantam, 1988.

Morse, Melvin. *Closer to the light: Learning from children's near-death experiences.* New York: Villard, 1990.

Morse, Melvin with Perry, Paul. *Transformed by the light: The powerful effect of near-death experiences on people's lives.* New York: Villard, 1992.

Nelson, Lee. *Beyond the veil: Volume one.* Springville, Utah: Cedar Fort, Inc., 1988.

Nelson, Lee. *Beyond the veil: Volume two.* Springville, Utah: Cedar Fort, Inc., 1989.

Nelson, Lee. *Beyond the veil: Volume three.* Springville, Utah: Cedar Fort, Inc., 1989.

Nelson, Lee and Nelson, Richard. *NDE—Near-death experiences.* Springville, Utah: Cedar Fort, Inc., 1994.

Petro, Andy. "NDE of Andrew Petro, Jr.," *IANDS Vital Signs,* Vol. XVI, No. 4, Fall 97, p. 6.

Rawlings, Maurice. *Beyond death's door.* New York, Toronto, London, Sydney, Auckland: Bantam Books, 1979.

Ring, Kenneth. *Life at death: A scientific investigation of the near-death experience.* New York: Coward, McCann and Geoghegan, 1980.

Ring, Kenneth. *Heading toward omega: In search of the meaning of the near-death experience.* New York: Morrow, 1984.

Ring, K. "Amazing grace: The near-death experience as a compensatory gift," *Journal of Near-Death Studies,* 10 (1), 1991, 11–39.

Ring, Kenneth and Evelyn Elsaesser Valarino. *Lessons from the light: What we can learn from the near-death experience.* New York, NY: Plenum, 1998.

Ring, Kenneth and Cooper, Sharon. *Mindsight: Near-death and out-of-body experiences in the blind.* Palo Alto, California: William James Center for Consciousness Studies, Institute of Transpersonal Psychology, 1999.

Ring, Kenneth. "Religious wars in the NDE movement: Some personal reflections on Michael Sabom's *Light and Death,*" *Journal of Near-Death Studies,* 18(4), Summer 2000.

Ritchie, George G. with Sherrill, Elizabeth. *Return from tomorrow.* Old Tappan, New Jersey: Spire Books, Fleming H. Revell Co., 1978.

Ritchie, George G. *My life after dying.* Norfolk, VA: Hampton Roads Publishing Co., 1991.

Rommer, Barbara R. *Blessing in disguise: Another side of the near-death experience.* St. Paul, Minnesota: Llewellyn Publications, 2000.

Sabom, Michael B. *Recollections of death: A medical investigation.* New York: Harper and Row, 1982.

Sabom, Michael. *Light & death: One doctor's fascinating account of near-death experiences.* Grand Rapids, Michigan: Zondervan Publishing House, 1998.

Sharp, Kimberly Clark. *After the light: What I discovered on the other side of life that can change your world.* New York: William Morrow and Company, Inc., 1995.

Shermer, Michael. "Demon-Haunted Brain," *Scientific American: Skeptic,* March 2003, 25.

Storm, Howard. *My descent into death: and the message of love which brought me back.* London: Clairview Books, 2000.

Sutherland, Cherie. *Reborn in the light: Life after near-death experiences.* Australia, New Zealand: Bantam Books, 1995. (First published as *Transformed by the light.* Australia, New Zealand: Bantam Books, 1992.)

Sutherland, Cherie. *Within the light.* Australia: Bantam, 1993.

Sutherland, Cherie. *Children of the light.* New York: Bantam, 1995.

Swedenborg, Emanuel. *Heaven and Hell.* Translated by George F. Dole. 58th printing. New York: Swedenborg Foundation, 1990.

Top, Brent L. and Top, Wendy C. *Beyond death's door: Understanding near-death experiences in light of the restored gospel.* Salt Lake City: Bookcraft, 1993.

Valarino, Evelyn Elsaesser. *On the other side of life: Exploring the Phenomenon of the near-death experience.* New York, London: Insight Books, 1984.

VandenBush, Bill. *If Morning Never Comes.* North Platte, Nebraska: The Old One Hundred Press, 2003.

Van Lommel W., Wan Wees R., Meyers V., Elfferich, I. "Near-death experience in survivors of cardiac arrest: A prospective study," *The Lancet,* 2001; 358: 2039–45.

Van Lommel, Pim. "A Reply to Shermer: Medical Evidence for NDEs," *Web site: www.skeptical investigations.org.* March 16, 2003.

Vincent, Ken R. "The Near-death Experience and Christian Universalism," *Journal of Near-Death Studies* 22, no. 1 (2003): 57–71.

Wade, Jenny. "Book Review: The eternal journey: How near-death experiences illuminate our earthly lives, by Craig R. Lundahl and Harold A. Widdison," *Journal of Near-Death Studies,* 18(1), Fall 1999, 51–57.

Wade, Jenny. "In a sacred manner we died: Native American near-death experiences," *Journal of Near-Death Studies*, 22(2), 2003, 83–115.

Wallace, Ranelle, with Taylor, Curtis. *The burning within*. Carson City, NV: Gold Leaf Press, 1994.

Wells, Amber D. "Reincarnation beliefs among near-death experiencers," *Journal of Near-Death Studies*, 12(1), Fall 1993, 17–34.

Widdison, Harold A. "Letters to the Editor: Review of Eternal Journey," *Journal of Near-Death Studies* 19 (Fall 2000): 57–64.

Widdison, Harold A. *Trailing Clouds of Glory: First-person Glimpses into Premortality*. Springville, Utah: Horizon Publishers, 2004.

Wilson, Ian, *The After-Death Experience: The Physical of the Non-physical*. New York: William Morrow and Company, Inc., 1987.

Williams, Kevin R. *Nothing Better than Death: Insights from Sixty-two Profound Near-death Experiences*. Website, www.Xlibris.com, Corporation, 2002.

Yorgason, Blaine M., Bruce W. Warren, and Harold Brown. *New Evidences of Christ in Ancient America*. Provo, Utah: Stratford Books, 1999.

Zaleski, Carol. *Otherworld Journeys: Accounts of Near-death Experiences in Medieval and Modern Times*. New York: Oxford University Press, 1987.

Indexes

Index of Persons Cited

Index of Elements of Near-Death Experiences and Research Cited